The Labour Movement in Britain from Thatcher to Blair

Keith Barlow

The Labour Movement in Britain from Thatcher to Blair

With a Foreword by Jim Mortimer

Extended and Updated Edition

PETER LANG
Frankfurt am Main · Berlin · Bern · Bruxelles · New York · Oxford · Wien

Bibliographic Information published by the Deutsche Nationalbibliothek
The Deutsche Nationalbibliothek lists this publication in the Deutsche Nationalbibliografie; detailed bibliographic data is available in the internet at <http://www.d-nb.de>.

The first edition was published in 1997 in the
European University Studies.

Cover design:
Olaf Glöckler, Atelier Platen

ISBN 978-3-631-55137-0

www.peterlang.de

Acknowledgements

This new book is the extended edition of the book *The Labour Movement in Thatcher's Britain* which was the published version of my doctoral thesis which I successfully defended at the University of Bremen in 1996 and then published by Peter Lang GmbH in 1997. I remain grateful to Professor Logie Barrow at the University of Bremen, for his careful supervision and to the University for allowing me submit and defend my thesis.

This new book is the result of continued research and reading in this subject area beyond the successful completion of my thesis. In this, I would like to acknowledge the value of numerous discussions I have had over a good many years with various people who have been active on the industrial relations scene as well as those specialising in this subject area in academic circles. I am especially grateful to Professor John Foster for reading through the first draft of this new book and for his valuable comments in preparation for publication.

During the course of my work, various bodies and institutions have supplied me with valuable material without which the work leading up to the publication of this book would not have been possible. In this, I would like to thank the Trades Union Congress in particular for kindly allowing me to make extensive use of its library facilities over the years.

I would also like to thank my colleagues at the *Deutsch-Russisches Zentrum Sachsen e.V.*, Leipzig, for their co-operation and support in the final stages of work for this book.

Finally, I would like to thank my parents and my partner Ute for their continued support at every stage of work leading to the completion of this book.

The arguments and conclusions reached in this book are entirely mine and I, and I alone, am responsible for any errors and mistakes which may have got through unnoticed.

Foreword

The special merit of this book is that it provides a searching analysis of the relationship in Britain in recent years between economic and social policy, the course of industrial relations and the strength and weaknesses of the labour movement. This is no mean achievement.

The author demonstrates also that a commitment sympathetic to labour is compatible with objectivity in dealing with evidence. Indeed, one of the strengths of this book is that it draws heavily on official statistics and reports. It is all the more persuasive for it. The author's sympathy for the interests of working people is clear but he is not uncritical of aspects of the labour movement and its official policies.

Britain's economic record during the period covered in this book is uneven. This is also true of the entire period since the Second World War. Even so living standards for the majority of the population are still higher than in some other economically developed countries. There are, however, serious problems remaining with the economy.

One of the main features of the economic record – which the author brings out – is the decline of manufacturing industry. Britain, once the 'workshop of the world' now runs a heavy adverse balance of trade in manufactured goods. Less than 3 million workers are now employed in manufacturing industry. This is less than one in every eight of the total workforce. Instead of manufacturing industry Britain now depends heavily for employment on financial and business services. No doubt some of this is essential but some of it is also parasitic. It is heavily influenced by speculation.

The problems arising from the adverse trade balance, including exchange rates, have troubled every British government for many years. They are described in this book. The difficulties have been made worse by Britain's commitment to heavy military expenditure and – in more recent years – by the cost of the war in Iraq.

All these problems have, as the author so rightly describes, been reflected in the controversies and policies of the trade union and labour movement. The 1945 Labour government carried out, with the support of the unions, an ambitious programme of social reform. It ran into into problems and eventual defeat largely as the result of the adverse economic effects of a massive rearmament programme launched partly because of pressure from the USA.

Labour governments elected in the 1960s and 1970s also introduced some progressive reforms but were eventually defeated because of economic problems and controversy with the unions about incomes policy and industrial relations.

This was followed by a long period of Conservative rule, associated mainly with the name of Mrs Thatcher. Severe legal restrictions were imposed upon the unions. In 1997 Labour were again elected to office but this time as 'New' Labour. As Keith Barlow rightly recognises 'New' Labour broke with some traditional Labour commitments and, in particular, has perpetuated some of the worst features of the restrictions imposed upon the unions by Mrs Thatcher. 'New' Labour has also continued with a policy sympathetic to the privatisation of sections of public service.

Today, with the decline of manufacturing industry and coal-mining, trade union membership is much lower than it was in 1980. On the other hand, many of the union leaders who have been elected in recent years are critical of the policies of the current Labour leadership. They reflect the mood of the membership.

Anyone seeking to understand the problems of the British economy, the effect of these problems on political developments and, in particular, the possible responses of the trade union and labour movement, will find this book an invaluable guide.

Jim Mortimer

Contents

Introduction

The aim of this book is to explain how the Conservative Party in Government from 1979 to 1997, judged on its own criteria, succeeded in bringing about a major restructuring of power in the British economy in the 1980s and 1990s and how this influenced the policies of the *New* Labour Government which was elected to office in the aftermath of the severe Conservative election defeat in 1997. The extent to which these criteria really served anyone's objective needs is a different matter.

This book concentrates on selected areas of Government policy and strategy since 1979 and on specific events. By placing these in an economic, political and legal context, a picture can be formed which will lead to three important conclusions.

Firstly, any claim that there was something specifically "new" about the British Government's policies in the 1980s and beyond is questionable. Secondly, the policies and strategy, initially of the Thatcher Government (1979-1990) can in no way be regarded as spontaneous to pressures of the day. They were an application of a long and carefully prepared strategy which continued to influence Government policy long after Margaret Thatcher ceased to be Prime Minister. Thirdly, the policies of the Thatcher Government had apparently had a sufficient enough impact that the Labour Party, as part of its endeavours of getting back into office, felt the need to fundamentally review its policies and, as it were, adapt to the political agenda which the Thatcher Government had put into effect.

On the first conclusion, the coining of the term "Thatcherism" before the 1979 general election led to some on the Left to argue that Britain was entering a new political phase. But was this term, the "New" Right (the political label associated with the forces which took over the Conservative Party following Edward Heath's downfall as Party leader in 1975), really "new"?

To help answer this question, the starting point must be the collapse of what is often referred to as "consensus"-era politics. Indeed, there is also the question of whether there was really "consensus" at all in British domestic policy following World War Two. If there was, then one must be clear to what extent "consensus" politics actually existed in Britain, how deep or shallow its roots were and when it ceased to exist. This is the aim of the first chapter.

In so far as any era of "consensus" actually existed in Britain, then the outcome of the May 1979 election would have formalised an end to this era. However, this did not mean that a Conservative Government replacing a Labour Government in 1979 automatically resulted in the introduction of completely new policies. Certainly, in some aspects, the Thatcher Government's policies meant a complete change; in other aspects, it was more a continuation of the policies of the previous Labour Government.

Chapter 2 helps to clarify those areas of policy where a change can be attributed to the outcome of the 1979 election and those areas where it was merely a continuation. This then links up with the second issue, the influence of historical events upon which the Thatcher Government could introduce a well thought-out and comprehensive strategy for its economic and social policies in as far as they could be described as being "social" at all.

Emphasising the interaction between "macro-" and "micro-" economic strategies helps to explain the complexities involved in forcing through economic and industrial restructuring on a national and/or industry-wide basis, and the implications of pursuing such measures in just one firm or company in a competitive industry. The range of industrial disputes in the 1980s shows that specific policies for bringing about industrial restructuring in one area of the economy or in one industry were not necessarily applicable elsewhere.

Not only were the actual policies important but so too were the tactics pursued for their realisation in each specific case. Working people and their trade unions in Britain have a long tradition of standing up for their rights and livelihoods and the Thatcher Government clearly took account of this.

One key factor which many analyses of the economic and political strategy of the Thatcher Government tend to overlook is the significance of the special historical character of British labour law and the fact that Britain has no written constitution, hence no constitutional court as such. Both of these exist in other advanced industrial nations, especially in Western Europe. Consequently in Britain, great emphasis must be attached to the specific role and development of case law, especially those aspects of it relating to the "resolving" of industrial disputes. It is therefore worth noting that the absence of a written constitution together with any resulting provisions for one guaranteeing various rights for workers gave the Thatcher Government a considerable degree of leeway in bringing about major changes in trade union and labour relations law, just on the basis of a simple majority vote in Parliament, in a way which would not have been possible elsewhere. In other countries, simple majority votes in Parliament alone would be insufficient if changes to workers' rights require constitutional changes.

The very fact that a revival of the common law in seeking to "resolve" industrial disputes was an essential element in economic and "social" strategy in the 1980s is clearly evident. This is so, not only in the ways in which the trade union laws of the Thatcher Government sought to narrow the scope of "immunities" for the individual organisers of industrial disputes, but also to expose trade unions themselves to tort liabilities thus, to a great extent, putting the law back to what it had been before the historic Trade Disputes Act, 1906, got onto the Statute Book. It is this crucial legal aspect which has been lacking in many analyses of British Government strategy of the 1980s and beyond.

Lord Wedderburn has made a most valuable contribution in filling this gap by his analyses of legal aspects of the Thatcher Government's economic and "social" strategy and by placing them in a historical context. He has demonstrated that there is a link between a "free"- market economic strategy and the part the common law can play in helping to make it work. On the basis of Wedderburn's findings, chapter 3 will attempt to show how significant this link is between the "macro-" and "micro-" economic strategies of the Thatcher Government.

The inviolability of the law of contract, the very foundations upon which the common law is based, tends in practice, especially where employer/employee relationships in a "free" market for labour are concerned, to come down more on the side of those who are better placed to shape the terms and conditions of the employment contract – namely the employers.

Nevertheless, it has been alleged by those who supported the "free"- market economic policies of the Thatcher Government e.g. the late Friedrich August von Hayek, that working people acting in unison, i.e. in trade unions, obstruct the "free" functioning of the labour market and that the removal of the "immunities" Parliament conceded to trade unions would be a precondition of any successful economic and industrial restructuring in the 1980s. The argument that legal "immunities" which made trade unions "privileged" bodies, thus being protected from claims in tort in the course of their normal functions and leading to allegations that they were responsible for Britain's declining position in the advanced industrial world, is by no means new. It is therefore necessary to determine whether these "immunities" were really "privileges" or, in the words of Lord Wedderburn, "social rights". But, whatever line of argument one takes in this respect, it can be shown that there is an interaction between a "free"- market economic strategy and the part the common law can help in making it work. Consequently, the practical applications of this whole strategy become clearer when it is related to specific events, especially in the 1980s with the 1984/1985 miners' strike and disputes in the British printing industry. This is the main objective of the fourth chapter.

It is therefore necessary to assess how the trade union and labour movement responded to this challenge. The Thatcher Government was well aware of the fact that, in the not so distant past (at the end of the 1960s and subsequently, in the early 1970s), a Labour Government followed by a Conservative Government (in which Margaret Thatcher herself was a Cabinet Minister) had been defeated in their industrial relations policies by the organised labour movement. Thatcher was therefore determined and careful enough to ensure that her Government was not going to be the third to suffer that fate.

However, before one can consider whether the Thatcher Government's policies were "successful", one has to determine the criteria by which "success" should be measured. If the criteria were to be based on the overall performance of the British economy and the well-being of the masses of ordinary people, opinions would be divided. However, a judgement on political grounds by those forces identifying themselves with the ownership of vast holdings of capital would, no doubt, be positive.

"New"-Right thinking would generally be that governments should not be determining economic policy anyway. Rather, their tasks should be limited to the pursuit of those measures which are deemed necessary to ensure that market forces can operate "freely" and "efficiently". Only then, according to this line of thinking, would the best economic results be attained.

Trade unions and their practices have often been seen as a factor impeding the efficient functioning of a "free"-market order. It is therefore necessary to determine whether or how successful the Thatcher Government was in its trade union laws. To what extent did these laws weaken the bargaining power of organised labour? There is also the question of whether the labour movement conceded defeat unnecessarily. In this respect, there is also the question of whether the review the Labour Party leadership authorised of the Party's policies in the aftermath of the Party's election defeat in 1987 (its third consecutive defeat) was necessary after all.

The fact is that despite Labour's policy review, the Conservative Party and Government led by Margaret Thatcher's successor John Major managed to avoid defeat in the 1992 election and by the time the Labour Party got back into office in 1997, public discontent with the Major Government was such that Labour, with or without a policy review, would have got back into office anyway. In this, it is necessary to examine what went wrong for Labour in the run-up to the 1992 election. In this, one should not overlook the implications of Labour supporting the decision of the Conservative Government in October 1990 (shortly before Thatcher was replaced as Prime Minister) to anchor sterling in the European Exchange Rate Mechanism (ERM) and the conditions attached to this. This is one purpose of chapter five. Another purpose of this chapter is to make an assessment of the policies of the Blair Government especially in the area of economic and social policy. There, the issue of trade union and labour relations law is especially important as this helps to illustrate the closeness between the policies of the Conservative Party in government from 1979 to 1997 and those of *New* Labour since then.

In view of the wide-ranging legislative measures enacted against trade unions and trade unionists since 1979, there has been the question as to whether the rights' of workers and trade unions to organise and bargain collectively fulfill the various norms and conventions which have been laid down at European and international level which in turn have been signed and ratified by the UK. This question has gained even more importance due to the Human Rights Act, 1998, the cornerstone of which is that British law should not contravene the European Convention on Human Rights and Fundamental Freedoms from 1950 and any of its subsequent protocols and subsequently, the ruling in the European Court of Human Rights in 2002 in the Wilson and Palmer case. Consequently, there is the question as to what extent the rights of workers and trade unions in Britain conform to the norms of this Convention (despite any limitations it may permit on countries which have ratified it and incorporated its provisions into their own laws). This is another objective of the fifth chapter.

Put simply, one could conclude that the Thatcher Government did, in the short term, have some success in achieving its major objectives – namely pushing back the strength and influence of the organised labour movement. Supporters of the policies of the Thatcher Government can also claim success in that these policies helped to shape government policy in economic and social areas long after Margaret Thatcher ceased to be Prime Minister. However, an assessment of the longer term consequences for the British economy as a whole and for working people and their families continues to remain wide open.

The Thatcher Government's economic and political strategy as well as those of the Major and Blair Governments can, in fact, be assessed from many angles. Through a detailed analysis of Government papers, political party documents, trade union and TUC documents, the viewpoints of other organisations and individuals involved in the controversies, together with a wide range of secondary sources, this book aims to provide a contribution to the understanding of economic and social developments in Britain since 1979.

Chapter One: The significance of the post-1945 "consensus" in Britain for the trade union movement

1.1. Economic developments interacting with social consensus

What is often, though misleadingly, referred to in Britain as the "post-war consensus" era, has its roots in the change in the balance of forces between labour and capital arising out of the 2nd World War, which brought full employment back to Britain.[1] With the generally accepted feeling that mass unemployment and large-scale poverty should never again be tolerated, as had been the case in the pre-war years, the trade union and labour movement was able to secure the most comprehensive reforms in social welfare ever known in Britain at the time. What was to become known as the "welfare state" had its origins in the Beveridge Report,[2] published at the end of 1942, which, significantly, was written with the assistance of a group of young Keynesian economists[3] reflecting a clear rejection of the *laissez-faire* policies of the inter-war years.

Equally significant was a governmental commitment[4], subsequently endorsed by all the major parties[5] to macroeconomic measures for maintaining a high and stable level of employment, i.e. "full employment". This commitment on the part of the State, it should be noted, was very much influenced by the Minister of Labour in the wartime coalition government under Winston Churchill, Ernest Bevin (formerly General Secretary of the Transport and General Workers' Union (TGWU)) who persistently pressed for full employment to be government policy irrespective of which party was to win the coming election.[6]

The incoming Labour Government under Clement Attlee in 1945 set about establishing the institutions and reforms to which the wartime coalition had agreed. At the heart of the programme of the Attlee Government (1945-1951) was the nationalisation of basic industries, reflecting their strategic importance in Britain's post-war economic recovery. What is often overlooked is that the nationa-

---

1 Coates, David, *The Crisis of Labour*, Philip Allan (Oxford and New Jersey), 1989, p. 10.

2 *Social Insurance and Allied Services*, Report by Sir William Beveridge, HMSO (London), Cmd. 6404, November 1942.

3 Grahl, John, The Liberal Revolutionary, in: *Marxism Today* (London), Vol. 27 No. 6, June 1983, p. 20.

4 See *Employment Policy*, HMSO (London), Cmd. 6527, May 1944.

5 See Craig, F. W. S. (Ed.), British General Election Manifestos 1900-1974, Macmillan (London and Basingstoke), 1975, p. 115 (Conservative Party), pp. 125f (Labour Party) and p. 113 (Liberal Party).

6 Bullock, Alan, *The Life and Times of Ernest Bevin – Vol. 2 Minister of Labour 1940-1945*, Heinemann (London), 1967, pp. 313-322.

lisation which took place under this Government was largely in response to reports of Conservative-dominated investigating committees[7] and, as the 1945 general election showed, most voters favoured such measures.

With the nationalisation programme in place, along with the commitment to "full employment" and the establishment of the "Welfare State", both sides of industry were expected to take part in daily economic and political life, with the government of the day, as it were, playing the role of "manager of the economy" in a way which was without precedent in peacetime. With the nationalisation of key industries e.g. coal mining and the railways, the 1945-1951 Labour Government based Britain's economic and industrial strategy on the basis of a "mixed economy" in which publicly-owned industries of strategic importance to the country as a whole would exist parallel with those in or remaining in the private sector.

Whatever criticisms may have been made of the various industries which had been nationalised from those who in any way were generally critical of public ownership, principally, up to 1979, the concept of a "mixed economy" had not been brought into question by any post-war government even if there had been individual industries which after nationalisation were then denationalised. There, a most notable example was the steel industry which had eventually been taken into public ownership in 1951 and then denationalised in 1953. Nevertheless, all this would imply that a "mixed economy" was seen to be an integral part of the post-war "consensus". All these measures enabled the government of the day, initially Labour and then from 1951 Conservative, to mobilise the productive forces of the economy in the early post-war years and, on the surface, brought about an era of economic prosperity around the 1950s.

However, the foundations upon which this "consensus era" was established were shaky for two reasons. Firstly, the masses of ordinary people were largely excluded from day-to-day decision-making processes – this being largely left in the hands of trade union leaders who could politically identify themselves with Labour's parliamentary leadership and the forces of capital. Secondly, policies implemented in an attempt to restore Britain as a world power – rearmament and large-scale overseas investments – were tolerated, even though they operated at the expense of modernising Britain's industrial base. The effect of this was that productivity was lower and grew more slowly than that of other countries in the advanced industrial world (see below). Such a phenomenon, being characteristic of British capitalism in peacetime since the 1880s, has been in striking contrast

[7] Sugden, Philip, Dissertation A: Post-war British Conservative Party economic, political and ideological strategy, with particular reference to the period 1974 to 1979, Humboldt University, (Berlin), 1985, p. 11 (unpublished).

to that of Britain's major competitors who had consequently grown faster.[8] With her major competitors concentrating on building up their economic strength and devoting substantial state support for modern technology, it is not surprising that Britain's standing in the world as a major economic power was increasingly challenged.[9]

In terms of economic growth, from 1950 right up to the early 1970s, Britain's performance, in comparison with other countries of the advanced industrialised world belonging to the Organisation for Economic Co-operation and Development (OECD), was weak (see Appendix 1, table 1). However, despite her relatively poor economic performance in this period, demand and output generally rose fast enough to maintain "full employment", although with imports rising twice as fast as exports in this period,[10] it was surely inevitable that balance of payments difficulties would put the brakes on Britain's economic expansion. "Stop-go" policies were therefore introduced in an attempt to keep the balance of payments in check. However, Britain's underlying economic difficulties became more exposed in the 1960s, oscillating between recession and recovery, with inflationary pressures as well as the negative trade balance plus large capital outflows holding back her economic advance.[11]

In recognition of her weak economic performance, the Macmillan Government (1957-1963)[12] embarked upon a two-pronged strategy. Firstly, it turned towards a corporatist concept which was characterised by setting up the National Economic Development Council (NEDC) and the National Incomes Commission. There, the emphasis was on tripartite collaboration consisting of the Government, employers and the trade unions. Secondly, with Britain's trade growing faster

---

8 Aaronovitch, Sam, *The Road from Thatcherism*, Lawrence and Wishart (London), 1981, pp. 5f.

9 Ibid.

10 *Cambridge Economic Policy Review*, Vol. 6, No. 1, University of Cambridge Department of Applied Economics, April 1980, p. 5.

11 See *Economic Policy Review*, No 4, University of Cambridge Department of Applied Economics, March 1978, pp. 1ff.

12 In October 1963, Harold Macmillan, whose government in June of that year had been shaken by the circumstances surrounding the resignation of the Secretary for War John Profumo (by attempting to conceal his involvement in a scandal which then raised serious doubts as to the effectiveness of the country's security), resigned following an operation. As national security ultimately was (and still is) the personal responsibility of the Prime Minister, this scandal dented Macmillan's personal standing and therefore his ability to lead his Party to another victory in a general election which in anyway was due in the following year at the very latest. After a "long drawn-out struggle", Sir Alec Douglas-Home (as Lord Home became after renouncing his peerage) "emerged" as Macmillan's successor. See Pelling, Henry, *A Short History of the Labour Party* (Fourth Edition), The Macmillan Press Ltd (London and Basingstoke), 1972, p. 130.

with the original member states of the European Economic Community (EEC) than with the European Free Trade Association (EFTA) or the countries of the Commonwealth, Macmillan sought Britain's entry into the EEC.

Attempts to keep the balance of payments and inflation under control by means of "stop-go" policies were highly resented on the shop floor. An indication of this can be seen through the increase in the number of strikes and the rising proportion of them over wages (see Appendix, table 2).

By the late 1950s, there appeared to be three features of industrial relations practice reflecting the fact that, with there being "full employment", the influence of the shop stewards grew. This became of growing concern, not only to most politicians and employers, but also to many trade union leaders who feared that their authority was being undermined. These three features became known as "wage drift", "restrictive practices" and "unofficial strikes".[13]

By "wage drift", it was meant that there was a widening gap between earnings and nationally agreed rates of pay, especially in manufacturing industry. In this, increases in earnings were said to be running ahead of increases in productivity, and local groups of workers, it was claimed, were able to exploit local shortages of skilled labour to their advantage. Regarding "restrictive practices", it was alleged, initially by the media that local groups of workers (often without official union support) were able to impose rigid forms of work control which were undermining industrial efficiency. "Unofficial strikes" (strikes without official union support) were, it was argued, increasing in number even though the number of "official" strikes showed no upward trend[14] (see Appendix, table 3).

So, with the domestic economy being sacrificed in pursuit of "imperial aims", the rising incident of industrial unrest was inevitably going to put into question the future of the "consensus era". For whatever claims the Conservatives could make in terms of falling unemployment and strong economic growth in the run-up to the 1964 general election, the extent to which they had any solid foundation became questionable (see Appendix, tables 4 and 5). In addition, a most notable factor questioning any such claims on the economic front was Britain's worsening balance of payments. In view of all this, not forgetting the events leading to the resignation of Profumo, the previous year, electoral support for the Conservative Party fell sharply enough for it to be narrowly voted out of office in the 1964 election.[15]

---

[13] Coates, David, ..., pp. 45f.

[14] Ibid.

[15] See Pelling, Henry, ..., pp. 130f.

When Labour was returned to office in October, 1964, it inherited a weakening economy and with what was then a record balance of payments deficit of £800m[16] which was aggravated by a large capital outflow.[17] Fully realising both the domestic and international implications of a weak economy, the incoming Labour Government under Harold Wilson, in line with its 1964 election manifesto commitments, introduced a National Plan with the dual purpose of expanding the economy and tackling Britain's negative trade balance.[18] But in addition to all this, Labour, under the obvious influence of the Treasury, was determined to maintain the value of sterling. In the absence of any decisive measures to divert outflowing capital into investment in manufacturing industry, the National Plan lacked a solid foundation upon which it could bring about the results it was intended to, i.e. for the economy to expand by 25% by 1970.[19]

However, the value of sterling could hardly be maintained unless investment and state support for manufacturing industry were put on a level comparable to that of Britain's major competitors. As a considerable amount of capital had been allowed to flow out of the country unhindered since the end of the War, the dual aim of economic expansion and maintaining the value of sterling could only be achieved by deflationary measures. In other words, incomes policies were, in effect, the undeclared "key" to the success of the Labour Government's National Plan.

Labour embarked upon what has been described as a "modernist" approach to the task of arresting Britain's economic decline. This consisted of four elements.[20] These were making industrial capital more effective, a major role for the state in restructuring key areas of industry, more prominence for tripartite collaboration and, increasingly after the effective collapse of sterling as a reserve currency in 1967, entry into the EEC. It can therefore be seen that Labour was, in effect, to continue with the type of policies which were introduced by Macmillan's Conservative Government.

In order to maintain the value of sterling, the negative trade balance had to be corrected. Initially, the measures taken were relatively modest: import surchar-

---

[16] Hamilton, Malcolm B., *Democratic Socialism in Britain and Sweden*, Macmillan Press (Basingstoke), 1989, p. 120.

[17] *Economic Policy Review*, ..., March 1978, p. 2.

[18] See Craig, F. W. S. (Ed.), ..., 259.

[19] See Kastendiek, Hans, "Gewerkschaftsmacht" und Arbeitskonflikte als Hauptthеme der britischen Politik, in: Jacobi, Otto, and Kastendiek, Hans (Hg.), *Staat und industrielle Beziehungen in Großbritannien*, Campus Verlag (Frankfurt/New York), 1985, p. 17.

[20] Jacques, Martin, Thatcherism: The Impasse Broken?, in: *Marxism Today* (London), Vol. 23 No. 10, October 1979, p. 7.

ges were imposed and also incomes policies to help keep inflation under control. To assist in this process, Labour established the National Board for Prices and Incomes on the same tripartite model as the NEDC and the National Incomes Commission. However, with only modest economic growth in the mid-1960s and with the balance of payments remaining in deficit, coupled with a big capital outflow in mid-1966, deflationary measures were more rigorously applied – largely through incomes policies.

This time, however, deflationary measures which had previously succeeded in correcting the negative trade balance failed. This, together with another large capital outflow, meant that the existing value of sterling could no longer be defended. In November 1967, Labour was forced to devalue the currency. By making the defence of sterling central to its National Plan (which is also an indication of the traditional influence the Treasury has over the formulation of British economic policy), Labour thus failed in achieving both of its objectives – the desired level of economic growth and the maintenance of the pre-November 1967 value of sterling.

Although sterling's devaluation led to a large rise in exports, the trade balance continued to remain in deficit. So, further deflationary measures were introduced. Not surprisingly, by the end of the 1960s, the economy had dipped into a full-scale recession coupled with rising inflationary pressures. This has been characterised as "slumpflation".[21] Inevitably, unemployment was also rising.

Failure on the economic front brought the Labour Government into conflict with the organised working class. 1968 had witnessed the highest degree of industrial militancy since the end of the 2nd World War (see Appendix 1, table 2). This was to mark a turning point for the Government.

Upon attaining office, the Wilson Government had foreseen that industrial unrest was not likely to subside. So, in 1965, using "unofficial" strikes as a pretext, a Royal Commission[22] was established to help find ways of lowering the degree of industrial unrest. Predictably, this Royal Commission (often known as the Donovan Commission) was able to show that, in the period 1964-1966, on the basis of figures submitted by the Ministry of Labour, 95% of all strikes were "unofficial";[23] its significance was more that it itself symbolised the way trade

[21] Hall, Stuart, The Great Moving Right Show, in: *Marxism Today* (London), Vol. 23 No. 1, January 1979, p. 15.

[22] This being the Royal Commission on Trade Unions and Employers' Associations - often known as the "Donovan Commission" after Lord Donovan who chaired this commission.

[23] *Royal Commission on Trade Unions and Employers' Associations 1965-1968*, HMSO (London), Cmnd. 3623, June 1968, p. 97, paras. 367f.

unions on the shop floor were being officially blamed for Britain's weak economic performance. In this, Labour sided openly with the opposition Conservative Party and employers' associations, and opened the door to legal intervention in industrial relations – a process which could not possibly be associated with "consensus" politics.

In official circles, there were two schools of thought[24] concerning the above mentioned features of industrial relations practice resulting from the growing influence of shop stewards. The "Tory Right" along with some employers' associations put the causes down to the "privileged" legal position of trade unions as a result of the 1906 Trade Disputes Act (see below). There was also then the so-called "Oxford School" associated with industrial relations professors Allan Flanders and Hugh Clegg, who put the causes down to deficiencies in the institutions of collective bargaining in conditions of "full employment".

The real concern in ruling circles was clearly summarised by the Inns of Court Conservative and Unionist Society (a group of prominent Conservative lawyers) in its evidence to the Donovan Commission in 1966. Clearly being aware that there had been conditions of "full employment", they claimed that: "In the last twenty-five years there has been a sellers' market for labour and the present power of the trade unions derives in the main from this. It is likely to persist".[25]

So, the task of the Donovan Commission was to determine how, in conditions of "full employment", the influence of shop stewards could be curbed. There, this Commission had to determine ways in which incomes policies (as already noted, the undeclared "key" to the success of Labour's National Plan) could be made to work effectively.[26] The Commission itself stated: "We are, however, convinced that incomes policy can make a contribution of outstanding importance to the economic growth of this country and a more ordered system of industrial relations, and that any proposals which we make for the reform of industrial relations should assist an incomes policy to work effectively. The proposals we have made ... will do so".[27]

It went on to say: "Our proposals are designed to provide effective control of industrial relations, including pay, at the level of the factory and company by means of properly constructed agreements between companies and trade unions.

---

24 Coates, David, ..., pp. 46f.

25 *Trade Unions for Tomorrow*, Conservative Political Centre (London SW1), CPC Number 346, p. 10.

26 See Ramelson, Bert, *Donovan Exposed: A critical analysis of the Royal Commission on Trade Unions*, Communist Party (published in London), 1968, pp. 4f.

27 *Royal Commission on ..., ...*, p. 52, para. 207.

If the decisions take accord with incomes policies, then incomes policy will work."[28]

By largely putting Britain's economic ills down to "unofficial" strikes and seeking a cure through the implementation of incomes policies, the Wilson Government set itself on a confrontation course with the organised labour movement. If "consensus" policies were still to have any meaning, it was clear that shop floor activists were to have no part in it. By the close of the 1960s, the basis of the "consensus" era was coming under strain on both the economic and industrial fronts.

On the economic front, any success that could be claimed e.g. the turn-around in Britain's negative trade balance (leading to a current account surplus of £735m in 1970 – the largest in real terms since 1950) together with the large reduction in the public sector borrowing requirement (PSBR), with there actually being a surplus in the financial year 1969-1970 (shortly before Labour's defeat in the June 1970 general election) was at the cost of economic stagnation and rising unemployment.[29]

On the industrial front, the rising degree of industrial militancy led to a "politicisation" of many shop-floor workers. This had a noticeable effect on a number of key trade union elections which were won by left-wing candidates (including those belonging to, or with the backing from, the then Communist Party of Great Britain (CPGB)). The most striking of these were the elections in 1969 of Jack Jones (succeeding Frank Cousins) as General Secretary of what was then Britain's largest trade union, the TGWU and in 1967 of Hugh Scanlon as President of what was then Britain's second largest union, the Amalgamated Engineering Union (AEU). Both Jones and Scanlon had risen through the shop-stewards' movement and were both supportive of militant tactics when they were elected.[30]

[28] Ibid., p. 53, para. 211.

[29] See Shaw, Eric, *The Labour Party since 1945*, Blackwell Publishers Ltd (Oxford), 1996, p. 80.

[30] Kelly, John, *Trade Unions and Socialist Politics*, Verso (London and New York), 1988, p. 109. NB The AEU, founded in 1920, became the Amalgamated Union of Engineering and Foundry Workers in 1968 with the accession of the Amalgamated Union of Foundry Workers. In 1970, this union became the Amalgamated Union of Engineering Workers (AUEW) upon amalgamation with The Draughtsmen and Allied Technicians' Association (DATA) and the Constructional Engineering Union. The amalgamation allowed for four sections of the AUEW: engineering, foundry, technical and supervisory (TASS) and construction with each section retaining its own organisation, hence affiliating separately to the TUC and the Labour Party, but coming together in a national conference. At the time of amalgamation, the combined membership was 1.4 million with the engineering section being the most influential with 1.2 million members. The ultimate objective was the creation of one union for the engineering industry however, a common rule book which was

This meant that a new generation of trade union leaders emerged who were more likely to be in conflict with Labour's parliamentary leadership than previously, even though in most cases, as with Jones and Scanlon, being members of the Labour Party.

This leftward swing in a number of key unions weakened the power structure in the Labour Party in the 1970s which had traditionally rested on a cohesion of the party's national executive committee (NEC), the party conference, the party's parliamentary leadership, the party leader and affiliated trade unions. This cohesion, having previously functioned for decades, brought about a system of integrated organisational control within the party which gave considerable authority to the party leader.[31]

The leftward swing in those unions helped the left in becoming a dominant force at the annual party conference and hence, on the party's (NEC). This development, it should be noted, did not lead to the left in gaining "control" of the party at any time. However, the traditional grip of those who supported Labour's parliamentary leadership was loosened and party leaders, particularly those of the parliamentary party, had to take account of this development.

Following the defeat of proposals to resolve the problem of "unofficial" strikes as formulated in its White Paper *In Place of Strife* of January 1969, the Labour Government needed to heal the rift this had caused with the trade union movement. This defeat came about, not only through intensive pressure from prominent trade union leaders e.g. Frank Cousins and Jack Jones of the TGWU and Hugh Scanlon of the AEU, but also through considerable opposition within the Parliamentary Labour Party (PLP) and subsequently within the Labour Government itself.[32] This change in the leadership of prominent trade unions not only influenced the events leading up to the defeat of this White Paper but was also to have the effect of influencing the degree of the TUC's opposition to the 1971 Industrial Relations Act a couple of years later (see pages 49f).

---

drafted in 1972 had never been fully implemented. See Marsh, Arthur and Ryan, Victoria, *Historical Directory of Trade Unions* (Volume 2), Gower Publishing Company Ltd. (Aldershot, Hants.), 1984, pp. 12f and 19. For details of membership of the four sections of the AUEW at the time of amalgamation, see *Report of 103rd Annual Trades Union Congress*, TUC (London), 1971, pp. 551-655. For the purposes of this book, the AUEW will mean the AUEW (engineering section).

31 Shaw, Eric, *The Labour Party Since 1979*, Routledge (London and New York), 1994, p. 159.

32 See Barnes, Denis and Reid, Eileen, *Government and Trade Unions*, Heinemann Educational Books Ltd (London), 1980, pp. 116-126.

Clearly, the "consensus" which had almost broken down through the publication of *In Place of Strife* could not be restored as long as there were threats of authoritarian and penal measures against trade unions and trade unionists as proposed in this White Paper (see below). As events had subsequently shown, Labour's failure on the economic front coupled with its loss of credit on the industrial relations scene led to its election defeat in 1970. Subsequent events were to show that the rupture the "consensus" era had suffered through this White Paper was never really healed and this episode in the eyes of the trade union movement is something which has never been forgotten.

The pursuit of "consensus" politics was hardly the intention of the incoming Conservative Government under Edward Heath in 1970. On the contrary, its strategy for tackling Britain's economic ills was to secure entry into the EEC, using this to weed out "inefficient" sectors of industry; and to strengthen the role of the state in industrial relations,[33] in the hope of succeeding in taming the trade union movement where Labour had failed.

The Heath Government started by dismantling the various tripartite institutions which the previous Labour Government had established e.g. the National Board for Prices and Incomes.[34] At first, by "officially" not having an incomes policy, it sought nevertheless to keep down pay settlements in the public sector and to use this as a norm for the rest of the economy (i.e. incomes policy via the back door).

However, with unemployment continuing to rise within a relatively depressed economy, the collapse of Rolls Royce in 1971 and the long campaign to prevent the closure of Upper Clyde Shipbuilders, the Heath Government was forced to intervene more directly in the economy. This led to what has been described as the "U-turn" of 1972.[35]

Although the policy of holding back public sector pay settlements had some initial success (e.g. against the post office workers in 1971), the Heath Government suffered a defeat in the same year against the miners.[36] It suffered a further defeat in the following year in another conflict against the miners and also against the railwaymen. The conflict against the railwaymen entailed, additionally, a humiliating defeat under an important provision of the 1971 Industrial Relations Act (see below). In effect, the policy of keeping down pay settlements

33 Sugden, Philip, ..., p. 25.

34 Gamble, Andrew, *The Free Economy and the Strong State* (Second Edition), Palgrave (Basingstoke and New York), 1994, p. 82.

35 Ibid., p. 84.

36 Ibid.

in the public sector had collapsed by the summer of 1972. In its attempt to weed out "inefficient" sectors of industry (the "no lame duck" policy) the Government was not only trying to get industry restructured but was also using this as a means of warning trade unions of mass unemployment if they did not keep down their pay settlements.[37]

Faced with the apparent collapse of its policy on pay, industrial restructuring and industrial relations, the Heath Government, it could be argued, sought to re-establish the various policy instruments which had been characteristic of "consensus" politics before 1970. This, in effect, was the political significance of the "U-turn".

Realising the economic and industrial implications of its "no lame duck" policy, the Heath Government was compelled to rescue Rolls Royce and Upper Clyde Shipbuilders (through nationalisation), and also to put through Parliament a special Act (the 1972 Industry Act) giving the Government powers to intervene directly in industrial restructuring.

Against its election pledge,[38] the Heath Government introduced statutory incomes policies as from autumn 1972. Also, in the aftermath of its failure on pay and industrial relations, attempts were made at re-establishing tripartite collaboration. This change in course appeared to work until the conflict with the miners in winter 1974 which resulted in the downfall of the Heath Government.

Britain's underlying economic weakness continued to become more exposed with balance of payments deficits holding back economic growth. Expansionary fiscal and monetary policies in the 1973 Budget were seen to have been a major factor behind the serious balance of payments deficit, that year. Furthermore, the Bank of England's minimum lending rate (MLR), since the introduction of this particular criterion for the Bank to intervene in the money markets as from October 1972, fluctuated at around 8% until around the middle of 1973. It then started to rise rapidly. MLR reached 13% on 13th November of that year and stayed at that rate until 7 January, 1974, when it started to fall gradually. All the same, MLR continued to remain high, almost constantly in double figures, until it started falling steadily in 1977.[39] All this helped to highlight the underlying weakness of the British economy. This was aggravated further by the sudden

[37] Sugden, Philip, ..., pp. 35f.

[38] Craig, F. W. S. (Ed.), ..., p. 331.

[39] Bank of England Money Market Intervention Rates: Changes in Bank Rate, Minimum Lending Rate, Minimum Band 1 Dealing Rate and Repo Rate, in: *Bank of England Statistical Abstract Part 1*, December 2002, Table 22.1.

increases in oil prices at the end of 1973[40] which led to a downturn in the world economy.

When Labour was returned to office at the beginning of March 1974, it thus inherited, as in October 1964, a balance of payments deficit though this time, on a magnitude hitherto unknown in Britain. This, to mention nothing of the effect of the miners' strike (which led to the introduction of the three-day week), contributed to the severest economic crisis since the end of the 2nd World War. On top of this, with the unpopularity of incomes policies on the shop floor, the period 1968-1974 witnessing the highest level of industrial unrest since the end of the War, Labour realised that Britain's economic difficulties could only be overcome through cooperation with the trade union movement. This was the basis upon which Labour's Social Contract came into being.

The Social Contract should be seen in the context of re-establishing "consensus" politics. This had been ruptured by *In Place of Strife*: it had subsequently been abandoned by the incoming Conservative Government in 1970, and briefly re-established in 1972. "Consensus" politics came under pressure again in consequence of the 1974 miners' strike.

In formulating the Social Contract, Labour's parliamentary leadership had to take into account the leftward shift in a number of key trade unions which in turn, as just noted, had an influence on Labour's NEC. One should not overlook the influence of the CPGB in this process. Despite its relatively small membership, it was able to exert considerable influence on the policies of some key unions and, indirectly, on the policies adopted by Labour Party conferences.[41] This was possible because it was well organised industrially and could work with many non-communist militants who had a similar political outlook on a wide range of everyday issues, particularly with regard to economic, social and industrial matters.

It was this leftward shift which influenced the formulation of *Labour's Programme 1973* which was adopted by the 1973 Labour Party Conference. One major significance of this was the adoption of "A New Economic Strategy"[42] which was based on an extension of public ownership of industry, price controls, more expenditure on social reforms and, most importantly, the often quoted

---

40 Between October 1973 and January 1974, the world price of crude oil quadrupled. So for countries like the UK which were net importers of oil, this led to the twin problems of inflation and a worsening of their balance of payments. See Hickson, Kevin, *The IMF Crisis of 1976*, Tauris Academic Studies (London and New York), 2005, p. 62.

41 See Flanders, Allan, *Management and Unions*, Faber and Faber (London), 1975, p. 18.

42 See *Labour's Programme 1973*, Labour Party (London) 1973, pp. 13-39.

commitment to "a fundamental and irreversible shift in the balance of power and wealth, in favour of working people and their families".[43] This was to form the basis of the Alternative Economic Strategy (AES). The formulation of a "New Economic Strategy" was influenced by an earlier document published by the TUC-Labour Party Liaison Committee in February 1973[44] which was approved by the TUC General Council, Labour's NEC and the Parliamentary Committee of the Labour Party.

When *Labour's Programme 1973* was adopted, it was unclear as to whether Britain would remain a member of the EEC, which she had joined at the beginning of that year. The Labour Party and the Labour Opposition had opposed Britain joining on the basis of the terms which were negotiated by the Heath Government and, unlike in other countries which had also joined then and later, there was severe criticism in that no referendum on this crucial question had taken place. Consequently, the Labour Party pledged to renegotiate the terms of Britain's membership with the British people having the final say in a referendum as to whether Britain should remain a member or whether it should seek withdrawal.[45] This decision was to be one vital element in determining whether the key policy commitments of the AES could be realised at all. In this, the position the Labour Government was to take on the question of Britain's continued membership of the EEC was to be indicative of the extent it really supported its own party's programme, especially the AES.

Based on *Labour's Programme 1973*, pledges respecting the above-mentioned "fundamental and irreversible shift" were made in the two general elections in 1974.[46] But of greater importance, especially for Labour's parliamentary leadership, was the need for a "far reaching *social contract* between workers and the

---

[43] Ibid., p. 13.

[44] *Economic Policy and the Cost of Living*, TUC-Labour Party Liaison Committee (London), February 1973.

[45] This promised referendum, in which the British people voted to remain in the EEC, took place on 5 June, 1975. There, the majority of Cabinet Ministers in the Wilson Government together with the Conservative and Liberal parties supported Britain's continued membership. However, there was considerable opposition within the Labour Party itself to its own government's position on this vital question and a special conference of the Party in spring 1975 decided to support Britain's withdrawal. The opposition in the Labour Party to remaining in the EEC was such that the Government was unable to carry the support of the majority of its own MPs. Instead, in the House of Commons vote on the "renegotiated" terms of membership, Wilson was particularly dependent on the support of the Conservative Opposition, which, it is worth noting, was then under its new Leader and future Prime Minister, Margaret Thatcher.

[46] See *Let us work together – Labour's Way Out of the Crisis: The Labour Party Manifesto 1974* (February), Labour Party (London), p. 2. See also *Britain will win with Labour – Labour Party Manifesto October 1974*, Labour Party (London), p. 30.

Government – a contract which can be renewed each year as circumstances change and as new opportunities present themselves".[47]

By stressing the need for a "fundamental and irreversible shift", this programme was, in effect, trying to re-establish "consensus" politics on a new footing. It recognised that meeting its objectives in economic management meant the control of inflation, the maintenance of full employment and the achievement of rising real standards of living – personal, social and environmental – for all sections of the community.[48]

However, this pledge did not appear so definite in Labour's October 1974 manifesto which stated: "We put forward in this manifesto a list of improvements we want to make in society. We put them forward in good faith; but many of them cost money, and we understand perfectly well ... that the timing of them will depend on how quickly and how completely we get on top of the economic problems".[49]

In all fairness to the Labour Government, the economic situation had deteriorated drastically since the publication of the *Labour's Programme 1973* in a way which could not have been envisaged when it was originally adopted. All the same, this statement in the October 1974 election manifesto, as formulated, is enough to question the extent to which the Labour Government had ever intended to bring about this "fundamental and irreversible shift".

On the positive side, for the trade union and labour movement, the period of the Social Contract brought about a series of significant reforms. Following the repeal of the 1971 Industrial Relations Act by the newly elected Labour Government in 1974, a series of statutes were passed giving working people, their organisations and their families more rights than they had ever had previously, e.g. more protection against dismissal, more rights for trade unions and the right to maternity leave.

On the negative side, these reforms were continually overshadowed by the difficulties Labour faced in overcoming the economic legacy it inherited upon taking office in 1974. All this coincided with a new phase in the economic fortunes of advanced capitalist countries which became apparent in the 1970s. On the one hand, there was economic stagnation associated with rising unemployment; on

47 *Labour's Programme 1973*, ..., p. 14.

48 Ibid., p. 13.

49 *Britain will win with Labour* ..., ..., p. 3.

the other hand, accelerating inflation. This phase became known as "stagflation"[50] and elements of this had already been evident in Britain in the late 1960s.

However, with inflation touching 30% in July 1975 together with a "run" on sterling, union leaders realised that they were not going to be able to block the return of incomes policies. Instead, they sought to shape their details. So, in the first year they were used under the Social Contract, pay increases were limited to £6 per week with no increases for those earning over £8,000 per year (on the initiative of the then TGWU General Secretary Jack Jones). Likewise, in the following annual pay round, it was the Amalgamated Union of Engineering Workers (AUEW), representing many skilled workers, which sought percentage increases so as to protect pay differentials and there, pay increases were limited to 4.5%. Initially, these policies met little resistance and there were no officially sanctioned strikes against them.[51] So, under the Social Contract, incomes policies were to be used in an attempt to bring down inflation as well as to reduce the balance of payments deficit. Not only that.

In 1974, the Wilson Government, shortly after taking office, introduced a budget which turned out to be reflationary. Furthermore, as Britain exported less than the new government had predicted, owing to the decline in world trade, Britain's balance of payments deficit was therefore higher than expected.[52] So, due to this deficit and rising inflation, Labour changed course which in turn would signify an abandonment of any commitment, in as far as there had ever been any, to the AES. So, parallel to the introduction of incomes policies, Labour started to implement deflationary measures through cuts in public expenditure. These cuts were initially announced in the 1975 Budget together with cuts of a further £1 billion in July, the following year. These cuts had the aim of reducing the PSBR by reducing public expenditure *in real terms* so as to reduce inflation. The method by which this was to be achieved was by using a system of *cash limits* which was initially introduced in July 1975. The use of *cash limits* was to be of more significance in the following year when Labour, due to the heavy selling of sterling on the major currency markets, felt compelled to seek a loan through the International Monetary Fund (IMF)[53] (see below).

---

[50] See Therborn, Göran; The Two-Thirds, One-Third Society; in: Hall, Stuart and Jacques, Martin (Ed.), *New Times*, Lawrence and Wishart (London), 1989, p. 103.

[51] Coates, David, ..., pp. 73f.

[52] Healey, (Lord) Denis, *The Time of My Life*, Michael Joseph (London), 1989, p. 393.

[53] Hickson, Kevin, *The IMF Crisis of 1976 and British Politics*, Tauris Academic Press (London and New York), 2005, pp. 57f. NB prior to the introduction of *cash limits*, public expenditure had been calculated in volume terms i.e. on the basis of the amount required to finance specific programmes even if these turned out to be more expensive than originally envisaged as was/is often the case. So, the principle behind the introduction of *cash limits* was that a nominal figure was to be set for each item of expenditure and then it became the

Although the rate of inflation fell from its peak of summer 1975 (falling from an average of 24.05% in that year to 16.62% in 1976), the extent to which this fall can actually be attributed to incomes policies is questionable as the inflationary pressures facing Britain at the time were caused by an excessive growth of the money supply.[54] Regarding the balance of payments situation, Britain's current account deficit fell from £3,186m in 1974 to £1,526m in 1975.[55] In 1977, according to Denis Healey (Chancellor of the Exchequer 1974-1979) Britain's balance of payments deficit had been eliminated. This had been achieved despite the burden on the balance of payments of the high costs of capital investment in North Sea oil extraction before oil had started to flow to any significant effect.[56]

So, despite any success Labour could claim in the fight against inflation and in seeking to reduce the PSBR and the balance of payments deficit, the cost of all this, not forgetting the economic legacy it inherited upon taking office in 1974 as well as the effect of Heath's conflict with the miners, was a major downturn in the UK economy with economic growth being negative in 1974 and 1975 (see Appendix, table 5). Consequently, there was not only a large increase in unemployment, rising from 542,000 in mid-June 1974 to 1,450,000 in mid-June 1977 (see Appendix, table 4), but in the period 1975-1977, living standards, even for those in work, fell more than at any time in post-war Britain.[57]

Leaving aside any progress that could be claimed in the fight against inflation etc., Labour was then to be confronted by a sterling crisis. Although there had been a rapid increase in oil prices, the main oil exporting nations such as Saudi Arabia, Iran and Nigeria had tended to hold a large amount of their sterling deposits in the City of London. So, through the sudden increase in oil prices, the deposits these countries held there also swelled and the Labour Government could initially benefit from this in its financing policy. However, when these countries started to spread their portfolios more widely, money started to flow out of the City of London. This was to make the value of sterling more volatile on the world's currency markets. It was the run-down of the sterling deposits held in the City of London in 1976 which turned out to be the principle factor behind the sterling crisis in that year.[58] This crisis became increasingly critical as the year progressed.

---

responsibility of government departments themselves to finance their expenditure programmes out of their block allocation of funding. See Hickson, Kevin, ..., pp. 57f.

54 See Ibid., p. 69, footnote 35.

55 See Ibid., p. 69, footnote 42.

56 Healey, (Lord) Denis, ..., pp. 400f.

57 Kelly, *John, Labour and the Unions*, Verso (London and New York), 1987, p. 21.

58 Keegan, William, *Britain Without Oil*, Penguin Books Ltd. (Harmondsworth), 1985, p. 24.

Whenever a country is confronted by such pressures on its currency, measures undertaken to try and counter these difficulties have often taken the form of enacting deflationary measures, raising interest rates, currency depreciation or to convert foreign currency reserves into the country's own currency. An additional option is to try and secure a foreign currency loan, as Britain had already done, for example, through the IMF, but any such loan would be subject to conditions.

Despite the reduction in Britain's current account deficit from 1974 to 1975, her external payments situation, as indicated by the size of the sterling balances held by central monetary institutions, had deteriorated throughout much of 1975. To prevent any worsening of this, the Labour Government in winter 1975/1976 (still under Harold Wilson) applied for and secured its first loan through the IMF. At that point, there were already indications that public expenditure cuts, in addition to those which had already been announced, would have to take place.[59] The stand-by facility which Labour had then secured through the IMF provided, at best, only temporary relief as the pressure on sterling was to resume with more serious consequences.[60]

By autumn 1976, the international pressure on sterling was such that the steep rises in MLR, which had already taken place at the time, appeared to have little effect in preventing further falls in its value.[61] This, together with the generally worsening economic situation coupled with concern over rising public expenditure from within prominent financial circles, despite the cuts which had already taken place, forced the Labour Government (under Wilson's successor James Callaghan)[62] to secure another loan through the IMF, knowing what its conditions were likely to be.

---

[59] See Hickson, Kevin, ..., pp. 58f. Between March and December 1975, the sterling balances held by central monetary institutions fell from £4,862m to £4,100m. See p. 69, footnote 43.

[60] See Ibid., pp. 74-99.

[61] This impact of the pressure on sterling can be seen in that on 13 September, 1976, MLR rose from 11.5% to 13%. This was to be quickly followed on 7 October by an additional 2% increase to 15%, then an a post-war high. See footnote 39. NB On 10 March, 1976, the exchange rate of sterling against the US dollar was £=$1.91. On 1 April, it fell to $1.88. On 28 May it fell to $1.76 with it falling to $1.72 on 2 June. Despite the rise in MLR to 13% on 13 September, the exchange rate fell to $1.63 on 28 September. It was only after the conclusion of the loan agreement with the IMF towards the end of 1976 when there was any notable recovery in the value of sterling after falling during the course of that year. See Hickson, Kevin, ..., pp. 232-238 (Appendix The 1976 IMF Crisis: A Chronology).

[62] James Callaghan took over as Prime Minister and Leader of the Labour Party in winter 1976 from Harold Wilson who, having led the Party since 1963 and having also been Prime Minister from 1964 to 1970, stepped down. Wilson was elected Party Leader upon the death of Hugh Gaitskell.

However, despite Britain being on the brink of becoming an oil-producing and exporting nation, seeking to secure a loan through the IMF on the security of the revenues which were yet to flow through North Sea oil extraction no longer appeared to be an option[63] even though this would have been feasible given the positive effect this was going to have on Britain's balance of payments within the foreseeable future. Instead, the IMF was to force Labour into making further cuts in public expenditure which meant it having to go against the grain of many of its manifesto commitments and much of what the Labour Party had always stood for even though in the financial year 1976/1977, according to Healey, public expenditure was £2.2 billion less than had originally been planned.[64]

The terms of this loan were to be of historic significance. The IMF insisted that public expenditure and money supply be controlled[65] and this was to be done through *cash limits*[66] with them being more vigorously applied than when they were originally introduced in the previous year (see above). In this, there were to be publicly stated targets for curbing public expenditure and for controlling the rate of growth of the money supply. By implication, the Government was also forced to abandon those parts of its October 1974 manifesto which were seen as controversial, i.e. plans it had for intervening in industry[67] and for stimulating the economy. Instead, it had to make further cuts public expenditure, despite high unemployment, trying not to recall the effect that such deflationary policies had had in the 1920s and 1930s. So this meant that in addition to the public expenditure cuts which were announced in July 1976, there were then to be a total of £1 billion of cuts for the financial year 1977/1978 and £1.5 billion for 1978/-1979. The Government decided to limit further cuts by selling £500m worth of shares in British Petroleum.[68]

By agreeing to the IMF's terms with unemployment at what was already then a post-war high, Labour was also effectively forced to abandon a key element of "consensus" politics – the commitment to "full employment" (even though this commitment was not officially revoked as government policy until March 1985).[69] So these cuts together with the unpopularity of incomes policies brought

---

63 Keegan, William, ..., pp. 22f.

64 See Healey, (Lord) Denis, ..., p. 401.

65 Maude, Angus (Ed.), *The Right Approach to the Economy*, Conservative Central Office (Westminster, London), October 1977, p. 9.

66 Ibid., p. 12.

67 Labour's plans for state intervention in industry had already had to be curtailed as a condition for Britain's continued membership of the EEC – now the EU.

68 Hickson, Kevin, ..., p. 148.

69 See Hanson, Charles G. and Mather, Graham, *Striking Out Strikes*, Institute of Economic Affairs (Westminster, London), Hobart Paper 110, 1988, p. 15. See also *Employment: The*

the Labour Government on a collision course with the organised labour movement and the mass of Labour Party activists.

Yet, the turnaround in the UK economy in 1977, as indicated, for example, by the elimination of her balance of payments deficit, that year (before the IMF agreement had time to influence any of this), the PSBR being lower than the Treasury had predicted[70] and the steady decline in interest rates from what was then a postwar peak with MLR at 15% in autumn 1976 with it falling to 5% on 17 October, 1977 (the lowest since 1971/1972),[71] enabled Healey, in his own words, "to introduce a reflationary budget in 1978 to undo the damage done by excessive deflation in 1977 ... [with] room to increase demand by £2.8 billion without infringing any ... undertakings to the IMF".[72] The turnaround in the UK economy in 1977 was aided by the initial flow of North Sea oil in measurable quantities. In that year, North Sea oil production was roughly equal to half the UK's total consumption and the UK's balance of payments benefited by around £2 billion.[73] So, all in all, the cuts attached to the IMF loan at the end of 1976 were unnecessary, as Healey himself later admitted. Furthermore, the Government, according to Healey, only drew half the loan offered by the IMF and all of it, or the equivalent, had been repaid by the time Labour left office in 1979.[74]

However, the upturn in the UK economy as from 1977, as already indicated, had no effect in overcoming the widespread discontent over the effect of incomes policies and the steep rise in unemployment from within the organised labour movement. When this upturn came, the effect this had on reducing the number of people out of work was minimal. Unemployment fell from 1,450,000 in mid-June 1977 to 1,446,000 in mid-June 1978 to 1,344,000 in mid-June 1979 shortly after Labour left office (see Appendix, table 4).

In the mid-1970s, a serious dilemma faced the Labour Government. The extent to which "stop-go" policies worked in the 1950s and 1960s can be questioned, but they were more obviously ineffective from the mid-1970s when Britain was faced with the dual problem of high inflation and high unemployment. This predicament was clearly expressed by the Labour Prime Minister James Callaghan in his speech to the 1976 Labour Party Conference: "We used to think you could spend your way out of a recession and increase employment by cutting taxes and

---

Challenge for the Nation, Cmnd. 9474, HMSO (London), March 1985, p. 3, para. 2.1.

70 Healey, (Lord) Denis, ..., p. 432.

71 *Bank of England Statistical Abstract Part 1*, December 2002, Table 22.1.

72 Healey, (Lord) Denis, ..., p. 433.

73 *The Challenge of North Sea Oil*, Cmnd. 7143, HMSO (London), March 1978, p. 6, para. 12.

74 Healey, (Lord) Denis, pp. 432f.

boosting government spending. I tell you in all candour: that option no longer exists. An insofar as it ever did exist, it only worked by injecting inflation into the economy. And each time that happened, unemployment rose. The cosy world which we were told would go on for ever, where full employment could be guaranteed by the stroke of the Chancellor's pen, is gone".[75]

The decisive fact was that, by the mid-1970s, Britain ceased to have what could be defined as "full employment". On the assumption that there are always people changing jobs, plus seasonal factors in sectors such as agriculture, "full employment" was once understood as everyone wanting work being in employment.[76] In fact, in 1944, Lord Beveridge had regarded an unemployment rate of 3% as being compatible with "full employment". At the time, this would have implied that around 550,000 people might be unemployed.[77]

On the basis of this 3% criterion, it can be argued that Britain had "full employment" from the early years of the 2nd World War up to and including 1970, the year when Labour was voted out of office (see Appendix, table 4). Even though unemployment rose in the latter half of the 1960s reaching a post-war peak of 600,000 in 1970 it still remained below this 3% mark.[78] By the early 1970s, "full employment" could only have been seen to be maintained through tolerating higher levels of the PSBR which in turn would have led to higher balance of payments deficits and/or higher levels of inflation. Consequently, the incoming Conservative Government in 1970 did not take any decisive measures to ease the restrictive fiscal policies of the outgoing Labour Government. So unemployment, as it were, was allowed to rise with the effect that in 1971 and 1972, Britain did not have "full employment". It was only in the aftermath of the "U-turn" in 1972 when the Heath Government began to take measures to tackle rising unemployment. Thus, it was only in 1973, when the easing of constraints on fiscal and monetary policy began to take effect, did the number of people out of work begin to fall. However, it only fell back to roughly what it was in 1970.[79] In 1973, there was rapid growth in the UK economy but this, as already noted, was coupled with a worsening of Britain's balance of payments and rapid increases in interest rates: all this before the impact of the heavy increase in oil prices at the end of that year and the implications of the conflict with the miners!

---

[75] See *Labour Party Conference Report*, Labour Party (London), 1976, p. 188.

[76] See *Donaldson, Peter, Guide to the British Economy* (Fourth Edition), Penguin Books (Harmondsworth), 1976, pp. 153ff.

[77] Beveridge, William H., *Full Employment in a Free Society*, Allen and Unwin (London), 1944, p. 128.

[78] See also *Economic Policy Review*, ..., March 1978, p. 2 and Statistical Appendix Table 2, pp. A8-A9.

[79] Ibid.

In 1973 and 1974, there was a brief return to "full employment" but from 1975, this key element of "consensus era" politics, as far as the Government was concerned, appeared to become unattainable and unemployment started rising once more. Significantly, when the economy experienced an upturn as from 1977, aided by the initial inflow of North Sea oil revenues, the impact on the unemployment figures, as already noted, was limited.

The terms of the IMF loan also eased the way for Callaghan to conclude a pact with the Liberal Party. With Labour's unpopularity resulting in some by-election defeats, the Party's slender parliamentary majority from the October 1974 election was more than eroded. This pact ensured that Labour, when faced with an Opposition motion of no confidence in early 1977, to stay in office. At the same time, however, it enabled the Callaghan Government to out-manoeuvre the left in the Labour Party and to proceed further in dropping policies which it had not been enthusiastic about in the first place.

Although this pact enabled Labour to remain in office for another couple of years, the absence of any noticeable improvement on the economic front as far as the masses of working people were concerned, made trade union support for the Social Contract harder to sustain. Eventually, opposition to the Social Contract rose to the point that it broke down. Nevertheless, the Callaghan Government pursued incomes policies further and tried to keep pay settlements down to just 5% in the 1978/1979 pay round when the rate of inflation was still more than double that. In so doing, it set itself on a confrontation course with the organised labour movement, which led to large-scale industrial unrest, particularly among low-paid workers in the public sector,[80] in what became known as the "winter of discontent".

On balance, Labour's handling of Britain's economic situation was "little more than pragmatic crisis-management in which the central element was securing working class acquiescence to cuts in real wages and public expenditure together with rising unemployment".[81] So, Labour left office in 1979, as it had in 1970, amidst discontent over incomes policies which reflected a general failure on the economic front.

Any element of "consensus" politics which remained after the commitment to "full employment" had effectively been abandoned, collapsed in the 1978/1979 pay round. The general election result of May 1979 brought this era to a close.

---

[80] See Kelly, John, *Labour and the Unions*, ..., pp. 21f.

[81] Jacques, Martin, ..., p. 9.

1.2. British labour law in the context of consensus politics

In a number of industrialised countries in Europe, three stages can be identified along the path leading to the legality of trade unionism.[82] Firstly, arising out of the industrial revolution with the resulting growth of the industrial working class, governments were compelled to repeal various penal laws making trade unionism illegal, as in Germany in 1869, France in 1884, Italy in 1889 and Sweden in 1864.[83] Secondly, there was the establishment of various forms of "positive rights" for workers to organise and bargain collectively. For these two stages to have any real significance, there had to be a further stage, which was for workers and their organisations to be protected from claims for damages in the event of industrial action and for such action not to be regarded as a breach of the employment contract.[84]

What is interesting about Great Britain was that the path taken to the development of modern-day labour law was different. When trade unions first emerged in Britain, they faced illegality, as elsewhere, under both the criminal and civil law. The Combination Acts of 1799 and 1800 were amongst 40 statutes which criminalised workers' organisations.[85] "Combination" was not only seen as a threat to the "free" functioning of the market, which was supposed to guarantee the well-being of society, but was also seen as a threat to the social and political status quo.[86]

In Britain, in line with other countries mentioned above, the first stage consisted of the repeal of various laws rendering trade unionism illegal. This process began in 1824/1825 through the repeal of the Combination Acts. On the other hand, with this repeal legislation re-enacting a list of criminal offences,[87] this "first stage" was to be a long and tedious process which in fact spanned half a century. As late as between 1858 and 1875, there were no less than 10,000 prosecutions a year in England and Wales alone for breach of the employment contract.[88] So, it was not until the passing of a series of statutes in the 1870s that

[82] Wedderburn, (Lord) K. W., Freedom of Association and Philosophies of Labour Law, in: *Industrial Law Journal*, Oxford University Press (Oxford), Vol. 18 No. 1, March 1989, pp. 4f.

[83] Wedderburn, (Lord) K. W., *The Worker and the Law* (Third Edition), Penguin (Harmondsworth), 1986, p. 19.

[84] Wedderburn, (Lord) K. W., Freedom of Association ..., ..., p. 5.

[85] McIlroy, John, *Trade Unions in Britain Today*, Manchester University Press (Manchester and New York), 1988, p. 66.

[86] Ibid.

[87] Ibid.

[88] Ibid.

strike action or the threat of it ceased generally to be a criminal offence. At that point, the most important statutes were the Trade Union Act, 1871, and the Conspiracy and Protection of Property Act, 1875.[89]

The 1875 Act was of particular importance in two ways. Firstly, it became "the first example of legal immunity [under the criminal law] for those involved in trade disputes".[90] Basically, this meant that no one was to be deemed liable for prosecution for criminal conspiracy if he committed an offence for actions "in contemplation or furtherance of a trade dispute".[91] Secondly, this Act repealed various statutes which had generally made it a criminal offence for workers to break their employment contracts. Most notably, this included the Master and Servants Acts which had made a breach of the employment contract, on the part of the employee, but not on the part of the employer, a criminal offence (see page 139).

However, unlike other countries mentioned above, Britain did not advance to the "second stage" of enacting a system of "positive rights" because trade unions in Britain rarely demanded this.[92] In these other countries, the trade union movement developed along with mass political parties rooted in the labour movement, so that political demands for workers' rights were made and eventually conceded. In Britain, in contrast, the "political wing" of the labour movement did not reach "maturity" until 1906 (through the formation of the Labour Party).

In the years up to 1906, trade unions were affected by a much more pressing problem than the call for "positive rights". This was that, as a result of a successful employers' offensive against the "New Unions" in the early 1890s, the ground was prepared for the judiciary to make court rulings in various cases which went against the spirit of the various statutes legalising trade unions and their activities.[93] This culminated in the House of Lords' ruling in the case of the *Taff Vale Railway Company v. the Amalgamated Society of Railway Servants* in 1901 (see pages 126f). Consequently, the pressing problem for trade unions was less to achieve "positive rights". Rather it was "directed towards the pragmatic objective of removing common law shackles"[94] so that unions could organise and bargain collectively without the risk of claims for damages.

---

89 *Trade Union Immunities*, Cmnd. 8128, HMSO (London), January 1981, pp. 11ff, paras. 39-43.

90 Ibid., p. 13, para. 43.

91 Ibid.

92 Wedderburn, (Lord) K. W., Freedom of Association ..., ..., p. 4.

93 Griffith, J. A. G., *The Politics of the Judiciary* (Fifth Edition), Fontana Press (Hammersmith, London), 1997, p. 64.

94 Wedderburn, (Lord) K. W., *The Worker and the Law* ..., ..., p. 22.

After the legality of trade unions was conceded in the 1870s, civil liability began to take shape in two ways. Firstly, the judiciary developed a new "civil liability for conspiracy", which meant that anyone who joined with another in a strike for purposes which the courts regarded as "illegitimate" could be sued for damages. Secondly, the organisers of industrial action risked being exposed in tort[95] for "inducing a breach of the contracts of employment" of those whom they called out on strike[96] (see page 142).

Thus, although industrial action may have ceased to be a criminal offence as far as Parliament was concerned, it could still be looked upon as being an offence from the point of view of the judiciary. In fact, nobody could have summed up these judicial developments of the time (from the early 1890s to 1906) better than the Thatcher Government itself when it said in its 1981 Green Paper *Trade Union Immunities*: "In short, it seemed that these new liabilities had put the law back almost to where it was before the 1870s".[97]

If there were any doubts about the position of the judiciary regarding the legality of industrial disputes, they would have surely been removed as a result of the House of Lords' ruling in the Taff Vale case. As this ruling caused the defendant union to pay legal costs and damages amounting to almost two-thirds of the union's annual income,[98] trade union anger was predictable. This ruling has been accurately described as leaving "a legacy of suspicion and mistrust ... to poison relations between the courts and the unions for many years".[99]

With the political wing of the trade union movement developing through the formation of the Labour Representation Committee (leading to the foundation of the Labour Party) and many Liberal MPs dependent on the votes of trade union members, demands for legislation to protect trade union funds in the event of industrial action received wide support. Clearly, the then Conservative Government was compelled to take account of these developments and a Royal Commission was established.[100]

---

95 A "tort" is a civil wrong other than a breach of contract.

96 *Trade Union Immunities*, ..., p. 13, para. 45.

97 Ibid., p. 13, para. 46.

98 Ibid., p. 14, para. 49.

99 Griffith, J. A. G., ..., p. 66.

100 This Royal Commission consisting of five members was established in June 1903 under the Chairmanship of Lord Dunedin. It was directed to inquire into the subject of trade disputes and trade combinations and the law affecting them. The (majority) report together with two dissenting reports were published in January 1906. See *Royal Commission on* ..., ..., p. 2, para. 5, and p. 226, para. 850.

The outcome of this Royal Commission was the historic Trade Disputes Act, 1906, although as a result of the general election in winter 1906, it was a Liberal Government which put through this piece of legislation. As this election also brought about the first real influx of Labour MPs, this enabled the trade union movement to secure the degree of legal protection it had long sought. This, misleadingly, became known as "immunities".

The purpose of this historic piece of legislation was not to put trade unions "above the law" as the term "immunities" might imply. On the contrary. The words of the then Solicitor General during the 2nd Reading of the 1906 Bill made clear that the proposed legislation was not intended "to confer any exceptional immunities, far from it; it was in order to remove exceptional disabilities imposed on those trade unions, disabilities which are contrary to the general spirit of our law".[101]

It should be further noted that the purpose of these "immunities" was to protect trade unions and those acting on their behalf from liability in tort for acts undertaken "in contemplation of furtherance of a trade dispute" which, itself, was defined by this Act. Other countries (mentioned above) had such provisions in other forms, so "immunities" were the way the equivalent of what came into being elsewhere were conceded in Britain.[102]

This Act of 1906 marked a watershed. Since then, there had been an established provision in the law, despite modifications at various stages (see below), protecting trade unions and those acting on their behalf from claims in damages arising out of industrial disputes. It "made trade unions immune from actions in tort and conferred protection on individuals, such as union officials, against liability for conspiracy to injure and including breach of contract where the acts were done in contemplation or furtherance of a trade dispute".[103] This Act also marked a watershed in that it was only at this point that the ability of trade unions to organise and bargain collectively without fear of repercussions, be these through the civil or criminal law, became firmly established. This Act, in effect, kept the judiciary at bay for a good many years and in a sense provided a basis whereby grievances at work could be resolved without the intervention of the courts.

As the Thatcher Government itself stated in 1981: "immunities are not simply legal privileges .... Without some legal protection – however circumscribed – it

[101] McIlroy, John, ..., p. 68.

[102] For a fuller explanation of the development of "immunities", see Wedderburn, (Lord) K. W., *The Worker and the Law* ..., ..., pp. 16-25.

[103] Rogers, W. V. H., *Winfield and Jolowicz on Tort* (Sixteenth Edition), Sweet and Maxwell Limited (London), 2002, p. 661.

would be impossible for trade unions or individuals to organise industrial action without risk of civil proceedings and the ultimate safeguard of a collective withdrawal of labour would be effectively nullified".[104] Thus, as industrial law professor Lord Wedderburn clearly states: "What the statutory 'immunities' protect are social 'rights'. In substance, behind the form, the statute provides liberties or rights that the common law would deny to workers. The 'immunity' is mere form".[105]

From 1906 up to 1971, there was no attempt by Parliament or the Government to go back on the provisions of the 1906 Act as a whole. However, in the aftermath of the defeat of the trade union movement in the 1926 General Strike, the Conservative Government under Stanley Baldwin was able to retaliate against it through the Trade Disputes and Trade Unions Act, 1927. With the defeat of the strike deepening the rift between the trade union leadership and the shop floor, with the latter being severely weakened,[106] the Government was then able to impose constraints on the main provisions of the 1906 Act.

Amongst the provisions of the 1927 Act were that general and sympathetic strikes became illegal, anyone leading or participating in an illegal strike was liable to be fined or imprisoned for up to two years, whilst union funds could be made vulnerable to claims for damages, thus removing the "immunities" conferred by the 1906 Act.[107] However, the Baldwin Government was reluctant to go as far as putting the law back to what it was before 1906. The 1927 Act was repealed in full in 1946.

After an era of what could be described as "judicial acquiescence", the courts, beginning in the early 1950s, once again sought to reassert "their" authority in defining the law in the filed of trade union and labour relations law. With the influence of the shop floor increasing in the 1950s and 1960s, and with concern in ruling circles at this, the courts appeared to find scope for reasserting the "authority" they had lost through the 1906 Act. This, in effect, gave the "green light" that was being sought in an attempt to curb the rising influence of the shop floor and the growing incidence of "unofficial" strikes.

---

[104] *Trade Union Immunities*, ..., p. 92, para. 384. Original source quoted in: Wedderburn, (Lord) K. W., *The Worker and the Law* ..., ..., p. 20.

[105] Wedderburn, (Lord) K. W., *The Worker and the Law* ..., ..., p. 20.

[106] Degen, Günther R., *Shop Stewards: ihre zentrale Bedeutung für die Gewerkschaftsbewegung in Großbritannien*, Europäische Verlagsanstalt (Frankfurt am Main and Köln), 1976, p. 121.

[107] Hutt, Allen, *British Trade Unionism*, Lawrence and Wishart (London), 1975, pp. 115f.

During the 1960s, a few important cases went before the courts in which the organisers of industrial action found themselves exposed to torts which, in the view of the judiciary, were not covered by the 1906 Act. In this, there were two ways of particular importance as to how common law liability was extended. Firstly, there was "the development of the indirect form of the tort of inducing a breach of contract" and secondly, there was "the development of liability for the tort of intimidation".[108]

Regarding the tort of inducing a breach of contract, the law was to develop in a way in which union officials found themselves liable, not for inducing a breach of the employment contract (which the 1906 Act protected), but interestingly, for the commercial contracts disrupted in the dispute. In this, there were two important cases – *Stratford v. Lindley* in 1965 and *Torquay Hotel Ltd. v. Cousins* in 1969.[109]

The first case came about as a result of a recognition dispute in a company in the Stratford group where two unions were seeking recognition – the TGWU (organising the majority of lightermen) and the Watermen's Union. When the TGWU was suddenly recognised, the watermen responded by placing an embargo on barges hired out and repaired by another company in the Stratford group thus bringing it to a standstill. There, the House of Lords ruled in favour of the plaintiff on the grounds that as the embargo came about as a result of union rivalry, there was no "trade dispute" as defined by the 1906 Act.[110]

The effect of the House of Lords' ruling in the case of *Stratford v. Lindley* was strengthened in the Court of Appeal ruling in the case of *Torquay Hotel Ltd. v. Cousins*.[111] This case, which was taken out against the then TGWU General Secretary, Frank Cousins, came about as the union was trying to organise hotel workers in Torquay much to the alarm of the hoteliers.

A recognition dispute came about at one hotel (the Torbay Hotel) concerning the TGWU. However, when the managing director of Imperial Hotel, a prominent member of the hoteliers' association, publicly stated that they would "stamp out" the TGWU in the town, the union responded by picketing Imperial Hotel (which was owned by Torquay Hotel Ltd. and having no TGWU members) and organised the blacking of oil deliveries. There, the Court of Appeal upheld the granting of interlocutory injunctions against the TGWU. The fact that there was a trade dispute at Torbay Hotel was not in doubt. However, the TGWU action against

[108] *Trade Union Immunities*, ..., p. 16, para. 62.

[109] See Wedderburn, (Lord) K. W., Freedom of Association ..., ..., p. 6.

[110] See Wedderburn, (Lord) K. W., *The Worker and the Law* ..., ..., pp. 565f.

[111] Griffith, J. A. G., ..., pp. 71f.

Imperial Hotel was not judged as being in furtherance of the trade dispute at Torbay Hotel.[112] In this case, the Appeal Court had obviously disregarded the fact that such a provocative statement by the managing director of Imperial Hotel had unnecessarily aggravated the dispute. From these two cases, it is clear that the courts sought to limit the degree of protection to the organisers of industrial action by, in effect, making rulings which aimed at narrowing the "definition of a trade dispute".

However, a judicial landmark was reached in January 1964 through the House of Lords' ruling in the case of *Rookes v. Barnard* (see pages 146f). There, it was ruled that the threat of strike action if the plaintiff (a non-unionist who had resigned from his union) were not removed from his place of employment (where a union membership agreement was in force) amounted to a threat of intimidation not covered by the 1906 Act.[113] This produced a situation in which, as the Thatcher Government itself in its 1981 Green Paper stated, "it seemed possible that whenever a trade union official threatened a strike he might be liable to be sued for intimidation".[114] From this, the conclusion can be drawn that the Law Lords' ruling not only went against the spirit of the 1906 Act, but can also be interpreted as an attack on the right to strike.

Consequently, a parallel can be drawn between the court rulings of the 1890s together with Taff Vale in 1901 and the ruling in *Rookes v. Barnard*, in which the judiciary had effectively undermined the will of Parliament. Just as in 1906, Parliament had to pass a new piece of legislation to reaffirm what it had intended in the 1870s, Parliament, as a result of *Rookes v. Barnard*, had to do the same again in order to reaffirm what it had decided in 1906. This it was to do through the Trade Disputes Act, 1965.

Meanwhile, the ruling in *Rookes v. Barnard* was significant in another respect: it gave the then Conservative Government the chance it was seeking in tackling the problem of "unofficial" strikes. It was this ruling which prompted the then Minister of Labour, Joseph Godber, in spring 1964 to announce the setting up of an inquiry into trade unions, one of its objectives being to review the operation of the 1906 Act.[115] However, as the Conservatives lost the 1964 election, it was a Labour Government which, against its election pledge,[116] established the Royal Commission, already referred to, under the chairmanship of Lord Donovan.

---

[112] Wedderburn, (Lord) K. W., *The Worker and the Law* ..., ..., pp. 565ff.

[113] For brief details of the case of *Rookes v. Barnard*, see pages 141f.

[114] *Trade Union Immunities*, ..., p. 17, para. 68.

[115] *Trade Unions for Tomorrow*, ..., p. 5.

[116] See Ramelson, Bert, ..., p. 1.

The incoming Labour Government was under pressure from trade unions to enact legislation to "nullify" the effect of the *Rookes v. Barnard* case, and from employers to take action regarding "unofficial" strikes. The 1965 Act and the establishment of the Royal Commission could be seen in the context of the newly-elected Labour Government trying to restore the pre-*Rookes v. Barnard* "status quo" in industrial relations whilst at the same time, seeking to reassure employers about Labour's concern over "unofficial" strikes.

Even if Labour was unsure of how the problem of "unofficial" strikes should be resolved, a group of prominent Conservative lawyers were already convinced that they had the answers. A few years previously, the Inns of Court Conservative and Unionist Society had considered this problem and related matters. In their 1958 publication *A Giant's Strength*, a series of recommendations were made which, even if they were not enacted upon at the time, won the sympathy of Conservative ministers. The most significant recommendation made by these Conservative lawyers was that the legal protection which trade unions had secured through the Acts of 1871, 1875 and 1906 (which they regarded as "privileges") should only be available to trade unions which "registered" with the Registrar of Friendly Societies.[117] Furthermore, proposals were made as to conditions for the Registrar to accept the registration of a trade union, and the basis for this was to be the union's rule book.[118] This would have given the state a degree of jurisdiction over how trade unions were to conduct their own internal affairs.

On the subject of strikes, the recommendation was that any industrial dispute, before becoming a strike, be referred to an independent tribunal for an inquiry. Once an inquiry had been conducted, it was proposed that there should be a pause of "perhaps fourteen days" before a strike could legally take place.[119] So, in this situation, it was clear that "unofficial" strikes would no longer be protected. On this basis, it was anticipated that the incidence of such strikes would be drastically reduced.

With trade unions already getting bad media publicity due to "unofficial" strikes, Labour, by setting up such a commission, allowed the initiative in resolving this problem to pass into the hands of the Conservative Opposition. Although the Royal Commission endorsed the Labour Government's action regarding the 1965 Act,[120] the proposals of the Conservative Opposition very much influenced its key recommendations, which were designed to provide effective control of

[117] *A Giant's Strength*, The Inns of Court Conservative and Unionist Society (London), undated (published in 1958), pp. 23 and 54.

[118] Ibid., pp. 41ff and 54f.

[119] Ibid., p. 22.

[120] *Royal Commission on ...*, ..., p. 226, para. 852.

industrial relations, including pay, at the level of the factory and company by means of properly constructed agreements. In that way, incomes policies could be successfully implemented.[121] The Royal Commission, like the Conservatives, proposed that company and factory agreements be registered so as to make them legally enforceable. The reason for this was that, in conditions of "full employment", it was felt that shop floor workers were able to force up actual earnings faster than wage rates, and in the absence of such agreements, the power of the shop floor was said to be increasing at the expense of trade union organisations and employers' associations. This proposal was very much in line with the Inns of Court Conservative and Unionist Society's recommendations in their evidence to the Royal Commission.[122]

An aim of the Royal Commission was to find a way of bringing shop stewards under the control of official union structures,[123] with the ultimate aim of the latter policing the implementation of incomes policies. In this connection, the Commission's "solution" to the problem of "unofficial" strikes was as follows: "A majority of us think it proper that the protection of the first limb of section 3 of the 1906 Act and the corresponding provision in the 1965 Act should be limited to those acting on behalf of a trade union, and make a recommendation to this effect".[124]

Section 3 (first limb) of the 1906 Act was designed to provide "immunity" for a person e.g. a trade union official who, "in contemplation of furtherance of a trade dispute", induced another person to break his contract of employment.[125] The Royal Commission recommendation that this "immunity" be limited to those acting on behalf of a trade union was very much in line with the thinking of these Conservative lawyers back in 1958. It meant that only "official" strikes would have continued to have legal protection (only about 5% of all strikes at the time).[126] Furthermore, a majority of the Royal Commission felt that: "the protection of any extension of section 3 should, like that of the section itself ... be restricted to those bodies which will be trade unions under the suggested new arrangements for incorporation and registration".[127]

---

[121] Ibid., p. 53, para. 211.

[122] *Trade Unions for Tomorrow*, ..., pp. 32-39.

[123] Degen, Günther R., ..., 331.

[124] *Royal Commission on* ..., ..., p. 132, para. 488.

[125] Ibid., p. 232, para. 880.

[126] Ramelson, Bert, ..., p. 10.

[127] *Royal Commission on* ..., ..., p. 235, para. 894.

Thus, with the combination of registration and legally enforceable collective agreements, shop stewards were clearly seen by the Royal Commission to be the main enemy on the industrial relations scene.

Regarding the tort of inducing a breach of contract as, for example, in the House of Lords ruling in *Stratford v. Lindley*, the Royal Commission felt that the provisions of the 1906 and 1965 Acts should be extended to cover all contracts.[128] But this, of course, would have only applied to registered unions when engaged in "official" disputes.

So, with registration making factory and company agreements legally enforceable, and only "official" strikes being legally protected, the Royal Commission tended to conform to the view that "consensus" politics would exclude shop-floor activists. In fact, the Royal Commission sought a strengthening of official union structures so as to bring shop floor activists under the latter's control as a means of reducing the incidence of "unofficial" strikes. So "registration" was therefore seen as the key to the "reform" of industrial relations.

The Conservative Party, anticipating the political line the Royal Commission was going to take on "unofficial" strikes brought out its own document *Fair Deal at Work* shortly before the Donovan Report was published.[129] With the trade union movement being made scapegoats for Britain's economic ills, this document not only aimed to capitalise on the apparent unpopularity of trade unions but also to put pressure on the Labour Government to introduce legislative measures along the lines argued for by the Royal Commission. As far as *Fair Deal at Work* was concerned, this meant "Corporate Legal Status"[130] for trade unions. This would have required more far reaching conditions for registration than those recommended by the Royal Commission. But, whatever disagreement there may have been over details, the important thing to note was the breadth of support for the principle of registration.

With the publication of the Donovan Report, the Conservative opposition was able to go on the offensive. Aided by general confusion within the ranks of the PLP on the Report's findings and recommendations, the Labour Government's pledge to tackle the problem of "unofficial" strikes by legislative means went without challenge in the House of Commons debate on the Report on 16 July, 1968.[131]

---

[128] Ibid., pp. 234f, paras. 892f.

[129] See Barnes, Denis and Reid, Eileen, ..., p. 110.

[130] See *Fair Deal at Work*, Conservative Political Centre (London), CPC Number 400, April 1968, pp. 18-27.

[131] For the House of Commons debate on the Report of the "Donovan Commission", see *Par-*

The Labour Government's proposals for tackling the problem of industrial unrest were outlined in its controversial White Paper *In Place of Strife* in January 1969, which proposed to establish a special tripartite body for mediating in industrial disputes – the Commission on Industrial Relations (CIR). The Government rejected a key recommendation of the Royal Commission that legal protection be limited to registered unions. This was because, firstly, most employers probably would not have been prepared to sue "unofficial" strike leaders, so that such a provision might not have been effective. Indeed, legal action against "unofficial" strike leaders could well have aggravated a dispute. Secondly, trade unions would have been able to get round such a legal change by automatically declaring all strikes "official" unless stated otherwise. Thirdly, in the event of legal action, "unofficial" strike leaders would have been defenceless no matter what the reason for striking was.[132]

However, the controversial aspects of the White Paper, which were to form the basis of "an Industrial Relations Act" centred on the proposals for the resolution of recognition disputes between unions (paragraphs 58-60), for union registration (paragraph 109), for compulsory ballots in the event of "official" strikes (with the wording of the ballot slip to be approved by the Secretary of State – paragraph 98) and for a statutory "conciliation pause" (of 28 days) in the event of "unconstitutional" stoppages undertaken in breach of procedure (paragraphs 93-96).[133] With "unofficial" strikes supposedly accounting for around 95% of all strikes, most of them, it was alleged, were also "unconstitutional" and, according to the White Paper, were "responsible for three-quarters of the working days lost because of strikes".[134] "Unconstitutional" strikes allegedly took place in breach of procedure[135] (which explains why calls were originally made for procedural agreements to be made legally binding). In all cases, there was provision by which the Secretary of State could refer cases to a new Industrial Board and for financial penalties to be imposed on trade unions, employers and individuals (i.e. shop floor activists) for refusing to abide by its orders.[136]

It was these provisions, particularly those for imposing penal sanctions on trade unions and trade unionists, which discredited this White Paper in the eyes of the trade union and labour movement. The intensity of the opposition to these proposals was such that they had to be retracted. In return, the TUC agreed to give a

liamentary Debates (Hansard), Fifth Series – Volume 768, Session 1967-68 Comprising Period from 8th - 19th July 1968, Cols. 1260-1383.

132 *In Place of Strife, Cmnd.* 3888, HMSO (London), January 1969, p. 27, para. 88.

133 As briefly summarised in: *Trade Union Immunities*, ..., p. 19, para. 73.

134 *In Place of Strife*, ..., p. 27, para. 90.

135 See Ibid, pp. 27f, paras 90ff.

136 Ibid., p. 20, para. 60.

"solemn and binding" undertaking to intervene in "unofficial" and "unconstitutional" stoppages so as to bring about the earliest resumption of work.

The White Paper, interestingly, proposed a change in the 1906 Act so as to enable a union to be sued in tort, except in trade disputes. Whilst the Government may have agreed with the TUC that this should only be possible if "the definition of a trade dispute is watertight",[137] it would give the impression that trade union funds would once again become vulnerable if union leaders didn't take sufficient action to deter "unofficial" disputes. This proposal, even if not acted upon at the time, was to give an indication of what was already being considered in official circles.

For the Labour Government, the collapse of *In Place of Strife* was humiliating and in the eyes of the trade union and labour movement, a black mark was placed against the history of the Labour Party in government. For the Conservative Opposition, this meant that Labour leaders were incapable of "standing up to the powerful pressures exerted by vested interests within their own ranks".[138] This whole episode suggested that, by the end of the 1960s, Labour was unable to offer any convincing solutions to Britain's worsening economic situation. So, in the run-up to the 1970 general election, the Conservative Party successfully capitalised on this failure.

The answer of the new Conservative Government under Edward Heath to Britain's industrial relations problems was its 1971 Industrial Relations Act, modelled on the earlier Conservative Party policy document *Fair Deal at Work*. In one single Act, the Heath Government sought to bring about the biggest overhaul in trade union and labour relations law Britain had ever known.

The 1971 Act repealed the 1906 Act while re-enacting its main "immunities" provisions. However, these provisions were only to apply to unions "registered" under this Act when engaged in "official" disputes – thus echoing the call made by these Conservative lawyers in 1958 and, subsequently, by the Conservative Party itself.

Like the Donovan Report, the cornerstone of the 1971 Act was "registration". In line with the Royal Commission's recommendation[139] and Labour's discredited *In Place of Strife*, the 1971 Act established a Registrar of Trade Unions and Employers' Associations. Although registration was not compulsory, it carried with it certain "privileges" under the Act and also tax benefits (which had previously

---

[137] Ibid., p. 33, para. 113.

[138] *'Fair Deal' Takes Shape*, Conservative Central Office (London), December 1970, p. 7.

[139] *Royal Commission on ..., ...*, p. 212, para. 792.

been available to unions). These, of course, were to be lost in the event of non-registration. The criterion for registration was to be the union rule books which would need to be approved by the newly appointed Registrar. So, under this Act, only those trade unions which registered and remained on the provisional register were recognised as trade unions. The status of those which were not registered or had de-registered was nothing more than an "organisation of workers". So any industrial action taken by any of them was unprotected.[140]

The 1971 Act established a new framework of industrial law which included the creation of a new kind of "industrial tort" – the so-called "unfair industrial practice" – and a special court to adjudicate on the Act's provisions – the National Industrial Relations Court (NIRC).

Many forms of activity established as normal trade union practices fell within this category of an "unfair industrial practice". This included calling strikes in breach of collective agreements, strikes to secure or maintain a "closed shop"[141] (a practice which this Act sought to prohibit), sympathetic strikes and strikes concerning union recognition.[142] But the key as to whether these provisions were to have any significance was how a plaintiff would act and how the union or unions would react in the event of a case going before the NIRC.

There was an important difference between *In Place of Strife* and the 1971 Act. The former tended to favour an authoritarian approach to solving industrial disputes by giving the Secretary of State discretionary reserve powers whilst the latter tended to favour the judicial process. Although the Conservative Party *may* have been critical of the authoritarian powers the 1969 White Paper envisaged, they welcomed Labour's acceptance that the reform of industrial relations required a new measure of law.[143] This helped to pave the way for the 1971 Act a couple of years later.

Provision, rejected previously by the Donovan Commission, was also made in the 1971 Act that, in the event of any industrial action leading to a national emergency, the Government could apply to the NIRC for an Order banning it for up to 60 days during which a compulsory ballot of the workers directly involved would take place[144] – very much mirroring the United States' Taft Hartley Act

[140] Morton, Gary, Labour's anti-union laws, *Communist Review*, No. 30, Communist Party (London), Autumn 1999, p. 23.

[141] A "closed shop" is where membership of a specified trade union is a necessary condition of employment.

[142] See Barnes, Denis and Reid, Eileen, ..., pp. 141ff.

[143] *'Fair Deal' Takes Shape*, ..., p. 7.

[144] Wedderburn, (Lord) K. W., *The Worker and the Law* ..., ..., p. 52f.

from 1947.[145] The Labour Government had thought along similar lines with its proposed 28 day "conciliation pause" in its 1969 White Paper.

For fear of the obvious consequences, the Heath Government refrained from seeking to impose a strike ballot during the winter 1972 miners' strike. However, such a ballot was imposed on all three rail unions (ASLEF, NUR, and TSSA) during the British Rail dispute in April 1972. On an 85% turnout and with an overwhelming vote in favour of continuing industrial action,[146] (with a 95% vote in favour by ASLEF members together with 87% of NUR members and 74% in TSSA)[147] the result clearly backfired on the Government and represented its first major defeat under this Act.[148] The scale of this ballot defeat, against the background of fierce opposition to this Act from the trade union movement, meant that this provision was never used again during the short life of this Act.

Due to the unpopularity of the Act, and to the defiant stand taken against it by the trade union movement, culminating in the dramatic events of summer 1972 in the Neap House Wharf dispute which forced the release of five London dockers (often known as the "Pentonville Five") jailed by the NIRC for "contempt of court", the Act became discredited further and represented a defeat more humiliating than the one suffered during the British Rail dispute. The Government's predicament was clearly summarised in one academic study which was published in 1975: "The Government was forced to draw a number of unpalatable conclusions about the possible consequences of using the Act. Trade unionists would not automatically obey the law, organised workers had a sanction against legal judgements, the law could make disputes harder to settle, and the operation of the IR Act could bring the law into disrepute".[149]

The leftward shift in a number of key unions at the end of the 1960s influenced the TUC's position in relation to the Act. With the cornerstone of the Act being registration, the TUC General Council initially "recommended" unions not to register. However, in response to the intense opposition to the Industrial Relations Bill, the TUC then went further and voted to "instruct" all affiliated unions not to comply with the Bill when it became law. This especially meant refusing to

[145] Ibid.

[146] *Democracy in Trade Unions*, Cmnd. 8778, HMSO (London), January 1983, p. 18, para. 62.

[147] Griffiths, Robert, *Driven by ideals- a history of ASLEF*, Associated Society of Locomotive Engineers and Firemen (Hampstead, London), 2005, p. 209.

[148] Degen, Günther R., ..., 357f.

[149] Weeks, B. C. M. et. al., *Industrial Relations and the Limits of the Law*, Blackwell (Oxford), 1975, p. 227.

register.[150] Those unions which registered were instructed to de-register and the failure of 32 unions (nearly all small ones) to de-register led to their expulsion from the TUC in September 1972.[151] Given the degree of opposition to this Act and the way it had become discredited, the TUC was strong enough to ensure that all its other affiliates abided by TUC policy.

With the "U-turn" in 1972 and the resumption of tripartite collaboration, the Heath Government, for its part, was forced to abandon the controversial parts of the 1971 Act. Further, it was eager that neither management nor individuals should use any parts of the Act which were likely to cause conflicts.[152] In other words, by autumn 1972, the Government realised that its own Act was, to all intents and purposes, unworkable.

The extent of the failure of the 1971 Act can be seen in that, due to TUC policy, almost no major union registered under it. As registration was the cornerstone of this Act, the newly appointed Registrar of Trade Union and Employers' Associations was denied any effective powers. Furthermore, the legal enforcement of collective agreements, as far as employers were concerned, had almost no positive effect. Other provisions of the Act, particularly regarding the closed shop, became ineffective due to the policy of non-cooperation with the NIRC and the CIR.[153]

With the Government effectively abandoning its own Act as from 1972, it was only the odd maverick employer who sought to use any of the controversial provisions under this Act. One such employer, and in fact the last to use the Act, was the small engineering company Con-Mech in its response to a recognition dispute involving the AUEW which escalated as from autumn 1973. The refusal of the union to appear before the NIRC and to abide by the court's rulings instructing it to stop picketing led to heavy fines on the union which it refused to pay. The dispute escalated further when the NIRC seized £100,000 for contempt of court from, interestingly, the union's political fund (with the result that the union was unable to make a donation to the Labour Party's election fund for the following year – i.e. 1974). The union's continued determination to seek recognition at Con-Mech by using industrial means which had previously been legal led to further fines and, in addition, the awarding of damages against the union for losses incurred by the company. Once again, the AUEW refused to abide by

[150] Kelly, John, *Trade Unions and Socialist Politics*, ..., p. 108.

[151] See Barnes, Denis and Reid, Eileen, ..., pp. 144f.

[152] Weeks, B. C. M. et. al., ..., p. 228.

[153] See The Industrial Relations Act: What the Engineering Employers think, in: *Tribune* (London), May 18th 1973, p. 2. See also Gill, Ken, Secret NIRC documents show how union solidarity beat the Tory Act, in: *Tribune* (London), June 8th 1973, p. 8.

the NIRC's rulings and this led, in early May 1974, to the court ordering the sequestration of the union's assets – ironically, at the very time when legislation seeking the repeal of the 1971 Act was going through Parliament! This attempted seizure of the union's entire assets by the NIRC led to an all-out strike of union members (a decision of the union's executive council which was only carried on the casting vote of the then President, Hugh Scanlon). This dispute was quickly settled when the court felt compelled to accept payment of the union's fines by a group of anonymous businessmen.[154]

The Con-Mech dispute not only underlined the urgency by which the 1971 Act had to be repealed, the AUEW's action also made certain that this was actually done especially as the Labour Government, which had only recently been installed, did not have a majority in Parliament. The outcome of this dispute thus ensured that MPs of other parties did not stand in the way of the Act's repeal.

The defeat of the Industrial Relations Act following that of *In Place of Strife* meant that attempts by two governments (one Labour and one Conservative) to impose legal constraints on organised labour had failed. The Labour Party and the incoming Labour Government in 1974 were well aware that such policies could not be repeated and that a new framework had to be found within which Britain's economic and industrial problems could be overcome.

As far back as July 1972, TUC and Labour Party leaders had reached agreement on the legislation and policies which would replace the 1971 Act. It was agreed that the Act should be repealed completely.[155] This meant two things. Firstly, the institutions set up by the Act which had become discredited or irrelevant had to be abolished – the NIRC, the Registrar of Trade Unions and Employers' Associations and the CIR (established by Labour in 1969 but placed on a statutory footing through the 1971 Act). Secondly, not only did this mean that the "immunities" provisions of the 1906 and 1965 Acts had to be restored, but it opened the way for them to be renewed, as Wedderburn says, in a "spring-cleaned form to take account of judicial creativity" since they had come into being.[156] This was particularly important owing to the development of new common law liabilities, especially those inducing breach of commercial contract.[157] The repeal Act had to be flawless so that cases like Taff Vale or *Rookes v. Barnard* could never be repeated.

---

[154] See *Action Defeats the Bill*, Liaison Committee for the Defence of Trade Unions (Barking, Essex), undated (published in 1982), pp. 12f.

[155] *Labour's Programme 1973*, ..., pp. 14 and 25f.

[156] Wedderburn, (Lord) K. W., *The Worker and the Law* ..., ..., p. 61.

[157] Ibid.

However, when Labour was returned to office in early 1974, it was well short of a parliamentary majority. Consequently, the repeal Act – the Trade Union and Labour Relations Act, 1974 (TULRA) – did not get onto the Statute Book in the original form intended.[158] This was because the Opposition, whilst accepting the realities concerning the 1971 Act, was able to insert amendments in the repeal Bill so that "immunities" were only restored to trade unions in cases where the employment contract was breached.

Upon attaining a parliamentary majority in the second general election in 1974, even though it was only a very small one, the Labour Government sought to place on the Statute Book the scope of "immunities" in the watertight form originally intended with TULRA in the middle of 1974. This it did with the TULRA (Amendment) Bill, but, as the House of Lords would not pass it, it did not become law until 1976.[159] In effect, it was only when the 1976 Act got onto the Statute Book that trade unions regained the degree of "immunities" that Parliament had originally intended back in 1906. In the often quoted words of Lord Scarman in the case of *NWL Ltd. v. Nelson and Woods* in 1979, the 1974 Act was intended: "to sweep away not only the structure of industrial relations created by the Industrial Relations Act 1971, which it was passed to repeal, but also the constraints of judicial review which the courts have been fashioning one way or another since the enactment of the Trade Disputes Act 1906 ... Briefly put, the law is now back to what Parliament had intended when it enacted the Act of 1906 – but stronger and clearer than it was then".[160]

An important precondition for securing acceptance of the Social Contract was the extent to which the long-standing demands of the labour movement in respect of measures for improving and extending collective bargaining and providing more rights and protection for people at work were to be fulfilled. This meant, for example, broadening the scope of existing health and safety legislation and introducing more effective measures to help secure equal pay for women. In this, the most important measures were taken in the Employment Protection Act, 1975.[161]

In an attempt to extend and develop collective bargaining, the newly-elected Labour Government in 1974 established the Advisory, Conciliation and Arbitration Service (ACAS). This was intended to replace the CIR, abolished through the repeal of the 1971 Act. However, the philosophy underlying the two bodies was completely different. The CIR was part of the failed process of bringing the

[158] Ibid.

[159] *Trade Union Immunities*, ..., p. 22, para. 85.

[160] Griffith, J. A. G., ..., p. 80.

[161] Wedderburn, (Lord) K. W., *The Worker and the Law* ..., ..., pp. 62-66.

whole system of industrial relations within the law. ACAS was founded on the assumption that the root causes of grievances at work could only be resolved by developing collective bargaining and that, given previous experiences, the law should be kept out of industrial relations as far as possible.

An important provision of the 1975 Act was to place ACAS on a statutory footing and to give it powers to issue Codes of Practice. Although these Codes did not have the full weight of the law, it was intended that they should be taken into account by industrial tribunals and the Central Arbitration Committee (CAC) established by the Act. Once again, the clear intention was to keep the judiciary as far away from collective bargaining as possible.[162]

The 1975 Act, for example, guaranteed payments to workers on short-time working, introduced maternity rights for women, written statements on reason for dismissal, additional protection against unfair dismissal and the prohibition of dismissal or discipline of workers on grounds of membership or activities in a trade union. Not only were these measures in response to trade union demands but they were also of great benefit to people in workplaces where trade union organisation was weak or non-existent. The Act also aimed to continue and expand upon procedures for compulsory arbitration which had existed in various forms since 1940 for workers whose terms and conditions of employment fell below a specified minimum. Such measures were seen as "props" or aids to collective bargaining.[163]

Great importance was attached to Sections 11-16 of the 1975 Act in which provision was made for trade union recognition claims to be pursued through ACAS. But the intention of the Act was that ACAS itself should determine the criteria upon which a recommendation was made for recognition. Although there was an obligation for ACAS to consult all interested parties, experience had shown that there were difficulties in attempting to define strict procedures for handling recognition cases because the actual circumstances surrounding them vary considerably.[164] The principle behind the Act was that such matters be handled on a voluntary basis, with ACAS trying to conciliate rather than being a tribunal.

However, the 1975 Act made provision for a union to complain to ACAS in the event of an employer refusing to comply with an ACAS recommendation favouring recognition of it. In this, there was the ultimate right of appeal to the CAC. In such a situation, if the union's complaint was justified, the CAC had the

---

[162] Ibid., pp. 62f.

[163] Ibid., pp. 64f.

[164] *ACAS Annual Report 1977* (London), pp. 45-48.

power to make an award by imposing improvements in the terms and conditions of employment of the workers affected.

However, as a result of a few court rulings (or judicial creativity!), most noticeably in the case of *Grunwick Processing Laboratories Ltd. v. ACAS*, a situation arose where the courts ruled that ACAS had a mandatory duty to ascertain the views of workers to whom a recognition dispute referred. At the same time, there was no such duty on a interested party to cooperate with ACAS.

In the Grunwick dispute in 1977, the trade union APEX (Association of Professional, Executive, Clerical and Computer Staff) pursued a claim for recognition at the company.[165] The company refused to cooperate with ACAS by supplying it with the names and addresses of its employees (those who had not already been dismissed in the dispute). Subsequently, the Court of Appeal (overturning a High Court decision) ruled that the report which ACAS issued under Section 12 of the Act recommending recognition of APEX be set aside. This ruling, which was upheld in the House of Lords in December 1977, meant in effect that the procedures for pursuing recognition claims under Sections 11-16 of the Act were not legally enforceable, and were therefore inoperable if an interested party refused to cooperate with ACAS.

These court rulings, as noted by the then Chairman of ACAS, Jim Mortimer, meant that ACAS was seen to be a tribunal when handling recognition cases[166] but, at the same time, there was no legal obligation on any of the interested parties to cooperate with it. In the light of these developments, Mortimer had to inform the newly appointed Secretary of State for Employment in 1979, James Prior, that the recognition procedures in the 1975 Act could not be operated as they stood.[167] The logical conclusion of the Grunwick dispute was that an apparent loophole in the 1975 Act was exploited by the judiciary to make a key part of this Act ineffective.

Altogether, the 1974-1979 Labour Government brought in a whole range of reforms giving trade unions and working people more rights than they had ever had. A further consequence was to bring about a growth in union membership by 1.7 million, so that membership reached an all-time high in 1979.[168] On the other hand, these reforms did not reach the standards then existing in most EEC

[165] For a brief account of the Grunwick dispute by the then Chairman of ACAS, see Mortimer, J. E. (Jim), *A Life on the Left*, The Book Guild Ltd. (Lewes, Sussex), 1998, pp. 318-322.

[166] *ACAS Annual Report 1979* (London), p. 112.

[167] See Ibid., pp. 108-112.

[168] See Kelly, John, *Labour and the Unions*, ..., pp. 20f.

countries.[169] Also, some of these reforms were not really effective. Not only did this apply to union recognition procedures but also to the law on unfair dismissal for there was no compulsion on an employer to reinstate or re-engage an employee even where an industrial tribunal had ruled that he/she had been unfairly dismissed. In such situations, unfairly dismissed workers received only modest compensation, with even less for those who pursued claims against discrimination under the Sex Discrimination Act or the Race Relations Act.[170]

On balance, Labour's legislative reforms on trade union and worker rights were welcomed from the union viewpoint but problems on the economic front anyway undermined their impact. Also welcome, from the union side, was Labour's acceptance that problems at work could only be resolved through the extension of collective bargaining; but Labour had not paid sufficient attention to the likelihood that the judiciary would think differently. It is therefore clear that Labour had not thought far or deeply enough about the operation of, and hence the accountability of, the judiciary to the elected representatives of the people. The unpopularity of the Labour Government widened the scope of the judiciary to render a number of Labour's reforms ineffective, as was clearly shown in the Grunwick case. Labour's unpopularity at the time meant that court rulings which undermined some of Labour's legislative reforms on the trade union front were unlikely to be reviewed, let alone overturned, by a re-elected Labour Government with a parliamentary majority.

1.3. Conclusion

The foundations of "consensus" politics in economic and social fields were thus uncertain. The failure to sustain adequate levels of growth and output made the key elements of this "consensus" – "full employment" and key reforms in social welfare harder to sustain. With growing industrial unrest, symptoms rather than root causes were singled out for attention in ruling circles and by the mass media, particularly regarding "unofficial" strikes. If "consensus" politics had any meaning at all, it was that trade union leaders were expected to police their own rank and file activists.

The failure of two governments (one Labour and one Conservative) by using "unofficial" strikers as scapegoats meant that a more subtle approach had to be found. This was because the trade union movement was strong enough to resist what it considered to be an attack by the State on its rights. So, a way had to be

[169] McIlroy, John, ..., p. 81.
[170] Ibid., pp. 81f.

found of taming industrial militancy. This was the underlying significance of the Social Contract.

An understanding had to be reached between the two wings of the labour movement (the industrial and political wings) on a concept of government or an agenda for a Labour Government spanning at least one legislative period. So, basically, reforms benefiting trade unions and working people in return for cooperation on economic matters (i.e. incomes policies) provided the framework in which the Social Contract came into being.

Under the Social Contract, Labour failed to maintain "full employment". Subsequently, in autumn 1976, it was effectively forced to abandon this aim. Thus, the cornerstone of "consensus" politics crumbled. Given the high levels of unemployment and falling living standards, reforms in trade union and worker rights were of little significance in the events leading up to the "winter of discontent" 1978/1979. With the Labour Government thus discredited, the outcome of the May 1979 election was a foregone conclusion. So far as any element of "consensus" politics still had any meaning, the result of the 1979 election formally brought the "consensus" era to a close.

One element of "consensus" era politics which had received too little attention was the role of the judiciary in public life. Governments may change but the judiciary remains intact. British legal history is full of examples where the courts have undermined the will of Parliament, not least regarding trade union and workers' rights. Taff Vale, *Rookes v. Barnard*, and Grunwick are just a few but very important examples illustrating this point. As clearly summarised by Lord Wedderburn: "from 1875 onwards Parliament provided for those organising industrial action 'immunities' in trade disputes against tort liabilities. The judges then expanded tort liabilities. Parliament then, belatedly, countered the judicial expansions by adjusting the 'immunities' (often with some gaps or uncertainties)".[171]

It is clear that in the era of "consensus" politics, the government of the day did not go beyond correcting the "wrongs" of the judiciary, and did not attempt to reform the whole institution to give it more public accountability. In the end, one thing became clear. The incoming Conservative Government in 1979 could be confident about one thing – it did not have to worry that the judiciary might undo what it was planning in the field of trade union and labour relations law.

[171] Wedderburn, (Lord) K. W., *The Worker and the Law* ..., ..., p. 577.

Chapter Two: The theoretical foundations of Conservative labour relations legislation during the 1980s and 1990s

2.1. The Conservative macroeconomic strategy

The acceleration in inflation from the late 1960s together with growing unemployment appeared to support the claim of the "New" Right that governments were unable to manage economies successfully.[1] This meant that macroeconomic measures pursued in an attempt to maintain adequate levels of growth and demand so as to ensure "full employment", were either becoming ineffective or counter-productive.

From the late 1950s, public expenditure in Britain had grown faster than GNP.[2] In such circumstances, higher public expenditure could only be brought about by raising taxation, raising public borrowing or printing more money. As state intervention seemed to be losing its effect, its appeal diminished and the call for public expenditure cuts to finance income tax cuts was welcomed by a significant section of the electorate, especially as the burden of taxation on incomes had risen steadily over the 1960s and 1970s.[3]

Principally, criticism from the "New" Right on post-war economic and social policy rested on two pillars – lack of monetary discipline and the degree of state intervention in the economy. The lack of monetary discipline was therefore seen to be responsible for rising taxation, public sector borrowing and inflation. The degree of state intervention in the economy meant not only lack of monetary discipline; it was also argued that it encouraged inefficiency, unnecessary waste and discouraged competition.

For the "New" Right, and in particular following the change of Conservative Party Leader in 1975, Britain's economic prosperity could only be brought about by "rolling back the frontiers of the state", with the government enacting tough monetary measures to fight inflation, to keep the rate of monetary expansion under control and to keep down the level of public borrowing. Labour's nationalisation plans had to be stopped, it was claimed, and there had to be drastic cutbacks in various state subsidies e.g. housing.

---

1 Gamble, Andrew, *The Free Economy and the Strong State* (Second Edition), Palgrave (Basingstoke and New York), 1994, p. 46.

2 Kavanagh, Dennis, Political Crisis in Britain, in: Rohe, Karl and Schmidt, Gustav (Hrsg), *Krise in Großbritannien? Studien zu Strukturproblemen der britischen Gesellschaft und Politik im 20. Jahrhundert*, Studienverlag Dr. N. Brockmeyer (Bochum), 1987, p. 220.

3 Bleaney, Michael, The Tories' Economic Strategy, in: *Marxism Today* (London), Vol. 23 No. 11, November 1979, p. 12.

The Conservative Party claimed that between 1970 and 1973, public expenditure as a share of national income had held steady whilst between 1973/1974 and 1976/1977 this share had risen by 11.5% in real terms.[4] This claim, implying a more efficient economic performance than under Labour, overlooks various factors. For instance, the incoming Labour Government in early 1974 had not been responsible for the miners' strike at the end of 1973/beginning of 1974, which led to the introduction of the three-day week in much of the industrial base of the UK economy. Furthermore, there was the serious effect of the quadrupling of oil prices at the end of 1973 on Britain's balance of payments and partially as a result of the sudden increase in oil prices, the world economy plunged into its deepest crisis since the 1930s. Under such circumstances, the scope for keeping down public expenditure had been limited. What is surprising is that, given the impact of the economic crisis in the mid-1970s, the large increase in the number of people out of work, the costs of extra state benefits and losses of tax revenue associated with this, public expenditure did not rise by more than the 11.5% as claimed in the above-mentioned period.

What was needed for the conquest of inflation, the Conservative Party argued, was a programme in which state spending and revenue would amount to a significantly smaller proportion of the nation's annual output and income each year.[5] Before 1976, no such programme in itself had existed[6] but one significance of the 1976 IMF loan conditions were that such a programme had to be introduced. This meant that the system of *cash limits* which Labour had already introduced in the public sector in summer 1975 as part of its attempt to fight inflation had to be more vigorously applied (see pages 31-34). One result of this programme was that in the period between 1975/1976 and 1978/1979, government expenditure relative to national income had actually fallen from 46½% of GDP to 42%.[7]

In accepting the terms of the 1976 IMF loan, there was acceptance on both sides of the House of Commons that money supply and government expenditure had to be controlled[8] more vigorously than previously in the post-war period. Looking at the period 1975/1976 to 1978/1979, one can see how far Labour actually went in fulfilling Conservative demands for government expenditure to be cut as a share of national output. However, unlike the Conservative Opposition, Labour remained committed to interventionist strategies in industry (in as far as

---

[4] Maude, Angus (Ed.), *The Right Approach to the Economy*, Conservative Central Office (Westminster), 1977, pp. 9f.

[5] Ibid., p. 10.

[6] See Pliatzky, (Sir) Leo, Cash Limits and Pay Policy, in: *The Political Quarterly*, Blackwell (Oxford), Vol. 53 No. 1, January-March 1982, p. 17.

[7] Bleaney, Michael, ..., p. 15.

[8] Maude, Angus (Ed.), ..., p. 9.

IMF constraints[9] and EEC regulations permitted) and also to prices and incomes policies.

Public expenditure *in real terms* could, therefore, only rise if the economy grew at an adequate enough rate. Under such circumstances, Labour was lacking in effective macroeconomic instruments in tackling the unemployment problem. Although Labour planned for growth in government expenditure to rise by 2% per annum in real terms, it had been hoped that real GDP would rise by at least 3% per annum, implying that government expenditure as a share of GDP would continue to fall.[10] Thus, nothing short of an upturn in the world economy and a sizeable inflow of revenue from North Sea oil exploration could have given Labour the opportunity to "take the initiative" on the economic front. When this did happen towards the end of the 1970s, the impact it had on the unemployment statistics, as already noted, was limited. In effect, Labour found itself "managing" an economy without a coherent strategy, trying to implement "Keynesian" macroeconomic measures within a monetarist framework. In this context, the imposition of "sound" monetary policies by the IMF gave the Conservative Opposition an enormous boost in arguing for the adoption of monetarism.

This IMF loan, or the conditions for it, should not just be seen in the British context but more in association with the deregulation of international economic relations. The breakdown of the Bretton Woods system of fixed exchange rates in 1971/1972 had undermined a key pre-condition of Keynesian macroeconomic management. This was that such management could really only function in a closed economy, or in an open economy where foreign trade was subject to a degree of governmental control with stable exchange rates.[11] Significantly, the breakdown of the system of fixed exchange rates happened at a time when the advocates of monetarism were becoming more influential in leading political circles in the West. Consequently, governmental macroeconomic policies were becoming more prone than ever to developments in the world economy, particularly in Britain whose position in the advanced industrialised world was being steadily undermined by relatively poor growth rates and industrial performance. An over-expansion of the money supply would have resulted in a deteriorating trade balance and to a loss of "confidence" in the currency and economy[12] – to a greater extent than previously.

The uneasy mix of Keynesianism and monetarism confronted Labour with allegations that it was denouncing monetarism while practising it – by threatening

---

[9] As part of the IMF's loan conditions at the end of 1976, the Chancellor of the Exchequer Denis Healey had to sign a Letter of Intent that, among other things, precluded financial assistance to nationalised industries.

[10] Bleaney, Michael, ..., p. 15.

[11] Gamble, Andrew, ..., p. 47.

[12] Ibid.

tough monetary measures and higher taxation if powerful trade unions did not moderate their pay claims.[13] For Labour, incomes policies continued to remain a key element in fighting inflation and bringing about economic prosperity. For the Conservative Opposition, only the "market" could determine pay rates and pay settlements with trade unions and trade unionists being threatened with mass unemployment if they sought pay settlements beyond what the "market" permitted. Government involvement in the economy, for the Conservatives, was limited to determining what the parameters of macroeconomic policy should be, i.e. spending and borrowing levels, and for setting targets for controlling the rate of monetary expansion with interest rates being allowed to rise to such levels as might be deemed necessary to ensure that monetary targets were met.

The macroeconomic strategy of the Thatcher Government rested on the notion that the key to securing Britain's economic future lay in strengthening the influence of the City of London as a major international financial centre. The hope was, also, the rising international competitiveness and profitability of the City would create employment in an expanded financial services sector based on London and the South East of England[14] which could, partly, offset any loss of employment in the manufacturing sector. Consequently, macroeconomic policy was formulated to achieve this objective. Manufacturing industry would only survive if it became more "efficient", and this meant that changes in working practices and new technology had to be forced through.

To achieve its principle macroeconomic objectives, the Thatcher Government had a three-pronged strategy. Firstly, the deregulation of financial markets. This entailed the lifting of any remaining exchange controls, as was done in autumn 1979. Secondly, there was to be a more rigid application of the measures the IMF had imposed on Labour towards the end of 1976 to control the rate of monetary expansion and reduce public expenditure as a share of GDP. Thirdly, the role of the State in the economy was to be reduced, not only through public expenditure cuts, but also through privatisation.

To help ensure that its monetary targets were met, the Thatcher Government allowed interest rates to rise irrespective of the effects this was going to have on manufacturing industry and other sectors of the economy. This, even if to a lesser extent, actually happened under the previous Labour Government. There, it is worth recalling that MLR, having fallen to just 5% on 17 October, 1977, from the then postwar high of 15% in autumn, the previous year (see page 35), started to rise again a just few weeks later. It jumped to 7% on the 28 November and

[13] Joseph, (Sir) Keith, *Solving the Union Problem is the Key to Britain's Recovery*, Centre for Policy Studies (London), 5 February 1979, p. 2.

[14] See Coakley, Jerry and Harris, Laurence, Financial Globalisation and Deregulation, in: Michie, Jonathan (Ed.), *The Economic Legacy 1979-1992*, Academic Press (London and San Diego), 1992, p. 38.

fell back to 6.5% on 9 January, 1978. Throughout 1978, MLR rose steadily to 12.5% and then reached 14% on 8 February, 1979. It fell back to 12% on 5 April[15] (shortly before Labour lost the 1979 general election).

Basically, there were two reasons for the rises in MLR as from autumn 1977. Firstly, interest rates were used to try and prevent any economic recovery from leading to any recurrence of the inflationary pressures which were witnessed in the mid 1970s (see pages 31-35). Secondly, following the IMF loan agreement at the end of 1976, and also in anticipation of North Sea oil which was about to start flowing in significant quantities, demand for sterling then grew thus more than reversing the decline in its value in that year. Furthermore, high interest rates would tend to encourage money to flow into the City of London anyway. So, all these factors would tend to lead to an increase in the exchange rate for sterling.

Thus, one additional factor behind the increases in interest rates and the exchange rate from autumn 1977 becomes apparent. Britain could only be seen to secure the maximum benefit from North Sea oil if there was a high exchange rate together with an improvement in the terms of trade, irrespective of the consequences this was going have on manufacturing industry and the livelihoods of those employed there.[16] At the same time, the rate of growth of the money supply had to remain under tight control. So one consequence of the steep rises in interest rates as from June 1979 (see below) can be seen in how the Thatcher Government was going to exploit the opportunities North Sea oil was going to offer in its endeavours to strengthen the international standing of the City of London. Although the previous Labour Government would not have overlooked the significance of having a high exchange rate, it saw in the potential revenues from the North Sea as an opportunity for modernising British industry and the country's infrastructure[17] in apparent contrast to the Thatcher Government. Only by taking account of the importance it placed on the City of London can the structural changes which took place in the British economy in the 1980s be understood.

When the Thatcher Government took office in May 1979, the apparent recovery in the world economy from the mid 1970s was nearing an end. This was to be followed by a slump (as with the crisis of the mid 1970s, triggered by a major increase in oil prices (see below)) which was to last until 1982.[18] With an im-

[15] See Bank of England Money Market Intervention Rates: Changes in Bank Rate, Minimum Lending Rate, Minimum Band 1 Dealing Rate and Repo Rate, in: *Bank of England Statistical Abstract Part 1*, December 2002, Table 22.1.

[16] See The two faces of recession, in: *Financial Times* (FT) (London and Frankfurt), 19 July 1980, p. 14.

[17] See *The Challenge of North Sea Oil*, Cmnd. 7143, HMSO (London), March 1978

[18] Gamble, Andrew, ..., p. 107.

pending downturn in the world economy, and Britain being particularly prone to such crises, the thinking behind post-war "consensus" politics might have been to favour measures so as to soften the impact of this – even more so as Britain had become an oil-producing nation by the end of the 1970s. However, the conquest of inflation by applying strict monetary discipline together with the "liberalisation" of the money markets took priority over all other matters.

In the first Budget of Mrs. Thatcher's new government on 12 June, 1979, for the financial year 1979/1980, public expenditure was to be cut by £1,500m with *cash limits* tightened to reduce public expenditure by a further £1,000m so as to reduce the Public Sector Borrowing Requirement (PSBR) to £8,250m. Major changes were to take place in the structure of taxation, with more emphasis being placed on *indirect* rather than *direct* taxation. Income tax rates were lowered, benefiting those on high incomes whilst VAT was almost doubled from 8% to 15% and there were also big increases in prescription charges etc.. Such measures, being enacted alongside the public expenditure cuts, meant that the costs of the 1979 Budget were to fall on those with low incomes. At the same time, in an attempt to keep the growth of money supply under control, MLR was raised from 12% to 14%.[19] On top of this, OPEC announced on the following 28 June, that oil prices were to be increased by 15%.[20] So, despite the drastic measures announced in this Budget and the worsening economic situation coupled with the latest increase in oil prices, the Government failed to keep down the rate of monetary expansion. Consequently, in November 1979, MLR was raised by a further 3% to 17% which meant that MLR rose by 5% within the first six months of the Thatcher Government taking office.[21]

Just one week after its first Budget, the Thatcher Government started its step-by-step programme of the privatisation of publicly-owned firms and corporations together with the selling off of stakes the Government had in the private sector.[22] Privatisation was a major feature of her government's policy and that of her successor John Major,[23] who replaced her as Prime Minister and Conservative Party Leader in autumn 1990. This policy went as far as returning to the private sector key industries which were nationalised under the first post-war Labour Government which were of strategic importance for Britain's post-war recovery (see below). Initially, the policy of privatisation meant that the National Enterprise

---

19 See Budget Summary, FT (London and Frankfurt), 13 June 1979, p. 1. (For full details of the June 1979 Budget, see FT, 13 June 1979, pp. 18-27).

20 Gamble, Andrew, ..., p. 108.

21 See Bank of England Money Market Intervention Rates: ....

22 Gamble, Andrew, ..., pp. 108f.

23 For a comprehensive list of the publicly-owned companies which were privatised under the premierships of Margaret Thatcher and John Major, see Florio, Massimo, *The Great Divestiture: Evaluating the Welfare Impact of the British Privatizations 1979-1997*, MIT Press (Cambridge, Massachusetts and London), 2004, pp. 40ff.

Board (established by the previous Labour Government as part of its strategy to boost manufacturing industry) was required to sell assets worth £100 million and for the British National Oil Corporation (also established by the previous Labour Government) to dispose of a number of its stakes and interests in North Sea oil exploration.[24]

The Thatcher Government's public expenditure plans were more clearly formulated in November 1979 in its White Paper *The Government's Expenditure Plans 1980/81* (Cmnd. 7746). In this White Paper, plans were outlined in which public expenditure was to be reduced by 4% in real terms by 1983/1984.[25]

The mechanism by which the Government sought to proceed with its economic strategy was unveiled in its Budget in March 1980. By more vigorously continuing with the policy of *cash limits* and controlling monetary expansion, the Government put into effect its Medium Term Financial Strategy (MTFS). This had three main objectives: firstly, to reduce the level of direct taxation so as to "encourage initiative"; secondly, to lower the real growth of public expenditure so that it would fall as a share of GDP and; thirdly, to reduce the PSBR.[26]

For these objectives to be fulfilled, a programme of public expenditure cuts was needed. As the Government was committed to increasing spending in certain areas, e.g. law and order and defence, the impact of the cuts would be mainly in those areas which contribute to what is known as the "social wage". Such measures included ending the link between the basic state pension and earnings (so that basic state pensions would not rise by more than retail prices, i.e. there would be no provision for raising the living standards of the large number of pensioners whose sole income was the basic state pension). Other measures included the reduction and abolition of the earnings-related supplement to unemployment and other benefits from 1982, with such benefits being subject to taxation, and cutbacks in the provision of sick pay and child benefit.[27] Parallel to the cutbacks in state benefits, national insurance contributions (a major source of funding for these provisions) were increased, implying an increase in taxation "via the back door",[28] with the effect that people had to start paying higher national insurance contributions for lower benefits.

Through these measures, the Government, on the basis of its own criteria, could claim a success in the fight against inflation in the period 1980 to 1984 together

---

24 Gamble, Andrew, ..., pp. 108f.

25 Ibid., p. 110.

26 Busch, Andreas, *Neokonservative Wirtschaftspolitik in Großbritannien*, Peter Lang (Frankfurt am Main) 1989, pp. 59f.

27 See Sturm, Roland, *Großbritannien: Wirtschaft – Gesellschaft - Politik*, Leske und Budrich (Opladen), 1991, pp. 133-143.

28 *TUC Economic Review 1982*, TUC (London), 1982, p. 40, para. 10.17.

with a reduction in the PSBR/GDP ratio. Rather than a deficit, there was, in fact, a public sector surplus in the financial years 1987/1988 to 1989/1990[29] – an unusual phenomenon as governments normally run deficits. A major factor influencing this was that economic recovery following the slump of 1979 to 1981 led to an increase in consumer spending which in turn led to rising VAT revenues. However, it should not be overlooked that privatisation revenues together with revenue from North Sea oil extraction assisted the Government in bringing down the PSBR in the course of the 1980s.

The social impact of these measures was evident. The burden of taxation was shifted onto those on low incomes to the benefit of those on high incomes. With benefits being cut back and national insurance contributions being increased, it was clear that the "welfare state", along with those it was supposed to serve, was going to have to shoulder the main burden of the Thatcher Government's economic strategy.

Clearly, as these measures were being put through parallel to a downturn in the world economy, they were bound to plunge the British economy into a deep recession. This particularly affected manufacturing industry. The Cambridge University Department of Applied Economics observed that, between 1979 and 1981, UK manufacturing output fell by 15% which was more than in any other industrial country and more than during the inter-war depression. The UK's drastic fall in manufacturing output in this period compared with an increase of over 10% in Japan and 4% in Italy whilst in the same period, manufacturing output fell in the United States, West Germany and France by 1.5%, 2.5% and 8% respectively.[30] It should also be noted that, despite the increase in oil prices, other industrial countries chose not to implement restrictive monetary measures on such a drastic scale as in Britain, which, moreover at that time, had not only become an oil-producing nation, but had also benefited considerably from higher oil revenues.

Significantly, the Cambridge economists observed that the main cause for this 15% fall in manufacturing output was to be found in the home market for manufactured goods, which contracted by 16% in this period. According to these economists, this was the result of restrictive monetary policies with excessively high interest rates leading to an over-valuation of the exchange rate, which in turn, pushed down investment and undermined "confidence" in manufacturing industry.[31] (Low investment in manufacturing industry in the UK had already

---

[29] *OECD Economic Surveys 1990/1991 – United Kingdom*, OECD (Paris), August 1991, p. 35.

[30] Begg, Ian and Rhodes, John, Will British industry recover?, in: *Cambridge Economic Policy Review*, Vol. 8 No. 1, University of Cambridge Department of Applied Economic, April 1982, pp. 18f.

[31] Ibid., p. 19.

been a problem for many decades which was clearly aggravated by these restrictive monetary measures). The Government's own statistics, quoted in the *TUC Economic Review 1984*, in fact gave support to these conclusions (see Appendix, table 6). So, on the one hand, Britain, as far as her foreign trade balance is concerned, benefited considerably from the rising oil revenues and the inflow of "hot" money (due to the high interest rates). On the other hand, she endured a massive weakening of her industrial base with its inevitable effects on unemployment (rising from 1.3 million in May 1979 to 1.5 million in May 1980 to 2.6 million in May 1981 and to 3.0 million in May 1982).[32]

Behind these predictable developments, the question which needs asking is whether the Government achieved the objectives it set for itself on the economic front. The three-pronged strategy that it embarked upon was in fact incompatible and inconsistent with the greatest inconsistency being between the monetarist policy of attempting to control finance and the competitive goal of deregulation.[33]

For the MTFS, the Government defined money supply in terms of sterling M3,[34] also known as "broad money". This consists of the notes and coins in circulation plus the sterling bank deposits of the public and private sectors.[35] The problem was that, due to the deregulation of international finance, the boundary between money and other financial assets kept changing and the demand for them rose faster than national income.[36] Furthermore, broad money-supply movements tend to mirror changes in bank lending and other forms of credit.[37] As deregulation encouraged competition among financial institutions, profitability could only be maintained by increasing lending at finer margins.[38] So, financial institutions were having to offer more attractive terms to savers and investors and at the same time, compete in a highly competitive market, thus tending to increase the volume of lending. As a result, the Government was unable to fulfill its financial targets under the MTFS. Consequently, these targets were frequently revised upwards thus, undermining the whole basis of its strategy[39] (see Appen-

---

32 The Tories' inflated record, in: *Labour Research*, Vol. 78 No. 5, Labour Research Department (LRD) (London), May 1989, p. 13, Table 1. Alternatively, see Appendix, table 7.

33 Coakley, Jerry and Harris, Laurence, ..., p. 38.

34 Gamble, Andrew, ..., p. 110.

35 Composition of monetary and liquid aggregates, and associated statistics, in: *Bank of England Quarterly Bulletin*, Bank of England (London), December 1982, Vol. 22 No. 4, p. 536.

36 Deakin, Simon et. al., *Inflation, Employment, Wage-bargaining and the Law*, The Institute of Employment Rights (London), March 1992, p. 23.

37 Coakley, Jerry and Harris, Laurence, ..., p. 42.

38 Ibid.

39 Ibid.

dix 1, table 8). In 1985, the Government was forced to abandon its MTFS criteria for controlling the rate of monetary expansion.

Whilst not underestimating the importance the Thatcher Government continued to attach to controlling monetary expansion as a means for fighting inflation, from the mid-1980s, more emphasis was placed on achieving this by seeking to maintain a relatively stable exchange rate. In this respect, high interest rates, as under the MTFS, were used.[40] But by placing more emphasis on exchange rate stability, the Government was taking account of developments in what was then the European Community (EC) to stabilise exchange rates within the European Monetary System (EMS) and for plans to establish European Economic and Monetary Union (EMU).[41] There, it is important to assess the significance which was attached to the establishment of the Single European Market.

In 1985, Margaret Thatcher launched a major policy initiative so as to radically extend the existing Common Market (as the EEC had often been referred to) into a "Single Market"[42] (in other words, a European free market). The basis for this was as the Community's internal tariffs on goods had been abolished by July 1968 (4½ years before Britain joined) and at the same time had become a customs union, which Britain had fully accepted in July 1977, there were, as far as Thatcher was concerned, the question of the "non-tariff" barriers.[43] In this, she wanted the extension of competition into services and utilities, the dismantling of non-tariff barriers and the extension of privatisation and deregulation.[44] In so doing, Thatcher thought that British firms would benefit from the opening-up of other countries' market in these areas.[45]

However, Thatcher believed that there were obstacles in the treaties from which the EC came into being involving "unanimity" among its member states in various decision-making processes which prevented a single market from coming into effect.[46] In view of her success at the Fontainebleau Summit of EC Heads of State and Government, the previous year, where she managed to secure a rebate and subsequent reductions in Britain's contributions to the Community Budget,[47] she apparently felt confident enough to put forward proposals for changes in the functioning of the EC which she deemed necessary to further the

[40] Ibid., p. 43.

[41] Ibid.

[42] See Shore, (Lord) Peter, *Separate Ways*, Gerald Duckworth and Co. Ltd. (London), 2000, p. 80.

[43] Thatcher, (Baroness) Margaret, *Margaret Thatcher: The Downing Street Years*, HarperCollins (London), 1993, p. 553.

[44] Shore, (Lord) Peter, ..., p. 80.

[45] Thatcher, (Baroness) Margaret, ..., p. 553.

[46] Shore, (Lord) Peter, ..., p. 80.

[47] Ibid.

"free" market policies for which she stood. She thus proposed to other EC member states the establishment of a "convention" so as to examine ways by which the necessary decision-making processes could be made by qualified majority voting (QMV), but within the scope of the existing treaties, except in areas where "vital national interests" were at stake[48] where unanimity would still be required. Thatcher, in her memoirs accepted that "the price we would have to pay to achieve a Single Market with all its benefits, though, was more majority voting in the Community" and "more power for the European Commission: but that power must be used in order to create and maintain a Single Market, rather than to advance other objectives".[49] However, in the eyes of those critical of Britain's membership of the European Union (EU), as the EC is now called,[50] Thatcher's initiative turned out to be a fatal mistake which was to overshadow the remaining years of her premiership.

At the EC Heads of State and Government meeting in Milan at the end of June 1985, other EC member states not only agreed to the general thrust of her proposals but went beyond what she wanted. Rather than establishing a "convention", it was decided instead to convene an Inter-Governmental Conference (IGC) which was then to formulate any amendments to the Treaty of Rome[51] which were deemed necessary for the "Single Market" to come into being. Thus, the predicament the Prime Minister found herself in was that the treaty amendments which then appeared could, in the words of the former Labour Cabinet Minister, the late Peter Shore, "hardly be vetoed by their principal author".[52]

The unintended outcome of Thatcher's policy initiative was the Single European Act (SEA) which she signed at the European Council meeting in Luxembourg in February 1986. The SEA was in fact the first major alteration to the Treaty of Rome and it had three important provisions. Firstly, a date (1 January, 1993) was set for the completion of the Single Market enabling "free" competition within the entire EU. Secondly, there was a to be an extension of qualified majority voting within the EU's Council of Ministers thus narrowing the range of issues which had previously required unanimity. Thirdly, there was a commitment to achieve EMU.[53] EMU was to be the cornerstone of the future Maastricht Treaty and the completion of the Single Market was to be part of the first stage of establishing EMU.

48 Ibid.

49 Thatcher, (Baroness) Margaret, ... p. 553.

50 EC (originally founded under the name European Economic Community (EEC) in March 1957) has been known as the EU since 1992 through the conclusion of the Treaty of Maastricht (officially known as the *Treaty on European Union*).

51 The Treaty which founded the EEC in March 1957.

52 Shore, (Lord) Peter, ..., p. 80.

53 Baimbridge, Mark et. al., *Britain and the European Union: alternative futures*, Campaign for an Independent Britain (London), April 2005, p. 115.

The SEA was passed by the British parliament in 1986 and became Community law in July 1987 and thus paved the way for the Single Market to come into being.[54] Although the former Prime Minister spoke of "the price" which had to be paid to achieve a Single Market, it was the advancement of these "other objectives", in particular to EMU which was to overshadow the remaining years of Thatcher's premiership.

The commitment to EMU involved the anchoring of the national currencies of the member states of the European Community in the European Exchange Rate Mechanism (ERM) of the EMS. In fact, the Thatcher Government had already been confronted with this issue before the SEA was signed. The Governor of the Bank of England had already advocated ERM membership as early as 1984.[55] This very issue was to divide the Thatcher Government, chiefly between the Prime Minister herself and then Chancellor of the Exchequer Nigel Lawson and was to remain unresolved until October 1990.[56]

Whilst the Cabinet was united over the need to fight inflation and for this to be done by cutting social expenditure, Thatcher argued that ERM membership was an abdication of control over monetary policy by claiming that it would then be "determined by the German Bundesbank".[57] Furthermore, the anchoring of sterling in a fixed exchange rate mechanism would have been a distortion of the "free" market principles she stood for. Thatcher firmly argued that "the only effective way to control inflation is by using the interest rates to control the money supply".[58] This, she, as already noted, had no hesitation of doing irrespective of the social costs, as was clearly shown in autumn 1979 when MLR was allowed to rise to 17%.

However, apparently unknown to the Prime Minister until 20 November, 1987, the Chancellor of the Exchequer had been pursuing a policy of "shadowing the deutschmark" since March of that year by setting interest rates according to the exchange rate with the aim of keeping the value of the pound below three deutsch marks.[59] In this, the Chancellor had allowed interest rates to fall. He also continued with this policy following the stock market crash in October of that year which helped to fuel what became known as the "Lawson boom" (see

---

[54] Burkitt, Brian et. al., *From Rome to Maastricht: A reappraisal of Britain's membership of the European Community*, Campaign for an Independent Britain (London), June 1992, p. 5.

[55] Coakley, Jerry, and Harris, Laurence, ..., p. 43.

[56] For a detailed personal account of the differences inside the Thatcher Government over the question of anchoring sterling in ERM, see Thatcher, (Rt. Hon. Baroness) Margaret, ..., Chapter XXIV(Floaters and Fixers), pp. 688-726.

[57] Ibid., p. 690.

[58] Ibid.

[59] Ibid., p. 701.

below).[60] However, by pursuing such a policy, the Chancellor had apparently, not only been undermining the importance to the way the Prime Minister believed that inflation ought to be fought, but "shadowing the deutschmark" meant, in the words of Peter Shore, Britain "covertly but effectively joining the ERM with a fixed sterling-DMark parity".[61]

However, the divisions within the Thatcher Government over ERM and EMU cannot be simply reduced to just one aspect of the measures which were deemed necessary to fight inflation. At the heart of these was (and still is) the conflict within ruling circles in Britain between those who saw the country's interests best served by placing more emphasis on the deepening of the special relationship with the USA and those who saw these interests better furthered by a deeper degree of integration within Europe and the structures of the European Union. Whereas Thatcher was in the former category, a number of her key ministers including the then Chancellor of the Exchequer Lawson were in the latter category. Whilst not being opposed to a confederative association within what is now the EU, Thatcher and her key allies saw the tightly-centralised federative structure envisaged by the Maastricht Treaty as preventing Britain from getting the best of both worlds.[62]

The crucial question is what was necessary to help secure the ability of the British economy to produce goods and services on a longer term basis and being able to compete in highly competitive markets. Note had to be taken of the fact that the value of sterling and other economic variables e.g. interest rates had been among the more volatile in the advanced industrialised world which in turn had often resulted in serious consequences for the masses of ordinary people. In other words, would the anchoring of sterling in ERM have helped place the British economy on a more stable footing and allow the development of her productive and technological base to match those of her major competitors.

One aspect of this problem is clearly demonstrated by the fact that during 1980, high interest rates (with MLR at 17%) together with rising oil prices helped to increase the value of sterling by 12% thus seriously eroded the competitiveness of much of British industry.[63] For example, during the period February 1979 to October 1980, the value of sterling rose from US$2.00 to US$2.42 and there were similar increases in the value of sterling against other major currencies and from then, the exchange rate of sterling steadily declined, most notably against the US dollar with it falling to just US$1.09 in February 1985[64] – then an all-

60 See Coakley, Jerry and Harris, Laurence, ..., p. 43.

61 Shore, (Lord) Peter, ..., p. 88.

62 See Star Comment: Not Major or Thatcher, in: *Morning Star* (London), 6 July 1992, p. 4.

63 Gamble, Andrew, ..., p. 110.

64 Table 16.1 Foreign exchange rates: against sterling: in, *Bank of England Statistical Abstract 1992 Part 1: Banking, capital markets, government debt and related statistics –*

time low which, in part, was influenced by the effects of the year-long miners' strike which ended in winter 1985.

However, in the period between July 1985 and February 1987, whilst the value of sterling against the US dollar rose from US$1.38 to US$1.53, against other major currencies, most notably against the West German mark, the value of sterling, largely due to falling oil prices, declined by 30% representing a fall from DM4.01 to DM2.79.[65] This fall was subsequently to be followed by the policy of "shadowing the deutschmark" which was to lead to a short-lived boom in the UK economy. Whereas the UK economy up to 1986 had only been growing modestly (i.e. not enough to prevent unemployment from continuing to rise), there was then to be a short period of rapid economic growth – the "Lawson boom". Whereas real GDP (over the previous year) grew by 3.6% in 1985, in 1986, 1987 and 1988, it grew by 3.9%, 4.5%, and 5.2% respectively (see Appendix, table 5). In this manufacturing output rose sharply as the exchange rate had fallen and unemployment, which had been rising from 1979 to 1986, started to fall.[66] However, this recovery in manufacturing output had not offset the major loss in industrial capacity due to the slump of 1979 to 1981.

However, rather than taking steps to ensure that this upturn in the UK economy had a secure and stable foundation so as to prevent the economy from overheating, the Chancellor of the Exchequer did the opposite. In his Budget on 17 March, 1987, Lawson cut the basic rate of income tax from 29% to 27%.[67] In his tax-cutting Budget on 15 March, 1988, he not only reduced the basic rate of income tax to 25%, he also cut the top rate of taxation to just 40%.[68] Whilst these measures may have brought some welcome relief for those whose incomes were modest, without any doubt, the major beneficiaries of these measures were those on high incomes. What is remarkable is that by implementing such measures at such a stage in the trade cycle, the advantages British industry gained by the fall in the value of sterling against the deutsch mark were short lived. As British industry had lost so much of its productive capacity during the slump of 1979 to 1981, it was hardly in a position to take full advantage of the consumer boom these tax cuts had helped to facilitate. Consequently, imports satisfied much of this extra demand and by 1989 and 1990, this led to the worst balance of payments crisis Britain had ever known (see below).[69]

Interest and exchange rates.

65 Ibid. See also, Jay, (Lord) Douglas (Ed.), *The European Monetary System: The E.R.M. Illusion*, Labour Common Market Safeguards Committee (London), June 1990, p. 9.

66 Jay, (Lord) Douglas, ..., pp8f. See also Appendix, table 7.

67 See Budget Summary, FT (London and Frankfurt), 18 March 1987, p. 1. (For full details of the March 1987 Budget, see FT, 18 March 1987, pp. 18-31).

68 See Budget Summary, FT (London and Frankfurt), 16 March 1988, p. 1. (For full details of the March 1988 Budget, see FT, 16 March 1988, pp. 12-25).

69 See, Jay, (Lord) Douglas, ..., p. 9.

The "Lawson Boom" also led to a rapid expansion of credit and a surge in estate prices which the financial markets could not sustain. Thus, the clearing banks' short-term base rate,[70] which had fallen to 7.5% in May 1988 (their lowest level during Thatcher's Premiership), started rising once again as from the following month. By November 1988, interest rates had risen rapidly to 13% and rose to 14% in May 1989.[71] In the following October, shortly before his resignation, Lawson, in response to a 1% increase in German interest rates and renewed fears of rising inflation, raised the Bank of England's base rate to 15%. Consequently, this expansion in credit and the surge in estate prices, upon which much of the City's expansion had been based, collapsed. This precipitated a severe crisis of the financial system which continued right into the 1990s. As a result, the international standing of the City of London as a major international financial centre was weakened[72] thus undermining a major economic objective the Thatcher Government had set for itself. In the process, much of Britain's manufacturing capacity was sacrificed through the combination of financial deregulation, tight monetary policies and the closure of "unprofitable" areas of publicly-owned industries, being triggered in part to further privatisation.

Initially upon succeeding Lawson, the new Chancellor of the Exchequer John Major resisted pressure for interest rates to be raised further.[73] This enabled the value of sterling to fall against the deutsch mark with the effect that its value by the end of 1989 was about 10% lower than it had been the year before.[74] As the "Lawson boom" had already come to an end, allowing the value of sterling to fall against the deutsch mark had the effect of easing the rate of slowdown in economic growth but did not prevent a major economic crisis which was to subsequently occur. Whereas in 1987 and 1988, real GDP grew rapidly, in 1989 it grew by only 2.2% and by just 0.8% in 1990 (see Appendix, table 5).

---

70 From 13 October, 1972 to 20 August, 1981, the Bank of England posted MLR as the *minimum* criteria for intervening in the money markets. From that date, the BoE ceased the "continuous posting of MLR". As from then, the *base rate* of the major clearing banks, then being Barclays Bank, Lloyds Bank, Midland Bank and the National Westminster Bank, were to give an indication as to *minimum* rates of lending. These can be referred to "as a benchmark interest rate comparable with the BoE's base rate and MLR". Until May 1997 (see below), the rates at which the BoE's intervened in the money markets were subject to the approval of the Chancellor of the Exchequer and this in turn determined the minimum rates for banks and other financial institutions. A change in the *base rate* normally signifies a marked change in the level of short-term market rates and could therefore be judged as an indicator of the broad level of interest rates. See Notes to Table 15, in: *Bank of England Statistical Abstract 1992 Part 1.....*

71 See footnote 15.

72 Coakley, Jerry and Harris, Laurence, ..., pp. 42f.

73 Junor, Penny, *The Major Enigma*, Michael Joseph Ltd (London), 1993, p. 178.

74 Jay, (Lord) Douglas, ..., p. 10.

It was against this downturn in the UK economy coupled with high interest rates when Thatcher, in October 1990, finally conceded to the anchoring of sterling in ERM. As ERM became the key element in the first stage towards EMU, which was to become the cornerstone of the Maastricht Treaty,[75] this decision was a victory for those forces within her party and government which favoured deeper "integration" within Europe. This then exposed the Prime Minister to additional pressures in supporting further moves towards EMU. This, she resisted and this was a factor which her opponents in her party used to secure a change of party leader and, by implication, prime minister the following month (see page 211). At this point, and on an issue of such immense importance, the Prime Minister's decision to give way on ERM was to show that the tight grip she had long held over her party and government had been loosened and was never to be regained.

Sterling entered ERM on 8 October, 1990, with a central rate of 0.696904 against the ECU and a bilateral central rate against the deutsch mark (the most dominant currency in ERM) of £1=DM2.95000. Although the value of currencies in ERM was allowed to diverge within a range of plus or minus 2.25% against the central rate, in the case of the Spanish peseta and sterling, a wider band of plus or minus 6% was permitted. So, as far as the deutsch mark was concerned, sterling could, theoretically, fluctuate between the upper rate of DM3.13200 and the lower rate of DM2.77800.[76] So, disregarding the economic downturn, Britain was then obliged to defend the value of sterling within these parameters and, if necessary, through deflationary measures and/or increases in interest rates.

Upon joining ERM in October 1990, the BoE imposed an MLR of 14% which enabled the main clearing banks' base rates to fall from 15% to 14%. From then up to 5 May, 1992, the base rates of these banks fell steadily to 10%.[77] However, according to a study published by the Campaign for an Independent Britain in 1992, in the first year of Britain's membership of ERM, *real* interest rates (being the difference between *nominal* interest rates (commercial banks' prime lending rate) and the retail price index (RPI)) had actually risen because the RPI in this period had fallen more sharply than *nominal* interest rates. In this period, where-

---

[75] Officially known as the *Treaty on European Union*. This was finally agreed at the summit of the EC's heads of state and government in Maastricht on 9-10 December, 1991 and signed in Maastricht by the EC's foreign and finance ministers on 7 February, 1992. This treaty came into effect on 1 November, 1993, once it had been ratified in all of the then 12 EC member states.

[76] Adams, J. J., The exchange rate mechanism of the European monetary system, in: *Bank of England Quarterly Bulletin*, Bank of England (London), November 1990, pp. 479ff. NB On Friday 5 October – three days before joining ERM, the BoE invoked an MLR of 14% to be effective on the day of joining. See Notes to Table 15, in: *Bank of England Statistical Abstract 1992 Part 1.....*

[77] See Table 15.2 Changes in Bank Rate, Minimum Lending Rate and Base Rates and Notes to Table 15, in: *Bank of England Statistical Abstract 1992 Part 1.....* See also footnote 63.

as *nominal* interest rates fell from 15.0% to 11.5%, the increase in the RPI fell from 10.6% to 4.1%, therefore *real* interest rates actually rose from 4.4% to 7.4%. In the same period in Germany, according to this study, *real* interest rates fluctuated between 7.4% and 8.0%.[78] This implies that an important criterion for maintaining the value of sterling in ERM was that *real* interest rates in Britain, despite the economic downturn, had to rise and then remain comparable to those in Germany. So, the anchoring of sterling in ERM, and at an overvalued rate, meant, that at that particular point in the trade cycle when there was already an economic downturn, a major economic crisis was inevitable.

Whereas real GDP grew by just 0.8% in 1990, in 1991, it fell by 1.4% and rose by just 0.2% in 1992 (see Appendix, table 5) implying that growth was negative throughout much of 1992. However one assesses the impact of ERM on the UK economy, one thing is clear. Under ERM, the British economy was subject to permanent deflation. This was because the central fault of the system was that it forced economically weaker countries, including Britain, to enact deflationary measures to defend high values of their currencies and this also involved high interest rates which then undermined investment plans.[79] ERM was also presented as a means of forcing firms to work more efficiently, but under conditions of high interest rates defending an overvalued currency, a lot of productive industrial capacity, as with the slump of 1979 to 1981, was to be permanently lost.

In 1992, barely a few months after the Maastricht Treaty (whose cornerstone being EMU – see above) had been signed, ERM, a crucial stage in this process had partially broken down. Basically, there were two reasons for this.

Firstly, on 2 June, 1992, the people of Denmark voted against ratification of this treaty in a referendum. This promptly led to France calling a referendum for the following 20 September with the prospect of it being rejected there as well. In addition, there was considerable opposition to this treaty elsewhere in Europe. This was especially so in Britain where the Major Government had considerable difficulty in getting Parliament to ratify it despite the *opt-outs* which it secured for Britain on the question of the single currency and the "social chapter" (see below). Consequently, it became questionable whether this treaty could come into effect at all as it had to be ratified in *all* of the member states of the EC.

Secondly, and partially in response to the uncertainty over this treaty, weaker currencies in ERM, especially the lira and sterling came under increasing market pressure towards the end of summer 1992.[80] This was also influenced by the weakness of the US dollar which undermined further the competitiveness of Bri-

---

78 Burkitt, Brian et. al., ..., p. 5.

79 See Kitson, Michael and Michie, Jonathan, *Coordinated Deflation – The Tale of Two Recessions*, Full Employment Forum (Watford), 1993, pp. 9f.

80 Mills, John, *Europe's Economic Dilemma*, Macmillan Press Ltd (Basingstoke), 1998, p. 64.

tain and other countries which compete directly with the US on the world market.[81] Furthermore, due to the higher than expected costs of German unification, the German Bundesbank sought to counter rising wages, rising budget deficits and rising inflation by raising interest rates.[82] In addition, the relaxation and subsequent abolition of any remaining capital controls, as required by the SEA, would expose EMS to massive speculative pressures on foreign exchange markets. Therefore, under such circumstances, the foundations upon which ERM was established were unstable as illustrated by the following sequence of events towards the end of summer 1992.

On 20 August, sterling fell close to the minimum value permitted under ERM and the US dollar fell to an historic low against the deutsch mark. On 27 August, record levels of intervention failed to raise the value of sterling appreciably. On the following day, the lira fell below the minimum rate permitted under ERM. On 3 September, Britain borrowed $14.5 billion in deutsch marks to raise her reserves and sterling rose to above DM2.80. On the following day, the Bank of Italy raised official interest rates sharply but the lira still remained below the minimum permitted rate under ERM. Despite intervention from the Bundesbank and the Bank of Italy on 10 and 11 September, the value of the lira continued to remain below the ERM's floor so the currency was officially devalued. On 15 September, not only was there new pressure on the lira but also on the peseta and again on sterling. On the following day, the BoE raised its base rate by 2% and at the same time announced an MLR of 12% and announced a rise to 15% taking effect on the following day. However, despite intervention from the BoE, the Bundesbank and the Bank of France, sterling fell below the ERM floor so Britain had no alternative other than to withdraw from ERM. So, the second rise in MLR could be rescinded. The same fate affected the lira leading to its suspension from ERM one day later.[83] Ironically, the ejection of sterling and the lira from ERM on 16 and 17 September respectively came just a few days before the crucial French referendum on the Maastricht Treaty – the outcome of which had been uncertain.

However, the real problem with ERM was not that it failed to achieve the aims it had originally set out – currency stability and convergence – for these, in any case, were really of only secondary importance to what the primary objectives of any economy should be – growth and full employment.[84] The problem with ERM is that its objectives were only seen as achievable through deflationary measures and as the cases of Britain and Italy had shown, the objectives which had originally been set out under ERM became unattainable. Furthermore, the

[81] Kenen, Peter B., *Economic and Monetary Union in Europe: Moving beyond Maastricht*, Cambridge University Press, 1995, p. 159.

[82] See Ibid., p. 138.

[83] Kenen, Peter B., ..., pp. 152f.

[84] Mills, John, ..., p. 64.

potential cost, both economically and politically, of staying in ERM would have been especially high for Britain as the recession had been long and deep and where increases in short-term interest rates are translated into higher mortgage rates.[85]

Britain's withdrawal from ERM enabled sterling to "float freely" on the foreign exchange markets once again. This enabled an immediate reduction of 2% in MLR[86] with further reductions in interest rates to follow. In January 1993, several central banks lowered official interest rates with MLR being lowered to 6%.[87] This meant that in the UK, interest rates had fallen to their lowest levels since October 1977. Throughout the rest of the 1990s and into the new millennium, interest rates remained relatively stable.[88] Thus, free of the tight monetary constraints of ERM, the UK economy could then embark upon a period of steady growth (see Appendix, table 5) without this being coupled with any major inflationary pressures.

However, in the period following the ejection of sterling from ERM right up to the end of John Major's premiership in 1997, unemployment had only declined modestly, remaining at over two million, despite there being steady economic growth (see Appendix, tables 5 and 7) coupled with the lowest interest rates for more than twenty years. This also means that up to the end of his premiership, the number of people out of work did not fall back to what it was before sterling was anchored in ERM in 1990.

Following the slump of 1979 to 1981, real GDP grew moderately up to 1988. However, 1979 levels of industrial output were not restored until 1985. As industrial output included North Sea oil extraction, which expanded rapidly in the late 1970s/early 1980s, the real picture of the British economy towards the end of the 1980s was more critical. As far as manufacturing industry was concerned, 1979 levels of output were not recovered until 1987 and in the period June 1979 to June 1987, the number of people employed in this key sector of the economy fell from 7.13 million to 5.06 million implying a loss there of a little over two million jobs.[89] As Britain's oil reserves are likely to have been used up within a space of a generation, it was more important to assess Britain's economic performance on manufacturing, alongside service and "high-tech" industries because her longterm prosperity depends on her being able to produce and sell goods and services in a highly competitive market.

---

85 Kenen, Peter B., ..., p. 157, footnote 7.

86 Ibid., p. 153.

87 Ibid., p. 154.

88 See Bank of England Money Market Intervention Rates: ....

89 See tables for "Industrial production/national output" and "Employees in employment" in: Economic Notes, *Labour Research*, Vol. 77 No. 7, LRD (London), December 1987, p. 24.

However, in comparison with other countries in the advanced industrialised world, Britain's performance in manufacturing industry during the 1980s was weak. For example, by 1991, manufacturing output was only 5.8% above what it had been in 1979 with Britain coming 20th of the 21 OECD countries.[90] Yet, in this same period, domestic expenditure on manufactured goods rose sharply, so imports had to meet the increased demand for these goods. This in turn led to a worsening of Britain's balance of payments. This, as already noted, had been aggravated through the shedding of a lot of productive industrial capacity in consequence of the slump of 1979 to 1981 as well as the effects of anchoring sterling at an overvalued rate in ERM between 1990 and 1992.

Britain's continued erosion as a major industrial nation reached a new point in the third quarter of 1982 when, for the first time in her trading history, she had a deficit in her trade in manufactured goods.[91] This trade deficit in manufactured goods continued to worsen throughout the 1980s,[92] reaching a record of £17 billion in 1989.[93] So, the effect of the "Lawson boom" may have been that the Exchequer, through rising consumer demand, benefited from extra VAT revenues but overshadowing this was the rapid deterioration in Britain's trade balance being largely due to the worsening of her trade in manufactured goods. By way of comparison, in 1979, Britain's manufacturing trade balance had been in surplus by 1.5% of GDP, but by 1989 it had fallen to a deficit of 3.5% of GDP.[94]

An additional point was that recovery in output and economic activity following the slump of 1979 to 1981 was not strong enough to prevent a continued rise in unemployment. The number of people out of work reached a peak of officially 3.4 million in January 1986.[95] However, considering that in the 1980s numerous changes had been made in the way the official unemployment statistics were calculated, the real picture was bleaker still. Due to these changes, many categories of unemployed people who once appeared in the official figures were no longer included.[96] One important category was unemployed men over 60.[97]

---

90 See Wells, John, Ministers burying heads in sand over unprecedented trade deficit, in: *The Guardian International* (London), 15 June 1992, p. 11.

91 Kimmig, Karl H., Politische und ökonomische Aspekte der "britischen Krise", in: Rohe, Karl and Schmidt, Gustav (Hrsg), ..., p. 161.

92 Coutts, Ken and Godley, Wynne, Does Britain's Balance of Payments Matter Any More?, in: Michie, Jonathan (Ed.), ..., p. 63.

93 The Budget: Red Book Details, in: FT (London), 20 March 1991, p. 22.

94 Coutts, Ken and Godley, Wynne, ..., p. 63.

95 Economic Notes, *Labour Research*, Vol. 75 No. 12, LRD (London), December 1986, p. 28.

96 According to the document *The Social Charter: How Britain benefits*, produced by the Labour Group of the European Parliament in 1989 (and published jointly with the Labour Party in that year), no less than 29 changes had been made in the way the official unemployment statistics had been calculated since 1979. See page 6 of the document.

97 See *A State of Collapse: The UK Economy under the Tories*, LRD (London), April 1987, p.

In the light of all these developments, Britain entered the 1990s with her standing in the advanced industrialised world severely weakened. This was very much due to the policy of seeking to strengthen the role of finance capital as the basis of Britain's future economic prosperity; but this was to the detriment of much of the productive base of the British economy which, since 1979, had been plunged into two slumps coupled with massive job losses. This was just one factor which led to an erosion of electoral support for the Conservative Party in the run-up to the 1997 election which brought an end to eighteen years of the Party in government.

2.2. The Conservative microeconomic strategy

The Thatcher Government's approach to the competitive weakness of British industry rested on the notion that its poor trading performance was due to a lack of market discipline on both sides of industry. The assumption was that this led to excessive wage costs and resistance to new technology and changes in working practices.[98] There, one notes a slight change in the line of argument. Previously, "unofficial" strikes had been looked upon as the main cause of Britain's industrial difficulties; then it became factors which supposedly obstructed the "free" functioning of the labour market which were blamed.

The extent to which such explanations of the weak state of British industry are accurate is not the point at issue here. Rather, it was more that in conditions of "full employment" and under the previous Labour Government's Social Contract (when "full employment", as it were, had ceased to exist), the trade union movement was able to secure additional reforms benefiting working people and their families. It was these reforms as well as the commitment to "full employment" itself which became regarded as factors obstructing the "free" functioning of the labour market. As a result, so the argument goes, industry was burdened with additional costs which undermined its competitiveness which in turn led to job losses.

In the context of the tight Conservative fiscal and monetary policies, together with the abolition of any remaining exchange controls in autumn 1979, industry was considered able to survive, only if it became more "efficient", in the sense that "management should have the right to manage", meaning that it should be able to put any restructuring programmes it desired into effect without any trade union opposition. Whether it be a case of "unofficial" strikes or "obstructions" in

---

24, Table 7: Fiddling away the unemployment figures. See also Appendix, notes to table 7.

98 Begg, Iain and Rhodes, John, ..., p. 21. See also Weinmann, Georg, Wandel oder Kontinuität? Britische Gewerkschaften in der Ära Thatcher, in: *1999 Zeitschrift für Sozialgeschichte des 20. und 21. Jahrhunderts*, Hamburger Stiftung für Sozialgeschichte des 20. Jahrhunderts (Hamburg), 6. Jahrgang Heft 3, p. 57.

the labour market, British industry was seen to have a future only if the power of organised labour was curbed.

Numerous factors were identified as "obstructing" the "free" functioning of the labour market (often looked upon as "outmoded concepts" in ruling circles in both government and industry). But in principle, five areas came in for particular criticism. These were minimum wage regulations, national and industry-wide pay bargaining, cost-of-living or automatic annual pay negotiations, trade union "immunities" and the "closed shop".

Minimum wage regulations were criticised in that they allegedly force employers to pay more that the "market rate" to many of their less-productive workers, by which unskilled workers were, it was argued, being denied the chance of working. Such regulations, it was claimed, discriminated against teenage workers and minority groups because people in these categories, tending to have less on-the-job training, would not be able to compete against adults for jobs.[99] This line of argument accurately reflected the thinking of the Thatcher Government[100] and tended to overlook the lack of resources Britain has traditionally devoted to training and retraining.

However, the biggest objection on the part of the Thatcher Government to minimum-wage regulations and particularly to wages councils (first established in the early years of the 20th century in response to public concern over excessively long hours of work and low pay) was the alleged interference with the "freedom" of employers, and with the "freedom" of potential employees to take jobs at wages regarded as "acceptable".[101] On this basis, it was argued that minimum-wage regulations destroy jobs. However, the evidence to date of the introduction of minimum wage regulations would show that this is not the case (see page 244).

National and industry-wide pay bargaining (which are largely concerned with establishing minimum terms and conditions of employment) have been criticised in that wage rates were said to have been set without any adjustment for the "relative" value of the same work done in different parts of the country.[102] The Thatcher Government claimed that national agreements disregarded differences

---

99 Forrest, David, *Low Pay or No Pay?*, Institute of Economic Affairs (Westminster, London), Hobart Paper 101, July 1984, p. 25.

100 See *Consultative Paper on Wage Councils*, Department of Employment (London), 1985, para. 11.

101 Ibid., para. 7.

102 Miller, Robert and Wood, John B., *What Price Unemployment? An Alternative Approach*, Institute of Economic Affairs (Westminster, London), Hobart Paper 92, January 1982, p. 38.

in individual circumstances or performance and were not reflected in the level of earnings where unemployment was particularly high.[103]

It is interesting to note that many employers' associations claimed that national-wage bargaining had helped to keep down pay increases and avoid "leap-frogging" through trade unions' targeting of profitable plants and companies. Also, it was felt that many non-pay issues were more efficiently handled at national level. In addition, smaller companies, lacking the resources for single-employer bargaining, found nationally-agreed procedures useful in limiting industrial disputes.[104]

In this, there appeared to be differences between the Conservative Party (and Government) and many employers' associations on how the labour market should operate. There is the "free-market" approach whereby terms and conditions of employment should be determined on the basis of supply and demand and "individual" performance etc. and the corporatist approach in which collective bargaining is felt to be best handled on an industry-wide or national basis involving trades and employers' organisations. "Free-market" thinking also includes criticism of automatic annual pay negotiations using the argument that these should be conducted on the basis of what the "market" permits and assessing "individual" performance, not on the basis of compensating working people and their families for increases in the cost of living.

Another major area of criticism, as already noted, was the "immunities" for trade unions and trade unionists from common law liability. Even though these social rights had originally come about as a result of social developments arising out of industrialisation in the 19th century, they were often denounced by many in the Conservative Party as "privileges" which supposedly put trade unions "above the law". In this, there was criticism that trade unions could pursue industrial disputes and secure terms and conditions of employment above what the "market" would permit and at the same time, be immune from common law liability in the process.

A further area of criticism was the "closed shop". Conservative opposition to the closed shop is well documented. The reason given was that it "forced" workers to join a specific trade union against their will. What is often overlooked was that many employers actually favoured this practice for basically two reasons. Firstly, it helped to force the shop-floor to conform with formalised agreements and procedures, with union officials being sufficiently insulated from shop-floor pressures, enabling unpopular negotiating decisions to be taken. Secondly, union membership meant that rank and file workers were tied to their unions' discipli-

---

[103] *Employment for the 1990s*, Cm 540, HMSO (London), December 1988, pp. 23f, para. 3.5.

[104] McIlroy, John, *Trade Unions in Britain Today*, Manchester University Press (Manchester and New York), 1988, pp. 50f.

nary machinery which was strengthened by linking the withdrawal of a union membership card to the loss of a job. This prevented protest resignations and increased the authority of union representatives.[105] Significantly, the Donovan Commission, although criticising the way the closed shop often operated, rejected the call for this practice to be prohibited[106] – this line of argument being consistent with the view that the shop floor should be brought under the control of official union structures.

The main reason for opposing the closed shop was that it help unions to secure better wage rates, "too often" above the "market rate".[107] This criticism was clearly confirmed in the Thatcher Government's 1989 Green Paper *Removing Barriers to Employment.* In this Green Paper, reference was made to research on the effects of the closed shop on industrial costs. It was argued that the existence of a "pre-entry" closed shop"[108] raised the earnings of manual workers "by over 10% on average" and, in plants with relatively little product market competition, "by about 20%". In the small proportion of plants in competitive markets which had both a "pre-entry" closed shop and a high level of union coverage in the industry, earnings could have been "up to 30% higher". The "pre-entry" closed shop was also said to have raised the pay of other manual workers in a plant, not just those it covered. Additionally, it was claimed to have "indirectly" pushed up "earnings levels more generally in local and national labour markets".[109] So, a more convincing reason for opposing the closed shop becomes evident: this had "an adverse effect on company profitability".[110] The Green Paper went on to claim that had the "pre-entry" closed shop never existed, and consequently labour costs been 10% lower for those directly covered by it, "aggregate employment would have been over 100,000 higher".[111]

---

[105] Dunn, Stephen and Gennard, John, *The Closed Shop in British Industry*, Macmillan (London and Basingstoke), 1984, p. 5. See also Hart, Moira, Why bosses love the closed shop, in: *New Society* (London), Vol. 47 No. 854, 15 February 1979, pp. 352ff.

[106] *Royal Commission on Trade Unions and Employers' Associations 1965-1968*, Cmnd. 3623, HMSO (London), June 1968, pp. 162ff, paras. 598-602.

[107] Miller, Robert and Wood, John B., ..., p. 38.

[108] There were two categories of the closed shop – the "pre-entry" and the "post-entry". The "pre-entry" closed shop was where membership of a specified trade union was a *precondition* for being able to take up employment in a particular firm or industry or for a certain type of job. There, union membership was often tied to having a recognised professional qualification as, for example, was once the case for various skilled jobs in the British printing industry. A "post-entry" closed shop was where membership of a specified trade union became a condition of employment upon commencement of the employment contract.

[109] *Removing Barriers to Employment*, Cm 655, HMSO (London), March 1989, p. 5, para. 2.11.

[110] Ibid., p. 5, para. 2.12.

[111] Ibid., p. 6, para. 2.14.

Although it is difficult to determine the number of workers who were covered by closed-shop agreements, surveys have shown that the closed-shop population rose from around 3¾ million or 16% of all workers in the early 1960s to a peak of at least 5.2 million or 23% of all workers in 1978[112] (the year before the Conservative election victory). It is also clear that under the Labour Government's Social Contract, trade unions were able to take advantage of the more favourable legal climate resulting from the repeal of the 1971 Act to extend the closed shop.

At this point, an additional factor has to be taken into consideration. This was the challenge posed to many trade unionists by technological developments. The introduction of new technology was to make obsolete many skills which had previously been acquired after successfully completing an apprenticeship and/or many years of work in the industry. Where trade union membership initially depended on the successful completion of an apprenticeship and with there also being a "pre-entry" closed shop, technological development threatened the job security and well-being of many skilled workers.

This situation was to become even more serious where new technology enabled work to be undertaken by unskilled workers requiring at most a minimum of training, where previously skilled workers had been needed. Such a dilemma confronted craft workers in the British printing industry and their unions, particularly the National Graphical Association (NGA) and the Society of Lithographic Artists, Designers, Engravers and Process Workers (SLADE) in the 1970s and early 1980s.

Through the "pre-entry" closed shop, craft unions had been able to control the supply of labour to the printing industry in three ways. To start with, the number of apprentices entering the industry was determined by apprenticeship ratios. Secondly, union membership and therefore skilled jobs were restricted to those who had successfully completed an apprenticeship (normally over a five- or six-year period), consequently, any new employee had to be cleared by the union. Thirdly, a control system was imposed to prevent employers from by-passing the union and seeking or getting work done elsewhere as union members were forbidden under union rules to handle work going to and from "unrecognised" sources.[113]

Prior to the introduction of new technology in the printing industry, in particular in the newspaper industry through 'direct entry' systems (integrating the editorial, advertising and composing processes leading to direct access to the printing stage), all production processes up to and including the printing stage were car-

---

[112] Dunn, Stephen and Gennard, John, ..., pp. 15ff and p. 145.

[113] Gennard, John and Dunn, Steve, The Impact of New Technology on the Structure and Organisation of Craft Unions in the British Printing Industry, in: *British Journal of Industrial Relations*, Blackwell (Oxford), Vol. XXI No. 1, March 1983, p. 18.

ried out by members of the NGA for whom a "pre-entry" closed shop had been secured. This meant that the NGA not only controlled the production process, it also helped to ensure that the high professional standards the industry required were maintained. The significance of the introduction of 'direct entry' systems was that the production processes became computerised and simplified and could then be carried out by less skilled people not requiring a craft qualification. This therefore meant that these people could be recruited from outside the industry and employed on inferior terms and conditions of employment.

Rather than trying to frustrate technological developments in the industry, the NGA (and also SLADE whose members were largely involved in the production of pictures and illustrations, mostly in advertising studios and publishing firms) embarked upon a series of strategies so as to try and influence the pace of its development. Such strategies included new technology agreements, attempts to return work to the composing room, attempts to organise new groups of workers entering the industry, seeking to revise, and securing new, training agreements, and amalgamations of the various trade unions in the industry.[114]

Like the NGA, SLADE also controlled the supply of labour to the industry via the apprenticeship system and the "pre-entry" closed shop. As a result of modern photographic techniques available to studios in publishing firms and advertising agencies, pictures and illustrations could then be produced independently of the production stages traditionally controlled by SLADE and the NGA.[115]

However, there were aspects of the attempts to try and regain control over print origination work which led to controversies; these were of significance in the drafting of the legislative changes to trade union and labour relations law in the 1980s. The most controversial in this respect concerned SLADE in the latter half of the 1970s.

Technological development led to the creation of an "alternative printing industry" which meant that print origination and reproduction work could be done in the growing number of art studios and advertising agencies which were mostly non-unionised but in a part of the industry where the craft unions had once been strong. In an attempt to protect the livelihood of its members, SLADE in the early 1970s sought to recruit the employees of these art studios and advertising agencies. It had only limited success and consequently revised its recruitment strategy. It founded a new section of the union called the "Slade Art Union" (SAU) for the purpose of recruiting and negotiating on behalf of members employed in art studios and advertising agencies. Once again, the union did not

[114] See Ibid., pp. 20-32.

[115] *Report of Inquiry into certain Trade Union Recruitment Activities*, Conducted by Andrew Leggatt QC, Cmnd. 7706, HMSO (London), October 1979, p. 4, para. 15. This Report is often referred to as the "Leggatt Report".

succeed in its recruitment drive to the extent it had wished. SLADE then responded to the problem by blacking work done by non-union labour, thus regarding it as coming from "unrecognised" sources. As the printing work of art studios and advertising agencies was done by members of SLADE, it meant that work coming from these places could not be handled unless their employees joined the SAU. This had the result, it was alleged in the Leggatt Report[116] that SLADE was operating a policy of "coercion" in its endeavours to recruit workers in art studios and advertising agencies.

The NGA operated a similar strategy to that of SLADE. To ensure that work being done came from recognised sources, the NGA, in December 1976, introduced a "label" so that it could "assist chapels in ensuring that work originated from NGA sources", and NGA chapels were subsequently instructed that "from the week beginning Tuesday 4 January 1977, NGA members shall not handle any origination i.e. typesetting and make-up that does not carry the completed NGA identity label, unless inquiries subsequently prove that the work in question was produced by SLADE members".[117] Subsequently, arrangements were made for NGA and SLADE branch secretaries to check the origin of all art work received for production purposes so as to make it difficult for any non-union work to be passed for production.[118] By April 1977, the NGA and SLADE had evolved a joint "Fair List" system for this purpose. However, in February 1979, SLADE decided to discontinue the "Fair List" system as there was evidence that the labelling system was producing a degree of resentment which was felt to be unhelpful to effective trade union organisation[119] although members were still advised to check the origin of any work produced.

Conservative criticism of the recruitment methods of SLADE were debated in the House of Commons on 29 June, 1977. They were subsequently raised in a debate on the newspaper industry on 18 May, 1978, on 8 March, 1979, on the Employment Protection Act and on 16 March, 1979, on trade unions.[120] The outcome of these criticisms was the Leggatt Report, already referred to.

This inquiry, however, should be seen more in the context of efforts by the newly-elected Conservative Government to try and gain acceptance for its proposed reforms in trade union and labour relations law. In view of such plans, the TUC and the print unions boycotted the inquiry. In the eyes of SLADE, the inquiry ignored the real problems of changes in technology, unemployment and the bad

---

[116] See Ibid.

[117] Ibid., p. 11, para. 37.

[118] Ibid.

[119] Ibid., p. 12, para. 40.

[120] Ibid., p. 17, paras. 57 and 60.

wages and conditions of employment for most people in the art and design part of the industry.[121]

The breaking down of established trade union practices and the strategy of deregulating the labour market were seen to be necessary by the incoming Conservative Government if it was to succeed with its macroeconomic strategy in the 1980s. The strategy of deregulating the labour market can therefore be looked upon as the Conservative Government's microeconomic strategy.

The Leggatt Report not only concerned the existence of certain established trade union practices which the Conservatives had long wanted to do away with. Its significance was also that a particular industry had been targeted in which trade union organisation was especially highly developed. This factor was taken into consideration in the drafting of the Employment Acts of 1980 and 1982.

With the battering the Heath Government had endured on the industrial relations front almost a decade earlier, the Thatcher Government sought to ensure that it would not be similarly humiliated. In its determination to cut state subsidies and to restore (what it regarded as) profitability to the public sector, it was made clear that there would be closures and redundancies and that it would back tough managerial policies to help bring this about.[122] Such measures should also be seen in the context of paving the way for eventual privatisation.

However, the Thatcher Government sought to avoid industrial disputes in the public sector unless it was confident of victory. Thus, it backed the management of the British Steel Corporation (BSC) in the national steel strike at the beginning of 1980 (which was concerned with a pay dispute and closures) and also backed the management of another publicly-owned company – British Leyland (BL) – in the dismissal of the trade union convener Derek Robinson (which should be seen in the context of trying to weaken shop-floor organisation in the company – see pages 156ff). When, however, in February 1981, the Government was faced with the prospect of a national miners' strike over planned pit closures, it backed down and provided the National Coal Board with the subsidies necessary to keep the threatened pits open.[123]

This makes it clear that the Thatcher Government was fully aware of the problems of the Heath Government's Industrial Relations Act. The conclusion which can be drawn is that it did not seek to achieve all of its objectives through a single Act as Heath had attempted. At the same time, although it can be argued

[121] See The Backlash Looms, in: *SLADE Journal*, SLADE (London), No. 81, November 1979, p. 1.

[122] Gamble, Andrew, ..., p. 109.

[123] Ibid., pp. 109 and 112f.

that the objectives of the 1971 Act and the laws of the Thatcher Government were similar, the approach of the two was, in fact, very different.

The 1971 Act was a long and complicated piece of legislation and experience revealed that it had a contradiction of aims reflecting a degree of confusion as to what was wrong with Britain's industrial relations and how the law should seek solve these problems.[124] A central contradiction of the 1971 Act was the purported encouragement of collective bargaining and the right given to individual workers to join or not to join a recognised union, and to use the law to seek the recognition of rival unions. In view of the fact that collective bargaining means that certain conditions of employment would be determined by collective negotiation rather than by individuals seeking special agreements, it was therefore inevitable that collective bargaining imposes some limitations on the "rights" of individuals.[125]

Another contradiction of the 1971 Act concerned the internal administration of unions. On the one hand, some of the Act's provisions enlarged the rights of individual union members on such matters as disciplinary procedures etc., so as to limit the ability of unions to "control" their members. These legal measures were brought about on the basis, emphasised by the media, that what was wrong with Britain's industrial relations was the political motivation of union leaders and that there would be fewer strikes if ordinary members controlled their unions. On the other hand, many commentators noted that the high proportion of "unofficial" strikes was because union leaders did not exercise enough control over their members.[126]

In contrast, the trade union laws of the 1980s were formulated on the basis that working people acting collectively obstructed the "free" functioning of the labour market and that common-law remedies should be reinstated in the event of industrial action occurring through a breach of contract. In addition, so it was argued, reforms and rights conceded to working people which imposed costs on employers had to be removed if industry was to prosper. This meant that unit production costs had to fall if British industry was going to flourish so a "micro-economic strategy" on the part of the Government was needed to help bring this about. An integral part of this strategy was therefore one of deregulating the labour market as part of the overall strategy of deregulating the economy.

Upon taking office in 1979, the Thatcher Government moved quickly but with caution in order to "put right" what was considered "wrong" on the industrial relations front. An early step was to issue an Order, taking effect on 1 October,

---

[124] See Weeks, B. C. M. et. al., *Industrial Relations and the Limits of the Law*, Blackwell (Oxford), 1975, Chapter 8, pp. 220-232.

[125] Ibid., p. 220.

[126] Ibid., p. 221.

1979, increasing the qualifying period of employment from 26 to 52 weeks before a claim for unfair dismissal could be heard by an industrial tribunal. Also an Order, taking effect on 30 November, 1979, was made reducing from 60 to 30 days the minimum period of consultation required before employers could dismiss between 10 and 99 employees.[127] These changes, according to the TUC, removed around one million workers from protection against unfair dismissal.[128]

Along the legislative path, the first step was the 1980 Employment Act. The aim of this first piece of legislation, according to the then Secretary of State for Employment James Prior, was to strike "a fair balance" between what is necessary to protect those organising industrial action and those whose jobs and businesses may be threatened by such action in which they had no part.[129] In this, it could be argued, an attempt was made to tackle some aspects of trade union practices which caused concern in ruling circles and which, as a result of media publicity, had become controversial.

The two main areas the 1980 Act concentrated on were so-called "secondary" industrial action and the closed shop. This Act created a new legal concept of "secondary" industrial action and "secondary" picketing, making both unlawful.[130] This left union officials engaged in sympathy strikes liable to claims in damages. Under this Act, "immunities" remained, but only for disputes with the immediate employer and for secondary action focused exclusively on direct customers or suppliers of that employer.[131]

As to the closed shop, rather than seeking to ban it, as the Heath Government attempted through the 1971 Act, the approach was to try and undermine support for it. A union could only secure a closed-shop agreement if it had the support of 80% of the workers affected,[132] the hope of course being that unions would have difficulty in reaching these figures. At the same time, more protection was given to employees who refused to join a union where a closed-shop agreement existed.[133] The 1980 Act, in response to the Leggatt Report, removed "immunity"

---

[127] *ACAS Annual Report 1979*, ACAS (London), pp. 47ff, paras. 3-5.

[128] *Industrial Relations Legislation: The Employment Act 1980 and Employment Bill 1982*, TUC (London), 1982, p. 8, para. 27.

[129] See *House of Commons The Employment Committee Session 1979-80: The Legal Immunities of Trade Unions and other related matters - Minutes of Evidence 20 February 1980 (The Rt Hon James Prior, MP)*, HMSO (London), p. 19.

[130] Tyler, Christian, Tebbit's Law: A Tory Dream Come True?, in: *Marxism Toady* (London), Vol 26 No 4, April 1982, p. 25.

[131] Coates, David, *The Crisis of Labour*, Philip Allan (Oxford and New Jersey), 1989, p. 121.

[132] Ibid.

[133] *Trade Union Immunities*, Cmnd. 8128, HMSO (London), January 1981, p. 68, para. 270.

from the organisers of any industrial action which had the purpose of compelling workers to join a trade union.[134]

Under the 1980 Act, provision was made by which trade unions could apply for public funds to finance strike ballots, ballots for union elections and changes in union rules.[135] This was introduced under the pretext, in the mass media and in ruling circles, that trade union leaders were often unrepresentative of their members. The hope was that unions would apply for public funds to finance postal balloting, thus enlarging the scope for media intervention in trade-union internal affairs which would lead to fewer "militant" union leaders and fewer strikes.

The 1980 Act also gave the Secretary of State for Employment the right to draft "Codes of Fair Industrial Relations Practice" which were largely aimed at restraining picketing, with there generally being a maximum of six pickets outside the workplace where the employees were in dispute with their employer. Although these "Codes" were not legally enforceable, they could offer guidance to judges and industrial tribunals and, of course, to the police when confronted with the prospect of mass picketing. The Act also took away from trade unions the right to claim recognition from unwilling employers or to claim the "going rate" from employers who were paying below "recognised" or "general" level of terms and conditions in the industry.[136] This was consistent with the thinking that the market should determine what individual employers pay their employees, and this provision in the Act should also be seen as an initial first step in trying to undermine national or industry-wide pay bargaining.

Although the then Secretary of State could argue that the provisions of the 1980 Act were designed to strike "a fair balance" and to correct "a number of specific abuses of trade union power",[137] many in the Conservative Party were far from convinced that the Act went far enough. In an attempt to appease his critics (and possibly the Prime Minister herself), Prior embarked upon a review of trade union "immunities" to map out the terrain for possible future legislation, even though it was not clear if he personally favoured any further legislative moves in that direction.[138] By the time further trade union legislation was presented to Parliament, there had in any case been a Cabinet reshuffle which included the appointment of a new Secretary of State for Employment (see below). This change was of significance in the subsequent formulation of policy in the field of trade union and labour relations law.

---

[134] Ibid., pp. 70f, paras. 283ff.

[135] Coates, David, ..., p. 121.

[136] Ibid.

[137] Tyler, Christian, ..., p. 25.

[138] Ibid.

The 1982 Employment Bill (which became the Employment Act, 1982) was published on 28 January of that year – four months after the Cabinet reshuffle. The popularity of the Thatcher Government had fallen considerably, unemployment was at three million and there were splits in the Cabinet, particularly over economic policy. So, the Prime Minister had to decide whether to modify her policies so as to appease her critics in the Cabinet, who had successfully limited the size of spending cuts which the Treasury (and the Prime Minister herself) demanded and had opposed the full implementation of the "free market" strategy, or to stick resolutely to that strategy.[139] The Prime Minister chose the latter – a gamble which paid off.

One major change in the Cabinet was the replacement of Prior (one of Thatcher's critics), who resisted every attempt to toughen his 1980 Act, by Norman Tebbit who was firmly committed to the doctrines and objectives of Margaret Thatcher and the "New" Right.[140] With the Falkland's war in spring 1982, a cyclical upswing in the economy after the slump and a reflationary budget in 1982, Thatcher and her closest allies were able to establish control over the Cabinet and the Conservative Party with the effect that her opponents in the Party and Cabinet were defeated.[141]

Furthermore, with the slump resulting in factory closures and layoffs on a large scale, industrial militancy fell sharply and likewise, the number of working people remaining to be industrially organised (on the basis of membership of TUC-affiliated unions) declined (see Appendix, tables 9 and 10 respectively). This factor was also influenced by the absence of a formally administered incomes policy which meant that the Government was able to distance itself from pay negotiations in many sectors of the economy.[142] In this, many workers managed to avoid a reduction in their real disposable incomes, so the costs of the slump fell on the unemployed and those employed in sectors on low pay where the potential for any effective trade union organisation was more limited.[143] So, with pay negotiations having the effect of segregating the industrially strong from the industrially weak, and further, separating those in work from those out of work, the Thatcher Government managed to avoid the degree of effective discontent

[139] Gamble, Andrew, Mrs Thatcher's Bunker: the reshuffle and its consequences, in: *Marxism Today* (London), Vol. 25 No. 11, November 1981, p. 6. There, the author spoke of the Conservatives' "social market" strategy. This term is misleading as people of various political persuasions claim to support such a concept. Further, it can be questioned whether the policies of the Thatcher Government were "social" at all. The term "free market" would be more accurate.

[140] Ibid., pp. 6f.

[141] Jessop, Bob et. al., *Thatcherism: A Tale of Two Nations*, Polity Press (Cambridge), 1988, pp. 63f.

[142] Winchester, David, Trade Unions and the Recession, in: *Marxism Today* (London), Vol. 25 No. 9, September 1981, p. 25.

[143] Ibid., p. 23.

from the organised labour movement which had afflicted previous post-war governments.

Given all these factors, the Government could proceed with its plans and the 1982 Employment Bill, in full confidence, as the new Secretary of State for Employment hinted, "there will be no Labour Government after the next election to repeal it".[144] All these events and, in particular, the outcome of the Falkland's war in June 1982 and the split in the Labour Party leading to the creation of the Social Democratic Party (SDP), the previous year (see page 186), meant that Thatcher's opponents inside and outside the Conservative Government and the Conservative Party itself were defeated. The Conservative Party surged into a massive lead in the opinion polls (virtually without precedent in the mid-term of a parliament)[145] making the outcome of the 1983 election a foregone conclusion. From then, with the sole exception of the miners' strike 1984/1985, Thatcher and her closest supporters were able to proceed with their economic and political programme without any significant opposition from outside the Conservative Party and Government until the autumn of 1990. At that point, a change of Prime Minister rather than a change of policy seems to have been sufficient in stemming the Government's rising unpopularity, thus helping to prevent what may well have been a Conservative defeat in the 1992 election.

Taking this decade as a whole, the autumn 1981 Cabinet reshuffle was to be of significant importance in the drafting of subsequent legislation in the field of trade union and labour relations law. From 1979 to 1981, Government policy, it could be claimed, had been that "immunities are not simply legal privileges which could be abolished outright. ... The debate, therefore is about the nature and limits of that legal protection".[146] Since then, "immunities", for the first time since the First World War, had come to be seen as "privileges" in Government policy.[147] As the Thatcher Government claimed at the beginning of 1983, "Trade union power ... springs from legal immunities and privileges" and "the law has granted these privileges".[148]

The second major piece of legislation in the field of trade union and labour relations law was the Employment Act, 1982 (often referred to as the "Tebbit Act" or "Tebbit's law"). This Act concentrated on two main areas: trade union funds and the closed shop.[149] The cornerstone of this Act was that it made trade unions

---

[144] Tyler, Christian, ..., p. 26.

[145] Kavanagh, Dennis, ..., p. 222.

[146] *Trade Union Immunities*, ..., p. 92, para. 384.

[147] Wedderburn, (Lord) K. W., Freedom of Association and Philosophies of Labour Law, in: *Industrial Law Journal*, Oxford University Press (Oxford), Vol. 18 No. 1, March 1989, p. 32.

[148] *Democracy in Trade Unions*, Cmnd. 8778, HMSO (London), January 1983, p. 1, para. 3.

[149] Tyler, Christian, ..., p. 24.

themselves liable in tort arising out of industrial action deemed as unlawful. It did this by repealing Section 14 of the 1974 Act and by introducing a code on vicarious liability (see page 126). In this, the law, to a great extent, was put back to what it was following the House of Lords' ruling in the Taff Vale case in 1901. This Act narrowed further "the definition of a trade dispute", which also meant that the scope of "immunities" for the organisers of industrial disputes was further restricted.[150]

The 1974 and 1976 Acts, as noted by the TUC, had been intended to enable workers and unions to take industrial action without the risk of court injunctions and claims for damages. In this, workers were normally free to organise strikes and other action without being taken to court, as long as the action was "in contemplation or furtherance of a trade dispute".[151]

The 1980 Act, as already noted, excluded "immunity" for "secondary action". The 1982 Act went further in narrowing the definition of a trade dispute to one between workers and their employer which was "wholly or mainly" about the terms and conditions of employment.[152] This was designed to exclude protection from industrial action arising out of disputes which were not between an employer and that employer's own employees, demarcation disputes and disputes which were merely "connected with" rather than related "wholly or mainly" to pay and jobs etc..[153] So, for example, industrial action taken to prevent redundancies might not have fallen into the 1982 Act's definition of a trade dispute; demarcation disputes, i.e. disputes between workers and workers which often arise out of managerial decisions, would not have been protected; and there were further restrictions imposed on solidarity or sympathetic action. Ultimately, the aim appeared to make the so-called "political strike" illegal.[154] As a result of all these measures, the scope for using the interlocutory injunction (see page 130) to restrain industrial action was widened considerably.

(The law covering "immunities" now falls under section 219 of the Trade Union and Labour Relations (Consolidation) Act, 1992, and, of course, apply providing that the action undertaken is "in contemplation or furtherance of a trade dispute". There, the definition of a "trade dispute", having been previously narrowed by the 1982 Act, is now regulated under section 244 of the 1992 Act.[155])

---

[150] Coates, David, ..., p. 122.

[151] *TUC Handbook on the Employment Act 1982*, TUC (London), 1982, p. 9, para. 2.2.

[152] Coates, David, ..., p. 122.

[153] *TUC Handbook on the Employment Act 1982*, ..., p. 9, para. 2.5.

[154] See *New Tory attack on union rights*, LRD (London), April 1982, pp. 4-8.

[155] *Law at work 2007*, LRD (London), May 2007, pp. 157ff. For brief details of the purpose of the 1992 Act, see Chapter 3, footnote 9.

The 1982 Act went further in trying to impose restrictions on the closed shop. Building on the provisions in the 1980 Act, a closed shop could only be lawful if supported by 80% of the workers affected or 85% of those voting.[156] The aim behind this measure was that this practice would fade out on account of unions not being able to secure the degree of support required by the 1982 Act. In fact, where closed-shop ballots had taken place, 80% of them had produced union victories.[157] What in fact was more likely to affect the future of the closed shop was the decline in Britain's manufacturing base and hence the number of people working in that sector of the economy. In 1984, there were an estimated 3.6 million workers covered by closed-shop agreements (a decline from a peak of over 5 million in 1978). In early 1989, there was still an estimated closed-shop population of 2.6 million workers[158] of whom around 1.3 million were covered by the "pre-entry" closed shop[159] – being more than the Thatcher Government had previously estimated.[160] One prominent labour lawyer Lord McCarthy had actually questioned this figure by asserting that it was doubtful that more than 150,000 were covered by such agreements at the time.[161] All the same, the Thatcher Government was going to make this practice illegal in the 1990 Act.

The 1982 Act also increased compensation for those who had lost their jobs through the closed shop in the period 1974 to 1980. This enabled them to claim higher levels of compensation than had been available for workers who had been unfairly dismissed.[162]

The Government's claim that many workers had been unfairly dismissed due to closed-shop agreements was strengthened by a ruling in a leading case before the European Court of Human Rights (ECtHR) in Strasbourg in 1981. There, it was ruled that the dismissal of three railway workers on the grounds of non-union membership where a closed-shop agreement was in force was in breach of Article 11 of the European Convention on Human Rights (ECHR).[163] There, it is worth noting that these dismissals had to be defended by a Conservative Attor-

[156] McIlroy, John, ..., p. 86.

[157] Kelly, John, Communists and the Unions, in: *Communist Campaign Review* (London), Vol. 2 Issue 3, Spring 1988, p. 13

[158] *Removing Barriers to Employment*, ..., p. 4, para. 2.6.

[159] Ibid., p. 5, para. 2.7.

[160] Ibid., p. 5, para. 2.8.

[161] Carty, Hazel, The Employment Act 1990: Still Fighting the Industrial Cold War, in: *Industrial Law Journal*, Oxford University Press (Oxford), Vol. 20 No. 1, March 1991, p. 4.

[162] *Employment Law under the Tories*, LRD (London), August 1986, p. 20.

[163] This being the case of *Young, James and Webster v. United Kingdom*. See Ewing, K. D., Article 11 and the right to freedom of association, in: Ewing, K. D. (Ed.), *Human Rights at Work*, The Institute of Employment Rights (London), 2000, pp. 87ff. NB Article 11(1) of the ECHR provides that "Everyone has the right to freedom of peaceful assembly and to freedom of association with others, including the right to form and to join trade unions for the protection of his interests".

ney General. Many labour lawyers, according to one prominent specialist, Lord McCarthy, felt that the Government, due to its opposition to the closed shop, did not argue its case before the ECtHR on the best possible grounds and that had it done so, this case might not have gone in their favour.[164] These railwaymen were, in effect, claiming a form of unfair dismissal which was not covered by the 1975 Employment Protection Act and, as Lord McCarthy noted, received substantial sums in compensation – far more than they could have otherwise obtained for unfair dismissal under the provisions of this Act.[165]

Given that the right to freedom of association,[166] as incorporated in Article 11 of the ECHR, was to give working people the right to form and join trade unions for the purpose of protecting of their interests, it would therefore be important to assess the implications of this ruling in Strasbourg ruling on this Article. There, the ECtHR had, in effect, construed an individual right not to associate, implying a freedom of non association thus, a weakening of the rights to form and join trade unions. This case, as with other cases under Article 11, has been less concerned with advancing union freedom but more with trying to undermine it. So, undermining support for the closed shop should be judged as one aspect of this.[167] Yet, in another case in Strasbourg under this article, the civil service unions, after having failed in the British courts, failed in their challenge to the ban imposed by the Thatcher Government at the beginning of 1984 on trade union

---

[164] McCarthy, (Lord) William E. J., *Freedom at Work: Towards the Reform of Tory Employment Laws*, Fabian Society (London), November 1985, Fabian Tract 508, pp. 19f.

[165] Ibid.

[166] The right to "freedom of association" is guaranteed under the ILO Constitution, which was originally incorporated into the Treaty of Versailles in 1919. In view of the outcome of the Russian revolution in 1917, revolutionary outbreaks in other European countries together with severe economic crises across Europe following World War One leading to "fears" of a "westward extension" of the Russian revolution, the signatories to Versailles had to acknowledge that "universal peace ... can be established only if it is based upon social justice". In 1944, when it became clear that World War Two would lead to a victory for the anti-Hitler coalition, this right became anchored in the Declaration of Philadelphia, which revitalised the ILO which then became a specialist agency of the UN. (Philadelphia is most notably known for its declaration that "labour is not a commodity"). The right to "freedom of association" then became anchored in two exceptionally important conventions from the ILO - Convention No. 87 on Freedom of Association and Protection of the Right to Organise adopted on 9 July, 1948 (coming into effect on 4 July, 1950), and its counterpart, Convention No. 98 on the Right to Organise and Collective Bargaining, adopted on 1 July, 1949 (coming into effect on 18 July, 1951). Additionally, "freedom of association" became incorporated in Article 20 of the Universal Declaration of Human Rights which was "adopted and proclaimed" by the UN General Assembly on 10 December, 1948. Regarding ILO Conventions No. 87 and No. 98, Britain, then under the first post-war Labour Government, was the very first country to ratify them. Convention No. 87 provides for the right to join workers' and employers' associations, the right of such organisations to organise their own administration and activities and the right to establish federations and confederations. This is especially important for trade unions and their members.

[167] Ewing, K. D., ..., pp. 88f.

membership for those working at Government Communications Headquarters (GCHQ). There, although the International Labour Organisation (ILO) criticised this ban, the ECtHR ruled that this did not constitute a breach of Article 11 on the grounds that workers engaged in the administration of the state could be excluded from this Article.[168]

The case of the three railwaymen can also be compared with the dismissal of the BL trade union convener Derek Robinson (see pages 156ff). Whereas the 1982 Act increased compensation to those who were dismissed on grounds of non-union membership, for dismissals arising out of legitimate trade union activity or other categories of unfair dismissal, no provision was made for any special level of compensation.

In response to the Leggatt Report, the 1981 Green Paper suggested that the law be reviewed in cases of workers refusing to handle work from non-union companies or refusing to work with non-union labour, and the practice adopted by some organisations of inserting clauses in contracts requiring contractors to employ union labour only on the contract.[169] In response, the 1982 Act removed "immunity" from industrial action to force "union only" labour agreements thus opening the way for claims in damages suffered by any third party whose contract was affected.[170]

The 1982 Act became law at the end of October 1982. The fact that in January 1983 another Green Paper, *Democracy in Trade Unions*, was published so soon afterwards, meant that the "reform" of trade union and labour relations law was going to be permanent feature under the Thatcher Government – with more vigour than before the Cabinet reshuffle. Indeed, a further hint that more legislation was in the pipeline could be seen in the 1983 election campaign. Despite the passing of the 1980 and 1982 Acts, the Conservative Party claimed that "... some trade union leaders still abuse their power against the wishes of their members and the interests of society" and went on to claim that they often obstructed technological change.[171]

---

[168] Ewing, K. D., *Britain and the ILO* (Second Edition), The Institute of Employment Rights (London), July 1994, p. 24, paras 5.4f. Although article 11(1) of the ECHR provides for the right to freedom of association (see footnote 163), article 11(2), however, states "No restrictions shall be placed on the exercise of these rights other than such as are prescribed by law and are necessary in a democratic society in the interests of national security or public safety, for the prevention of disorder or crime, for the protection of health or morals or for the protection of the rights and freedoms of others. This article shall not prevent the imposition of lawful restrictions on the exercise of these rights by members of the armed forces, of the police or of the administration of the State".

[169] See *Trade Union Immunities*, ..., pp. 70-75, paras. 282-304.

[170] *Employment Law under the Tories*, ..., p. 17.

[171] *The Conservative Manifesto 1983*, Conservative Central Office (London), 1983, pp. 12f.

With Labour resoundingly defeated in the 1983 election, the way was clear for the Government to proceed with further legislation on the trade union front. The 1983 Green Paper was based on the pretext that trade union leaders were out of touch with their members. Three areas were singled out with a view to further legislation: strike ballots, the election of trade union leaders and the payment of contributions into unions' political funds.[172] These were to form the basis of the Trade Union Act, 1984.

Meanwhile, in autumn 1983, the 1980 and 1982 Acts were put to the test in the Mercury and Messenger Newspaper Group disputes and were proved to be effective (see Chapter 4). At about that time, the miners imposed an overtime ban in response to a pay claim. This was then to be followed by an announcement of numerous pit closures which led to the 1984/1985 miners' strike. Nevertheless, the Government felt confident enough to proceed with further legislation. Whereas the courts, through the 1980 and 1982 Acts, sided with the employers in the Mercury and Messenger Newspaper Group disputes, these Acts were not the point at issue in the miners' strike (even though attempts were made to use them against the miners). These two Acts, designed to tackle various established trade union practices, proved effective in these two disputes and, subsequently, in the News International dispute (see Chapter 4).

The 1984 Act was presented as having the aim of "giving the unions back to their members".[173] On the issue of strike ballots, the Thatcher Government was well aware of the fact that externally-imposed strike ballots tended to rally union members behind their leaders and unions, with the result that the membership would be more likely to support such action. As already noted, such a provision had already existed under the 1971 Act which had been used only in the British Rail dispute in 1972, with the result decisively backfiring on the Heath Government. The Thatcher Government was also aware of the experience in the United States of externally-imposed ballots under the Taft Hartley Act and had noted that during the 35 years it had already been in force, 163 ballots had been held. Of these, the employer's last offer was rejected in 155 cases and accepted in only eight.[174] Although it can be argued that the prospect of a mandatory ballot would make union leaders more careful in ensuring that they really did have the backing of their members before embarking upon a strike, it had also been noticed at the same time that some strike ballots which had not been imposed on the unions rejected a strike call.[175] Whatever the arguments, the idea of ballots had an appeal, anyway, as extending democracy even though that in itself might not have been the real motive.

---

[172] Kelly, John, Tebbit changes tack, *Marxism Today* (London), Vol. 27 No. 3, March 1983, p. 22.

[173] Coates, David, ..., p. 122.

[174] *Democracy in Trade Unions*, ..., pp. 18f, para. 62.

[175] Ibid.

The Thatcher Government's answer to this problem was quite simple. Provision was made in the 1984 Act for trade unions to be protected in the event of strike action only after a secret ballot amongst the members concerned had taken place and endorsed such action. This also meant that the scope for employers to seek interlocutory injunctions to restrain industrial action was widened still further.

Thus, in the provisions of the 1980, 1982 and 1984 Acts, the Government saw a solution to industrial relations problems lying in the restoration to the judiciary of much of the legal terrain it had lost as a result of the 1906 Act. In other words, the revitalisation of the common law meant that the judiciary could be relied on to play a bigger role in "resolving" industrial disputes (see Chapter 3), enabling the Government to "keep its distance".

Concerning trade union elections, the 1984 Act stipulated that elections to union executives were to take place every five years by secret ballot. The motives behind insisting on a secret ballot, and subsequently under the Employment Act, 1988, a secret postal ballot (which had been intended in the 1984 Act though not explicitly stated), must be seen partly in response to the leftward advances in a number of prominent trade unions in the late 1960s. The effect of these advances was that the traditional grip of forces in the trade union and labour movement who were firm supporters of Labour's parliamentary leadership was loosened. This had not only alarmed many in the leadership but also those to the right of the Labour Party including the Conservative Party, employers' federations and the mass media.

Prior to the 1984 Act, different unions elected their executives and either elected or appointed their officials in ways which best suited their circumstances. In some unions, officials were elected and subject to periodic re-election. In others, officials were elected for life and there were also unions where officials were appointed. In some unions, leaders were elected by branch ballot or by members going in person to vote, openly in meetings or by secret ballot, at their branch or local office, whilst in others, members voted by postal ballot.

The 1983 Green Paper noted that in the AUEW (Engineering Section), where voting had taken place at branch offices, the turnout had been low, normally in the range of 6 to 11%, but since the introduction of postal balloting in 1972, participation had risen to as much as 50%.[176] Interestingly, the Green Paper made no mention of the experience of electoral procedures in other unions. It should be noted that in the NUM, voting took place in the form of pithead ballots, with participation levels often higher than 70%,[177] and that in 1981, the left-wing miners' leader, Arthur Scargill, was elected NUM president receiving 70% of the

[176] Ibid., pp. 3f, para. 9.

[177] McIlroy, John, ..., p. 153.

vote on a turnout which was greater than in the 1979, 1983 and 1987 general elections.[178]

By way of broader comparison, Article 3 of ILO Convention No. 87, which came into effect in 1950, says: "1. Workers' and employers' organisations shall have the right to draw up their own constitutions and rules, to elect their representatives in full freedom, to organise their administration and activities and to formulate their programmes. 2. The public authorities shall refrain from any interference which would restrict this right or impede the lawful exercise thereof." The word "activities" includes taking industrial action, and "public authorities" means the state and government.[179]

However, in 1985, the ILO Committee of Experts rejected complaints from the TUC that the 1984 Act violated the freedom of association guarantees of ILO Convention No. 87. There, the Committee of Experts stated that "no violation of the principles of freedom of association is involved where legislation contains certain rules intended to promote democratic principles within trade union organisations or to ensure that the electoral procedure is conducted in a normal manner and with due respect for the rights of union members in order to avoid any dispute arising as to the result of the election".[180]

Similarly, other complaints to the ILO Committee of Experts from the TUC due to this Act, concerning strike ballots and ballots for political funds, were rejected for similar reasons.[181] So there, the Thatcher Government could claim legitimacy from an agency of the UN, originally established to advance and defend workers' rights, for the provisions it introduced under the 1984 Act, whatever its real motive may have been. For despite the Committee of Experts' rejection of the TUC's complaints against the 1984 Act, one thing remained indisputable. No other Western European country had such legislation seeking control trade union internal affairs.[182] Furthermore, trade unions alone, not employers' associations or any other bodies or voluntary organisations, were singled out for government attention with its claim of extending democracy. This would suggest the real motive of the 1984 Act was less to extend democracy than to reduce the number of strikes and to secure the election of more "acceptable" union leaders.[183]

---

[178] Ibid., p. 127.

[179] Hendy, John QC, *A Law Unto Themselves. Conservative Employment Laws: A National and International Assessment* (3rd edition), The Institute of Employment Rights (London), September 1993, p. 79.

[180] Ewing, K. D., *Britain and the ILO* (Second Edition), ..., p. 38, para. 7.4.

[181] See Ibid., pp. 38f, paras. 7.5ff.

[182] *Unions Attacked: LRD's Guide to the Trade Union Bill*, LRD (London), December 1983, p. 8.

[183] See McIlroy, John, ..., p. 155.

The other main provision of the 1984 Act was to require trade unions possessing political funds to ballot their members every ten years on whether or not these should be retained.[184] Owing to the 1913 Trade Union Act, no union can devote resources to political activities and this includes donations and/or payment of affiliation fees to political parties unless there is a special fund for this purpose which is financed solely through union members paying a political levy in addition to their union subscriptions. As the Labour Party's major source of income was (and still is) trade union affiliation fees, the intention behind this provision in the 1984 Act can be judged as self-evident.

In the first round of voting among trade union members on whether or not their unions, in line with the provisions of the 1984 Act, should retain their political funds, the membership in *all* 38 unions voted 'Yes'. This represented the wishes of 84% of the union members who voted. Furthermore, in over 20 other unions, which previously didn't have political funds, and were therefore not affiliated to the Labour Party, the membership voted to establish them.[185] This in turn gave them the option of affiliating to the Labour Party. So, this provision of the 1984 Act totally backfired on the Thatcher Government in that the historic links between the trade unions and the Labour Party were legitimised – the direct opposite of what had been hoped and intended. In the second round of balloting on the retention of political funds (1994-1996), the results were similar with the support of 82% of union members who voted.[186]

Nonetheless, with the 1980, 1982 and 1984 Acts on the Statute Book, the Thatcher Government had largely succeeded in redrawing the boundaries of how trade unions should go about their business. Subsequent legislation in this field was largely aimed at closing "loopholes" which came to light in the operation of or in the interpretation of these Acts or to "attend to some unfinished business" as was the case with the closed shop. In addition, one should not underestimate the impact of the 1979-1981 slump on the morale of trade unions and their members, with the Thatcher Government clearly taking advantage of this in its trade union policies. No further legislative moves concerning trade union practices were made until 1988 – after a third election victory in 1987. In the meantime, the trade union movement suffered major setbacks in some major industrial disputes in the mid-1980s. In addition to the Messenger Newspaper Group dispute and the 1984/1985 miners' strike, another setback occurred in the News International dispute of 1986/1987.

---

[184] *1984 Trade Union Act: The Trade Union Response to the new Legislation*, TUC (London), August 1984, p. 11, para. 31.

[185] Leopold, John W., Trade unions and the third round of political fund review balloting, in: *Industrial Relations Journal*, Vol. 37 Issue 3, Blackwell Publishing Ltd. (Oxford), May 2006, p. 191.

[186] Ibid. NB The results of the third round of political fund voting (2003-2005) were similar with 78% support from those taking part in the balloting. See Leopold, John W., ..., p. 197.

However, trade union practices were not the only concern of the Thatcher Government's microeconomic strategy. Parallel to the introduction of the 1980, 1982 and 1984 Acts, the Government set about removing various regulations which imposed minimum terms and conditions of employment. Between 1980 and 1984, a number of statutes ensuring minimum "fair wages" were repealed.[187] In 1982, the Fair Wages Resolution of the House of Commons was rescinded. This had originally been introduced in 1891 in response to the "evils of sweating" and brought into a more up-to-date form in 1946. The purpose of the Fair Wages Resolution was to ensure that government contractors and subcontractors observed currently "accepted" standards of pay and conditions; that they should not be less favourable than those for the trade or industry concerned, with the ultimate sanction of public contracts being lost.[188] The position of the low paid was weakened further by the Wages Act, 1986. One provision of this Act was that the powers of wages councils (originally established in 1909 by Winston Churchill in response to widespread public concern over low pay and bad working conditions before being ultimately abolished in 1993) were reduced to setting just one basic rate and, in addition, around half a million workers under the age of 21 were no longer to be covered by them.[189] Wages councils provided protection for up to three million workers. However, given the Government's argument that "impediments" to the "market order" had to go, this also entailed two ILO conventions having to be denounced.[190]

Once the 1987 election was out of the way, the Government proceeded with yet further trade union and labour legislation. The next piece of legislation, the Employment Act, 1988, concentrated on the "rights" of individual union members and also sought to close any "loopholes" which had come to light in previous Acts. Under this Act, individual union members were given rights to restrain their union(s) from calling on them to take industrial action which had not supported by a secret ballot, protection against dismissal for non-union membership in all circumstances, the right to inspect unions' accounting records (to an extent way beyond that given to shareholders),[191] protection against unions disciplining their members in cases such as working during a dispute, to elect all principal union leaders by secret postal ballot under independent scrutiny and the right to

---

[187] Wedderburn, (Lord) K. W., ..., p. 17.

[188] Wedderburn, (Lord) K. W., *The Worker and the Law* (Third Edition), Penguin (Harmondsworth), 1986, p. 347.

[189] Meggison, Doug, The rise and fall of the Wages Councils, in: *Communist Review* (London), No. 18, November 1993, pp. 28-32. Wages councils were ultimately abolished by section 35 of the Trade Union Reform and Employment Rights Act, 1993; see Simpson, Bob, A Milestone in the Legal Regulation of Pay: The National Minimum Wage Act 1998, in: *Industrial Law Journal*, Oxford University Press (Oxford), Vol. 28 No. 1, March 1999, pp. 2f.

[190] Wedderburn, (Lord) K. W., Freedom of Association and Philosophies of Labour Law, ..., p. 17.

[191] Ibid., p. 26.

take legal action against trustees if they permitted their funds to be used unlawfully.[192]

In this, the 1988 Act created a new Commissioner for the Rights of Trade Union Members (CROTUM) to "assist" union members in taking out court proceedings against their own unions.[193] Under this Act, the resources of the State were made available for any dissident union member to take steps against his union on causes set out and enlarged by the State, because the task of the State was seen to be that of protecting the market for individuals.[194] The argument was that, if the labour market was to function effectively, the "rights"of individuals have to be promoted and those of the collective group (meaning trade unions) curbed.

The "rights" of individuals can, in this context, only be advanced in a "free" market for labour. One notes the difference between the 1988 Act and the 1971 Act (both the product of Conservative administrations). In 1988, unlike in 1971, there was to be no State Registrar, for that, as Lord Wedderburn comments, "would be to commit the venal sin of corporatism".[195] So the State was to retain a formal distance by "assisting" the individual, this being clearly a follow-on from the provisions of the previous Acts in the 1980s.

So CROTUM, established for this very purpose, in the expectation that union members would seek its help, including the payment of legal costs, in bringing cases against their own unions, turned out to be of almost no significance. In the period of its existence, it assisted on average just nine applications per year. Even more insignificant was the Commissioner for Protection Against Unlawful Industrial Action (established under the Trade Union Reform and Employment Rights Act, 1993). In the six years of its existence, it assisted just one application and this did not even lead to a court case. Interestingly, both of these offices were held by the same person![196] Both these bodies were abolished by the Blair Government in 1999 through its Employment Relations Act.

Under the 1988 Act, the "rights" of individual union members went as far as them being protected in cases where they wilfully sought to undermine the democratic decisions of their own unions. Most notably, unions could no longer discipline their own members who, in a lawful strike, crossed picket-lines even if the majority of the employees concerned supported it.[197]

---

[192] *Removing Barriers to Employment*, ..., p. 2.

[193] Ibid.

[194] Wedderburn, (Lord) K. W., Freedom of Association and Philosophies of Labour Law, ..., p. 27.

[195] Ibid.

[196] See *Fairness at Work*, Cm 3968, Department of Trade and Industry (London), May 1998, p. 29, paras. 4.30f.

[197] Taylor, Robert, *The Future of Trade Unions*, André Deutsch Limited (London), 1994, p.

One important provision of the 1988 Act was for all principal union leaders to be elected by secret postal ballot under independent scrutiny – an extension of the provisions in the 1984 Act. The 1983 Green Paper (see above) made reference to the introduction of postal balloting in the AUEW in 1972. It had been noted that, before this rule-change, there had already been media interference in the election campaigns of Hugh Scanlon to the union's executive council and subsequently for the presidency.[198] It had also been noted that as a result of the introduction of postal balloting, the scope for media interference in union election campaigns and for the denunciation of certain candidates by the media was widened with considerable effect.[199]

An example of media interference in this union's elections took the form of a long article in the *Sunday Mirror* on 12 October, 1975, in which union members were "advised" whom to vote for in the coming round of union elections, with members being given the option of writing to this newspaper if they needed further "advice".[200] The left suffered a number of electoral defeats in this union in the latter half of the 1970s (their gains of a decade earlier, in effect, being reversed) and the left regarded outside interference in the union's elections as being one reason for this.

In the 1987 Green Paper, *Trade Unions and Their Members*, the Government stressed the need for union elections to be "free from interference",[201] but the evidence of postal balloting has been shown to encourage the opposite. It also stressed the need for the avoidance of both malpractices in union elections and voting at inconvenient branch meetings.[202] However, the Green Paper largely based its case on irregularities which came to light in the 1984 election for the post of TGWU General Secretary and subsequently in elections for the posts of General Secretary and Treasurer in the Civil and Public Services Association (CPSA). In neither of these unions were the elections conducted by postal ballot,[203] but there, they were won by the left or candidates supported by the left.

The Green Paper, however, made no reference to the fact that in the second ballot (postal) for the election of General Secretary of the AUEW in 1982, the left candidate – Communist Party member Ken Brett – who narrowly lost, had com-

46.

[198] Frow, Edmund et. al., *Democracy in the Engineering Union*, Institute of Workers' Control (Nottingham), 1982, p. 11.

[199] Ibid.

[200] Ibid.

[201] *Trade Unions and Their Members*, Cm 95, HMSO (London), February 1987, p. 22, para. 5.2.

[202] Ibid.

[203] Ibid., p. 23, para. 5.8 and pp. 24f, paras. 5.13-5.18.

plained of irregularities *before* the election result was known.[204] So, by being selective in its examples, the Green Paper was a further indication that achieving the election of "acceptable" union leaders was one of its main objectives.

Although the 1984 Act made an impact on the way unions conducted their affairs, particularly the balloting provisions for industrial action and the election of union executives,[205] the Government did not succeed in getting all the results it desired. Hence, there was further legislation in 1988. Not only was there the total failure with the political fund ballots, but there was also the fact that the great majority of strike ballots endorsed the call for industrial action. In addition, the balloting provisions failed to throw out the left *en masse* from union positions or to return candidates of the right.[206] With the possible exception of the AUEW in the mid to late 1970s, the introduction of postal balloting has, on balance, not led to any significant changes in the political orientation of union leaderships.

However, the process of bringing changes to trade union and labour relations law went beyond the 1988 Act. In 1989, another law was passed – the Employment Act, 1989 – whose provisions included the reduction of protection for women and young people, restricting time off work for trade union duties and making access to industrial tribunals more difficult.[207] This Act, although not directed specifically at trade union practices, could be seen as another move towards "freeing" the labour market.

The Government proceeded with further legislation in 1990 – the Employment Act, 1990. This Act was largely designed to put "the last nail in the coffin" of two specific features of British industrial relations practice the Conservatives had long wanted to do away with. Firstly, this Act made the "pre-entry" closed shop illegal, thus putting an end to this aspect of industrial relations practice. In this, the steps taken in 1980 and even more so in 1982 should be seen as interim measures with the ultimate aim of abolishing the closed shop. Secondly, this Act removed "immunities" from trade unions in the event of "unofficial" strikes. This measure seems to have been in response to a spate of "unofficial" industrial action among dockers, British Rail and London Underground workers in 1989. There, the 1990 Act widened the code on vicarious liability, having already been introduced in the 1982 Act, so that if union funds were to be protected, trade union leaders would have to take effective measures in distancing themselves from "unofficial" action[208] (see pages 132).

---

204 See Why the left must fight on, in: *Morning Star* (London), 24 May 1982, p. 2.

205 McCarthy, (Lord) William E. J., ..., p. 8.

206 Kelly, John, Communists and the Unions, ..., p. 13.

207 *Trades Union Congress 1990 General Council Report*, TUC (London), 1990, p. 3, Para. 4.

208 See Carty, Hazel, ..., pp. 4-9.

The 1990 Act also tightened up on "loopholes" which came to light regarding "secondary" industrial action under the 1980 Act. So under this Act, all forms of such action were made illegal except that on a picket line by workers at or near their own place of employment for the purpose of peacefully communicating or persuading, which fell within Section 15 of the 1974 Act, and later, substituted by a provision under the 1980 Act.[209]

So, briefly, with the passing of the 1990 Act, the legal situation regarding industrial action was that any action to induce workers, other than those in dispute, to take industrial action became unlawful. The only form of "secondary" action which was still permissible was peacefully picketing at the workplace in dispute. Unions became liable for any "unofficial" industrial action by their members unless it was "repudiated". Employers were then able to select for dismissal anyone taking part in "unofficial" action which also meant them losing their right to claim unfair dismissal. "Immunities" ceased to apply in the event of industrial action in support of "unofficial"strikers who had been dismissed. Unions could no longer support a call for industrial action before a ballot had been held. Any industrial action had to commence within four weeks of a ballot, unless delayed by court action.[210]

The imposition of such stringent regulations on trade unions in the event of industrial action had, in effect, two aims. Firstly, of course, the 1990 Act sought to frustrate such action further. Secondly, this Act widened the scope by which unions themselves were to be "coerced", as it were, on behalf of employers and the State into "policing" ordinary union members with the ultimate threat of unions themselves being made liable in tort for any "unofficial" industrial action which they had not officially "repudiated". The provisions of the 1990 Act, are now incorporated in the 1992 Act.

It is therefore not surprising that by spring 1992, according to the TUC, Britain's record on employment rights, very much due to the policies which had been enacted since 1979, had already been criticised by the ILO on eight accounts[211] – all this before Thatcher's successor John Major had got down to proceeding with further legislation in this field, especially with the Trade Union Reform and Employment Rights Act, 1993.

Firstly, as already noted, was the ban imposed on union membership at GCHQ in 1984. Secondly, in early 1987, there was the withdrawal of negotiating rights for teachers. Thirdly, employers being allowed to blacklist union members. Fourthly, under the 1988 Act, as already noted, restrictions were imposed on

[209] Ibid., p. 7.

[210] See *Making the Unions Pay: A Guide to the 1990 Employment Act*, LRD (London), June 1991, p. 3.

[211] See *Employment Law: A TUC Briefing*, TUC (London), Spring 1992, p. 9.

unions' rights to discipline members. Fifthly, under the 1988 Act, unions were banned from paying fines on members' behalf. Sixthly, already starting with the 1980 Act, was the imposition of restrictions on sympathy action. Seventhly, by narrowing the "definition of a trade dispute", the scope was widened by which employers could artificially split companies to limit industrial action which would be legally protected. Finally, on the basis of strike action being regarded as a breach of the employment contract, employers had already been able to dismiss workers who go on strike but with the 1990 Act, employers were then able to selectively dismiss "unofficial" strikers. However, breaches of ILO Conventions appeared to be of little concern to the Conservative Government.

The purpose of the 1992 Act was to *consolidate* the various statutes in the field of trade union and labour relations law into one single Act, thus supposedly addressing concerns, including those voiced by the ILO, over the complexity of Britain's industrial relations legislation. The Act itself neither changed the law nor did it prevent the Major Government from introducing further legislation in the following year[212] – this being the 1993 Act.

So, the stringent balloting provisions for industrial action became incorporated in the 1992 Act. Most notably, unions became required to give employers notice of any intention to conduct a strike ballot. In this, a detailed procedure was stipulated under sections 226-235 of this Act. Firstly, employers have to be notified in writing at least seven days in advance that the union intends to hold a ballot for industrial action, giving the date when it believes the balloting will begin and describe the employees who are entitled to vote. Secondly, no later than three days before the ballot begins, the employer must have received a sample copy of the ballot paper. Thirdly, as soon as the ballot result has been declared, the union has to notify the employer of the outcome. Fourthly, at least seven days before the start of such action, the union has to inform the employer in writing giving information on the number, category or workplaces of those being called upon to take such action. This includes giving the date such action will begin or if the action is to take the form of a series of stoppages, the dates on which they'll take place.[213] Subsequently, the 1993 Act went on to stipulate that all industrial action ballots be fully postal and independently scrutinised.[214] However, in view of the already exhausting balloting procedures, the obvious aim of imposing additional regulations through the 1993 Act should be judged as trying to frustrate such action as much as possible.

---

[212] See McColgan, Aileen, Recent Legislation: Trade Union and Labour Relations (Consolidation) Act 1992, *Industrial Law Journal*, Oxford University Press (Oxford), Vol. 22 No. 1, March 1993, pp. 32f.

[213] See *Law at work 2007*, ..., pp. 162-167.

[214] Eighteen Years of Worker-Bashing, *Labour Research*, LRD (London), May 1997, p. 19.

In the 1993 Act, the Government claimed that it sought to enhance the rights of individual union members. In this, there are two especially important areas which need to be noted. Firstly, the implications of the Wilson and Palmer cases, arising out of employer attempts to trade away union negotiating rights, and secondly, the operation of the TUC Disputes Principles and Procedures which were adopted at the Bridlington Congress of the TUC in 1939 (often known as the Bridlington Agreement).

Firstly, at a late stage in the passage of the Trade Union Reform and Employment Rights Bill in the House of Lords in 1993, an amendment was inserted which became known as the Ullswater Amendment (after the Minister who introduced it). This came about because there were cases, which eventually went before the ECtHR,[215] in which employers sought to trade away collective agreements with trade unions by trying to persuade their employees to sign new personal contracts with them being "rewarded" by pay increases.

In one such case, David Wilson, a lay official of his union (the National Union of Journalists – NUJ) was informed in 1989 by his employer, the Daily Mail, that the company was not going to renew the recognition agreement it had with his union. Any worker there who agreed to sign a new personal contract with the company was to receive a pay increase of 4.5% backdated three months. Wilson refused to sign the new contract and complained to an industrial tribunal which ruled in his favour on the basis that the 1978 Employment Protection (Consolidation) Act prevented employers from penalising workers who sought to be members of and be represented by independent trade unions. (The corresponding provisions of the 1978 Act are now to be found in Section 146 of the 1992 Act). The Employment Appeal Tribunal overturned this decision but it was subsequently restored by the Court of Appeal in 1993, which in the same case, restored an industrial tribunal decision in favour of Terry Palmer and a number of other RMT members who were denied pay increases by their employers due to them refusing to surrender their right to representation by their union.

Fearing that this ruling in the Court of Appeal would open the way for other claims against employers who sought to de-recognise trade unions in this way, the Government took steps to protect them: hence this amendment. As it turned out, this amendment became superfluous as the House of Lords in 1995 restored the Employment Appeal Tribunal ruling. However, in 2002, these cases were handled by the ECtHR which ruled in favour of Wilson, Palmer and others.[216]

---

[215] This was the case of *Wilson and the National Union of Journalists; Palmer, Wyeth and National Union of Rail, Maritime and Transport Workers; Doolan and others v United Kingdom*, other wise referred to as the Wilson and Palmer case. See Ewing, K. D., The Implications of *Wilson and Palmer*, in: *Industrial Law Journal*, Oxford University Press (Oxford), Vol. 32 No. 1, March 2003, pp. 1-22.

[216] Ibid., pp. 1f.

The second issue was that the Major Government claimed that the TUC's Bridlington principles constituted an unwarranted restriction on the freedom of an individual to join a union of his/her choice.[217] Bridlington is "designed to minimise disputes between unions over membership questions".[218] This is particularly important where more than one union is capable of representing a particular grade of worker. So, in a workplace where recognition rights have been secured by a specified TUC-affiliated union for a certain category of workers, other affiliated unions would cease in attempts to recruit them. Prior to the 1993 Act, those workers who had already been recruited by other unions would have been excluded from continued membership and urged to join the union which gained recognition rights. Due to this Act, the TUC had to review its disputes principles and procedures with the effect that membership of a trade union can not be excluded on the grounds of membership of another union and that a union which has recruited or organised in breach TUC disputes principles and procedures may have to provide financial compensation to a union which lodges a complaint.[219]

Bridlington has never sought to place restrictions on the "freedom of individual workers" even if cases occur where individual workers find themselves being represented by unions which are not of their personal choice. But judging Bridlington as a whole, it in fact widened the scope by which workers' economic, social and industrial interests can be best defended and advanced *collectively*. At the same time, by helping to prevent inter-union rivalry, it was seeking to prevent a possible source of industrial conflict. So the basis of Bridlington becomes clear. By joining the TUC, unions give it authority to resolve disputes between them, which, in fact, are comparatively rare, and whenever they occur, they are mostly amicably resolved through a process of conciliation under TUC auspices. Whenever conciliation fails, the case is referred to a disputes committee, which is chaired by a member of the TUC General Council who has no connection whatsoever with the issue in dispute. There is then the ultimate sanction of disciplinary measures against any union which refuses to abide by the Disputes Committee's decisions.[220] (In 1988, however, the failure of the EETPU to comply with the TUC Disputes Committee decisions in two specific cases initially led to its suspension, and subsequently, to its expulsion from the TUC in that year.)

It is worth comparing the Major Government's criticism of the TUC's Bridlington procedures with the words of Lord Diplock, supported by four other law lords, in a legal challenge to these procedures in the House of Lords ten years earlier: "I know of no existing rule of public policy that would prevent trade uni-

---

[217] *Guide to the Trade Union Reform & Employment Rights Act 1993*, TUC (London), 1993, pp. 15f.

[218] Ewing, K. D., Article 11 and the right to freedom of association, in: Ewing, K. D. (Ed.), *Human Rights at Work*, ..., p. 95.

[219] Ibid., p. 98.

[220] *The EETPU Suspension : A TUC Information Note*, TUC (London), July 1988, pp. 5f.

ons from entering into arrangements with one another which they consider to be in the interests of their members in promoting order in industrial relations and enhancing their members' bargaining power with their employers; nor do I think it a permissible exercise of your Lordships' judicial power to create a new rule of public policy to that effect".[221] So, rather than advancing the rights of individuals, the Government's aim in the 1993 must be judged in the context of seeking to undermine the authority of the TUC as a cohesive authority.

Together with the enactment of labour relations legislation, the Government's policy of "freeing" the labour market included resisting moves for the inclusion of social rights for workers in the negotiations which led to the conclusion of the Maastricht Treaty towards the end of 1991. In order to win the support of the European trade unions for the Single European Market and subsequently for EMU, which was then to become the cornerstone of the Maastricht Treaty, the European Community could not overlook the crucial issue of workers' rights. Consequently, eleven of the then twelve member states of the EC concluded the *Community Charter of the Fundamental Social Rights of Workers* at the EC Summit in Strasbourg on 9 December, 1989. Although this Charter only had the status of a political declaration rather than a legal instrument,[222] Britain would not sign it even though it was narrower and more limited in scope than the *European Social Charter*[223] which had been signed by the governments of the member states of the Council of Europe in Turin on 18 October, 1961. This, it should not be forgotten, included Britain under the Conservative Government of Harold Macmillan and it was under his premiership when the House of Commons ratified it, the following year.

The purpose of the 1989 Charter was to promote "social dialogue" as part of the process towards establishing the Single European Market. So the formulation of this Charter had to take account of the "free" market principles behind the Single European Market. Consequently, in certain key areas, this Charter does not fulfil the standard of social rights for workers which had already been achieved at European and international level and also in the constitutions of a number of countries in Western Europe. One notable omission is the absence of "the right to work".[224] Even though this Charter in no way questioned the main thrust of Thatcher's economic and trade union policies, she wouldn't sign it. If she had

[221] This was the case of *Cheall v. Association of Executive, Clerical and Computer Staffs* in 1983. See Ibid., p. 5 and Ewing, K. D., Article 11 and the right to freedom of association, in: Ewing, K. D. (Ed.), *Human Rights at Work*, ..., pp. 99ff. NB In 1986, this case was heard by the European Commission on Human Rights and this Commission agreed with the ruling in the House of Lords.

[222] Hepple, Bob, *European Social Dialogue – Alibi or Opportunity?*, The Institute of Employment Rights (London), August 1993, pp. 32f.

[223] See Barlow, Keith, The EU Constitution's Implications on the Right to Work, in: *Communist Review*, Communist Party of Britain (London), No. 44, Summer 2005, pp. 20-24.

[224] Ibid.

still favoured the establishment of the Single European Market (see pages 68f), she would have had little difficulty in conceding ground on specific aspects of this Charter.

Her refusal to sign it should be judged more in her opposition to moves towards creating EMU and could therefore be seen as an attempt to frustrate this process. It was originally intended that this Charter be the "Social Chapter" in the Maastricht Treaty but owing to the "opt-out" her successor, Major, secured on this[225] together with the "opt-out" on the third stage of EMU (the introduction of the euro) in the final stages of the Maastricht negotiations towards the end of 1991, the "Social Chapter" only became an addendum to the Treaty with its provisions not being applicable to Britain.[226]

2.3. Conclusion

Overall, it is not easy to judge how successful the Thatcher and Major Governments were with their macro- and microeconomic strategies in the 1980s and 1990s. True, if the main objective was purely to curb the influence of the trade union and labour movement, then a success can be claimed. But the fact that the Government persisted with legislating in this area right into the 1990s would show that whilst the Government did not attempt to achieve everything with just one piece of legislation, as Heath had tried in 1971, it nevertheless did not get all the results it had hoped for. This, for example, can be seen in persistently trying to make balloting provisions for union elections, strike action and for the maintenance of political funds more and more stringent. Results, rather than claims of trying to improve democracy in trade unions, were the main criteria behind these measures. If the main objective of these laws was to make the British economy more efficient and to improve its longer term prospects, then the criteria for measuring success have to be defined very carefully.

As already noted, the aim of strengthening the City of London as a major financial centre failed and, in the endeavours to achieve this, much of Britain's manufacturing base was sacrificed as a result of tight monetary policies and high interest rates. Under these circumstances, manufacturing industry could only survive if it became more "efficient". Among other measures, the use of labour had to be

[225] The "opt-out" Major secured on the "Social Chapter" in the final stages of the Maastricht negotiations towards the end of 1991 was agreed in exchange for Britain conceding to Germany's demands for the European Community to recognise Croatia which, earlier that year, had "broken away" from Yugoslavia. See Wareing, Robert, How the EC pushed Yugoslavia towards civil war, in *Socialist Campaign Group News*, No. 78, Campaign Group News Ltd. (London), May 1993, p. 7.

[226] Following the 1997 election, the newly elected Labour Government reversed this "opt-out" and accepted the provisions of the Social Chapter in the 1997 EU Treaty of Amsterdam. See page 228, footnote 95.

more "efficient" in that labour costs per unit of output had to be reduced relative to those of Britain's major competitors.

On the surface, this policy may sound plausible. However, a strategy of reducing labour costs through undermining employment rights could prove to be a short-sighted policy, even from an employer's perspective. A low-wage policy tends to produce a low-skill, high-turnover, low-productive and poorly managed work-force. By the time the Major Government left office, Britain, in comparison with other countries in Western Europe, remained a low-waged economy and was less productive. As already noted, Britain's standing in the advanced industrialised world had continued to weaken. So, better terms and conditions of employment can lead to a more productive, more highly-skilled workforce and hence a more stable economy. This, for example, had very much been the experience of one of Britain's major rivals in Europe – Germany – prior to unification.[227]

A key element in the legislation of the 1980s was the revitalisation of the common law in "resolving" industrial disputes. As already noted, from 1875, Parliament provided for those organising industrial action "immunities" in trade disputes against tort liabilities. The judges then expanded tort liabilities. Parliament countered such judicial expansions by adjusting the "immunities" (see page 58). The point about the laws in the 1980s is that Parliament, as it were, "changed sides". It began to narrow or destroy the "immunities" it created.[228] In effect, Parliament gave back to the judiciary much of what it had "lost" from 1906.

The question which needs to be asked is, why exactly did the Thatcher Government and the Parliament it controlled do this? Furthermore, one needs to consider what role was envisaged for the judiciary in the Conservative macro- and microeconomic strategy following the Conservative election victory in 1979.

---

[227] See Hendy, John QC, ..., pp. 32f.

[228] Wedderburn, (Lord) K. W., *The worker and the Law ...*, ..., p. 577.

Chapter Three: The link between Conservative macro and micro policies in shaping social strategy following the breakdown of the post-war "consensus": the significance of the common law in preserving the "free"- market order

The judiciary has traditionally regarded industrial action as an illegal act. This is because it invariably brings the organisers and participants of such action into conflict with a central feature of the common law – the inviolability of the law of contract. In this, the results of such action are that employment contracts are invariably breached.

The common law is a body of law which, especially in England, evolved over the centuries as a result of judges making decisions in cases which went before the courts; the outcome of these, in turn, becoming the law of the land. Traditionally, Parliament rarely intervened in the development of this body of law and, when it did, it did so to clear up doubtful points.[1]

The absence of a written constitution and the traditional lack of legislative involvement in shaping the course of the common law enabled the judiciary in Britain to evolve into an institution of particular significance with a large degree of influence. As a central feature of the common law is the inviolability of the law of contract, this in turn has been of great significance in influencing the way judges would rule on various cases arising out of industrial disputes going before the courts.

In Britain, with the absence of a written constitution and a constitutional court, the development of case law (subject to any Statutes passed by Parliament[2]) has been of greater importance in shaping the course of the law of the land than would have been the case with the presence of a written constitution. The common law, in the words of a well-known 18th century judge, Lord Mansfield, "does not consist of particular cases, but of general principles, which are illustrated and explained by those cases".[3] In this way, judges could derive rules which could be applied to new cases.[4]

---

1 See Hayek, F. A., *Law Legislation and Liberty*, Routledge and Kegan Paul (London), 1982, Vol. 1, p. 85.

2 Through the Human Rights Act, 1998, UK law should not contravene the *Convention for the Protection of Human Rights and Fundamental Freedoms* and any of its subsequent protocols. This Convention was originally adopted by the Council of Europe in Rome in 1950 and is more commonly known as the European Convention on Human Rights (ECHR). See page 233. See also Gearty, Conor A., The Human Rights Act 1998: an overview, in: Ewing, K. D. (Ed.), *Human Rights at Work*, Institute of Employment Rights (London), 2000, pp. 1-23.

3 Hayek, F. A., p. 36.

4 Ibid.

So, where as Parliament normally kept clear of influencing the development of the common law, the introduction of "immunities" in the 19th and 20th centuries, enabling trade unions to exist and bargain collectively, marked a new turn in the standing of Parliament in relation to the judiciary. The "immunities" conceded by Parliament, especially those under the 1906 Act, had, as it were, the effect of impeding the operation of and, consequently, the development of the common law in connection with industrial disputes.

However, the 1906 Act did not prevent judges from deciding what they thought the law ought to be in industrial disputes altogether. From time to time, judges were able to "create new liabilities out of older principles", and these enabled them to outflank the "immunities" Parliament had originally conceded to trade unions.[5] It was on this basis, as Lord Wedderburn has noted, that judges were able to introduce tort liabilities for strikes interfering with commercial contracts, and the tort of intimidation arising out of the very right to strike itself[6] (see pages 43ff).

When Parliament legislated to protect trade unions from, what by modern-day standards, would be the most negative aspects of common law liability when undertaking strike action, it still did not grant any actual right to strike. This meant that, despite the passing of the 1906 Act and its "immunities" provisions (later renewed, in Lord Wedderburn's phrase, in a "spring-cleaned form" following the repeal of the 1971 Act), industrial action, in the eyes of the judiciary, continued to be regarded as a breach of the employment contract.

Whereas one prominent judge, Lord Scarman, spoke of the 1971 Act's repeal legislation as putting the law back to what Parliament decided through the Act of 1906 – but stronger and clearer than it was then (see page 52), this would not be representative of judicial thinking generally.[7] Indeed, more representative of such thinking, reflecting a high degree of frustration over "immunities" impeding what it would regard as the natural development of the common law, can be seen in the often quoted words of another prominent judge, Lord Diplock, in the case of *Duport Steels v. Sirs* in 1980. Diplock described "immunities" conceded to trade unions as being "intrinsically repugnant to anyone who has spent his life in the service of the law or the administration of justice ... It involves granting to trade unions a power, which has no other limits than their own self-

[5] See Wedderburn, (Lord) K. W., Freedom of Association and Philosophies of Labour Law, in: *Industrial Law Journal*, Oxford University Press (Oxford), Vol. 18 No. 1, March 1989, p. 6. (NB This article is based on a lecture delivered by Lord Wedderburn on 29 February, 1988, to the First Division Association of Civil Servants in honour of the civil servants working at GCHQ who, in 1984, lost their jobs for refusing to surrender their trade union membership).

[6] Ibid.

[7] Ibid., p. 7.

interest, to inflict by means which are contrary to the general law, untold harm to industrial enterprises unconcerned with the particular dispute, to the employees of such enterprises, to members of the public and to the nation itself"[8].

When Parliament passed the Act of 1906, it legislated so as to protect trade unions from tort for the actions of their members and this also included the actual organisers of industrial action, providing this was "in contemplation or furtherance of a trade dispute". It should be noted that in this Act, as well as in the 1974 Act (which repealed the 1971 Act) and subsequently, the TULRA (Consolidation) Act, 1992,[9] no provision has ever been made to protect the individual workers from common law liability when taking strike action. This means that right up to the present day, individual workers can still risk being sued if they went on strike and employers could also regard strike action as a termination of the employment contract.[10] Although it may not be normal practice for an employer to sue his striking employees for damages, he is more likely to try and dismiss them.[11]

In the path taken in many advanced industrial countries, and in particular in Western Europe, leading to the legality of trade unions and their rights to organise and bargain collectively, as already noted, strike action, to varying limits, became lawful. In this, strike action did not become regarded as a "breach" or "termination" of the employment contract but a "suspension" of it.[12] Consequently, where a "right" to strike exists, it would be unthinkable for an employer to sue or dismiss his striking employees.[13] This is precisely where Britain differs from most of her counterparts in Western Europe; there, where a legal right to strike exists (irrespective of the degree of this right), employers do not have a right to dismiss their striking employees solely on account of lawful industrial action.[14]

If one compares Britain with, for example, Germany and Italy, one can see how different the British situation is. In Germany, there is no formal right as such to

---

8 See Griffith, J. A. G., *The Politics of the Judiciary* (Fifth Edition), Fontana Press (Hammersmith, London), 1997, p. 311.

9 The Trade Union and Labour Relations (Consolidation) Act, 1992, is a Consolidation Act incorporating the numerous changes which had subsequently been made to the 1974 Act, especially those during the 1980s.

10 Wedderburn, (Lord) K. W., Laws about Strikes, in: McCarthy, (Lord) William E. J. (Ed.), *Legal Intervention in Industrial Relations: Gains and Losses*, Blackwell Publishers (Oxford, UK and Cambridge, USA), 1992, pp. 152f.

11 Wedderburn, (Lord) K. W., Freedom of Association ..., ..., p. 5.

12 Wedderburn, (Lord) K. W., Laws about Strikes, ..., p. 152.

13 Wedderburn, (Lord) K. W., Freedom of Association ..., ..., p. 5.

14 Wedderburn, (Lord) K. W., Laws about Strikes, ..., p. 152f.

strike, and this is especially so for full-time public servants.[15] However, strike action in Germany can be lawful if conducted by a trade union and if it pursues an aim that can be regulated by collective agreement. At the same time, such action must not violate the "peace obligation" deriving from an existing collective agreement. The union must follow the strike procedure laid down in its standing rules and a strike must represent the last resort of achieving the aim in dispute; and at the same time, the "fairness principle" must be observed. An unlawful strike gives rise to entitlements to damages and, in particular, mutual entitlements to a restraining injunction between those involved.[16] There is also provision for unions to call "token strikes", although these can only take place for a fixed duration and can only be used to back up negotiations during collective bargaining after the expiry of the "peace obligation".[17]

In the opinion of Lord Wedderburn, the widest right to strike is enjoyed by workers in Italy, this being guaranteed by Article 40 of the country's Constitution. In Italy, the Constitution provides for the right of association, the right of peaceful assembly, the right to form and join trade unions and to conduct union activity, at both the workplace and generally, as well as a right to strike.[18] This means that strike action there need not be limited to the actual terms and conditions of employment. It can also be pursued in support of "political-economic demands" e.g. for a better social security system or better housing, and that such action can be lawful even though the employer may not be the prime target. Whenever strike action is lawful, those taking part in it cannot be penalised. Article 40 of the Italian Constitution does not, however, provide a legal right to strike on purely political grounds.[19]

So, comparing Britain with the examples of Germany and Italy, one can see that there are important differences regarding the legality of strikes and the right to take strike action without the risk of being sued for damages or being dismissed.

A significant point is that, in Germany, strike action appears to be lawful only within the context of an institutionalised structure of industrial relations, a situation which in many ways seems to resemble the thinking of the Donovan Commission in the mid to late 1960s. Although the Donovan Commission did not call for a legal right to strike, it did make the recommendation that only the small minority of "official" strikes be protected by the "immunities" provisions

---

[15] *Trade Union Immunities*, Cmnd. 8128, HMSO (London), January 1981, Appendix, p. 99, para. 93.

[16] Weiss, Manfred, *European Employment and Industrial Relations Glossary: Germany*, Sweet and Maxwell (London), 1992, p. 296, para. 673.

[17] Ibid., p. 341, para. 778.

[18] Hendy, John QC, Article 11 and the right to strike, in: Ewing, K. D. (Ed.), *Human Rights at Work*, ..., pp. 125 and 146 footnote 63.

[19] Wedderburn, (Lord) K. W., Laws about Strikes, ..., p. 154.

of the 1906 Act and the corresponding provision of the 1965 Act. This recommendation, as already noted, was rejected by the then Labour Government. So, despite the institutionalised structure of industrial relations in Germany, German workers still have more rights than their British counterparts to use the strike weapon without the fear of reprisals (i.e. through damages or dismissals).

In Britain, "immunities", rather than "positive rights" to take strike action, came into being. As already noted, the scope of these "immunities", was narrowed by the 1982 Act. Although "immunities" reached a peak towards the end of the 1970s due to the legislative measures of the 1974-1979 Labour Government, industrial action, nevertheless, invariably remained "a breach of the employment contract, a common law rule as fundamental today as it was in 1800".[20]

Thus, one cannot argue that the trade union laws put through by the Thatcher Government placed limitations on the right to strike (even though that was their obvious intention and effect) because such a right has never, in strict fact, actually existed in Britain. An important aim of the laws passed in the 1980s, most notably in the 1982 Act in narrowing "the definition of a trade dispute", was to return to the judiciary much of the terrain it had lost in determining what it felt the law should be when called upon to judge what is lawful or unlawful in an industrial dispute.

The laws of the 1980s did not go as far as removing all of the "immunities" which Parliament had conceded to trade unions in 1906 or as far back as the 1870s. However, the Thatcher Government's laws had a strong enough effect for calls to be made for the Government to go the whole way and abolish all remaining "immunities" which would have the effect of bringing trade union action into conflict with the law.[21]

Criticism of "immunities" has largely boiled down to claims that they allegedly give "legal privileges" to trade unions,[22] meaning that they supposedly "put unions above the law". Without offering any evidence based on surveys or commissions, one very prominent critic of "immunities", the late Friedrich August von Hayek, claimed that "the spectacular legal privileges granted ... to trade unions" had "since become the chief cause of the progressive decline of the British economy".[23] Trade unions, allegedly, "create a unique form of monopoly"[24] – labour monopoly – and "labour monopoly is due to the coercive suppression of

[20] Wedderburn, (Lord), Freedom of Association ..., ..., p. 5.

[21] Ibid., p. 11.

[22] See, for example, Hayek, F. A., *Law, Legislation and Liberty*, ..., Vol. 1, p. 179, footnote 32. - See also Vol. 3, pp 31f.

[23] Ibid., Vol. 3, p. 32. See also Wedderburn, (Lord) K. W., Freedom of Association ..., ..., p. 8.

[24] See Wedderburn, (Lord) K. W., Freedom of Association ..., ..., p. 8.

competition", while, interestingly, "enterprise monopoly is the result of better performance".[25] So the root cause of "labour monopoly" lies in the "immunities" conceded by Parliament and, by implication, the latter needed to be abolished.

What is often overlooked by those who regard trade union "immunities" as being "privileges" is, in the words of Lord Wedderburn, "the greatest legal privilege of all" – that of limited liability whereby the law, citing the words of Lord Diplock in a case in 1984, permits "the creation of corporations as artificial persons ... to enable business to be undertaken with limited liability in the event of the business proving to be a failure".[26]

The 1980, 1982 and 1984 Acts, as already noted, had "significantly reduced the legal immunities for trade unions and their officials" but "the hard core of immunity" remained.[27] Clearly mirroring the sentiments of Hayek, a 1988 publication from the Institute of Economic Affairs argued for a "bolder approach which goes all out to eliminate labour monopoly power" and this "should include the repeal of remaining trade union immunities and a return to the ordinary common law of contract and tort in industrial relations".[28] By implication, this could have also meant a call for the revival of the common law doctrine of a "restraint of trade" and, as a consequence, reopen the question as to what extent trade unions would have continued to be legal (see below). Even if such a move were not to make trade unions, as such, illegal, organising and seeking to bargain collectively would, in the eyes of the common law, of course be as illegal as they have always been. Damages and high legal costs would then, once more, become "fines" for committing such action.

By the time the Major Government left office in 1997, the Conservatives had not gone as far as abolishing all remaining "immunities" during their eighteen years in government. Nevertheless, by the time they left office, trade unions were only protected when authorising industrial action if the criteria as outlined in the 1992 Act was diligently followed. This has remained to be the case despite the longest ever period of the Labour Party in government. Principally, for trade unions to be protected when authorising industrial action, the following criteria have to be met:

Firstly, the action has to fall within a "definition of a trade dispute", as defined by the 1992 Act, which, ten years previously, had been narrowed by the 1982 Act, in that it had to be "wholly or mainly" about the terms and conditions of employment. Secondly, a ballot authorising such action has to take place cou-

25 Hayek, F. A., *Law, Legislation and Liberty*, ..., Vol. 3, p. 83.

26 Wedderburn, (Lord) K. W., Freedom of Association ..., ..., p. 12.

27 Hanson, Charles G. and Marther, Graham, *Striking Out Strikes*, Institute of Economic Affairs (Westminster, London), Hobart Paper 110, 1988, p. 76.

28 Ibid.

pled with periods of notice of such a ballot being given to both employers and those eligible to take part in it together with employers being informed of those employees who are eligible to vote in the ballot. Thirdly, the action has to be "official" in that it has to be endorsed by the union concerned, meaning that it has to ensure that all procedures, statutory or otherwise, have been fulfilled.[29]

So in fulfilling the above conditions before unions can be protected from claims in damages when engaged in industrial action, situations can occur where such action could be crippled at the very outset with the law *itself* denying workers and their union any opportunity of fulfilling these very conditions to any effect. This can occur in situations where the only chance workers have of securing a satisfactory outcome to their grievances is through embarking upon industrial action immediately with the full backing of their union. This very predicament was to confront catering workers employed by Gate Gourmet at British Airways at London Heathrow airport as recently as summer 2005. Ironically, this was eight years after the landslide Labour election victory in 1997 in which the Blair Government could have easily enacted legislative measures so as to restore some degree of legal parity between workers and employers in industrial disputes in the aftermath of the legislation passed over the previous 18 years had it had the intention of doing so.

Gate Gourmet is a trans-national concern and the world's second biggest concern specialising in airline catering. In 1997 British Airways (BA) transferred its airline catering services to Gate Gourmet on a ten-year contract. At the time of the dispute in 2005, the company claimed it had 109 kitchens in 29 countries with a total workforce of 22,000 employees worldwide. In 2002, this company was taken over by the US-based finance investor Texas Pacific Group.[30]

As part of the company's strategy of cutting labour costs, with existing catering workers at Heathrow airport and their union (the TGWU) fearing redundancies, the TGWU had been engaged in discussions with the company in an attempt to save their jobs and to prevent any worsening of their terms and conditions of employment. Then suddenly, on 10 August, without the union being consulted, the company took on 130 seasonal workers on terms and conditions of employment even worse than those of the existing caterers (being mainly middle-aged Asian women). Thus, by implication, a strike by the existing caterers had been provoked. Whilst the catering workers were meeting to discuss the implications of the recruitment of these seasonal workers, they were given a "three-minute"

---

[29] See *Law at work 2007*, Labour Research Department (LRD) (London), May 2007, pp. 157-171.

[30] Hendy, John and Gall, Gregor, British Trade Unions Today and the Trade Union Freedom Bill, in: Ewing, K. D. (Ed.), *The Right to Strike: From the Trade Disputes Act 1906 to a Trade Union Freedom Bill 2006*, The Institute of Employment Rights (Liverpool), 2006, p. 248.

ultimatum over a megaphone to return to work or be dismissed with the result that the company immediately dismissed 667 catering workers.[31] Those who turned up for work the following day were confronted with the option of either signing new employment contracts on worse terms and conditions than those previously or being made unemployed. In solidarity with the catering workers, BA baggage handlers and some check-in staff (also TGWU members) stopped work for the day on 12 August.[32]

The 1992 Act left the catering workers' union, the TGWU, unprotected in claims for damages in the following ways. Firstly, as the strike action was spontaneous, no ballot as required by this Act had (or could have physically) taken place. Secondly, in the absence of such a ballot, not only was the TGWU prevented from actually supporting the strike, it was also required to officially repudiate it. Thirdly, as the strike action by the baggage handlers was deemed as being "secondary" (being one of solidarity and with their employer being BA, rather than Gate Gourmet, and therefore not being directly party to the dispute) their action was also unprotected (which wouldn't have been the case hadn't the catering services been transferred). A further consequence of the strike action by the catering workers is that as it was neither "lawful" nor "official", the very limited right to claim unfair dismissal under the 1992 Act was not available.[33] As the strike by the caterers was spontaneous with the above conditions not having been fulfilled for it to be deemed "official" and "lawful", it could therefore be judged by management, on the basis of common law principles, as being a breach of the contract of employment thus opening the way for it to treat this "breach", as it were, as a "termination" of it.

Although the strike by the catering workers left BA without any catering on its flights for over a month the law physically stood in the way of the TGWU giving the catering workers the degree of support needed to keep their jobs on the basis of their existing terms and conditions of employment without the risk of being sued for heavy damages. In the end, a total of 813 workers were dismissed. 272 of them were reinstated and 411 workers were given the equivalent of their redundancy pay entitlement. For the remaining 130 workers, there was nothing with the result that the company was able to shed 541 jobs by only paying the equivalent of redundancy pay to 411 workers.[34]

---

[31] Ibid., see also *Law at work 2007*, ..., pp. 161f.

[32] Hendy, John and Gall, Gregor, ..., p. 248.

[33] Ibid., pp. 249f.

[34] Ibid., p. 249. Once the Gate Gourmet dispute at Heathrow airport was over, there was a pay dispute lasting from October 2005 to April 2006 involving catering workers at the same company at Düsseldorf airport in Germany. For details on the Gate Gourmet dispute at Düsseldorf airport, see, for example, Hendy, John and Gall, Gregor, ..., pp. 250-253.

The strike by catering workers at Gate Gourmet in 2005 has shown that the 1992 Act lacks flexibility for trade unions if the very nature of a specific dispute is such that whatever steps are undertaken to comply with the law, it can still remain impossible for them to support such a strike in any effective way, no matter what the workers' grievances may be, and to retain the protection of the law at the same time. Of course, the 1992 Act, as such, didn't prevent the TGWU from going through all the necessary procedures to enable it to make the strike "official" but the only chance these catering workers had of preserving their jobs and preventing any worsening of their existing terms and conditions of employment was to take immediate strike action with the full backing of their union before the company could take any further steps to undermine their action. But the law is such that the time and all the formalities this would have involved had the effect of the catering workers being "robbed of the initiative" with management, as it were, being given a free hand to render any "official" strike action ineffective before it could begin.

But whatever the nature of the strike may be, if there is the slightest doubt as to whether all the strike procedures have been correctly fulfilled, leaving aside any difficulties in fulfilling the above-mentioned statutory requirements, the union authorising such action could be taken to court and, initially, an injunction could then be secured restraining such action. There, the way is open for the courts to grant employers injunctions restraining industrial action over a very minor technicality as was most recently demonstrated in the Royal Mail dispute in October 2007.

The Royal Mail dispute centred on the question of pay, pensions and general terms and conditions of employment for postal workers. At one point in the dispute, a High Court injunction was obtained by the Rail Mail against the postal workers' union (Communication Workers' Union (CWU)) restraining strike action "on less than three hours notice". There, the union "was unable to put in evidence or even get a representative to court to give its lawyers a full briefing" so "there was no time to prepare any documents for the court or a written legal argument". The union's lawyers "had 30 minutes to read a substantial file of evidence prepared by Royal Mail and its written argument and to get some information over the 'phone from the CWU". The injunction was granted on the grounds that the strike notice was "defective".[35]

In line with the 1992 Act, the CWU had given details of "every workplace" where its members were intending to strike, the "number in each grade at each workplace", the "total number in each workplace and the total overall". However, the union "did not provide the totals in each grade overall, though they were easily

[35] Ewing, Keith and Hendy, John, Why Mr Brown should back the Bill, in: *Morning Star* (London), 18 October 2007, p. 7.

calculable by the Royal Mail from the figures given" hence the injunction was granted.[36]

However, during the firefighters' dispute 2002/2003, which developed into the most serious industrial conflict in Britain since the mid 1980s, the trade union laws as such were not the point of issue. Though in response to the strikes which took place in this dispute, legislation was pushed through Parliament giving the Government the option of withdrawing firefighters' negotiating rights and of placing the fire service under central government control (see pages 235-239).

So powers of the State to intervene directly in industrial disputes should be seen as going hand in hand with the whole range of statutes passed in the 1980s and 1990s so as to restore to the courts many of the powers they had earlier lost to intervene in industrial disputes. It is therefore important to determine the mechanisms and common law principles which enable the courts to do this. There are three especially important judicial mechanisms which have traditionally operated to the disadvantage of trade unions. These are the interlocutory injunction, vicarious liability and the doctrine of restraint of trade.

The Interlocutory Injunction

An injunction is a court order requiring the party subject to it to do or refrain from doing something. On this basis, an injunction can be used as an "initial first step" to prevent industrial action if its legality is treated as being in doubt. Leaving aside the merits of any particular case, whenever an injunction is sought, it can be seen as a way a plaintiff can accuse a defendant of doing something or being about to do something he regards as being "illegal". It is in this context that the use of injunctions needs to be assessed, especially in the aftermath of the trade union laws which were enacted following Labour's election defeat in 1979.

Before the law on the granting of labour injunctions was modified in the 1992 Act, injunctions could have been granted on an *interlocutory* basis pending trial (which might not have taken place for many months) or, in cases of great urgency, on an *ex parte* basis (i.e. in the absence of the defendant and/or his representative).[37] This meant that in an attempt to stop an industrial dispute, if its legality appears to be in doubt, an employer, claiming great urgency, could apply for, and judges could then grant an *ex parte* injunction in the absence of the defendant trade union thus denying it the chance of stating its case or cross-examining witnesses. On this basis, a union could be "robbed of the initiative" in an indus-

---

[36] Ibid.

[37] Rogers, W. V. H., *Winfield and Jolowicz on Tort* (13th Edition), Sweet and Maxwell (London), 1989, p. 534.

trial dispute.[38] The reason for this is that in reality, very few cases concerning industrial disputes ever come to trial because the granting of the injunction itself has already served the purpose of stopping the dispute.[39]

In the process of repealing the 1971 Act, the incoming Labour Government in 1974 recognised the unfairness of this practice and, even if only symbolically, attempted to rectify this injustice in section 17(1) of the 1974 Act. In this, guidelines as to when injunctions could be granted were inserted to ensure that trade unions would not be unfairly handled in the courts when injunctions were sought providing the action in question was "in contemplation or furtherance of a trade dispute".[40]

In deciding whether an injunction could be granted, the court had to be satisfied that the plaintiff had shown *prima facie* evidence or a probability that his legal rights were being infringed. He would also had to have shown that he would suffer more harm than the defendant if the interim remedy were not granted, this being based on the "balance of convenience".[41]

However, in 1975, the House of Lords, in the case of *American Cyanamid Ltd. v. Ethicon*, claimed that this test caused confusion.[42] In this case, Lord Diplock stated that the court need only be satisfied that the applicant's claim was not "frivolous or vexatious" and that there was "a serious question to be tried".[43] Even though this case concerned patents rather than an industrial dispute, this ruling made the granting of an interim or interlocutory injunction easier to obtain with the effect of it undermining what the 1974 Act had originally intended. Although the "balance of convenience" still had to be shown by the plaintiff to be in his favour, Lord Wedderburn commented that the threat of irreparable harm to the employer's "property" in his business interests could not, in such a context, be outweighed by the interests of the defendant union.[44]

In response to the House of Lords ruling in the Ethicon case, a clause was inserted into the 1974 Act by the 1975 Employment Protection Act such that, in deciding when an interlocutory injunction should be granted, and the party against whom it's sought shows the action is "in contemplation or furtherance of a trade dispute", the court would have to take into consideration the chances of the plaintiff succeeding at the trial of the action at a later date.[45] This measure in

---

38 Ibid.

39 *Law at work 2007*, ..., p. 169.

40 Rogers, W. V. H., ..., p. 534.

41 Griffith, J. A. G., ..., p. 91.

42 Ibid.

43 Ibid.

44 Ibid.

45 Rogers, W. V. H., ..., p. 534.

the 1975 Act could be judged in the context of the Labour Government seeking to get Parliament to confirm what it had actually intended in the previous year through the repeal of the 1971 Act in that trade unions should not be unfairly disadvantaged in the courts whenever employers seek to stop industrial disputes through injunctions. But however well intended these attempts in the 1974 and 1975 Acts may have been, they failed to counter the crucial problem of controlling the power of High Court judges to issue injunctions because ultimately it is one of their *own* discretion.[46]

Perhaps the best example of the ineffectiveness of Labour's attempt to moderate even the *ex parte* injunction in the 1974 Act, as Lord Wedderburn noted, became clearly evident when in 1987 a judge granted an injunction, without notice to the defendant union, from his home over the telephone on a Sunday afternoon![47] Lord Wedderburn went on to note that a further provision to modify the range of labour injunctions, through section 17(2) of the 1974 Act, which had been inserted through the 1975 Act, had "had scarcely any effect at all" because of the power and degree of discretion judges have in issuing them.[48]

In any case, in considering an application for an interlocutory injunction in an industrial dispute, any claim that the court was seeking to maintain the "status quo" pending trial at a later date would still be difficult to sustain even if the law on granting injunctions was "fairly balanced". Even if "right" was on the defendant union's side, the granting of an injunction would legally prevent the union from pursuing the industrial action further whilst the employer would secure valuable time in making contingency plans which could undermine the union's position.

If a strike were called as a result of a dismissal, an injunction could not maintain the "status quo" as it would not result in the dismissed employee being reinstated. Likewise, if a strike was called over terms and conditions of employment, an injunction could well result in the union securing less than would be otherwise possible.[49] In fact, very often in industrial disputes, a full trial never takes place because the dispute had already been resolved.[50]

The scale of the trade union laws passed in the 1980s and subsequently in the 1990s enabled the courts to intervene in industrial disputes to a greater extent than at any time since the passing of the 1906 Act, with the possible exception

[46] See Wedderburn, (Lord) K. W., Laws about Strikes, ..., p. 171ff.

[47] This was in the case of *Barretts and Baird (Wholesale) Ltd. v. IPCS*. See Wedderburn, (Lord) K. W., Laws about Strikes, ..., p. 171 and p. 201, footnote 76.

[48] Ibid., p. 171.

[49] McIlroy, John, *Trade Unions in Britain Today*, Manchester University Press (Manchester and New York), 1988, p. 69.

[50] Griffith, J. A. G., ..., p. 91.

of the short-lived period of the 1971 Act. Consequently, the scope for the initial "first step" to be taken in preventing industrial action was widened considerably. An injunction is a powerful weapon, for, if it is defied, it exposes the guilty party to "contempt of court" which can then result in imprisonment or heavy fines and, as far as trade unions are concerned, the sequestration of their assets and the loss of their property.

The law covering the issuing of injunctions in industrial disputes is now regulated in section 221 of the 1992 Act. In this, an attempt was made, even if only on paper, to tackle the injustice of behind the issuing of injunctions in such cases, especially through what were previously *ex parte* injunctions, whereby unions had often been "robbed of the initiative" in an industrial dispute without them being given a chance to state their case. Section 221 of the 1992 Act provides that when an application for an injunction is made without notice and the defendant union claims, or in the opinion of the court is likely to claim, that it is "in contemplation or furtherance of a trade dispute", the court shall not grant the injunction unless it is satisfied that all reasonable steps have been taken to ensure that notice of the application and an opportunity of being heard have been given. Even if this reduces the risk of a defendant union being taken unaware in an industrial dispute, it contains nothing about how the court should proceed once the parties are before it.[51] Thus, the crucial question of the degree of discretion judges have in issuing injunctions with the result that a strike can be broken before any attempt can be made in attending to the root causes of the dispute still remains unresolved.

The scope by which injunctions can be issued against trade unions was widened in the Trade Union Reform and Employment Rights Act, 1993. Under this Act, an individual who claims that a trade union or other person has done, or is likely to do, an unlawful act to induce any person to take part in industrial action and that the effect or likely effect of this is to prevent or delay or affect the supply of goods or services to the individual may apply to the High Court for an order requiring him to desist from this inducement and to take steps to terminate the effect of any prior inducement.[52] The effect of this is that a member of the public likely to be affected by such action, even if he has no contractual claim to the delivery of the goods and services likely to be affected by the dispute, can all the same apply for an injunction to stop the dispute[53] and, in the event of one being granted, the union would have to take all necessary steps to comply with it.

The Messenger Newspaper Group dispute at the end of 1983 (see below) provides the best example in living memory of how effectively injunctions can be

[51] See Rogers, W. V. H., *Winfield and Jolowicz on Tort* (Seventeenth Edition), Sweet and Maxwell Limited (London), 2006, p. 843.

[52] Ibid., p. 844.

[53] Ibid.

used. Further, even while police tactics in industrial disputes were being revised, the State was still able to take effective measures to ensure that the "law" was upheld.

In a survey of injunctions sought to restrain industrial action covering the period 1980 to August 2005, published by industrial relations specialist Gregor Gall in the *British Journal of Industrial Relations* in June 2006, it can be seen that employers were becoming more prepared to seek injunctions on the basis of the trade union laws which had just come into effect (see Appendix, table 11).[54] Whereas in 1980, just one injunction was sought, in 1981, in both 1982 and 1983, there were ten and in 1983, there were twelve. There, it is worth noting that of the twelve injunctions which were sought in that year, four were secured by the Messenger Newspaper Group on account of the dispute with the National Graphical Association (NGA) – three of them being against the NGA itself and one against the National Union of Journalists (NUJ). Furthermore, injunctions were also taken out against the NGA in connection with this dispute when, in protest against the fines and the sequestration of its assets, it planned a national strike in the British printing industry for the 14 December (see pages 177ff).

Gall's survey shows that in the period 1980-1994, a total of 39 injunctions were sought on account of picketing, 39 concerning "secondary action", 58 due to balloting and 46 on "other grounds". From 1995 up to the end of August 2005, just seven injunctions were sought on account of picketing, none due to "secondary action", though there were 35 on account of balloting and 50 due to "other grounds".[55] As a result of the 1984 Act, injunctions were sought and granted in connection with strike ballots e.g. through claiming that there had been irregularities in the balloting procedures. There, it is also worth noting that there were changes to the balloting rules regarding strike action on account of the 1993 Act with the effect that judges apparently became more willing to grant interim injunctions restraining strike action if it was clear that the case would never go to a full trial.[56]

---

[54] Gall, Gregor, Research Note: Injunctions as a Legal Weapon in Industrial Disputes in Britain, 1995-2005, in: *British Journal of Industrial Relations*, Blackwell (Oxford), Vol. 44 No. 2, June 2006, p. 330. See also Rise in Legal Actions against Unions, in: *Labour Research*, LRD (London), Vol. 74 No. 10, October 1985, p. 259. NB In this article and subsequent articles, LRD published surveys of injunctions which had been *granted* whereas the survey published by Gregor Gall was for injunctions which had been *sought*. A comparison of the surveys conducted by Gall and LRD shows that the overwhelming majority of applications for injunctions had been granted – see also footnotes 55 and 56.

[55] Gall, Gregor, ..., p. 333. See also Appendix, table 11. NB According to Gall, in the period January 1995 to August 2005, there were a total of 87 applications for injunctions in industrial disputes of which 59 were granted, 14 rejected, seven withdrawn, five overturned on appeal with the outcome of the remaining two unknown. See Gall, Gregor, ..., p. 332 (Table 2),

[56] Employers Step Up Legal Challenges, in: *Labour Research*, LRD (London), Vol. 83 No. 9, September 1994, p. 8.

According to an earlier survey published in the *British Journal of Industrial Relations* in November 1987, covering the period May 1984 to April 1987, 80 injunctions were granted, eleven on account of picketing, 16 for "secondary action" and 47 concerning strike ballots.[57] In this survey, not only the number of injunctions and the reasons for them being sought are of interest, but also the industrial sectors from which they originated. Appendix 1, Table 12 shows that in the period May 1984 to April 1987, most of the injunctions were secured in three sectors – printing, shipping/transport and public services. The wide use of the injunctions in the printing industry can be associated with employers' strategies for forcing through the introduction of new technology and changes in working practices.[58] The fact that over a third of the injunctions in the said period were taken out in the printing industry would confirm the view that undermining effective trade union organisation in that particular industry was one major aim of the trade union legislation in the first half of the 1980s. There, it should also be noted that as this survey only covered the period May 1984 to April 1987, no account would have been taken of the injunctions taken out against the NGA and the NUJ as a result of the Messenger Newspaper Group dispute in autumn 1983.

The very fact that trade union organisation in the printing industry was targeted on account of the trade union laws was also confirmed in the survey published by Gregor Gall. In the period spanning 1980-1994, five industrial sectors accounted for 73% of the 185 injunctions which were sought and there, printing featured most prominently with 19% of them compared with transport (16%), manufacturing (15%), public sector (15%) and communications (8%).[59] This survey also shows that in the period 1980-1994, most of the injunctions sought were in the private sector. In the period 1995 to 2005, however, of the 82 injunctions sought, the public sector including the Royal Mail/Post Office accounted for 38% of them with transport accounting for 28% whereas there was just one injunction sought in the printing industry.[60]

Whereas in the period, 1980-1994, many of the injunctions sought were to prevent picketing and "secondary action", since 1995, injunctions have largely been sought concerning balloting for strike action through claiming irregularities in balloting procedures and on the basis of "other grounds". These "other grounds" have concerned questions as to the actual interpretation of the "definition of a trade dispute" e.g. whether industrial action is possible to protect existing terms

---

57 Evans, Stephan, The Use of Injunctions in Industrial Disputes May 1984 – April 1987, in: *British Journal of Industrial Relations*, Blackwell (Oxford), Vol. XXV No. 3, November 1987, p. 421, Table 1.

58 Ibid., p. 425.

59 See Gall, Gregor, ..., p. 333.

60 Ibid., pp. 333f.

and conditions of employment of union members in the event of a transfer of undertakings.[61]

Given the widened use of injunctions, it is therefore necessary to determine how they became such an effective method of restraining industrial action. This is where, with its extension into industrial disputes as from 1982, the common law principle of vicarious liability was to fit in.

Vicarious Liability

The concept of vicarious liability signifies the liability which A may incur to C for damage caused to C by the negligence or other tort of B, whether or not A has participated in the wrong committed to C.[62] (The very fact that A may be liable does not have the effect of protecting B from any possibility liability.[63]) On this basis, an employer can be held responsible for the actions of his employees on matters regarding the fulfilment of their employment obligations. This principle can therefore be extended to a trade union being held responsible (i.e. liable in tort) for the actions of its members and officials.

As already noted, one major aim of the 1982 Act concerned trade union funds (and property). In this, this Act did three things. Firstly, it made unions liable in tort, secondly, through Section 15 of the Act, a code on vicarious liability was introduced and, thirdly, it limited damages against unions in certain actions in tort.[64] By making unions liable in tort, the 1982 Act, as already noted, repealed Section 14 of the 1974 Act which had given them this protection.[65]

The 1906 Act, as already noted, provided immunity in tort for trade unions arising out of the actions of their officials and members. The exemption from tort, putting unions "outside the law of the land", was precisely because the Taff Vale case had dispelled any illusion there may have been in that "the law of the land" (in the eyes of the judiciary) could be neutral and just[66] when it came to industrial disputes.

The Taff Vale case came about because a signalman, who had led a movement for a pay rise, complained that he had been victimised by his company (the Taff Vale Railway Company). As a result, a strike was organised in support of the

61 Ibid., pp. 331f.

62 Rogers, W. V. H., ... , p. 879.

63 Ibid.

64 Wedderburn, (Lord) K. W., *The Worker and the Law* (Third Edition), Penguin (Harmondsworth), 1986, p. 530.

65 Ibid.

66 See Ibid., p. 528.

signalman, and the union (the then Amalgamated Society of Railway Servants) made it "official". The Union organised picketing at Cardiff to prevent the company from bringing in "blackleg" labour. The company took out a High Court injunction, not only against the individual organisers of the strike but, interestingly, against the union itself and the Court gave the go-ahead for the union to be sued. The Court of Appeal overturned the High Court decision but, subsequently, the House of Lords reinstated it.[67]

The outcome of this case was unexpected because it was not thought that a union could be sued in its own name for the actions of its officials and cases in the 1890s had seemed to indicate that the union itself was protected by virtue of the 1871 Act.[68] The implication of the Taff Vale case meant that the courts, in the eyes of the trade union movement and Parliament, had forfeited any claim to competence they may have had in handling industrial disputes. So the principle had to be established, or restated, that the courts be kept out of industrial disputes in order that grievances at work could be resolved without judicial restraint. This, indeed, was the historic significance of the 1906 Act.

The 1906 Act was repealed in 1971. With registration being the cornerstone of the 1971 Act, this meant that those unions registering under it got full corporate status, and only those unions registered under this Act were allowed the title of "trade union". The rest, as far as this Act was concerned, were "organisations of workers".[69]

Through the repeal of the 1906 Act, the 1971 Act's corporate "trade unions" became exposed to tort liabilities, but a "privilege" of registration was that limits were imposed on the damages they could incur (depending on their size). A non-registered union, however, could be sued "in the name of the organisation" with no limits on the damages being imposed.[70]

By repealing the 1906 Act, the 1971 Act revived the concept of vicarious liability in industrial disputes. This then raised the question, to what extent could a union (whether registered or not) be held responsible for the actions of its officials and members? The 1971 Act left aside the issue of vicarious liability to common law principles which meant that judges had to apply concepts of "expressed and implied authority" in order to determine the extent to which a union could be liable for the "unofficial" action of its shop stewards.[71]

---

[67] See *Trade Union Immunities*, ..., pp. 13f, paras. 47f.

[68] Ibid., p. 14, para. 50.

[69] Wedderburn, (Lord) K. W., *The Worker and the Law* ..., ..., p. 528f.

[70] Ibid., p. 529.

[71] Ibid., p. 532.

In this context, an important case was that of *Heatons Transport St. Helens Ltd. v. TGWU* in 1972 which involved "blacking" (deemed an "unfair industrial practice" under the 1971 Act) at the Liverpool and Hull docks. In this case, the House of Lords ruled that the "unofficial" action of the shop stewards fell within the scope of "general implied authority", so the TGWU itself was responsible for this action.[72] This ruling meant that, as far as the common law was concerned, dockers, whose jobs were affected by containerisation, were denied effective means of pursuing their dispute unless they were prepared to place the funds of their union in jeopardy.

In the Heatons case, the House of Lords also ruled that it would have been necessary for the union to have taken "positive steps" to restrain the "unofficial" action of its shop stewards by going as far as withdrawing a shop steward's credentials to act on the union's behalf.[73] This, the TGWU did not do as part of its policy of non-cooperation with the 1971 Act and the institutions established under it, including the NIRC. The same case, according to the 1981 Government Green Paper, *Trade Union Immunities*, involved issues such as "implied authority" and "custom and practice", which were "inherently imprecise".[74] The Green Paper went on to state that "The experience of the 1971 Act suggests that it would be unsatisfactory to remove the Section 14 immunity [of the 1974 Act] without attempting to deal specifically with the issue of vicarious liability".[75]

Resulting from this analysis, the Green Paper drew three conclusions with regard to the application of the principles of vicarious liability in cases of unlawful, "unofficial" action. Firstly, establishing effective trade union liability for unlawful actions of its officials and members would require detailed legislative definition of vicarious responsibility; otherwise a wide discretion of judgement would be left to the courts. Secondly, since different unions have different structures, rule books and customs etc., courts might experience considerable problems in determining the extent of vicarious responsibility in individual cases. Thirdly, given this uncertainty, the extent to which the courts would hold trade unions responsible in cases of unlawful, "unofficial" action was questionable.[76]

In seeking to strike a "fair balance" between what was felt necessary to protect those organising industrial action and those who had no part in it (see page 88), the then Secretary of State for Employment, James Prior, saw a solution in extending liability to the individual organisers of unlawful action.[77] Prior expressed

[72] *Trade Union Immunities*, ..., pp. 30f, para. 117.

[73] Ibid.

[74] Ibid., p. 31, para. 118.

[75] Ibid., p. 31, para. 120.

[76] Ibid., p. 32, para. 122.

[77] See *House of Commons, The Employment Committee Session 1979-80, The Legal Immunities of Trade Unions and other related matters, Minutes of Evidence 20 February 1980*

doubts as to whether changing or repealing Section 14 of the 1974 Act would be effective. He indicated that in the event of a strike, an employer would be more concerned with securing an injunction to enable work to continue than in seeking damages. He also indicated that the experience of various cases under the 1971 Act, especially the Con-Mech case (see pages 52f) should be considered before making any changes to Section 14.[78] Further, damages and legal costs could eliminate a union altogether, with the result that the sums might never be recovered.

However, by making individual organisers of industrial action more liable, as Prior had proposed, increased the risk of "martyrdom" (self-imposed or otherwise). Defiance of court orders could lead to union officials being imprisoned for contempt of court. Most notably, the imprisonment of the five London dockers in 1972 (see page 51) had the effect of rallying the trade union movement behind them and securing their release, thus discrediting the 1971 Act still further. It was therefore significant that in 1980, one very prominent judge, Lord Denning, warned that, in industrial cases, the "weapon of imprisonment" for contempt of court must never be used again: "Some better means must be found".[79]

Precisely this was achieved in the 1982 Act by repealing Section 14 of the 1974 Act and by introducing a code on vicarious liability. The fact that these "better means", in Lord Dennings's words, were not included in the 1980 Act but were to form the cornerstone of the 1982 Act would confirm the observation that the impact of the autumn 1981 Cabinet reshuffle was to change the direction of the Thatcher Government's labour relations policies from one that had initially spoken of "immunities" being "not simply legal privileges" to one which emphasised "privileges" as such – a point made by Lord Wedderburn (see page 91). Prior's removal from the Department of Employment in autumn 1981 was, in effect, a precondition for this policy change to be executed.

Individuals could still be fined and sued, but that in itself would not be enough to make the liabilities arising out of the trade union laws of the 1980s effective, as such fines are often paid by anonymous businessmen. The point about the 1982 Act was that it made the trade union *itself*, rather than its official, the defendant.[80]

This solution could be seen to work where trade unions derived their strength from their members and their contributions,[81] because, in Britain, the member-

(The Rt. Hon. James Prior, MP), HMSO (London), p. 24.

78 Ibid., pp. 24f.

79 Wedderburn, (Lord) K. W., Freedom of Association ..., ..., p. 31.

80 Ibid.

81 Ibid.

ship and property-base of the trade union movement offers the legal process "a sharp point of leverage, one readily grasped by the 1982 Act".[82] Thus, in the aftermath of the 1979-1981 slump, which had witnessed a rundown of much of Britain's industrial base, loss of trade union membership and a dampening of industrial militancy (see below), the economic and political climate of the early 1980s created the conditions by which the 1982 Act could take hold.

As succinctly put by Lord Wedderburn in a lecture in 1988: "The reintroduction of the union as the defendant, above all in the common case where an interlocutory injunction is the remedy sought, has proved how justified were the fears of Parliament in 1906 when it provided protection against the Taff Vale doctrine of tort liability. It is in these injunction cases that the texts of labour law come to life. ... So, in the 1980s the sweeping reductions of immunities readmitted the tides of the common law and put the union, its property and its organisation increasingly at risk, a law based and judicially developed upon those very principles which saw unions as an improper restraint of trade in the market and industrial action as an unlawful interference with contracts and property rights ... The exposure of union property to civil liability under that common law is the key which makes the machinery work. The interlocutory labour injunction is the oil that makes the engines hum smoothly".[83]

The code on vicarious liability, which was introduced through section 15 of the 1982 Act, made a trade union liable for the authorisation or endorsement of unlawful industrial action by three types of "specified person": firstly, top officers of the union – President, General Secretary or the principle executive committee; secondly, persons empowered by union rules; and thirdly, employed officials and committees to which employed officials regularly reported.[84] Under this Act, a union could only escape liability for unlawful action in the event of it taking effective measures in repudiating it.[85]

However, despite the trade union laws which had been passed by the end of the 1980s, the Thatcher Government claimed that "unofficial" industrial action was "subject to fewer constraints" than "official" action. In this, it expressed concern that industrial action called by a shop steward or another union official who is not authorised to do so under union rules still had the protection of statutory "immunities" even if such action had not been endorsed by a secret ballot.[86]

---

82 Ibid., pp. 31f.

83 Ibid., p. 32. See footnote 5.

84 Carty, Hazel, The Employment Act 1990: Still Fighting The Industrial Cold War, in: *Industrial Law Journal*, Oxford University Press (Oxford), Vol. 20 No. 1, March 1991, p. 7f.

85 Ibid., p. 8.

86 *Unofficial Action and The Law: Proposals to reform the law affecting unofficial industrial action*, Cm 821, HMSO (London), October 1989, p. 4, para. 2.1.

What is often overlooked about "unofficial" disputes is that the vast majority of them arise suddenly and are short lived and therefore resolved before the union has an opportunity to issue any "repudiation".[87] All the same, the Thatcher Government complained that "unofficial" action could still be used as a means of putting pressure on an employer before or during negotiations and went on to claim that a union may "formally repudiate unofficial action ... confident that its members [would] ignore the repudiation". So, "unofficial" action, it was alleged, could be "secretly encouraged by union officials".[88] If this can be shown, as was apparently so in the case of *Express and Star Ltd v. NGA* in 1985, the union would still be prone to common law liabilities.[89] So the outcome of this case in the courts made it unnecessary for the Government to have legislated further on that particular point but by doing so, it placed heavy and unrealistic burdens on trade unions.[90]

Nevertheless, under the Employment Act, 1990, this list of "specified person" was widened considerably to include "any other committee of the union or any other official (whether employed or not)".[91] For a union to avoid liability for unlawful action under the 1990 Act, more stringent procedures were introduced for it to distance itself from such action. This meant the action having to be repudiated in writing by the principal executive committee or the president or general secretary at the earliest opportunity, together with the actual organisers of the strike, the individual strikers and the employers concerned being informed that the strike has been officially repudiated.[92] So, in this, the introduction of the

---

87 Carty, Hazel, ..., p. 13.

88 *Unofficial Action and The Law: ...,* p. 5, para. 2.7.

89 In a dispute over the introduction of 'direct entry' systems (see page 84) in the advertising department at the *Wolverhampton Express and Star* newspapers in February 1985, the NGA was confronted by management plans to end the closed shop at the company, impose severe limitations in the right of the union to represent its members coupled with major reductions in earnings of the print workers. Before the union's chapels had the opportunity to consider management's proposals, 'direct entry' systems had been introduced provoking the NGA into "blacking" work for the company forthwith. The spontaneousness of this action, as deemed necessary by the NGA, meant that a ballot under the 1984 Act among the print workers involved could not have taken place. An injunction was subsequently issued against the NGA ordering its members to stop "blacking" work for the company and the NGA declared its intention to comply with it which meant it having to repudiate any continuation of this action. However, the High Court found that a national officer of the union together with a branch secretary had encouraged the boycott of work for the company to continue thus making the repudiation, in the view of the court, nothing more than "a conditional and half-hearted reprimand"so the union was fined £15,000 for "contempt of court" and the Court of Appeal agreed. See McIlroy, John, *The permanent revolution?: Conservative law and the trade unions*, Spokesman (Nottingham), 1991 p. 73 and *Unofficial Action and The Law* ..., ..., p. 5, para. 2.7.

90 Carty, Hazel, ..., p. 13.

91 Ibid., p. 8.

92 Ibid., p. 9.

code on vicarious liability in the 1982 Act, with its extension in the 1990 Act was, as already noted, intended to force unions, in effect, to "police" the activities of their own rank and file membership. This code on vicarious liability is now incorporated in section 21 of the 1992 Act.[93]

Similar to the 1971 Act, but only for those unions which registered under it, the 1982 Act imposed limits on the damages for which unions could be liable in the event of unlawful action, depending on the size of the union. However it would be a mistake to interpret this as a sign of the 1982 Act being even-handed. If, in the course of an industrial dispute a union found itself in "contempt of court", there would be no limits on the fines, to mention nothing of a possible sequestration of the union's assets, a judge can impose. The Messenger Newspaper Group dispute at the end of 1983 (see below), in which the NGA incurred fines and costs totalling £675,000, shows the extent to which the very existence of a trade union could be at stake when engaged in industrial action and, in this particular case, using means which before the passing of the 1980 and 1982 Acts were legally protected.

The 1990 Act, as just noted, imposed further extensions on the code on vicarious liability which had been introduced in the 1982 Act. This was clearly in response to a spate of "unofficial" industrial action in 1989 in the docks, British Rail and London Underground disputes. With this code being widened to include "any other committee of the union or any other official (whether employed or not)", not only shop stewards could render the union liable in the event of action deemed unlawful but even an unauthorised member.[94] This then puts unions under greater pressure to take even more stringent measures to repudiate "unofficial", unlawful action if they are to escape liability.

So, the conclusion can be drawn that, by reviving the principles of vicarious liability in the 1980s, the Thatcher Government sought to bring rank and file union activists under the control of official union structures in a way which attempts by the Donovan Commission and the 1971 Act had not achieved. What this clearly amounted to was a revival of the very principles which the Taff Vale case had established.

Thus, a parallel can be drawn between the endeavours of Donovan in the 1960s and the revival of the principles of vicarious liability in industrial disputes in the 1980s. Whereas in the 1960s, the purpose of Donovan was to find ways of bringing rank and file union activists under the control of official union structures so as to help make incomes policies work more effectively, in the 1980s, the purpose was for unions to "assist" the State in the policing of the "free" market order. The revitalisation of vicarious liability in industrial disputes by making the trade

[93] See Rogers, W. V. H., ... , pp. 831f.

[94] Carty, Hazel, ..., p. 8.

union itself the defendant was therefore just one measure by which the judiciary could limit the scope by which trade unions could upset the "free" market for labour with their funds and their property being put in jeopardy should they found themselves in "contempt of court".

Trade unions regarded as an unwarranted "restraint of trade"

Legal intervention in determining relations between labourers and their "masters" can be traced back over the centuries to the initial emergence of a "labour market" so as to prevent labourers from exploiting any labour market situation which could lead to improvements in their wages and other conditions of service. As far back as 1306, for example, a Royal Proclamation was issued forbidding building workers from "combining" in order to demand higher wages in the midst of a building boom in London at a time when there was a shortage of building workers.[95]

The various statutes, in England itself beginning under the reign of King Edward III in 1349 with the Ordinance of Labourers and subsequently in 1351 through the Statute of Labourers, were passed to set maximum wages so as to prevent workers from taking advantage of any labour market situation in the aftermath of the Black Death (1348/1349), which had wiped out a third of the population and led to a severe labour shortage. These Statutes and others following them over the centuries, which had brutally enforced the regulation of wages with the full thrust of the penal law, were only repealed in 1813.[96] "The spirit of the Statute of Labourers ... and of its offshoots", as noted by Karl Marx, "comes out clearly in the fact, that a maximum of wages [was] dictated by the State, but on no account a minimum".[97]

Up to the beginning of the industrial revolution in the 18th century, employment relationships had largely been of a feudal nature characterised by a complex of rights and duties which the courts upheld.[98] However, entrepreneurial desire for bigger profits from exploiting expanding new markets required greater labour market flexibility such that workers could be taken on and dispensed with, as and when the need arose. Thus, steps such as the ultimate abandoning of wage fixing in 1813 (whereby the State, through local magistrates, determined what

95 Hendy, John QC, *A Law Unto Themselves. Conservative Employment Laws: A National and International Assessment* (3rd edition), The Institute of Employment Rights (London), September 1993, p. 13.

96 Ibid., p. 13. See also Marx, Karl, Bloody Legislation against the Exploited, from the end of the 15th Century. Forcing Down of Wages by Acts of Parliament, in: Marx, Karl, *Capital* (Volume 1), Progress Publishers (Moscow), first published in 1954 (reprinted edition from 1986), Part VIII, Chapter XXVIII, pp. 690f.

97 Marx, Karl, ..., p. 690.

98 Hendy, John QC, ..., p. 9.

wages ought to be) were taken, not to improve the well-being of workers, but to fulfill entrepreneurial demands for labour market "flexibility".

The repeal of the Combination Acts in 1824/1825 may have lifted the ban on trade unions, but it did not prevent the Lord Chief Justice a few decades later, in the historic case of *Hornby v. Close* in 1867, from ruling that, even though trade unions were no longer criminal, they were nevertheless "in restraint of trade" as being illegal[99] (see below). This was because the courts, with the help of various statutes which made industrial action illegal, continued to judge unions, in effect, as being "conspiracies" under the criminal law and associations as being "in restraint of trade" under the civil law.[100] In this manner, trade unions were treated as a threat to the "free" functioning of the market order.

Parallel to the industrial and legislative developments in the 19th century was the evolving of the doctrine "freedom of contract". The notion of "the contract" enabled employers to take on workers on a contractual basis and lay down its terms and conditions. This arrangement proved beneficial for the employers as it enabled them to dismiss workers almost instantly. On the other hand, a breach of the employment contract by employees remained a criminal offence until the ultimate repeal of the Master and Servants Acts in 1875.[101]

The injustice of the Master and Servants Acts can be seen in that a breach of the employment contract on the part of the employees was a criminal offence but not that of the employer. So in the event of the employment contract being breached, workers were not only liable for prosecution under the criminal law but, by implication, also risked being sued for losses suffered by their employer under the civil law. However, a breach of the employment contract on the part of the employer was not deemed a criminal offence and whenever this occurred, he would have, at most, only been liable for civil action which would imply having to compensate his workers far any loss of wages they may have suffered.[102]

The concept "freedom of contract" is supposed to mean that parties enter into it freely so its terms and conditions would be upheld by the courts (unless it contained something illegal). On this basis, one might have expected the same principle to apply in the employer/employee relationship. But there was, and still is, a fundamental difference. In employment situations, workers, on account of their objective economic disadvantage vis-a-vis the employers, were hardly in a position to negotiate their terms and conditions of employment. Under the com-

---

99 See Webb, Sidney and Beatrice, *The History of Trade Unionism*, Longmans Green and Co. (London), 1920, pp. 261f.

100 McIlroy, John, *Trade Unions in Britain Today*, ..., p. 66.

101 Hendy, John QC, ..., p. 9.

102 See Laybourn, Keith, *British Trade Unionism c. 1770-1990*, Alan Sutton Publishing Limited (Stroud, Gloucestershire), 1991, pp. 66f.

mon law, this meant that judges would automatically uphold the terms of an employment contract, no matter how unfair these might be.[103] This is because the common law, the principles of which presupposed the inviolability of "the contract", did not traditionally consider the economic and social circumstances in which employment contracts were made or, in effect, imposed.

Common law attitudes were later modified in this respect, but only to the extent of judges realising that the changing reality of capitalism meant that entrepreneurs needing the growth of a big working-class market for mass production if the capitalist system were to flourish. Traditional judicial attitudes which in practice treated workers "as a subhuman species" were hardly compatible with them also being consumers of mass production. So, although capitalism's further development may have led to an apparent "change of judicial tone", the common law has remained firmly on the side of the employer. This means that as far as the judiciary is concerned, "managerial prerogative must be preserved unfettered".[104]

Additionally, under the common law, workers found themselves at another disadvantage. Breaches of the employment contract, especially through industrial action, leaving aside any "immunities" provisions, made the organisers of such action liable for heavy damages and legal costs and also from the time of the House of Lords' ruling in the Taff Vale case in July 1901 to the ultimate passing of the Trade Disputes Act towards the end of 1906 and, subsequently, once more since 1982, the unions themselves. But, what remedies under the common law were available if it was the employer who breached the employment contract? Leaving aside the various statutes giving workers limited degrees of protection against dismissal, workers could only claim for loss of wages,[105] which would in any case have been minimal if the employment contract provided for just a short period of notice before dismissal.

It is clear that there can hardly be any comparison between, on the one hand, loss of wages and, on the other hand, losses and/or damages suffered by those employers for business contracts which may have been disrupted by the dispute.

Given these factors, it can therefore be seen that, as "the contract" was sacrosanct, the common law was in practice geared to preserving the economic imbalance between employers and workers or, more precisely, between capital and labour. Leaving aside the various statutes which generally lifted the constraints on trade unions and their activities under the criminal law during the 19th century, the *Hornby v. Close* case demonstrated, that trade unions in principle continued to be regarded as being "in restraint of trade" under the common law. As

[103] Hendy, John QC, ..., p. 10.

[104] Ibid.

[105] Ibid.

the 1981 Green Paper stated: "Under the common law it is considered unlawful that unreasonable obstructions should be placed in the way of trade, and this includes trade in labour as well as in commodities. As a result, at common law the purposes of trade unions were regarded as unlawful for being 'in restraint of trade'".[106]

"Unreasonable obstructions", in this context, would of course include activities undertaken by trade unions which might stand in the way of a "free"-market order. The same principle could, in theory, be also applied to employers and their associations. In practice, however, it has tended to apply in the first instance against trade unions. In this context, the late Friedrich August von Hayek went as far as calling for the common law doctrine of "restraint of trade" to be generally enforced by declaring "invalid and legally unenforceable all agreement in restraint of trade, without any exceptions"[107] so as to no longer legitimise the "organisational activities" of unions.[108] In this, Hayek wasn't only referring to activities which had long received bad media publicity such as the closed shop, picketing, secondary strikes and boycotts, but also nation- and industry-wide pay bargaining for all these, he claimed, "coerce" individual workers, upset the market, reduce labour productivity and therefore reduce real wages all round and raise unemployment.[109] This, he also claimed, had certainly been "true of most countries of Europe, where union policy [was] strengthened by the general use of restrictive practices of a 'make-work' character".[110] Hayek may not have called for the prohibition of trade unions but in the "free"-market order he advocated, they would have been stripped of their industrial function and their role would, in effect, be reduced to one of resembling a staff association.

During the course of the long struggle to lift the legal constraints on trade unions, the *Hornby v. Close* case in 1867 was something of a turning point. This case concerned embezzlement by the treasurer of the Bradford branch of the Boilermakers' Society. As the Friendly Societies Act, 1855, enabled trade unions which deposited their rule books with the Registrar to proceed against defaulting individuals, it had therefore been thought that registered unions too would secure legal protection of their funds. However, with the Lord Chief Justice ruling that trade unions were "in restraint of trade" and thus illegal, trade unions were, in effect, deprived of any legal status and, therefore, protection of their funds.[111]

---

[106] *Trade Union Immunities*, ..., p. 12, para. 40.

[107] See Hayek, F. A., *Law, Legislation and Liberty*, ..., Vol. 3, pp. 86f.

[108] See Wedderburn, (Lord) K. W., Freedom of Association ..., ..., p. 10. See also Hayek, F. A., *The Constitution of Liberty*, Routledge and Kegan Paul Ltd. (London and Henley), 1960, p. 275.

[109] See Hayek, F. A., *The Constitution of Liberty*, ..., pp. 271-275.

[110] Ibid., p. 271.

[111] See Webb, Sidney and Beatrice, ..., pp. 261f. See also Wedderburn, (Lord) K. W., *The Worker and the Law* ..., ..., pp. 521f.

Given the outcry against the unions at the time and the Government decision to appoint a Royal Commission of Inquiry into trade unions shortly after the court ruling in this case, the limited degree of legality unions secured through the repeal of the Combination Acts appeared to be in jeopardy.[112] Trade union anger plus the election of a Liberal Government on the new urban franchise cleared the way for the Trade Union Act, 1871. The key provision of this Act was its section 3, in which the purposes of a trade union were not to be deemed unlawful merely by reason of being "in restraint of trade".[113]

But despite the passing of this Act, Karl Marx, fully aware that prosecutions in support of strike action still continued, questioned the sincerity of the motives behind this Act by noting the following observation a couple of years later: "The provisions of the labour statutes as to contracts between master and workman, as to giving notice and the like, which only allow of a civil action against the contract-breaking master, but on the contrary permit a criminal action against the contract-breaking workman, are to this hour (1873) in full force. The barbarous laws against Trades' Unions fell in 1825 before the threatening bearing of the proletariat. Despite this, they only fell in part. Certain beautiful fragments of the old statute vanished only in 1859. Finally, the act of Parliament of June 29, 1871, made a pretence of removing the last traces of this class of legislation by legal recognition of Trades' Unions. But an act of Parliament of the same date (an act to amend the criminal law relating to violence, threats, and molestation), re-established, in point of fact, the former state of things in a new shape. By this Parliamentary escamotage the means which the labourers could use in a strike or lock-out were withdrawn from the laws common to all citizens, and placed under exceptional penal legislation, the interpretation of which fell to the masters themselves in their capacity as justices of the peace ".[114]

By what "vanished only in 1859", Marx was referring to the Molestation of Workmen Act, 1859. This Act, provided for some relief from the judicial interpretation of "molestation" by excluding from liability peaceful persuasion to stop working, but only in strikes that concerned wages or hours and did not induce a worker to break an employment contract.[115] In this, such action ceased to be deemed as "molestation" or "obstruction" and was therefore no longer liable for a prosecution for conspiracy.[116]

---

[112] Musson, A. E., *The Congress of 1868: The origins and establishment of The Trades Union Congress*, Trades Union Congress (London), July 1982 Edition, pp. 19f.

[113] Wedderburn, (Lord) K. W., *The Worker and the Law* ..., ..., p. 522.

[114] Marx, Karl, ..., p. 691.

[115] Wedderburn, (Lord) K. W., *The Worker and the Law* ..., ..., p. 518.

[116] *Royal Commission on Trade Unions and Employers' Associations 1965-1968*, Cmnd. 3623, HMSO (London). June 1968, p. 228, para. 860.

Regarding the Act amending the criminal law relating to "violence, threats, and molestation", Marx was referring to the Criminal Law Amendment Act, 1871. This Act was passed in response to the Royal Commission on Trade Unions which had been appointed in 1867 in response to the outcome of the *Hornby v. Close* case. This Act repealed the 1825 and 1859 Acts with the effect that it reopened possibilities of prosecution under the criminal law in connection with trying to persuade workmen to stop working but, at the same time, stipulated that, providing that methods deemed as illegal under this Act were not used, no one would be liable for prosecution for actions tending to restrain the free course of trade.[117]

Although the Trade Union Act, 1871, may have settled the question of "restraint of trade", together with the Criminal Law Amendment Act (supposedly) not rendering any trade union member liable for prosecution through a mere threat to strike, prosecutions in support of strike action continued beyond the passing of these two Acts. Of particular importance was the case of *R. v. Bunn* in 1872 – the following year! There, a threat by certain London gas stokers to go on strike unless a certain workman, who was discharged for union activities, was reinstated resulted in their conviction on a charge of criminal conspiracy and a prison sentence of twelve months with hard labour.[118]

Following the reform of the Master and Servant Act in 1867, there would have normally been a fine or at the most a prison sentence of three months for a breach of the employment contract. Furthermore, due to the 1871 Trade Union Act, such a prosecution as had occurred in the Bunn case should have been thrown out in the courts. The protests against the prison sentences were so strong that Queen Victoria, on the advice of her Home Secretary, reduced the sentences to four months though they were still one month longer than the 1867 Act had intended.[119]

So, the union anger over these convictions was not going to be appeased by the appointment of yet another Royal Commission[120] – not so long after the one appointed in the aftermath of *Horny v. Close.* But being fully aware of the growing influence of the working-class vote at the time, the then Conservative Prime Minister, Benjamin Disraeli, as it were, "took the initiative". He offered a Bill that fulfilled most union demands.[121] In so doing, Disraeli could not have overlooked the fact that two European countries, Germany in 1869 and Sweden

[117] Ibid., p. 228, paras. 861f.

[118] Ibid., p. 221, para. 824. See also Steinmetz, Willibald, *Begegnungen vor Gericht: Eine Sozial- und Kulturgeschichte des englischen Arbeitsrechts (1850-1925)*, R. Oldenbourg Verlag (München), 2002, p. 33.

[119] Steinmetz, Willibald, ..., p. 33.

[120] This being the Royal Commission on Labour Laws.

[121] See Wedderburn, (Lord) K. W., *The Worker and the Law* ..., ..., p. 520.

in 1864 had already lifted the most repressive penal laws rendering trade unions and their activities illegal (see page 38). He would have also been aware of the growing industrial strength of the working class through the industrial revolution and hence, the possible consequences if workers, whose only means of overcoming grievances at work being by the withdrawal their labour, were to continue to find themselves up against the full thrust of the criminal law. Out of all this came a new Act, the historic Conspiracy and Protection of Property Act, 1875. Through this Act, Parliament, despite judicial interruptions over the decades, concluded a long and tedious process, already begun half a century earlier through the repeal of the Combination Acts, in which it, even if only grudgingly, lifted the various penal laws rendering trade unions and their activities illegal together with the wide-ranging penal sanctions judges had been able to impose on those participating in industrial disputes.

The historic significance of the 1875 Act is that strike action, or the threat of it, ceased generally to be a criminal offence. The key points about this Act was that it repealed the various statutes that rendered a breach of the employment contracts on the part of employees a criminal offence, in particular, the Master and Servants Acts and, as Lord Wedderburn stated, "invented a golden formula that became the bedrock of British workers' rights to organise and take effective industrial action".[122] This Act also repealed the Criminal Law Amendment Act[123] which, as already noted, had come into law on exactly the same date as the 1871 Trade Union Act. In this, through section 3 of this Act, a ruling in the Bunn case was reversed such that providing that a combination to do or procure any act "in contemplation or furtherance of a trade dispute" should not be deemed a criminal conspiracy *unless* the act itself would be punishable as a crime.[124] This Act, as earlier noted, became "the first example of legal immunity for those involved in trade disputes" (see page 39). All in all, the legislative measures which were enacted in the 1870s, especially the 1875 Act, can be interpreted as the "legal settlement of the 1870s".

Not withstanding the historic significance of the 1875 Act, it should, however, be noted that this Act codified yet again crimes connected with "intimidation", "molestation" and "picketing" and made provision for workers to be prosecuted for criminal liability for taking part in strikes in breach of their employment contracts where this concerned public utilities and in cases where there is a danger to life and property.[125] Thus, almost a hundred years later, these "crimes" under an Act that otherwise "became the bedrock of British workers' rights to organise

[122] Ibid., pp. 520f.

[123] *Royal Commission on Trade Unions and Employers' Associations 1965-1968*, ..., p. 228, para. 863.

[124] Wedderburn, (Lord) K. W., *The Worker and the Law* ..., ..., p. 520.

[125] Ibid., p. 520.

and take effective industrial action" were to be used in the trial and conviction of the Shrewsbury pickets in 1973.

In summer, 1972, there was a three-month national strike in the building industry which led to major improvements in pay and conditions of employment. The motives for pursuing such a trial against the Shrewsbury pickets need to be judged in the context of the defeats the Heath Government had already suffered earlier that year against the miners, the railwaymen and the dockers and the need to seek some degree of "justification" for its discredited industrial relations policies. So, the terrain chosen was an industry where trade union organisation was not so strong and cohesive as in other industries, where the 1971 Act itself was not the point of issue, with the Heath Government being confident that any convictions would not lead to the intense degree of trade union solidarity action which, most notably, had only recently secured the release of the five London dockers.

So, it initially ordered a police investigation into alleged instances concerning picketing by building workers in Shrewsbury on 6 September, 1972. These inquiries had been fruitless and normally this would have been the end of the matter. Astonishingly, however, five months after these alleged instances, the police were to press charges of conspiracy against the pickets. On 14 February, 1973, the first six of 24 pickets were arrested and charged with "Conspiring to intimidate people to abstain from their lawful work".[126]

What was actually meant by "lawful work" is highly questionable, a point which was vigorously challenged by the defence lawyer John Platts-Mills QC in the trial, for one major grievance among trade unionists in the building industry, which featured prominently in the building workers' strike, concerned the illegal practice of the "lump" or labour-only sub-contracting.[127] This point, important in

[126] See Warren, Des, *Shrewsbury – Whose conspiracy? The Need for an Inquiry* (Second Edition), New Park Publications Ltd. (London), January 1980, pp. 5-10.

[127] The "lump" or labour-only sub-contracting embraces many of the most negative aspects of the casualisation of labour and has often been associated with illegal practices, especially in the construction industry. This practice became widespread in the post-war period as property developers bought land on which to build houses houses for sale and looked for ways of cutting labour costs. In this, they often entered into agreements with individual craftsmen for the various jobs, which would be undertaken on the basis of all materials supplied, with payment made once these tasks were completed. Such craftsmen formed gangs to do these jobs, but not on the basis of having proper contracts of employment, and this opened the way to various illegal practices such as tax evasion, non-payment of national insurance contributions, the evasion of regulations on health and safety at work (a most serious matter given the high rate of accidents in the industry) and poor workmanship etc.. The "lump" angered trade unionists as it posed a grave threat to the terms and conditions of employment of those workers in the industry who were properly employed. The urge to make quick money whether among the contractors or the "lump" labourers themselves, especially in a building boom, took priority over the advantages of a proper contract of

itself, was dismissed by the Judge. This trial led to the imprisonment of six of the pickets – three for six months, nine months for Ken O'Shea, two years for Eric Tomlinson and Des Warren received the severest sentence of all being for three years. Not only that. In upholding the convictions of the Shrewsbury pickets in 1974, the Court of Appeal widened the scope by which workers could be prosecuted whilst engaged in industrial action beyond what had remained possible through the 1875 Act so as to include all threats of force and violence.[128]

So, there were two implications of the outcome of these trials. Firstly, for the Heath Government, this could be judged as an act of revenge against the trade union movement for the defeats it suffered on the industrial relations front. In this, it should also be noted that despite Labour being returned to office in winter 1974, in the midst of the downfall of a discredited government, the new Labour Home Secretary Roy Jenkins refused to honour the demands from the trade union movement and from within his own party for the release of the Shrewsbury pickets and to order an inquiry into these trials. In this, the intensity of trade union solidarity which secured the release of the London dockers did not extend to the Shrewsbury pickets.

The second implication of these trials was that the judiciary took the chance of reclaiming some of the competence it had lost through the 1875 Act in deciding the extent to which activities in support of a strike become a criminal offence. So, the outcome of these trials widened the scope in which the criminal law could be used against those involved in strike action. This, together with the severity of the jail sentences, represented, under the criminal law, one of the most severe attacks on the right to strike since the passing of the 1875 Act. So, the outcome of these trials would suggest that traditional judicial attitudes towards trade unions and trade unionists appeared to have changed very little a century after the passing of this Act.

Leaving aside the case of the Shrewsbury pickets, prosecutions under the 1875 Act had hardly been heard of in recent years though its provisions were used against the miners in the 1984/1985 miners' strike. By the end of September 1984, for example, 226 miners had been charged with "besetting", being an offence under the 1875 Act for which it carried the possibility of a fine or up to three months imprisonment.[129]

Even though the 1875 Act was to generally exclude the use of the criminal law in industrial disputes, this in no way meant that trade unions and working people

---

employment and the benefits associated with this e.g. possible pension schemes, defined working hours with agreed rates for overtime whenever the need arose etc..

[128] Wedderburn, (Lord) K. W., *The Worker and the Law* ..., ..., p. 541.

[129] *The miners case*, LRD (London), 1.10.1984, p. 17.

were to be free of repercussions in the courts even if strike action was "in contemplation or furtherance of a trade dispute". As already noted, as part of a successful employers' offensive against the "New Unions"[130] in the early 1890s, the ground was prepared by which the courts could make rulings in various cases which went against the spirit of what Parliament had intended when it decided to lift the various laws which had rendered trade unions, their activities and industrial action as illegal. Civil liability against unions, as earlier noted (see page 43), began to take shape in two ways. Firstly, the judiciary developed a new "civil liability for conspiracy", which meant that anyone who joined with another in a strike for purposes which the courts deemed as "illegitimate" could be sued for damages. Secondly, organisers of industrial action became liable in *tort* for "inducing a breach of the contracts of employment" of those whom they called out on strike. There, the judiciary, as it were, set about demolishing key aspects of the "legal settlement" of the 1870s with the effect that in many cases which went before the courts, the labour movement endured major defeats. In the period 1890 to 1906, the most significant judicial blow the trade union movement suffered was the House of Lords' ruling in summer 1901 in the case of *Quinn v. Leathem* just weeks after Taff Vale.[131]

Henry Leathem, a skilled flesher, had for many years supplied a butcher with meat. In 1895, in attempts to safeguard the livelihoods of its members as well as the professional standards of work in the meat trade in and around Belfast, the trade union (the Belfast Journeymen Butchers and Assistants' Association) sought to persuade Leathem not to employ non-union labour.[132] When this failed, the union instructed its members working for the butcher that if he continued to buy Leathem's meat, they would stop working. So the butcher took no more meat from him, who brought an action against the union officials for conspiracy to injure him. The House of Lords unanimously ruled in his favour.[133] The implication of this ruling is that the protection the 1875 Act provided to those acting "in contemplation or furtherance of a trade dispute" against prosecutions for *criminal* conspiracy did not extend to actions for *civil* conspiracy.[134] This case was also significant in that it was also decided that those using industrial sanctions as

---

[130] During the last decade of the 19th century, there was the emergence of the "New Unions" which sought to organise unskilled workers. The unions which were already established were able to rely upon the skill of their members as a crucial bargaining weapon but the "New Unions" were subject to constant pressures from an "over-stocked" labour market and employers sought to take advantage of this. See Griffith, J. A. G., ..., p. 64.

[131] McIlroy, John, The Belfast Butchers: *Quinn v Leathem* after a Hundred Years, in: Ewing, K. D. (Ed.), *The Right to Strike: From the Trade Disputes Act 1906 to a Trade Union Freedom Bill 2006*, The Institute of Employment Rights (Liverpool), 2006, p. 31.

[132] See Ibid., pp. 33-37.

[133] Griffith, J. A. G., ..., pp. 65f.

[134] *Royal Commission on Trade Unions and Employers' Associations 1965-1968*, ..., p. 226, para. 850.

a result of an agreement, that is through collective action, could be liable in tort in circumstances in which an individual acting alone would not be.[135]

The outcome of the *Quinn v. Leathem* case had the effect of the House of Lords reversing its *own* decision in the case of *Allen v. Flood* in 1898. In this case, a dispute arose between the iron-workers' union and the woodworkers where the former objected to certain work being done by the latter. The iron-workers told one of their officials that they would stop working if the woodworkers continued in employment. Subsequently, the employers lawfully dismissed the woodworkers who then took legal action against the official.[136]

The case of *Allen v. Flood*, interestingly, was heard in the House of Lords twice! It was initially heard in December, 1895. However, in his endeavours to secure a ruling in favour of the plaintiff and realising that he would be unable to carry a majority of his colleagues with him, the then Lord Chancellor, Lord Halsbury, decided that the case should be reheard in an enlarged body of Law Lords whereby High Court judges, many of whom were his own appointments, were summoned to "advise" – a practise which had long been though obsolete. This case was reheard in March/April 1897 but this attempt to "engineer" a ruling in favour of the plaintiff ultimately failed when, in December 1897, a majority of the House of Lords' judges hearing this case, including the former Lord Chancellor Lord Herschell,[137] decided that no action lay against a person for interfering with another's trade, business or employment unless he did so by means unlawful in themselves.[138]

Assessing the outcome of this case, Lord Wedderburn, commented: "This liberal judgement was a reaction, it is said, to Lord Chancellor Halsbury's efforts to engineer the opposite result".[139] Lord Wedderburn subsequently noted that: "Three years later he [Lord Halsbury] was to pack the court when two liberal Law Lords were not invited to sit so as to make his counter-attack in *Quinn v. Leathem*, 1901, where the Law Lords created the tort of conspiracy to injure".[140] Lord Halsbury's endeavours were also eased in that Lord Herschell, one of his strongest opponents in *Allen v. Flood*, had died the year before *Quinn v. Leathem* reached the House of Lords.[141] In effect, the ruling which Lord Halsbury

[135] Ibid.

[136] Griffith, J. A. G., ..., pp. 64f.

[137] See Ibid., 65. See also Wedderburn, (Lord) K. W., *The Worker and the Law* ..., ..., p. 612. NB Lord Herschell was Lord Chancellor twice: in 1886 and from 1892 to 1895. On both occasions, he was preceded and succeeded by Lord Halsbury who was Lord Chancellor from 1885 to 1886, 1886 to 1892 and from 1895 to 1905.

[138] *Royal Commission on Trade Unions and Employers' Associations 1965-1968*, ..., p. 235, para. 896.

[139] Wedderburn, (Lord) K. W., *The Worker and the Law* ..., ..., p. 612.

[140] Ibid.

[141] McIlroy, John, The Belfast Butchers: ..., ..., p. 41.

had sought in *Allen v. Flood* was achieved three years later in *Quinn v. Leathem*. So, whereas the final outcome of *Allen v. Flood* had the effect protecting trade unions from claims in tort from civil conspiracy to injure, the outcome of *Quinn v. Leathem* was to do the very opposite by creating this very tort.

Assessing the outcome of this case from a viewpoint similar to that of Lord Wedderburn, *Quinn v. Leathem*, in the words of John McIlroy, professor of industrial relations at the University of Keele, "was a landmark in the judicial development of the law of tort: it consolidated civil conspiracy in order to compensate employers for the removal of criminal conspiracy from industrial relations in 1875; it also maintained the possibility of another new tort, intentional and unjustified interference with the 'right to trade'".[142]

The House of Lords' ruling in *Quinn v. Leathem* was also seen to be at variance with its ruling in 1892 in the case of *Mogul Steamship Company v. McGregor Gow and Co.*. In this case, there was an important ruling in that the tort of civil conspiracy is not committed where, although someone is injured, those who combined and caused this injury were acting with the predominant objective of advancing their own legitimate interests and used no unlawful means.[143] If this principle could apply to employers and their associations, surely this principle could be applied to workers and their organisations. Whereas *Allen v. Flood* can be seen as conforming to the spirit of the Mogul Steamship case, the ruling in *Quinn v. Leathem* seemed to be inconsistent with this. Consequently, trade unions viewed the outcome of *Quinn v. Leathem* as an attempt to erode their power when seeking to strengthen their position against the employers.[144]

However, in the period 1890 to 1906, the most significant judicial development, without any doubt, came through the Taff Vale case. There, the crucial question was whether, due to the 1871 Act, a trade union could be sued in its own name in tort with the consequence that its funds were answerable for any damages awarded. There, the majority of the Lordships held that, while a trade union was not a corporation or a legal entity distinct from its members, the "privileges" conferred upon registered unions under the 1871 Act "imported a correlative liability" for it to be sued in its registered name for liabilities in tort incurred by those acting on its behalf.[145] This ruling was unexpected as it had not been previously thought that a union could be sued in its own name for damages incurred

[142] Ibid., p. 46.

[143] See *Royal Commission on Trade Unions and Employers' Associations 1965-1968*, ..., pp. 226f, para. 853.

[144] Griffith, J. A. G., ..., p. 66.

[145] *Royal Commission on Trade Unions and Employers' Associations 1965-1968*, ..., pp. 207f, paras. 770f and p. 226, para. 850.

by those acting on its behalf. The outcome of various cases in the 1890s seemed to indicate that the union itself was protected by the 1871 Act.[146]

Through the 1871 Act, registered unions were compelled to hold their property in the names of trustees and they would have been expected to hold such property for the benefit of the union's members since the union itself was not a legal entity and any property acquired was paid for by its members' subscriptions. Section 8 of the 1871 Act vested all the property of registered trade unions in their trustees for the use and benefit of the union and its members. In the Taff Vale case, this provision was interpreted as meaning that the property so held was the property of the union and that the union was the beneficial owner.[147] In this case, an injunction had initially been issued against the Amalgamated Society of Railway Servants by a High Court judge. The Court of Appeal unanimously disagreed with the injunction by stating that a registered union could not sue or be sued as it was not an entity known to the law. If anything, the 1871 Act implied "the exact contrary" of the judge's decision. However, the House of Lords agreed with the judge[148] and this ruling, as earlier noted, had left "a legacy of suspicion and mistrust [which was] to poison relations between the courts and the unions for many years".[149]

Not only was the Taff Vale ruling unexpected but also the size of the damages awarded against the union when in December 1902, the action for damages arising out of this case was finally heard. There, it was decided that the union should pay damages and legal costs amounting to a total of £42,000, almost two-thirds of the union's annual income. So the outcome of this case meant that any form of industrial action exposed trade unions to "incalculable financial risks".[150]

In view of this ruling in the Taff Vale case, the TUC, the following year, called for legislation so as to secure complete protection for trade union funds and a trade-union sponsored Bill to this effect in the House of Commons. Although defeated, this ruling set a motion in process which the Conservative Government at the time could hardly ignore.[151] This case was also significant in that it precipitated a rapid expansion in trade union affiliation to, and individual membership of, the Labour Representation Committee (LRC) which in turn led to the foundation of the Labour Party in 1906.[152] Being aware of the intense degree of

---

[146] See *Trade Union Immunities*, ..., p. 13, para. 44 and p. 14, para. 50.

[147] *Royal Commission on Trade Unions and Employers' Associations 1965-1968*, ..., , p. 209, para. 778.

[148] See Wedderburn, (Lord) K. W., *The Worker and the Law* ..., ..., p. 526.

[149] See Griffith, J. A. G., ..., p. 66.

[150] Steinmetz, Willibald, ..., p. 34.

[151] See *Trade Union Immunities*, ..., pp. 14f, paras. 49-54.

[152] See Pelling, Henry, *A Short History of the Labour Party* (Fourth Edition), The Macmillan Press Ltd., London and Basingstoke, 1972, pp. 11f.

trade union and working-class anger at the Taff Vale ruling together with the rising support for the LRC, the then Conservative Government was confronted with a major problem which it could not simply ignore. So, in a similar manner following the outcome of *Hornby v. Close* in 1867 and *R. v. Bunn* in 1872, another Royal Commission was to be established.

The main purpose of the Royal Commission, which was established in June 1903, was to consider the effect and if necessary the reform of the law as it had emerged from court rulings at the turn of the century, most notably in the *Quinn v. Leathem* and the Taff Vale cases.[153] The outcome of this Royal Commission plus the election of a Liberal Government in the 1906 general election, which also resulted in the first real influx of Labour MPs, was the 1906 Trade Disputes Act. The main provisions of this Act, as already noted, was that trade unions became immune from tort and this provision was extended to the organisers of industrial action, providing that it was "in contemplation or furtherance of a trade dispute". Thus, the historic significance of this Act was that it was only at that point when, generally, strike action or the threat of it ceased to be actionable, be it through the criminal or the civil law.

Leaving aside judicial attempts to undermine the provisions of the 1906 Act in later years, most notably through the House of Lords' ruling *Rookes v. Barnard* in 1964, where the Law Lords introduced the tort of intimidation, and the House of Lords' ruling in the case of *Stratford v. Lindley* in 1965 where the tort for breach of commercial contract was created (see pages 43f), the principle which had been established was that the judiciary be kept away from industrial disputes as far as possible. The reason for this is that any degree of impartiality one could claim the judiciary had ever had in the handling of industrial disputes was well and truly dashed in the Taff Vale case.

The ruling in the case of *Rookes v. Barnard* is the best example of illustrating that what Parliament had originally intended when it passed the 1906 Act was in no way "water-tight". In 1955 the Association of Engineering and Shipbuilding Draughtsmen (AESD) had a 100% registered membership agreement (closed shop agreement) at the design office of the British Overseas Airways Corporation (BOAC) at London airport. Due to a dispute between AESD and the BOAC, Rookes, having failed to persuade his union to take "direct action" against the company (favouring instead a resolution of the dispute through BOAC's negotiating procedure) resigned from the union. Therefore, under the terms of the membership agreement, which, incidentally, Rookes himself had helped to negotiate, he was no longer able to continue working there. Attempts to persuade Rookes to reconsider his decision failed. Eventually, the union threatened industrial action at the company if it didn't honour the terms of the membership agreement. Consequently, BOAC initially suspended Rookes and in March 1956 gave him

[153] See pp. 38f, footnote 99.

notice of dismissal. Rookes then sued three of the union's officials (the union's local branch chairman Barnard, one other local branch official Fistal and the union's divisional organiser Silverthorne) on the grounds that they wrongfully induced BOAC to dismiss him.[154] This case reached the High Court in 1961 which awarded damages totalling £7,500 against the defendants. In February 1962, the Court of Appeal unanimously overturned this ruling by maintaining that the plaintiff "had no cause of action in tort at common law; and if he had, the defendants would have been protected by the 1906 Act". In January 1964, however, the House of Lords upheld the original ruling in the High Court and thereby created a new liability – civil intimidation".[155]

Yet, as explained by Lord Wedderburn, there appeared to be no basis for the House of Lords to rule as it did. Firstly, there was no conspiracy to injure as the defendants had pursued legitimate trade union objectives. Secondly, there could be no liability for inducing a breach of contract as the plaintiff's employment contract had not been broken. Thirdly, even if either of these torts had been committed, the defendants would have been protected by the 1906 Act on the basis that they had acted in furtherance of a trade dispute.[156] Whereas the Court of Appeal had accepted that one of the major arguments against liability had been that intimidation as a tort should be confined to threats to commit acts of violence, the Law Lords, in justifying their ruling in *Rookes v. Barnard*, could be understood as placing the threat of strike action on a par with threats to commit acts of violence.[157] Thus, in the words of the Thatcher Government itself, "it seemed possible that whenever a trade union official threatened a strike he might be liable to be sued for intimidation"[158] (see page 44).

So the purpose of the 1965 Trade Disputes Act was not only to protect trade union officials from being sued for intimidation but also to reaffirm the original thinking behind the 1906 Act in that the judiciary should be kept out of industrial disputes (see page 41). The "policy" of seeking to keep the judiciary out of industrial disputes changed as from 1979, most notably through the 1982 Act.

---

[154] See Wedderburn, (Lord) K. W., *The Worker and the Law ...*, ..., pp. 39-42. See also Foley, Tony, *A Most Formidable Union: The History of DATA and TASS*, Manufacturing Science Finance (London), 1992, pp. 26f. NB In 1961, after a long and tedious process, AESD changed its name and became "The Draughtsmen and Allied Technicians' Association" (DATA) – see Foley, Tony, ..., pp. 5-8. See also pp. 24f, footnote 30.

[155] Wedderburn, (Lord) K. W., *The Worker and the Law ...*, ..., pp. 40f.

[156] Ibid., p. 41.

[157] See Welch, Roger, Judicial Mystification of the Law: Rookes v Barnard and the Return to Judicial Intervention, in: Ewing, K. D. (Ed.), *The Right to Strike: From the Trade Disputes Act 1906 to a Trade Union Freedom Bill 2006*, The Institute of Employment Rights (Liverpool), 2006, pp. 207-212.

[158] *Trade Union Immunities*, ..., p. 17, para. 68.

The key point in the 1982 Act was that the protection trade unions had from claims in tort was totally abolished though a union continued to have such protection as an "individual" where industrial action is taken "in contemplation or furtherance of a trade dispute",[159] subject of course to what remained within "the definition of a trade dispute" as narrowed by this Act. So, this Act revived the doctrine behind the House of Lords' ruling in the Taff Vale case from 1901 with the effect that unions themselves became once again liable to claims in tort for the actions of their officials if any industrial action fell outside "the definition of a trade dispute" as defined by this Act. Through this Act, the Thatcher Government opened the way for the judiciary to become involved in "settling" industrial disputes to an extent which had not been possible since 1906. Subsequently, the 1990 Act extended this provision to cover any "unofficial" action of its members unless the union took all possible steps in repudiating it. So, in making once again the union itself the defendant in industrial disputes, the Thatcher Government saw in the judiciary a powerful institution which could generally be relied upon to constrain industrial action with the added provision of unlimited fines and the sequestration of assets should the union find itself "in contempt of court".

The current status of a trade union, as defined by the 1992 Act, is that it is "not a body corporate" but it gives it "certain attributes of a body corporate". In this, a trade union can make contracts and sue and be sued in its own name and it can also be prosecuted.[160] It therefore seems, even if the Act itself is not specific, that where a claim does not concern a trade dispute, a union's liability in tort is the same as that of a natural person or corporate body.[161]

A further indication as to how the civil law was developing to restrain strike action can be seen in the outcome of the case of *Lyons v. Wilkins* (which, in fact, had been heard by the Court of Appeal twice – in 1896 and again in 1899). Although the 1875 Act restated the criminal offence of "watching or besetting" but excluded from that activity "attending at or near the house or place where a person resides, or works, or carries on business, or happens to be ... in order to obtain or communicate information", the Court of Appeal in the case of *Lyons v. Wilkins* in 1896 and subsequently again in 1899 decided against the officers of a trade union who, having made goods for the plaintiffs only, organised pickets to persuade workers not to work for them. There, it was ruled that the picketing went beyond obtaining and communicating information in that it was putting pressure on the plaintiffs by persuading people not to enter their employment. It was also decided that watching and besetting might be a nuisance under the

[159] Rogers, W. V. H., ... (Thirteenth Edition), ..., p. 527.

[160] Rogers, W. V. H., ... (Seventeenth Edition), ..., p. 831.

[161] Ibid.

common law and hence illegal.[162] The outcome of this case appeared to question the right to picket peacefully.[163]

The Trade Union Act, 1871, protected unions from the effects of the ruling in *Hornby v. Close* in what has been described as "a first step in an unspoken accommodation which was to last until 1979".[164] This "accommodation" was supposed to have been a "tacit treaty of mutual coexistence", whereby "trade unions were not to attempt to destroy capitalism and capitalism was not to attempt to destroy trade unionism".[165] Although there were skirmishes at various stages,[166] this "tacit treaty", by and large, remained intact until 1979.

For almost a century, the 1871 Act was thought to have confirmed the lawful civil status of union rules. Then, in a case in 1971 in which a worker had been wrongly excluded from membership of the then Society of Graphical and Allied Trades (SOGAT),[167] the judge ruled that the union executive's right to exclude membership "for any capricious reason" was invalid because it was "in restraint of trade". Interestingly, the judge was able to draw a distinction between the *rules* of the union and its *purposes*, and decided on this basis that the rule by which the SOGAT executive excluded this worker from membership was "not proper to the 'purposes' of this or indeed any trade union". This apparent loophole in the 1871 Act, which the judge had exploited, was then closed in the 1974 Act. Without this, a trade union could, in modern times, have once again become an unlawful association in the civil law.[168] In effect, the legality of trade unions under the civil law rests only on an "immunity" from the common law doctrine of "restraint of trade".

This "immunity" confirms one historical trend which is a special feature in the development of British labour law. The rights of workers to organise and bargain collectively, leading to the development of trade unions did not come into being on the basis of them being granted any positive rights. They were founded by working people and came into being in conditions of illegality.

The repeal of the Combination Acts should therefore not be seen in the context of trade unions being "allowed" to exist, but more of an "immunity" which was supposed to have lifted the bar on them under the criminal law. Almost half a century later, the "immunity" from the "restraint of trade" doctrine, in the aftermath of *Hornby v. Close*, was supposed to have erased their illegality under the

[162] Griffith, J. A. G., ..., p. 68.

[163] See Wedderburn, (Lord) K. W., *The Worker and the Law ...*, ..., p. 542.

[164] Hendy, John QC, ..., p. 15.

[165] Ibid.

[166] Ibid.

[167] See Wedderburn, (Lord) K. W., *The Worker and the Law ...*, ..., p. 522.

[168] Ibid.

civil law. Subsequently, the 1875 Act was passed to make workers immune from criminal proceedings in the event of industrial action resulting in a breach of the employment contract. Finally the Act of 1906 was passed in order to provide "immunities" in tort to trade unions and their officials when undertaking industrial action.

This whole historic development shows that the basis of workers' rights to organise and bargain collectively in Britain was founded on a system of "immunities" which lifted various bans and constraints on them, but did not, in effect, grant them any "positive" rights. The legislative measures in the 1980s should therefore be seen in the context of trying to reverse this historic development which, from the repeal of the Combination Acts right up to 1906, took the best part of a century to build up.

The 1974 Act confirmed the protection of trade unions from the "restraint of trade" doctrine. Even if in modern times, trade unions were still looked upon as being "in restraint of trade" under the common law, the 1982 Act, not withstanding its reintroduction of tort liabilities against trade unions themselves, did not go as far as altering the way in which the 1974 Act had generally settled the question of trade union status.[169]

Thus, on balance, the laws of the 1980s, which are now incorporated in the 1992 Act, have put legal protection to trade unions back to what it was before 1906 but have not gone as far as reviving the "restraint of trade" doctrine whose absence has provided a wide degree of protection to trade unions since 1871.

Conclusion

Following the downfall of the 1974-1979 Labour Government, the Thatcher Government saw in the judiciary as a powerful institution which could be relied upon to uphold its economic and "social" strategy in the event of an industrial challenge from organised labour. Thus a key element of its trade union laws was to revive the role of the judiciary, not only to expose trade union officials but, more importantly, the unions themselves in tort for industrial action deemed unlawful whereas, from 1906 to 1982 (leaving aside the period of the short-lived 1971 Act for unions which refused to register), they had this protection. In the 1982 Act (with its provisions being extended in 1990), a code on vicarious liability was introduced to expose trade union funds in tort unless union leaders and/or their officials and representatives were to take effective measures to "police" their rank and file.

[169] See Ibid., p. 529.

To put this another way, unions were told that they would have to take effective measures to ensure that their rank and file (and they themselves) did not do anything to disrupt the "free" market (outside the limited areas where industrial action remained protected by the law). Otherwise, their funds would be put in jeopardy. This in itself raises the question of what legality trade unions would have in a "free" market economy, even if such a thing were to become a reality. Workers organising and bargaining collectively would appear to be incompatible with such a concept. Calls for the repeal of all remaining "immunities" etc. would tend to confirm this conclusion.

The common law has proved to be an ideal legal system in the kind of management the "New" Right appears to have in mind for a "free" market economy. Its concept of "restraint of trade", as defined by the common law, means that trade unions obstruct the "free" market. The common law has the advantage for such "New" Right thinkers in that it enables the judges, on the basis of the laws passed in the 1980s, to restrain the unions without the Government being seen to become directly or indirectly involved in the way it was under the 1971 Act.

Indeed, a most revealing comment was made on this aspect of the matter by Lord Donaldson, then Master of the Rolls (previously, President of the short-lived NIRC), in a leaked conversation with the permanent secretary-designate at the Department of Employment in 1982. He described the law then as "putting the courts in the position of being almost entirely in the business of restricting or penalising the unions and not of remedying their grievances".[170]

Parallel to the legislative developments in the 1980s was the increasing role of the police and the revision of police tactics in countering mass picketing. If workers were prepared to take measures to defend their unions and livelihoods from what they see as unjust laws and court rulings, it is clear that the State understood, as the Thatcher Government clearly did, that contingency plans would have to be made and constantly reviewed and updated to ensure that the police would never again be "defeated" as they were at Saltley Gates during the 1972 miners' strike. Otherwise, laws, court rulings and injunctions deemed as unjust may not take hold.

All this leads to a further question which now needs answering. How did the labour movement respond to the degree of economic and industrial restructuring in the 1980s, the persistent passing of legislative measures so as to remove legal protection or to make illegal industrial practices on the part of trade unions and those acting on their behalf which previously had the protection of the law and more effective police tactics against workers actively involved in the pursuit of industrial disputes? And, perhaps more importantly, did the labour movement (both its political and industrial wings) offer any clear alternatives then and sub-

[170] Dickinson, Mark, *To Break a Union*, Booklist Ltd. (Manchester), 1984, p. 10.

sequently in the 1990s in the expectation of the Labour Party getting back into office?

Chapter Four: Fundamentals of the labour movement response to the economic and social developments of the 1980s and 1990s and to Conservative trade union legislation

4.1. The impact of the economic and social policies of the Thatcher Government on the trade union movement

There has been controversy, both within academic circles and in the labour movement itself, on how the trade union movement withstood the economic crisis of 1979-1981 and the subsequent developments on the economic and social fronts in its aftermath. Basically, two lines of argument can be identified.

On the one hand, one can point to some prominent industrial disputes where the unions lost or were weakened and draw the conclusion that the trade union movement had limited influence on the pace or form of industrial structuring which would lead to redundancies, particularly in manufacturing industry. One can then go on to claim that, as a result of this development trade unions lost a lot of influence. Without any doubt, increases in trade union membership in the latter half of the 1970s were more than wiped out by 1985, with membership continuing to decline throughout the rest of the 1980s (see Appendix, table 10). On this basis, in the aftermath of the 1984/1985 miners' strike, prominent historian Eric Hobsbawm could say that "British union militants" had "taken a good few beatings over the past six years",[1] but the question remains as to what extent they were weakened during the 1980s and what was their standing in the 1990s.

On the other hand, Jim Mortimer (formerly Chairman of ACAS and then Labour Party General Secretary) stated in 1987 that the loss of union membership had not been "as disproportionately heavy" as during previous periods of industrial depression. Pay increases negotiated for millions of workers, he noted, were at least equal to the rise in the cost of living. Further, at workplace level, unions had maintained their organisational roots and had even extended them.[2]

However, what needs to be remembered was that, while in opposition, the Conservative Party had made careful preparations on how economic and industrial restructuring was going to take shape in the context of their future monetarist framework without running the risk of repeating the experiences of the Heath Government. In this, in obvious recognition of the strength and influence of key sections of the trade union movement, the Conservative Government realised that there were limits on how far to go and what could be achieved in the short term.

---

[1] Hobsbawm, Eric, The Retreat into Extremism, in: Hobsbawm, Eric, *Politics for a Rational Left*, Verso (London and New York), 1989, p. 88.

[2] See Kelly, John, *Labour and the Unions*, Verso (London and New York), 1987, pp1f.

By officially having no incomes policy, the Thatcher Government was able to keep a formal distance from pay negotiations, especially in the private sector. This enabled many skilled and industrially well-organised groups of workers to negotiate wage increases which they found acceptable. On the other hand, unskilled workers and those industrially weak found themselves unable to secure satisfactory pay increases and their bargaining position was weakened further due to fears of unemployment. In this situation, the Thatcher Government, as it were, was able to divide skilled workers from the unskilled, the industrially strong from the industrially weak. Given the very high rates of interest (reaching record levels in Britain towards the end of 1979) leading to rising industrial fixed costs, an over-valued exchange rate and greater import penetration etc., those in relatively secure jobs were set against those whose jobs became more vulnerable. As result, many trade unions were hampered in developing united strategies for defending jobs and living standards.[3]

However, the policies of the previous Labour Government in carrying out "rationalisation" programmes in the public sector (as, for example, in British Leyland (BL) and the British Steel Corporation (BSC)) had in fact laid the foundations for the Thatcher Government to proceed further in that direction. This process was further assisted through the original introduction of *cash limits* in the public sector (see pages 60f). So, in a sense, no new government "initiative" on the economic front was needed as the pressure of high interest rates alone would have been enough to quicken the pace of industrial "restructuring". Industry, in general, had to become "leaner and fitter" and in the public sector, two corporations in particular were singled out in the initial phase: BL and the BSC. The National Coal Board (NCB) was to follow in a second phase (see below).

BL, a major producer of motor vehicles, collapsed in 1974/1975 due, according to a government enquiry conducted by Lord Ryder, to poor management and a lack of investment in the company.[4] Given the company's strategic importance to Britain's industrial base, the Labour Government was compelled to rescue it. This it did by bringing BL into public ownership (upon the recommendation of the Ryder Report). The Ryder Report envisaged major investment programmes so that BL could be re-established as a major producer of a broad range of motor vehicles. However, the prospect of a major publicly-owned company realising its full potential alarmed opponents of nationalisation, especially in industry, in prominent political circles and in the media. Bad media publicity (which was further aggravated by industrial relations problems) together with the difficulties the company had in overcoming the years of neglect under private ownership undermined continued Government support for the company on the basis of the

---

[3] See Winchester, David, Trade Unions and the Recession, in: *Marxism Today* (London), Vol. 25 No. 9, September 1981, pp. 23ff.

[4] See Interview with Derek Robinson, in: *Marxism Today* (London), Vol. 24 No. 3, March 1980, p. 6.

Ryder Report. Thus, the appointment of a new company chairman, Sir Michael Edwardes, in autumn 1977 must therefore be seen in the context of a change in Government policy on the future of BL.[5]

In so far as any commitment to Ryder remained, investment plans envisaged for expanding vehicle production were to run in tandem with "rationalisation" programmes. The first major step in this process was the announcement by the new BL chairman in winter 1978 that the company was to be split up into four companies as part of a major reorganisation programme. This aimed to cut the workforce by at least 12,500 and for this to be accompanied by plant closures.[6] So more emphasis was to be placed on short-term financial criteria than the long-term investment plans as envisaged by the Ryder Report. By autumn 1979, the company's workforce had been reduced to 165,000 employees,[7] representing a loss of 18,000 jobs since the winter 1978 reorganisation plan.[8] When one considers that in autumn 1979, for example, a total of 454,000 workers depended on BL for a job, not only those employed directly by the company but also those in firms making components for BL,[9] its importance for Britain as a manufacturing nation could not be underestimated.

The significance of the reorganisation programme became clearer in BL's "recovery plan" in September 1979. This involved further measures to "rationalise", or in Edwardes' term, to "streamline" the company. In what otherwise became known as the "Edwardes Plan", further plant closures were announced together with a further cut in the workforce "by not less than 25,000" over the following two-year period.[10] In anticipation of any possible resistance to the "recovery plan", ways were sought of forcing acceptance of it, and this is where the wider significance of the experiences at BL for the implementation of the Thatcher Government's policies towards organised labour becomes evident.

Although workers' interests in BL were represented by the various trade unions which were part of the Confederation of Shipbuilding and Engineering Unions (CSEU), there were often differences among the unions reflecting, for example, the various trades, skilled and unskilled workers and the problems of representing their interests collectively.[11] There were also differences between the shop

---

5 Ibid., pp. 6f.

6 See Address by Michael Edwardes to BL management and employee representatives in Birmingham on 1 February 1978 (unpublished).

7 Robinson, D. et. al., *The Edwardes Plan and your job*, Leyland Combine Trade Union Committee (Cookley, Nr. Kidderminster), undated (published autumn 1979), p. 10.

8 Ibid., pp. 7 and 14.

9 Ibid., p. 10.

10 Edwardes, Michael, Statement to all BL employees from the Chairman, 10 September 1979, p. 3 (unpublished).

11 See, Adams, Jack, in: Where are we now? A Roundtable Discussion, in: *Marxism Today*

stewards and full-time trade union officials. Additionally, in the words of the dismissed BL convener, Derek Robinson, implying criticism of his own union, "the AUEW used their inbuilt majority on the National Confed. to collapse the resistance to Edwardes shown by other unions".[12] On the pretext of "politically motivated shop stewards" not being "relied upon to put a balanced view [of the "recovery plan"] to employees", the company embarked upon the tactic of "appealing directly to the workers" by balloting them on this plan over the heads of the shop stewards.[13] In an 80% poll, the company secured the backing of 106,062 workers to 15,541 in support of its "recovery plan",[14] a 7 to 1 majority in favour.

So another aspect of the winter 1978 reorganisation plan became clear. It had the effect of putting plant against plant and worker against worker. Significantly, whereas the AUEW leadership supported the "recovery plan", the TGWU together with the company's leading shop stewards did not.[15] So, in the absence of unity among the company's workforce representatives, management was able to adopt a "divide and rule" policy and undermine the authority of the shop stewards in a company which was then Britain's seventh largest employer.

In the aftermath of this ballot, an alternative to the company's "recovery plan" challenging the closures and redundancies was published by a group of leading BL shop stewards.[16] For this, shop stewards' convenor, Derek Robinson, was subsequently dismissed by the company. It was clear that such a move must have been planned in advance,[17] for it seemed inconceivable by modern-day standards in Western Europe that a leading trade unionist could be simply dismissed by his employer for publishing proposals for safeguarding of jobs and the future of the company even if they differ from those of the company. The unions found themselves totally unprepared and virtually powerless when they attempted to mobilise industrial action to secure Robinson's reinstatement.[18]

In the wider context, this dismissal raises the question of why the previous Labour Government had originally made such an appointment to the chairmanship of BL. Partly, it no doubt relates to the long-standing policy of Labour's

(London), Vol. 24 No. 9, September 1980, pp. 21f.

12 Interview with Derek Robinson, ..., p. 8. When using the term "National Confed.", Robinson was referring to the CSEU in which the AUEW was a highly influential force.

13 McIlroy, John, *Trade Unions in Britain Today*, Manchester University Press (Manchester and New York), 1988, pp. 189f.

14 Pike, Alan, Massive backing for BL recovery plan, in: *Financial Times* (London and Frankfurt), 2 November 1979, p. 1.

15 See Smith, Arthur, The Sacking of Derek Robinson: Why BL risks crossing a bridge too far, in: *Financial Times* (London and Frankfurt), 24 November 1979, p. 20.

16 See footnote 7.

17 See Adams, Jack, ..., p. 22.

18 Ibid.

parliamentary leadership of seeking to curb the influence of shop stewards. It would have been linked in part to the aim of forcing through "rationalisation" measures in the public sector – its significance becoming clearer after the Conservative election victory in 1979 – to prepare for the eventual return of publicly-owned companies to the private sector. In BL, this involved taking on and breaking the influence of the shop stewards. This was to lead to the dismissal of the most prominent representative of the shop-floor workers in the company. So, whatever plans the Thatcher Government may have envisaged for BL, one thing became clear. An "industrial problem" was well on the way to being "solved" before it had taken office. In this, one cannot underestimate the significance of this particular appointment to the chairmanship of BL.

It is perhaps in the events leading up to and surrounding the dismissal of Derek Robinson where the impact of the changes in the leadership of the AUEW in the mid to late 1970s were to become openly evident. In a series of elections, the advances made by the left over the previous decade were reversed. This culminated in spring 1978 with the election of Terry Duffy to succeed Hugh Scanlon as the union's president. Whereas the AUEW and the TGWU, under the influence of the left, had often "spoken with one voice" on key industrial issues which then "set the pace" for the entire labour movement e.g. in resistance to the 1971 Act, this was neither the case when it came to the BL recovery plan, as already noted, nor was this so when BL workers at the company's Longbridge plant in Birmingham reacted to Robinson's dismissal by instantly walking out. Whereas the TGWU was expected to make the strike "official",[19] the executive council of the AUEW (Robinson's own union), through the influence of its then general secretary, Sir John Boyd, had unexpectedly stopped short of endorsing such action – the reason given that there was "too much at risk with the jobs of thousands of car workers"![20] So, the spontaneous strike action collapsed.

The AUEW, by supporting BL's "recovery plan", then found itself in a tricky situation in how to respond to this dismissal. The only option available which could have secured Robinson's reinstatement was industrial action with the full support of all the unions organised in BL. For the AUEW leadership as with any other union in the company, there was no "middle way". For whatever reservations may have been expressed, one thing would have been certain. Had the AUEW made such action "official", an all-out strike by workers at BL would have had wide-ranging economic implications on much of Britain's manufacturing base, particularly in the Midlands. No government could have ignored this. But faced with the choice of giving Robinson the industrial support needed to secure his reinstatement or not, the decision of the AUEW executive council had the effect of leaving Robinson to his fate.

[19] Smith, Arthur, ...

[20] Pike, Alan, Man of the Week: Back from the brink, in: *Financial Times* (London and Frankfurt), 1 December 1979, p. 35.

Comparing Robinson's dismissal with the recognition dispute at the engineering firm Con-Mech in 1973/1974, there were for the AUEW, as would have been the case with any other union, fundamental principles at stake. Whereas the then leadership of the AUEW, even if only on the casting vote of its then president, Hugh Scanlon, called an all-out strike when the National Industrial Relations Court ordered the sequestration of the union's assets for its persistent refusal to abide the NIRC's rulings (see pages 52f), the AUEW leadership in autumn 1979 stopped short of reacting in a similar way to secure Robinson's reinstatement. Similarly, the extent of the AUEW's uncompromising stand against the 1971 Act as a whole was in no reflected when it came to the Thatcher Governments trade union laws a decade later (see below).

Similarly, one can see how the way was cleared for a drastic "rationalisation" programme in the British steel industry. Indeed, there is an interesting comparison between BL and the BSC in that the steel industry under private ownership was, like BL up to 1974, poorly managed and in financial difficulties and had to be rescued by the state because of the industry's strategic importance. So, it was rescued by the Labour Government in 1967 through renationalisation (the steel industry had previously been nationalised in 1951 and then "denationalised" in 1953).

The main purpose of re-nationalising the steel industry was to "socialise" the costs of the massive modernisation programme required to bring the industry up to the technological level of Britain's major competitors, reverse the flow of imports and move into export markets.[21] BSC's modernisation programme envisaged the closure of small plants and the concentration of steel production in five big sites. In its *Ten Year Development Strategy* published in 1973, BSC envisaged the concentration of steel production in South Wales, Scotland, Teeside, Sheffield and Scunthorpe, with an annual production capacity expanding from 27 to 36 million tonnes.[22]

However, British Steel's modernisation programme depended on a continual expansion in the demand for steel in the latter half of the 1970s. In the aftermath of the world economic crisis in 1974, this did not materialise. In fact, expanding world demand for steel in the post-war years peaked in the early 1970s, and subsequently, with a contraction in demand for steel, British Steel had difficulties in marketing its products. The problem was aggravated in part by the poor quality of its output in comparison with that of other steel-producing nations. Additional problems for the renationalised industry were the provision for generous compensation for the assets taken into public ownership and its concentration on the production of bulk steel while a profitable private sector which concentrated on

[21] Kelly, John, Steel – an irreversible decline?, in: *Marxism Today* (London), Vol. 25 No. 6, June 1981, p. 10.

[22] Ibid.

special steels remained. In this, the division between the public and private sectors operated in a way that the former guaranteed the profitability of the latter.[23]

Following the renationalisation of the steel industry in 1967, the steel unions, particularly the Iron and Steel Trades Confederation (ISTC), could legitimately claim to have cooperated with the industry's modernisation and efficiency programmes. In the ten-year period up to 1979, the then General Secretary of the ISTC, Bill Sirs, was able to point to the union's "moderate" wage settlements and to a long list of agreed plant closures leading to the loss of over 100,000 jobs over the ten-year period as a whole, 40,000 of them being in the final two years.[24] The loss of jobs in this two-year period had been intensified by the imposition of *cash limits* on British Steel (a consequence of the IMF loan conditions at the end of 1976) leading to an even faster programme of closures so that investment in new capacity could be funded.[25]

An additional problem facing the steel industry seemed to be the apparently unfair treatment meted out to Britain in the EEC through the allocation of steel production quotas among its member states. In the period 1972 to 1984, for example, Britain appeared to be required to carry out a disproportionately large share of the contraction in steel production while Italy was able to increase her output. Similarly, regarding steel producing capacity in the EEC in the ten-year period 1973 to 1983, Britain was obliged to cut back whilst other member states were able to increase theirs (see Appendix, table 13). Put differently, in 1978, Britain produced 15% of the EEC's steel but had to shoulder 40% of the planned cutback in steel production in 1980.[26] However, the EEC's steel policy appeared to be compatible with the British Government's policy of seeking to "rationalise" the steel industry and the implications of such a policy on the future of Britain's coal mining industry is self-evident.

A further problem for the British steel industry was that many European governments subsidised the coking coal used in steel production to a greater extent than in Britain[27] (this factor, of course, was also significant for the coal mining industry). In addition, energy costs had been reported as being 40 to 50% higher in Britain than in many other European countries[28] (even though Britain was then

---

23 Fine, Ben and Poletti, Clara, Industrial Prospects in the Light of Privatisation, in: Michie, Jonathan (Ed.), *The Economic Legacy 1979-1992*, Academic Press (London and San Diego), 1992, pp. 325f.

24 The General Secretary (Bill Sirs), Notes and Comments, in: *Man and Metal*, The Journal of the Iron and Steel Trades Confederation (London), Vol. 56 No. 10, December 1979, p. 293.

25 Fine, Ben and Poletti, Clara, ..., p. 326.

26 Kelly, John, ..., p. 11.

27 Ibid.

28 Ibid.

the only EEC member state which was self-sufficient in coal, oil and gas). Taking all these factors together, other European steel producing nations seemed to be able to sell their steel more cheaply and make higher profits than was possible for BSC.[29]

With demand for steel not reaching the levels as had originally been anticipated for the latter half of the 1970s, the Department of Industry published a revised programme for the corporation in 1978, *The Road to Viability*, which envisaged further plant closures and job losses.[30] On the basis of this revised programme, the then BSC Chairman in December 1979, Charles Villiers, announced that the workforce of 167,000 would have to be cut by a further 50,000 and capacity reduced to a little over 15 million tonnes.[31]

However, it was the announcement in autumn 1979 of the planned closure the following year of the steel works in Corby which indirectly led to the national steel strike at the beginning of 1980. Previously, the Corby works had supposedly had "an assured long term future as a major tube making plant".[32] When, early in 1979, it was hinted that the steel works in Corby might be closed, the steel workers in the town formed a local defence committee involving other sections of the community. As a result, when the closure announcement was made on 1 November, 1979, the steel workers' reaction was immediate. The ISTC called for an overtime ban and for a series of selective sanctions against the BSC with the aim of forcing the Government to keep Corby open and to stem the tide of closures.[33]

The already severe financial constraints on the BSC had been made worse due to the fact that the Bank of England's MLR reached record levels by the end of 1979, having jumped from 12% to 17% within the first six months of the Thatcher Government taking office. So, the scene was set for an industrial conflict. A pay offer of just 2% on basic rates at the end of 1979 (at a time when inflation was running at 17%)[34] should be judged in this context. The wider question is whether a confrontation was provoked in order to force through further closures and redundancies in BSC and if so, could a parallel be drawn to the "rationalisation" measures in BL? One thing is certain. As far as the public sector was concerned, the "Ridley Report", leaked to the weekly journal *The Economist* in

---

29 Ibid.

30 Ibid.

31 Ibid.

32 Ibid., p. 12.

33 Rowthorn, Bob, Corby and the Steel Crisis, in: *Marxism Today* (London), Vol. 23 No. 12, December 1979, p. 2.

34 Kelly, John, ..., p. 12.

1978 (whilst the Conservatives were in opposition) saw BSC and BL as easy targets for a future Conservative Government's "rationalisation" plans.[35]

On the other hand, the fact that the steel strike lasted for three months suggested that the Government and the BSC had underestimated the determination of the steel workers who finally secured an increase of 11% on basic rates with an additional productivity bonus of 4.5%. The loss of earnings over this three-month period was a high price to be paid for this settlement. It caused disunity within the ranks of the ISTC and other unions organised in BSC. This, the newly appointed BSC Chairman in 1980, Ian MacGregor, exploited. In December 1980, in a manner similar to that of Michael Edwardes in British Leyland, he successfully imposed a ballot on the BSC's survival programme on the company's employees, by-passing the unions. As a result, the steel unions were unable to resist further closures and redundancies.[36] This is evident in that, in the first four years of the Thatcher Government, BSC shed 105,000 jobs[37] representing the bulk of its workforce. In this, the endeavours on the part of the Thatcher Government for its longer term aims for the industry paid off: it was "re-privatised" in November 1988. In that year, the output of steel, having fallen to just 11.9 million tonnes in 1981 (compared to 24.7 million tonnes in 1971) had risen to almost 15 million tonnes whereas the total workforce fell to just 52,000.[38]

On the part of the ISTC leadership, there were tactical errors in its conduct of the dispute. Although wages were an important issue, there was the failure to couple the wages struggle as part of a coordinated campaign to guarantee the long-term future of BSC and Britain as a major steel-producing nation. The fact that the ISTC did not call out steel workers in the private sector at the beginning of the strike[39] can be regarded as another tactical error on the part of the union's leadership.

So the outcome of the steel strike and the events leading up to the dismissal of Derek Robinson in BL were milestones for the longer term future the Thatcher Government, even before it had taken office, had envisaged for these industries: privatisation or, more precisely, "re-privatisation". There, it was the policies of the previous Labour Government, imposed or otherwise, which had laid the foundations for these "rationalisation" programmes in BL and BSC to be forced through.

As far as the trade union movement was concerned, an important outcome of the steel strike was the formation of the Triple Alliance involving the steelworkers,

35 Appomattox or Civil War, in: *The Economist* (London), 27 May 1978, p. 22.

36 Kelly, John, ..., p. 14.

37 *Coal, Rail and Steel*, NUM et. al. (London), undated (published 1983), p. 5.

38 Fine, Ben and Poletti, Clara, ..., pp. 326f.

39 Kelly, John, ..., pp. 12f.

miners and railwaymen.[40] These publicly-owned industries were inter-related in that the fortunes of one directly affected the fortunes of the other two. As a result, workers in these three industries realised that a coordinated strategy was needed to defend their jobs and livelihoods.

Thus, during its first period in office (1979-1983), the Thatcher Government succeeded in securing a significant degree of "rationalisation" in the public sector without having to take much in the way of policy initiatives. The more significant confrontation – the year-long miners' strike – was yet to come.

If the Thatcher Government was going to succeed with its economic and industrial policies, it had to be able to overcome any possible opposition to them, especially from trade unions contemplating industrial action to protect the jobs and livelihoods of their members who were likely to fall victim to any mass "shaking out" of British industry. The "winter of discontent" (autumn 1978/-winter 1979) was a clear reminder of the fact that the trade union movement was a force to be reckoned with and that the Conservatives could ill afford another battering on the industrial relations scene such as the Heath Government had endured.

It was therefore significant that, whilst in opposition, the Conservative Party under Thatcher's leadership had commissioned a series of studies on the problems a future Conservative Government might face from the unions. There, two reports were of specific importance.

Firstly, there was the so-called Carrington Report, commissioned in 1975. This sought to draw conclusions from Heath's downfall. It looked at how strategically placed groups of workers, particularly power workers and miners, with strong unions, could confront the power of the state, assuming they were prepared to use the strike weapon. In this case, the feeling was that alternatives had to be sought to a full showdown with the miners[41] because it was feared that, in such strategic sectors of the economy, the Government might not be able to win an all-out industrial confrontation.[42] However, if the economic and industrial policies of a future Conservative government were to have any credibility in the eyes of its supporters, it could not resign itself to the fact that certain trade unions were likely to be more powerful than the government so a second report was commissioned. This was the Ridley Report, already referred to. This Report sought how to deal with the problems which had been raised in the Carrington Report.

---

[40] Ibid., p. 13.

[41] McIlroy, John, *The permanent revolution? Conservative law and the trade unions*, Spokesman (Nottingham), 1991, p. 21.

[42] Geary, Roger, *Policing industrial disputes: 1893 to 1985*, Cambridge University Press, 1985, p. 96.

The Ridley Report suggested that there should be no direct government control over prices or wages in nationalised industries. This would enable workers in key industries to secure above-average wage increases while the government took on those who were not so industrially strong. It also went on to call for the recruitment of strike breakers, building up the strength and flexibility of the police, planning carefully before taking on any challenge in a strategic industry (e.g. mining or power) and legislating to control picketing and "to cut off the money supply to the strikers, and make the union finance them".[43]

Whilst the Ridley Report predicted that there would be conflicts in the public sector, a confrontation with the miners was felt to be the most likely ground upon which a battle would be fought.[44] The traditional strength of the miners as a powerful industrial force was something the Conservative Party was clearly all too aware of. However, if a future Conservative Government was to succeed in restructuring nationalised industries within its tight monetary framework (i.e. as a first step towards eventual privatisation), an industrial confrontation, especially with the miners, had to be prepared for. The Conservatives had to make preparations that would ensure victory on a terrain where Edward Heath had previously been defeated.

In preparation for a possible conflict with the miners, the following measures were felt necessary: building up stocks of coal, particularly at power stations; making contingency plans for importing coal; encouraging hauliers to recruit non-union drivers; introducing dual coal/oil firing in all power stations; creating a large, mobile squad of police to deal with picketing; cutting off money (i.e. social benefits) to strikers and making the union finance them.[45]

It was clear that the full resources of the State had to be mobilised in the event of a national miners' strike. However, with the experience of the discredited 1971 Act still in the minds of Conservative leaders and realising that legislative measures may be ineffective or could make matters worse, the Ridley Report made no specific recommendations as to industrial relations legislation as part of any preparations for a miners' strike or come to that any other major strike in the public sector. The only legislation this Report recommended, to which it itself referred to as "a nasty little bill" would be to end "statutory monopolies in the public sector"[46] so as to expose nationalised industries, with specific emphasis on the NCB, to increased competition from the private sector.

Picketing as a means of pursuing an industrial dispute had long been seen as an established industrial practice, even if employers and the State disapproved of it.

---

[43] Appomattox or Civil War, ..., pp. 21f.

[44] Ibid., p. 22.

[45] Ibid.

[46] Ibid., p. 21.

However, this practice took on a new form during the 1972 miners' strike which alarmed the Heath Government especially after the events at the Saltley coke depot in Birmingham. Instead of picketing just at their own pits, miners were sent to picket coal depots and power stations (becoming known as "flying pickets").

The successful use of mass picketing by the National Union of Mineworkers (NUM) at Saltley marked a turning point in the 1972 miners' strike. The strike had already resulted in stocks of coal and supplies of electricity falling to "dangerously low levels" which was affecting other industries and leading to workers being laid off. (By 18th February, 1.6 million workers had been laid off and coal stocks were only sufficient for about two weeks supply of electricity.) The Government declared a state of emergency on 9th February, 1972, and the introduction of a three-day week as from the 11th coupled with restrictions on office heating and display-lighting. It was when, on 10th February, 15,000 pickets, compared with just 800 police, successfully forced the closure of the Saltley coke depot (the only major coal distribution point still in operation), that the Government realised that it could not "win" the dispute. Consequently, a Court of Inquiry (under Lord Wilberforce) was set up to settle the dispute. The strike ended on 25th February.[47]

Mass picketing had also been resorted to in the summer of the same year in the Neap House Wharf dispute which arose out of the NIRC issuing arrest warrants on the five London dockers (the "Pentonville Five").[48] In this dispute, the police were determined that they were not going to be overwhelmed as they were at Saltley. With smaller numbers of pickets involved, the police, who had also revised their tactics following Saltley, were able to match the numerical strength of the pickets. Mass picketing was not resorted to again in industrial conflicts until the Grunwick dispute in 1977.[49]

The events at Saltley, in which it can be said that the police "lost" in the face of mass picketing, led to a review of police tactics and organisation so as to guard against any repetition of this. This review of police organisation led to the revitalisation of their mutual aid system, the establishment of the National Recording Centre and the introduction of techniques such as the "wedge" in police order training.[50] Through the National Recording Centre, a mechanism was developed by which the police could centrally coordinate the mobilisation of large numbers of its personnel through Police Support Units (PSU) from various parts of the country and deploy them at "trouble spots", be they industrial or otherwise. Every PSU consisted of 34 officers who trained once a month on public order operations, with the rest of their time being devoted to normal poli-

[47] See Geary, Roger, ..., pp. 73-77.

[48] Ibid., p. 78.

[49] Ibid., p. 83.

[50] Ibid., p. 134.

cing duties. In this, they differed from Special Patrol Groups (SPG) which constituted a permanent mobile reserve force.[51] So, in the event of any industrial disputes, the police would be able to tackle mass picketing with greater effect and efficiency than ever before. Examples of this could be seen in the Neap House Wharf dispute in 1972, the Grunwick dispute in 1977, the national steel strike in 1980 and in the Messenger Newspaper Group dispute in autumn 1983.[52]

Although the police were able to cope with mass picketing in the national steel strike (which mostly occurred in South Yorkshire), difficulties had been noticed in their response to this. For half a century, the police had had mutual aid arrangements at local level whereby they could call upon other local police forces for reinforcements when necessary. However, the steel strike had shown that the cost of financing such operations could cause problems for local authorities with the police having to work for longer hours which included having to travel considerable distances to picket lines.[53] As a result, the then Chief Constable of South Yorkshire, James Brownlow, suggested that a national contingency fund to cover the cost of policing national strikes might be needed and, possibly, also a stand-by force when national emergencies or problems arise.[54]

Rioting in the St. Pauls district of Bristol in April 1980, even though it was not in any way connected with an industrial dispute, also confirmed that there were weaknesses in the police mutual aid arrangements.[55] In anticipation of a national miners' strike, this apparent weakness had to be attended to.

Although the Home Office rejected the suggestions made by the then Chief Constable of South Yorkshire for a permanent mobile reserve force on a national basis, what emerged was a revised command structure whereby PSUs at local level could be centrally mobilised, coordinated and deployed.[56] This meant that the policing of national strikes could be handled by the National Recording Centre with the Association of Chief Police Officers coordinating local forces. It should be added that, in such situations, the police would come under the direct control of their own hierarchical and internal disciplinary structures, so that any "democratic accountability" at local or national level would be by-passed. In addition, PSUs had been formed, trained and equipped for riot control.[57]

---

[51] Ibid., p. 101.

[52] Ibid., pp. 134f.

[53] Kettle, Martin, The National Reporting Centre and the 1984 Miners' Strike, in: Fine, Bob and Millar, Robert, *Policing the Miners' Strike*, Lawrence and Wishart (London), 1985, p. 28.

[54] Ibid.

[55] Ibid., pp. 28f.

[56] Ibid., p. 29.

[57] See Fine, Bob and Millar, Robert, Introduction, in Fine, Bob and Millar, Robert, ..., p. 13.

Parallel to the police revising mutual its aid arrangements, there was a further extension of police powers which was to be of importance in the 1984/1985 miners' strike. As most of the miners in Nottinghamshire, then a major coal field, refused to support this strike, it was inevitable that this coalfield would witness major clashes between pickets and the police. In view of this, the police assumed powers allowing them to control tightly the movement of pickets from one part of the country to another. In this way, the police wanted to make sure that they would not be "defeated" again as they had been at Saltley in 1972 and the ultimate aim of this was to help the Thatcher Government break the strike.

At the same time, especially in Nottinghamshire, the police sought to arrest as many of the pickets as possible so as to take them out of circulation. In addition, the courts appeared to support the police strategy by imposing bail conditions on arrested pickets which, in effect, prevented them from taking any further active part in the strike. Such bail conditions included preventing miners from picketing except at their usual place of employment. In the case of miners from Yorkshire, bail conditions often included them being prevented from entering Nottinghamshire.[58] These developments were to show how far the State had moved in preparing for a major industrial conflict so the revision of police tactics were to be a factor which influenced the final of the 1984/1985 miners' strike.

The 1984/1985 miners' strike, lasting three days short of a year, was the longest national industry-wide strike in British history. The cause of this strike was the Government's policy of "rationalising" the coal mining industry through the closure of what it regarded as uneconomic pits. After nearly two decades of "enforced contraction" of the coal mining industry, the sudden increase in oil prices at the end of 1973 led the newly elected Labour Government the following year to review official policy towards the industry as coal had become cheaper than oil. The aim of this policy review as outlined in *Plan for Coal* was for Britain to make full productive use of her vast coal reserves so as to reduce her dependence on oil, to give the industry a more strategic role in the economy and for public funds to be made available for new investment in the industry.[59] *Plan for Coal* envisaged a major capital investment programme of up to £1,400m (at 1974 prices) for the ten-year period up to 1985.[60]

Plan for Coal was also supported by the NUM since it envisaged a modern efficient industry with a long-term investment programme. One reason for the miners' strike lay in the Thatcher Government's departure from *Plan for Coal* in favour of what were regarded as commercial criteria with a view to the eventual privatisation of the industry. Another reason for this strike must be seen in the

[58] Christian, Louise, Restriction Without Conviction: The Role of the Courts in Legitimising Police Control in Nottinghamshire, in: Fine, Bob and Millar, Robert, ..., p. 124.

[59] See *Plan for Coal*, National Coal Board, June 1974.

[60] Ibid., p. 12.

Government's response to the standing of the NUM as probably the most powerful and militant trade union in Britain at the time. It must also be remembered that the previous Conservative Government had been defeated twice in industrial conflicts with the miners – in 1972 and 1974. These two reasons are connected because if the Government was to succeed in the privatisation of the coal mining industry, it had to take on and defeat "the leading arm" of the trade union movement and this had an added degree of urgency especially after the experiences of 1972 and 1974. The only question facing the Thatcher Government was when to act as such a conflict had to be well prepared.[61]

The events leading up to the strike are worth noting. In February 1981, plans were announced for the closure of between 20 and 50 pits and this brought Britain to the brink of a national miners' strike. In face of this, the Government temporarily withdrew the closure plans, relaxed the financial constraints on the NCB and reduced coal imports.[62]

However, in the following period (1981-1983), the NUM leadership was defeated in three successive membership ballots over pit closures and pay. The Thatcher Government capitalised on this in portraying the NUM leadership as being out of touch with its members.[63] In the four-year period 1979/1980 to 1982/-1983, jobs in coal mining fell from 232,500 to 207,600 with many of them lost through the closure of 36 pits. Almost half of these jobs, i.e. 10,900, were lost in the year 1982/1983 alone.[64] This showed that the NCB was able to close pits on a one-by-one basis. In 1982, the NUM made public NCB documents showing 75 pits as having a "short life" along with plans to reduce the workforce by 70,000 over the following four years. The following year, Norman Siddall, the then NCB chairman, stated that 65,000 jobs would have to be lost for the Coal Board to break even by 1987/1988.[65] Clearly, *Plan for Coal* had long since been abandoned.

The Government based its case for pit closures on its own profit and loss criteria. These criteria were questionable. For example, a large part of the subsidies to the industry went back to the Government in the form of interest payments which, by the time the miners' strike began, had already been high for some years. Also, it was shown in a study prepared for the NUM, which included a pit-by-pit analysis, that the value of the output of coal from the threatened pits was well in excess of any losses which could be claimed in keeping them open.[66]

---

61 Hain, Peter, *Political Strikes*, Penguin (Harmondsworth, Middlesex), 1986, p. 226.

62 *The miners' case*, Labour Research Department (London), 1.10. 1984, p. 5.

63 Hain, Peter, ..., p. 226.

64 *Coal, Rail and Steel*, ..., p. 5.

65 *The miners' case*, ..., p. 5.

66 See Glyn, Andrew, *The Economic Case Against Pit Closures*, National Union of Mineworkers (Sheffield), undated – published 1984.

Additionally, state subsidies to the coal mining industry and the cost of coal production per tonne of output in Britain were shown to be low in comparison with those of other EEC member states. In 1982, for example, the cost of coal production per tonne of output was £61 in Belgium, £45 in France, £47 in West Germany and £41 in Britain. Likewise for the same year, state subsidies per tonne of output in these countries were £16.97 in Belgium, £17.63 in France, £9.48 in West Germany and in Britain just £3.24.[67] Clearly, the Coal Board's case for pit closures on economic grounds was not convincing. The motive for closing "uneconomic" pits appeared to be more political – related to the eventual aim of privatising the industry and, associated with this, the goal of weakening "the leading arm" of the trade union movement.

With the 1983 election out of the way, the final touches were made to what very much looked like a planned showdown with the miners. Note was also taken of what was felt to be the provocative appointment of the previous BSC Chairman, Ian MacGregor, to the chairmanship of the NCB in September 1983, especially following the large number of plant closures and redundancies in British Steel under his chairmanship. At the same time, note was also taken of an unwillingness of miners to strike against pit closures in South Wales and Scotland in winter 1983/1984,[68] although a national overtime ban had already begun in autumn 1983 in pursuit of a pay claim.[69]

The Government avoided a national miners' strike in winter 1981 through the temporary withdrawal of pit closure plans as the then Energy Secretary, David Howell, later inferred, "neither the Government nor I think that society as a whole was in a position to get locked into a coal strike". In "those days stocks weren't so high ... The whole NUM and trade union movement tended to be united on one side".[70] On this basis, the Government "held its fire" until March 1984 when stocks of coal were high, when the police and road haulage companies were ready, when summer was coming, and when morale among trade unionists amidst mass unemployment was low, following major defeats in BL and British Steel etc..[71] Thus, the announcement in March 1984 of a large number of pit closures leading to the loss of at least another 20,000 jobs provoked the strike.[72]

The miners had been united in 1972 and 1974 when the issue was pay which directly affected all miners. This was not the issue in 1984/1985. One group of miners, largely Nottinghamshire based, refused to support the strike. The reason

[67] *The miners' case*, ..., p. 4, Table 1.

[68] Hain, Peter, ..., p. 226.

[69] *The miners' case*, ..., p. 5.

[70] See Coates, David, *The Crisis of Labour*, Philip Allan (Oxford and New Jersey), 1989, p. 129.

[71] Ibid.

[72] See *The miners' case*, ..., pp. 5, 9, and 12.

given was that the NUM had recently decided that a delegate conference should have the final say in calling a national strike rather than the individual miners through a pithead ballot as had previously been the practice of the union.

The fact that the NUM did not conduct a pithead ballot has raised questions of whether its leadership made a tactical error in pursuit of the strike by not seeking the "legitimacy of the ballot". One thing is clear. The overwhelming majority of miners supported the strike by actively taking part in it – a point which the NUM President at the time, Arthur Scargill, has persistently emphasised. Furthermore, even if there had been such a ballot endorsing the strike, it is by no means certain that miners in "moderate" areas like Nottinghamshire would have respected its outcome[73] even though some of them claimed they would have. One reason for doubting this is that when in 1977/1978, a national NUM ballot rejected a productivity scheme, the Nottinghamshire miners, followed by other "moderate" areas, agreed to its introduction on a local basis.[74]

The Nottinghamshire miners had a "right wing tradition" dating back to the inter-war years[75] when they broke away from the Miners' Federation of Great Britain (MFGB, today, the NUM) after the 1926 General Strike and formed what was in effect a "company union". This was the Notts. Miners' Industrial Trade Union, better known as the "Spencer Union" after the Nottinghamshire Miners' leader and Labour MP, George Spencer.

The eventual collapse of the "Spencer Union" in 1937 was the culmination of a ten-year struggle by the MFGB and its Nottinghamshire area body – the Notts. Miners' Association – for one union in the industry independent of the employers. Up to then, the NMA had existed in conditions of semi-legality and the Nottinghamshire mine owners only recognised the "Spencer Union". The prelude to its collapse occurred in November 1936 when miners at a local pit in the Nottinghamshire village of Harworth went on strike in support of 25 miners who had been dismissed for simply being NMA members. This strike, which resulted in the imprisonment of eleven of the 25 miners plus one miner's wife destroyed any remaining credibility of the "Spencer Union". In the midst of all these developments, the MFGB felt confident enough to organise a national strike ballot in April 1937 to enforce recognition of the NMA. In a 98.9% poll, 444,456 miners voted for strike action with 61,445 against. The decisiveness of this strike ballot was also reflected among NMA members. The Nottinghamshire mine owners were compelled to accept the outcome of this ballot and terms were agreed by what was left of the "Spencer Union" to merge with the NMA.[76]

[73] Hain, Peter, ..., p. 228.

[74] Ibid.

[75] Ibid.

[76] See Westacott, Fred, Struggle for miners' unity, in: *Morning Star* (London), 19 February 1987, p. 6.

Spencerism, as this development became known, emerged again in the 1984/-1985 strike, once more in Nottinghamshire by miners opposed to the strike by breaking away from the NUM. This came about through the formation of the so-called Union of Democratic Mineworkers (UDM) whose membership was largely Nottinghamshire based. Whether this development was really aggravated through the absence of a pithead ballot remains a controversial question.

One reason for this was that as the planned pit closures were largely concentrated in the Scottish, Yorkshire and South Wales coal fields rather than in the Midlands areas like Nottinghamshire, it is by no means certain that the Nottinghamshire miners, given their past, to mention nothing of higher earnings through more technologically advanced pits, would have displayed any degree of solidarity with miners in other coal fields.[77] It is also worth noting that in the 1979 and 1983 elections, a number of traditional mining constituencies in the Midlands went Conservative.[78]

It is worth noting that in the miners' strike (in contrast to the two major disputes in the printing industry – see below), the NCB and the Government hesitated about using the provisions of the 1980 and 1982 Acts against the miners. On 14 March, 1984, for example, the NCB secured a High Court injunction against the Yorkshire area of the NUM to stop it from organising "flying" pickets (i.e. picketing in other areas) and to order it to withdraw instructions to its members to picket. Yet, although the Yorkshire miners disregarded the injunction and continued picketing, five days later, the NCB sought and was granted "an indefinite adjournment of its contempt of court application" against the Yorkshire area.[79] This strange turnabout on the part of the NCB can lead to the conclusion that, either it subsequently felt, or was "advised", that this court action, if continued further, would have perhaps unnecessarily widened the dispute which was still in its early stages.

Although attempts were made to use the civil law against the miners, this was only done by individual miners who did not support the strike and by one private company – Read Transport Ltd.. These actions led to the NUM at both area and national level being fined and having their assets sequestrated, but their actual impact was of limited significance. Apart from this, the NUM, in anticipation of legal action against it, had secretly moved most of its funds abroad.[80]

However, the reluctance on the part of the State or any public corporation to use the trade union laws against the miners (British Rail and British Steel, for exam-

[77] Hain, Peter, ..., p. 228.

[78] Ibid.

[79] Hanson, Charles G., Economic Significance of British Labor Law Reform, in: *Cato Journal*, Vol. 6(3), Cato Institute (Washington D. C., USA), Winter 1987, pp. 859f.

[80] Ibid., p. 860.

ple, could have done so due to the "blacking" of the movement of coal) can also be seen in the context of not wanting to widen the dispute. Nevertheless, when the authorities decided that the law on picketing was going to be upheld, ruthless use was to be made of what was in effect a new military-type police force. This had marked a qualitative change in the policing of industrial disputes in comparison with those of the previous decade. The policing of the News International dispute of 1986/1987 (see below) took on a similar form.

Ultimately, the key to the outcome of the strike would depend on whether or not the economy continued to function without major disruptions. The miners' strikes of 1972 and 1974 had resulted in power cuts, the introduction of a three-day week and, in the end victory for the miners. In 1984/1985, however, detailed advanced planning on the part of the Thatcher Government succeeded in avoiding power cuts and economic disruption on the scale of 1972 and 1974. Coal supplies, using private haulage companies, got through and additionally, oil supplemented coal in power stations. An additional factor in influencing the outcome of the strike was that unions in the power industry, especially the EETPU, refused to support the miners with its future General Secretary Eric Hammond actually insisting that its members "would carry out their normal duties, and that means crossing [NUM] picket lines",[81] fully disregarding a long-standing trade union practice in that trade unionists should never cross a trade union picket line. These factors, rather than any failure to seek the "legitimacy of the ballot" were, on balance, decisive in influencing the outcome of the strike.

As Bert Ramelson (national industrial organiser of the Communist Party of Great Britain (CPGB) from 1965 to 1977) clearly stated in a 1986 lecture: "The miners had one choice. Stand up or capitulate. ... As with any major class confrontation, the outcome was decided by the existing balance of forces". There was "the total mobilisation of all the state agencies – including the creation and use for the first time of a national military-type police force". There was also "the failure of Kinnock, the majority of the TUC council and the Communist Party to mobilise solidarity action on the scale required, particularly in the power industry and transport. ... The balance of forces was therefore on the side of the state, which was ready to use all its resources against the miners, and had already made contingency plans to do so before the strike began. ... The outcome was determined by this unfavourable balance of forces".[82]

The widespread support for the strike from miners' support groups all over the country, from individual trade unions and trade unionists, local trades councils, women's action groups, constituency labour parties (CLPs), branches of the

[81] See Richards, Andrew J., *Miners on Strike: Class Solidarity and Division in Britain*, Berg (Oxford and New York), 1996, pp. 135f.

[82] Ramelson, Bert, *Consensus or Socialism?: The 1986 Ralph Fox Memorial Lecture*, Ralph Fox Memorial Committee (Halifax), 1986, pp. 6f.

CPGB as well as other political parties and groups on the left was not mirrored in any corresponding degree from the Labour Party leadership and the TUC. This lack of official support clearly led politics professor Andrew Gamble to conclude that the strike "ended in complete defeat for the miners, once they had split and been successfully isolated from the rest of the Labour movement".[83]

Assessing the outcome of the strike purely in terms of victory or defeat has been a controversial issue. In a narrow sense, one can assess the outcome of the strike in such terms but the issue is wider than that. The strike centred on the future of an entire industry and its strategic role in the economy. The miners based their case on their continued support for *Plan for Coal*. The Thatcher Government abandoned the previous Labour Government's commitment to *Plan for Coal* and reasons which can be claimed on economic grounds for doing so were not convincing at all. Rather, the reasons for abandoning this commitment were, as already noted, "political" with the eventual aim of privatising the industry and breaking the influence of the miners as a major industrial force.

It must also be noted that on the side of the Labour Party leadership, there was no coordinated strategy to initiate action in support of the miners, no attempt to explain the reasons for the strike, no courage to stand up to the media campaign against the miners and altogether, a refusal to back the strike in full.[84] The miners, it can be argued, were campaigning to safeguard the future of an entire industry and the livelihoods of those who were dependant on it. Given the Labour Party's lack of open support for the strike, it can therefore be questioned whether Labour's leadership really had any sympathy for it at all. If it had any, it certainly found the strike "embarrassing and distasteful".[85] So, one cannot doubt that there was reluctance on the part of the Labour Party leadership and the TUC to give the miners the degree of support that was needed, to mention nothing of the fact that certain unions, most notably in the power industry, refused to support the strike at all, but is it really correct to assert, as Gamble has done that the miners "had split and been successfully isolated from the rest of the Labour movement"?

The following examples of solidarity with the miners, to mention nothing of the numerous miners' support groups throughout the whole of Britain, should be noted. The 1984 TUC Congress passed a resolution in support of the strike and for the NUM's campaign for an expanding coal industry in line with *Plan for Coal*.[86] A number of trade unions donated large sums of money to support the NUM e.g.

[83] Gamble, Andrew, *The Free Economy and the Strong State* (Second Edition), Palgrave (Basingstoke and New York), 1994, p. 125.

[84] See Coates, David, ..., pp. 131f.

[85] Kelly, John, *Trade Unions and Socialist Politics*, Verso (London and New York), 1988, p. 128.

[86] *The miners' case*, ..., p. 1.

the General, Municipal, Boilermakers and Allied Trades Union provided over £1 million in support for the miners.[87] Railwaymen supported the miners by boycotting the movement of oil, coal and iron ore for which many NUR and ASLEF members were sent home by their employer, British Rail. Another example of solidarity was industrial action by print workers at the *Sun* newspaper in protest against a management decision refusing to print a disclaimer from unions regarding a front page editorial which described miners as "the scum of the earth".[88]

Much of the solidarity for the miners and their families took the form of local trades councils and women's support groups through raising money and organising collections of food, clothing and toys. Yorkshire and Humberside Regional TUC, for example, raised over £400,000 together with trades councils in this region raising as much again as well as collecting food, clothing and toys.[89] The activities of women's support groups ranged from the collection of financial and material support for miners and their families to the organising of strike kitchens in the coal-mining communities to ensure that miners and their families were fed and whilst the miners themselves were free to carry out their strike duties.[90]

In addition, there were actions of solidarity with the miners from trade unions and trade unionists from outside Britain. Such examples include the introduction of a membership levy by the Swedish miners' union, the German miners' union IGBE made an initial donation of 20,000 DM and organised regular collections at local collieries, regular donations were made by the French trade union federation CGT and together with the International Confederation of Trade Unions (ICTU) there was the provision of holidays for miners' children in France and the Soviet Union by supporting trade unionists.[91]

Such examples of solidarity should surely refute any claim that the miners "had split ... from the rest of the Labour movement". A more accurate assessment of the strike was made by John Kelly, leading professor of industrial relations, in saying that concrete solidarity action was lacking in the areas where it really mattered.[92] Realistically, Gamble's assessment of the strike can be directed at the TUC and the Labour Party for the reasons already stated.

---

[87] Winterton, Jonathan and Ruth, *Coal, crisis and conflict: The 1984-85 miners' strike in Yorkshire*, Manchester University Press (Manchester and New York), 1989, p. 120.

[88] *The miners' case*, ..., p. 13.

[89] Winterton, Jonathan and Ruth, ..., p. 120.

[90] For an insight of women's initiatives in support of the 1984-1985 miners' strike, taking the example of Yorkshire, see Ibid., pp. 121-125.

[91] Ibid., p. 121.

[92] Kelly, John, *Trade Unions and Socialist Politics*, ..., p. 128.

4.2. The interlocking of political confrontation with employers' strategy for the introduction of new technology and changes in working practices

The confrontation in British Leyland, British Steel and most notably with the miners centred on the issue of the balance of forces in industry from a quantitative standpoint. On the other hand, disputes such as those in the printing industry illustrate an issue of fundamental qualitative importance where the introduction of new technology and changes in working practices were to be applied without regulative constraints.

Technological change and changes in working practices were at the centre of many industrial conflicts in the 1980s but it was in the printing industry where these problems really came to light. The most significant disputes centred on the Messenger Newspaper Group (autumn 1983) and News International (1986/-1987).

The Messenger Newspaper Group (MNG) was an independent newspaper group in the northwest of England. It was founded in 1974 and by 1983, it produced and distributed six weekly newspapers free of charge, its revenue being derived solely from advertising.[93]

Rapid technological developments in the British printing industry in the 1970s and 1980s brought about the development of an "alternative printing industry" in which the main production processes no longer needed skilled craftsmen. As a result, people outside the printing industry could enter it and produce freesheet newspapers, often employing non-union labour on inferior terms and conditions of employment than those of skilled print workers.

During the 1970s and 1980s, the growth in the number and circulation of freesheet newspapers was considerable. In 1974, there were 194 such newspapers in the country but this number had risen to 580 by 1983. Most of these were owned by provincial newspaper groups but over 200 of them were owned by individual businesses, one of them being the Messenger Newspaper Group.[94]

This development, together with the expansion of the use of radio and television, resulted in the provincial newspapers' share of advertising revenue falling whilst that of freesheet newspapers rose considerably.[95] It was supposedly against this background that the Newspaper Society[96] launched "Project Breakthrough" in

[93] Gennard, John, The implications of the Messenger Newspaper Group dispute, in: *Industrial Relations Journal*, Blackwell (Oxford), Vol. 15 No. 3, 1984, p. 8.

[94] Ibid.

[95] Ibid.

[96] The Newspaper Society represented regional and local newspapers in England, Wales and Northern Ireland.

July 1982, by which the provincial newspaper groups were to regain their competitive position for advertising revenue.

The NGA launched a counter-offensive to "Project Breakthrough" with "Project Seethrough" and questioned the extent to which there was really a crisis in the provincial press. There had, after all, been a considerable increase in advertising revenue over the years and, in any case, Newspaper Society members owned more than half of the freesheets.[97]

"Project Breakthrough" was supposed to lead to the introduction of "single keystroking"/direct entry systems throughout the provincial press by the end of 1984. The aim was to transfer work from the composing room, where it was carried out by NGA members for whom there was a pre-entry closed shop, to the editorial and advertising areas. Technological developments in the newspaper industry had the effect, as already noted, of integrating the various newspaper production processes up to and including the printing stage (see pages 83f). This made the skills of many compositors obsolete.

Bearing in mind that "Project Breakthrough" was launched in the year when Parliament passed the 1982 Act, the real motive on the part of the employers looked like an attempt to de-unionise the provincial press[98] a suspicion which the General Secretary of the National Graphical Association (1982) later underlined in a report to the union's 1988 Delegate Meeting. It is in this context that the Messenger Newspaper Group dispute (often known as the "Warrington dispute") needs to be assessed.

The origin of the dispute can be traced back to early 1982 when the Messenger Newspaper Group sought a new technology agreement at its Stockport office which wasn't concluded with the NGA until September of that year. Meanwhile, the company began negotiations with the union concerning a new typesetting plant at Bury and for this, a closed-shop agreement with the NGA was concluded.

However, the two sides could not reach agreement on hours of work and pay. The problem was that in Bury (in the company's view), hours of work were less unsociable than at Stockport and consequently, it wanted to pay its staff at Bury £40 per week less than at Stockport. The NGA insisted that the same conditions of employment should apply at both places.

In response, the company cancelled the closed-shop agreement at Bury and started recruiting non-union labour. At the same time, it opened a printing plant in Warrington and in late 1982/early 1983, started recruiting non-union labour for

[97] See Dickinson, Mark, To Break a Union, Booklist Ltd. (Manchester), 1984, pp. 40ff.

[98] Ibid., p. 41.

this as well. Following unsuccessful attempts to resolve the problem of the recruitment of non-union labour, the NGA declared an official dispute with the company. As the recruitment of non-union labour posed a threat to the terms and conditions of employment of NGA members, the NGA instructed its members to "black" all work from or intended for any MNG company.[99]

The dispute entered a new phase on 4 July, 1983, when six NGA members at Fineward Ltd., Stockport (an MNG company) withdrew their labour and were subsequently dismissed. These six union members were supported by ten journalist and photographer members of the National Union of Journalists (NUJ) who refused to cross picket lines.

In conciliation talks under the auspices of ACAS, the NGA sought membership agreements comparable with those in the newspaper industry generally (i.e. closed-shop agreements), while the company insisted that it would not restore such provisions unless it was the wish of the majority of the employees affected[100] i.e. including those who had been subsequently recruited by the company. In addition, the NGA sought the reinstatement of the six strikers (who became known as the "Stockport Six").

Both sides were clear that fundamental principles were at stake. The NGA was defending the principle that typesetting should be done by NGA members, that the MNG should abide by agreements with it and that the union had the right to defend its members using all industrial means. The company was defending the "principle" that employees should be able to choose whether or not to join a union and that unions should abide by the law[101] (meaning, of course, the legal constraints on trade unions which had only recently come into effect).

As the dispute escalated, the company withdrew all previous membership agreements with the NGA, the union began to exert pressure on the MNG's advertisers and suppliers to "black" the company and instructed its members not to supply origination work to it. In addition, the NGA started picketing at the company's Bury and Warrington offices. The industrial methods by which the NGA sought to pursue this dispute would have been effective and were established trade union practices which, being "in contemplation or furtherance of a trade dispute" had, since the 1870s, the protection of the law. This changed as a result of the 1980 and 1982 Acts. On the basis of these Acts, the company was able to obtain three injunctions against the NGA.

One injunction was against "secondary" picketing (picketing at a workplace other than at one's place of employment) which had been made illegal under the

[99] See Gennard, John, ..., pp. 8f.

[100] *ACAS Annual Report 1983* (London), 1984, pp. 26f, para. 2.9.

[101] Gennard, John, ..., p. 7.

1980 Act. As the dispute originated at the Stockport office, picketing at the Bury and Warrington offices was regarded as "secondary" even though they were both owned by the same parent company and that the recruitment of non-union labour in these two offices had clearly aggravated the dispute. The second injunction restrained the union from instructing its members not to supply origination work to the company. The third was to restrain the NGA from putting pressure on advertisers and other suppliers to the company. The second and third injunctions were obtained because "blacking" became unlawful under the 1982 Act. In addition, the company secured an injunction against the NUJ to prevent the NGA from spreading the dispute to journalists employed by the company who were not party to the dispute.[102]

Due to the 1980 and 1982 Acts, the law gave clearcut support to the company. It almost seemed as if such a dispute had actually been anticipated by those who drafted the law: all that the union could legally do in furtherance of the dispute was to station a maximum of six pickets outside the Stockport office.[103] The Stockport office was indeed picketed, but legally, there was nothing the NGA could do to prevent the work from being carried out elsewhere.

This situation left the NGA with two choices: either abandon the dispute, or to pursue it, going beyond the new laws, seeking the support of the trade union movement as a whole. As clearly stated by industrial relations specialist, John McIlroy, early in 1984: "If Wembley [see below] and TUC opposition to the law had any significance, the terrain for a conflict offered by the NGA could not have been bettered. It was fighting for its life. In the face of new technology, its survival depended on maintaining the closed shop and utilising industrial practices which are now illegal".[104]

The NGA pursued the dispute in the way it would always have done. This meant disregarding the High Court injunctions (granted on 14 October, 1983) and the union organised mass picketing. A month after the granting of the injunctions, Eddie Shah, the company owner, returned to the High Court to complain that on November 9th, the NGA had organised a demonstration which turned out to be a mass picket and he applied for the sequestration of the union's assets. While the High Court judge did not accede then, he stated that the union action of November 9th had been a "blatant breach" of the injunction and fined the NGA £50,000 plus costs.[105] The NGA refused to pay the fine[106] and picketing continued. At the same time, the union continued to seek a negotiated settlement to the dispute

[102] Ibid., pp. 10 and 14.

[103] Dickinson, Mark, ..., p. 187.

[104] McIlroy, John, The Unions: is There Life After Warrington, in: *Marxism Today* (London), Vol. 28 No. 2, February 1984, p. 31.

[105] Dickinson, Mark, ..., p. 101.

[106] Ibid., p. 102.

through ACAS. This appeared to be possible on the basis that the NGA would offer to settle for a "post-entry" closed shop with union members, contrary to union rules, working alongside non-union members. However, Shah refused to reinstate the "Stockport Six".[107]

Support for the NGA's position among trade unionists grew and picketing at the company's premises, in defiance of the injunctions, was stepped up. On November 25th, Shah returned to the High Court and made another application for the sequestration of the union's assets due to continued picketing as demonstrated by a mass picket on November 22nd. The judge imposed a fine of £100,000 on the union and ordered the sequestration of the union's assets.

In this dispute, the police successfully countered the mass picketing, even though, at one point, there were as many as 4,000 pickets. The overhauling of police tactics in industrial disputes following the experience at Saltley during the 1972 miners' strike enabled the police to ensure that Shah got his newspapers out on time.[108]

It became clear that the dispute had to be widened if the NGA was to secure the reinstatement of the "Stockport Six". Arguing that the 1980 and 1982 Acts prevented the union from pursuing the dispute peacefully and legally (plus the fact that Shah had the full support of the state apparatus), NGA members throughout the national newspaper industry took industrial action with the result that no national newspapers were printed over the weekend 25th/26th November, 1983. Following this, all national newspapers, with the exception of the *Morning Star*, issued writs for damages against the NGA for lost production.[109]

With the dispute escalating, and faced "with the dilemma, obedience or bankruptcy",[110] the NGA had little alternative other than to ask the TUC for support in line with the Wembley Conference decisions. What the NGA required was support from other print unions on the picket line at Warrington, financial and other assistance to ensure that the union could keep functioning and, most significantly, full support under Recommendation 5 of the Wembley Conference decisions[111] (see below).

On December 9th, the NGA was fined again for "contempt of court", this time £525,000, making a total of fines on the union of £675,000 plus, not forgetting legal costs and damages to the company. As a result, the NGA National Council called a 24-hour strike throughout the British printing industry on 14 December.

[107] Ibid.

[108] Geary, Roger, ..., pp. 134ff.

[109] Gennard, John, ..., p. 10.

[110] McIlroy, John, The Unions: is There Life After Warrington, ..., p. 31.

[111] Dickinson, Mark, ..., p. 122.

The dispute was discussed at the TUC's Employment Policy and Organisation Committee (Epoc) on 12 December. Reference was made to the fact that the 1983 TUC Congress had not backed a resolution calling for all-out opposition to the Government (see below) and the then TUC General Secretary, Len Murray, argued that the TUC should support the NGA only within the constraints of the law. However, Epoc voted 9 to 7 to support the NGA in line with the Wembley Conference decisions. This decision had to be approved by the TUC General Council but, seemingly without precedent, the TUC General Secretary publicly repudiated a decision of a key TUC committee and made clear his determination to get the General Council to overturn it. In the light of this, the NGA suspended its planned strike for December 14th. In the meantime, seven national and more than 20 provincial newspapers had been granted High Court injunctions ordering the NGA to withdraw its planned stoppage.[112]

On 16 December, the TUC General Council voted by 31 to 20 to overturn Epoc's decision and hence, only agreed to assist the NGA in so far as the law permitted. This effectively meant that the NGA could pursue the dispute no further. For whatever sympathy there may have been from the General Council with the NGA, the majority of its members took the view that the dispute was not winnable and consequently justified their stance in that supporting the NGA beyond what the law permitted would have brought the TUC itself into legal difficulties without knowing what the consequences would have been.[113]

At the following TUC Congress in September 1984, the TUC General Secretary was censured for his actions but, by then, the dispute had long been over. Various reasons had been offered at the time in justification of the TUC's position, e.g. fear of writs on account of the 1980 and 1982 Acts and that some unions were not prepared to support the NGA.[114] However one interprets the reasons for the General Council's decision, one thing became clear. Any commitment the TUC had in defying the trade union laws became one of acquiescence.

This dispute was significant in that it gave the Thatcher Government its first major victory on the industrial front on the basis of its own legislation. But, that was not all. This legislation was applied in such a way in that it forced the TUC to comply with laws which were designed to place legal curbs on trade unions so as to clear the way for the unrestrained introduction of new technology and changes in working practices.

---

[112] Gennard, John, ..., p. 11.

[113] See Gennard, John, *A History of the National Graphical Association*, Unwin Hyman Ltd. (London), 1990, p. 314.

[114] See McIlroy, John, *The permanent revolution? Conservative law and the trade unions*, ..., pp. 71ff.

The Messenger Newspaper Group dispute was also significant in that it was the first major industrial dispute since Taff Vale where the common law succeeded in restricting the traditionally accepted rights of trade unions to defend their members' interests. It was in this dispute, through the unrestrained use of the injunction against the NGA, where the 1980 and 1982 Acts came to life. It was a similar application of these laws which was to hit the print unions again in the 1980s and this was in the News International dispute. The experience of the trade union union laws in the Messenger Newspaper Group dispute and the police tactics in the miners' strike were applied comprehensively in the News International dispute.

News International was a subsidiary company of News Corporation Ltd (Australia), which was dominated by Rupert Murdoch and his family. Traditionally, newspapers had been Rupert Murdoch's main area of business, but over the years he had greatly expanded his operations, going into publishing, television and the new media as well as other industries, all on a global scale. Through numerous company takeovers, Murdoch had been able to establish himself as the world's most powerful person in the media industry. At the time of the News International dispute, it was estimated that Murdoch's company controlled six billion (US) dollars worth of assets.[115]

Murdoch also extended his business interests into television in the United States by buying out the film company "Twentieth Century Fox" for US $550m and the company "Metromedia", together with its six television stations, for US $1,550m in the mid 1980s.[116] To finance his acquisitions in US television, Murdoch had to secure massive loans at high rates of interest. This meant that, initially, success in Murdoch's TV venture in the US depended on his other subsidiary companies making high enough profits to enable him to repay these loans. This requirement, of course, also applied to News International.

At the beginning of the 1980s, News International owned two national newspapers in Britain – the *Sun* and the *News of the World*. In 1981, the Thatcher Government allowed News International to takeover *The Times* and the *Sunday Times*. The Government evidently felt an obligation to Murdoch because both he and his newspapers had given Margaret Thatcher vital support, especially in winning over working class voters in the "winter of discontent" leading up to the Conservative election victory in 1979.[117]

---

[115] Whitfield, David, Murdoch multi-media dictator, in: *Communist Review* (London), Winter 1986/1987, p. 25.

[116] Ibid., p. 26.

[117] Hodgson, Godfrey, Private Power and the Public Interest: The Case of Times Newspapers, in: *The Political Quarterly*, Blackwell (Oxford), Vol. 52 No. 4, October-December 1981, p. 412.

This takeover meant that Murdoch owned two national daily newspapers and two Sunday newspapers giving him control of about 30% of the national newspaper market at that time. Following a major newspaper promotion battle in the early 1980s, News International gained the largest share of the UK national newspaper markets altogether, overtaking Mirror Group Newspapers (owned by the late Robert Maxwell).

As a result of technological development, newspapers were eager to reduce manning levels and impose changes in working practices. Following on from his victory over the NGA in the Messenger Newspaper Group dispute, Eddie Shah launched a national newspaper *Today* in March 1986 – a colour tabloid using the most advanced technology and employing relatively few staff.[118] In October the same year, *The Independent* was launched on the same basis as *Today* – new technology and low staffing levels.[119]

The *ACAS Annual Report 1986* states that the catalyst for proceeding with technological change in national newspapers was probably through the launch of *Today*.[120] This may be so, but Murdoch had already been making such plans for his newspapers before he acquired *The Times* and *Sunday Times* in 1981.[121]

The background to the News International dispute (often known as the "Wapping dispute") can be traced back to the early 1980s when Murdoch started building his new printing works in Wapping in the East End of London. It was intended that he would produce the *Sun* and the *News of the World* there, instead of in the centre of London, and in 1983, Murdoch began negotiations with the print unions about production at Wapping.[122]

These negotiations were going to be difficult as News International wanted a substantial reduction in the workforce from around 6,000 to just a few hundred. Despite these difficulties, the print unions were confident that they could have been overcome e.g. through early retirement, voluntary redundancy, retraining and natural wastage. However, suspicion grew that Murdoch had never really intended that these negotiations should succeed. They dragged out for over 18 months. In the view of the print unions, the aim was to give Murdoch valuable time in which he could get his Wapping plant ready and draw up plans for dismissing his unionised workforce.[123]

---

[118] *ACAS Annual Report 1986* (London), 1987, p. 27.

[119] Ibid.

[120] Ibid.

[121] An NGA (1982) Briefing Paper: News International Dispute, National Graphical Association (1982) (Bedford), February 1986, p. 18, para. 11.2 (unpublished).

[122] Ibid., p. 8, para. 3.2.

[123] Ibid., p. 9, paras. 4.2f.

The next stage in this process came in March 1985, when Murdoch announced plans to launch a new London evening paper (The Post) in March 1986 which would be printed at Wapping. In fact, Murdoch never intended to launch such a newspaper – it was simply a ploy with the aim of recruiting the workers who would operate his new machinery at Wapping. The new workers he recruited were not members of any of the print unions but of the EETPU. Despite this, the print unions proceeded with their negotiations with News International concerning production of "The Post" despite expressing concern over the recruitment of EETPU members for the jobs normally done by print union members.

In the course of these negotiations, which never got round to discussing actual staffing levels and conditions of employment, News International put before the unions (NGA (1982), SOGAT '82, NUJ, AUEW and the EETPU) four "non-negotiable" points:

1. all agreements to be legally binding on the unions and individual;
2. no industrial action whatsoever under any circumstances;
3. no "closed shop";
4. complete and total "unfettered right" of management to manage.[124]

No trade union could agree to the above points and still function normally. All unions except the EETPU rejected them.

The prospect of newspapers being produced at Wapping posed a clear threat to the print workers at existing plants in Gray's Inn Road and Bouverie Street (both in the centre of London). The print unions insisted that, in the event of newspaper production being transferred to Wapping, existing terms and conditions of employment for the print workers should be protected. In addition, they sought recognition rights in the event of their members being transferred to Wapping. This was rejected by the company.

As with the Messenger Newspaper Group dispute, the unions and their members were being forced into a position which they could not accept. Consequently, being left with no alternative, the print unions balloted their members on industrial action which, it should be noted, was conducted in line with the new trade union laws. At the eleventh hour, the TUC, at the request of the print unions, sought to mediate, but without success.

It became clear all along that Murdoch had been secretly preparing to transfer the production of his newspapers to Wapping and to another plant at Kinning Park in Glasgow, both of these containing the most modern direct input typesetting equipment such as would bypass skilled NGA printers. In addition, Murdoch got one of his subsidiary companies – the Sydney-based TNT international

[124] Ibid., pp. 12f, para. 7.1.

transport company – to distribute his newspapers so as to bypass SOGAT members who were normally responsible for distribution.[125]

The News International strike began on 24 January, 1986. So effective were Murdoch's plans that, when the print workers took strike action, he was able to dismiss them instantly while at the same time continuing to produce and distribute his newspapers.[126] To dismiss workers in an industrial dispute, as already noted, would be deemed unthinkable in a country where a right to strike exists, as is generally the case in Western Europe, especially as this strike action had been authorised by ballots in line with the trade union laws brought in by the Thatcher Government.

All along, not only had Murdoch quite clearly been drawing up plans for dismissing his workforce, but News International had actually sought legal advice on the best way of doing this. This was to catch the workers when they were participating in a strike or other industrial action. Proof of this came to light when a copy of a secret legal document giving advice on how a company could dispense with its unionised workforce was leaked to the *Morning Star*, which printed it in full.[127]

Thus, the company was able to provoke a strike as a means of dismissing its unionised workforce. The strike fell within the category of a "trade dispute" as defined (or rather, narrowed) by the 1982 Act and the ballots authorising it had been conducted in line with the provisions of the 1984 Act. Yet, as far as the common law was concerned, the strike was a breach of the contract of employment which meant that the strikers had no right to claim redundancy pay or unfair dismissal.

The activities of the EETPU in this dispute were brought to the attention of the TUC but the real question was whether it was prepared to "use its authority" and take disciplinary action against the EETPU so as to help the print workers in getting their jobs back. The TUC ruled that the EETPU had brought the trade union movement "into disrepute" and had acted in a way that was in direct contradiction to TUC policy.[128] To put it simply, the EETPU had stolen the jobs of the existing print workers.

The TUC General Council issued the EETPU with a "six-point directive" which was to be met by 12 February, 1986, i.e. within six days of it being issued. The points included:
1. a ban on assisting further recruitment of workers to Wapping and Glasgow;

[125] Power, Mike, A Tale of Wapping Woe, in: *Marxism Today* (London), March 1987, p. 40.
[126] Ibid.
[127] See Murdoch deceit unmasked, in: *Morning Star* (London), 4 February 1986, p. 4.
[128] An NGA (1982) Briefing Paper: News International Dispute, ..., p. 34, para. 16.33.

2. not to recruit into membership anyone employed by News International or its associated companies without the agreement of the other unions;
3. to inform members working at Wapping and Glasgow that they were doing the work normally done by sacked members of the print unions;
4. not to enter into any agreements with News International without the agreement of the other unions;
5. not to enter into unilateral negotiations with News International, and to try to bring about fresh negotiations between the company and all five unions, itself included;
6. not to enter into a sole negotiated or union membership agreement by which other unions would be deprived of their existing rights, except by prior consultation.[129]

The EETPU was to be suspended from the TUC until the following annual congress if these directives were not met.[130]

The outcome was that these directives were not fulfilled, modest though they were, and the EETPU was not suspended from the TUC at the time. This meant that the General Council, as in the Messenger Newspaper Group dispute, opted to leave the print unions to their fate. So, the EETPU, as it were, violated basic trade union rights and got away with it.

Throughout the dispute (which lasted over a year until 5 February, 1987), Rupert Murdoch, as had Eddie Shah in the Messenger Newspaper Group dispute before him, made full use of the Thatcher Government's trade union laws which prevented the print unions from pursuing the dispute effectively within the scope of the law.

Very early in the dispute, News International used the courts to restrain the unions from undertaking "secondary action". For example, on 29 January, 1986, the company obtained a High Court injunction against the TGWU (which organised TNT drivers) preventing it from issuing instructions to its members not to cross the Wapping picket line. Three days later, the Scottish courts banned SOGAT from interfering with the distribution of the company's papers, and the TGWU was ordered not to encourage its members employed by TNT to boycott the company's papers, or even to stop at picket lines. On 7 February, the High Court ordered the post office workers' union to stop encouraging its members not deliver *Sun* bingo cards to homes throughout Britain.[131]

[129] Ibid., pp. 34f, para. 16.34.

[130] Ibid., p. 35, para. 16.35.

[131] Trask, Roger, *Anti-trade union legislation in Britain*, International Centre for Trade Union Rights (London), February 1989, p. 17.

As with Messenger in autumn 1983, SOGAT, the main union in News International, was left with the choice of abandoning the dispute or defying court injunctions. It decided to pursue the dispute and defy the injunctions. The legal action against SOGAT escalated on 11 February when a High Court judge fined the union £25,000 for "contempt of court" and sequestrated its assets (estimated at £17m at the time).[132]

The print unions supported the dispute to the point that, in the case of SOGAT, it became financially crippled. The SOGAT leadership felt that it could only proceed further with the dispute if union members were willing to pay a weekly levy of 58p for as long as the dispute lasted.[133] Having failed to secure support for this levy, the SOGAT leadership on 5 February, 1987, called off the dispute. Subsequently, the other unions involved did likewise.

The print unions in this dispute had reacted too late, a fact which Murdoch himself pointed out in an interview a few weeks after it had begun. Had the strike begun before Christmas (1985), it could have been more effective. Preparations at Wapping for the production of newspapers were not then complete and any industrial disruption earlier could have lost the company a considerable amount of advertising revenue as pre-Christmas advertising in Murdoch's papers had been heavy.[134]

As with the Messenger Newspaper Group dispute and the miners' strike, the police were out in force to prevent picketing at the entrances to the Wapping plant. Although pickets were arrested for alleged violence, a "blind eye" was turned to lorry drivers who raced through picket lines. In one such incident, a 19-year old demonstrator, Mike Delaney, was knocked down and killed by a TNT lorry driver leaving Wapping. No charges were brought against him.[135] This compares with another incident in which SOGAT executive member and Wapping strike leader, Mike Hicks, was arrested and imprisoned for allegedly assaulting a police officer. As Hicks played such a prominent role in the dispute, his arrest was widely felt to be an act of victimisation on the part of the State authorities aimed at putting more pressure on SOGAT to call off the dispute.[136]

The above mentioned examples showed that the mid 1980s witnessed some very significant industrial disputes. But for unions to pursue them effectively meant breaking the law, being found in "contempt of court", suffering large fines and the sequestration of their assets and having to face the full armoury of the state

---

[132] Ibid.

[133] See *SOGAT Journal – Special Issue: Union in Crisis*, SOGAT (Hadleigh, Essex), November 1986.

[134] Power, Mike, ..., p. 40.

[135] Trask, Roger, ..., p. 18.

[136] Ibid.

authorities. Faced with the choice of defiance and acquiescence, TUC leaders backed down rather than risk confrontation.

4.3. Attempts in the labour movement to counter the Conservative trade union legislation

In the 1983 election, Labour polled 28.3% of the popular vote, its lowest share of the poll since 1918. Although the Conservative Party won a landslide victory in terms of parliamentary seats, it won the election on "the lowest winning percentage of the vote" any Conservative leader had had since Bonar Law.[137]

The polarisation of the traditional left/right divide in the Labour Party following the 1979 election defeat, leading in 1981 to the foundation of the Social Democratic Party by a group of prominent Labour MPs on the right of the Party, the political consequences in Britain of the Falkland's war in 1982 together with an economic upswing following the 1979-1981 slump left the Labour Party in a weak position in the run-up to the 1983 election. It therefore became clear that neither the Labour Party nor the trade union movement would halt, let alone reverse, the Thatcher Government's economic and social policies in the foreseeable future. The trade union and labour movement had originally pledged to oppose the trade union laws of the Thatcher Government and called on the next Labour Government to repeal them. A commitment to do this in respect of the 1980 and 1982 Acts was made in Labour's 1983 election manifesto.[138]

Although the TUC mounted a campaign against the 1980 Act, it was limited in scope. It largely amounted to the then TUC General Secretary, Len Murray, trying to impress upon the Government that a "voluntary" approach and the TUC's own machinery could more effectively deal with problems arising out of picketing and the closed shop rather than legislation. However, the major plank of the TUC's opposition to the 1980 Act was that TUC-affiliated unions should not apply for Government cash to fund ballots under this Act.[139]

It was only when the 1982 Employment Bill was published at the end of January 1982 that the TUC decided to take a more rigorous stand against the trade union laws being enacted by the Thatcher Government. At a conference of executives

---

[137] Gamble, Andrew, Thatcher: The Second Coming, in: *Marxism Today* (London), Vol. 27 No. 7, July 1983, p. 8. NB For details of general election results during the 20th century, see, for example, Harmer, Harry, *The Labour Party 1900-1998*, Longman (London and New York), 1999, pp. 29-41.

[138] *The New Hope for Britain: Labour's Manifesto 1983*, The Labour Party (London), 1983, p. 9.

[139] See McIlroy, John, *The permanent revolution? Conservative law and the trade unions*, ..., pp. 50f.

of TUC-affiliated unions in Wembley on 5 April, 1982, an eight-point plan of opposition to the union laws, which became known as *The Wembley Principles*, was agreed.

Briefly, the main points of *The Wembley Principles* can be summarised as follows. Firstly, no TUC-affiliated union should participate in secret ballots on union membership agreements under the terms of the 1980 Act or the 1982 Bill. Secondly, unions should observe existing Congress policy of neither seeking nor accepting public funds for ballots under the 1980 Act. Thirdly, no trade union member of any industrial tribunal or the Employment Appeal Tribunal should serve on cases arising from the application of a union membership agreement or arrangement. Fourthly, affiliated unions should continue to observe strictly the requirements of the TUC Disputes Principles and Procedures. Fifthly, and most importantly, under Recommendation 5, if the TUC General Council feels that a request for support is justified, to coordinate support for an affiliated union in the event of it experiencing legal action from an employer under those laws, including industrial action against the employer concerned and to provide financial support to the union in the event of it experiencing financial difficulties arising out of such action.[140]

In effect, all the Wembley Conference did was to reaffirm the powers the TUC had already had. It is also worth noting that Recommendation 5 was worded in such a way that the General Council was not automatically compelled to help an affiliated union experiencing difficulties under these laws.[141] Consequently, the real question was how the TUC would react in the event of an affiliated union facing the full thrust of these laws. Or, put it another way, would the TUC be prepared to break the law and instruct its affiliated unions to do likewise if the need arose?

Although under the 1980 Act, a few cases went before the courts, they were handled "carefully". A good example concerned the case of the then EETPU's Fleet Street branch secretary, Sean Geraghty, who was found to be in "contempt of court" arising out of an injunction restraining industrial action in support of the NHS pay claim in August 1982. For this, a nominal fine of £350 was imposed on him with the threat of a one week prison sentence if it was not paid within two months. The fact that this fine was paid by an anonymous donor would confirm the view that employers were reluctant to get involved in a confrontation with the unions over the trade union laws.[142] The handling of this case would also indicate that the judiciary was worried about the prospect of "martyrdom", especially as the 1982 Employment Bill was still going through Parliament (it only received Royal Assent on 28 October, 1982).

[140] See Ibid., pp. 64-67.

[141] Ibid., p. 67.

[142] Ibid.

However, from the time of the Wembley Conference to the first major dispute under the trade unions of the early 1980s (i.e. the Messenger Newspaper Group dispute), 18 months had passed which had not only witnessed a severe Labour defeat in the 1983 general election but also, in consequence, the election of a "New Realist" Labour Party leadership under Neil Kinnock and Roy Hattersley.[143] In addition, one factor, often overlooked, was that the 1981 TUC annual congress voted to change the method of election for members of the TUC General Council. The previous principle by which General Council members were elected in "trade groups" by the whole of the Congress was replaced by a system in which most members were to be appointed by the individual unions themselves depending on the size of the union. This change, which came into effect in September 1983, was to result in the leaders of a number of medium-sized unions on the "right" of the movement in joining the General Council whilst the seats of up to nine left wingers became vulnerable.[144] By implication, the extent to which the TUC would exercise its powers in the event of an affiliated union facing the full thrust of the 1980 and 1982 Acts would be influenced by the change in the composition of the General Council. The significance of this change is that the TUC would have been more reluctant to sanction industrial action which was against the law. Also significant was that the 1983 TUC Congress rejected a resolution calling for all-out opposition to the Government (see page 179).

The first case of any importance under these laws (though not as dramatic as the Messenger Newspaper Group dispute just a little later) was the Mercury dispute (*Mercury Communications Ltd. v. Post Office Engineering Union*) in autumn 1983. As part of its campaign against the privatisation of British Telecom (which the POEU believed would lead to job losses among its members), the union instructed its members not to connect Mercury, a new company, into the British Telecom network. The High Court's refusal to grant Mercury an injunction was overturned in the Court of Appeal. The High Court ruled that the POEU's action fell within the "definition of a trade dispute" under the 1982 Act as it was "wholly or mainly" about the terms and conditions of employment. The Court of Appeal, on the other hand, viewed the union's action as being political rather than industrial, motivated by opposition to privatisation rather than fear of job losses.[145] This may suggest that one motive behind the trade union laws was to frustrate any possible union opposition to Government privatisation plans.

Due to the Appeal Court's ruling, the union held a special conference to decide whether the injunction should be complied with. With Len Murray advising the

---

[143] Ibid., p. 68.

[144] Kelly, John, TUC Reforms, in: Marxism Today (London), Vol. 25 No. 11, November 1981, pp. 4f.

[145] See McIlroy, John, *The permanent revolution? Conservative law and the trade unions*, ..., pp. 68f.

union that it was not TUC policy to encourage unions to break the law, the POEU decided to comply.[146] Although the Mercury case may not be judged as a "landmark", it was, nevertheless, a victory for the 1982 Act. This, together with the recent TUC Congress decision rejecting the call for all-out opposition to the Government showed that the trade union laws were beginning to take hold on influential sections of the trade union movement. These developments, together with the recent effects of the change in electing TUC General Council members, clearly influenced the General Council's decision in the Messenger Newspaper Group dispute. So, the TUC's commitment to the Wembley Principles had, to all intents and purposes, been shelved by the end of 1983, even if they had ever been of any real significance.

This dispute in autumn 1983 showed more than anything else that the General Council (with its weakened left influence) was not going to sanction any action in support of trade unions and trade unionists if it involved breaking the law. This, together with the demoralised state of the labour movement following the 1983 election, showed that the 1980 and 1982 Acts, to be followed by the 1984 Act, were going to remain on the Statute Book for the foreseeable future. So, the question facing the trade union and labour movement was whether the demand for the repeal of these laws remained a realistic option and, if not, what should replace them? If the key aspects of these laws were not going to be resisted, then, by implication, they would remain in being.

The case for repeal may not have been convincingly put as was so with the 1971 Act. This Act of the Heath Government had become unworkable, been abandoned and ultimately repealed because the trade union movement succeeded in defying it. This also came about because the TUC was strong enough and, more significantly, determined enough to ensure that Congress policy regarding this Act was honoured by all affiliated unions, and that disciplinary measures were taken against those which did not.

By the mid-1980s, the TUC's declared opposition to the Thatcher Government's trade union laws was being undermined by what the Left regarded as a "right-wing block" centred on the AUEW and the EETPU. Both of these unions, because of their support for secret postal balloting and in view of their financial difficulties as well, were eager to seek state funding for this provision under the 1980 Act.[147] Parallel to this, other unions, despite their opposition in principle to the 1984 Act, were going to abide by the Act's balloting provisions concerning strikes and union elections. Indeed, shop stewards had already been taking part in balloting under the 1982 Act over the maintenance of the closed shop.[148]

---

[146] Ibid., p. 69.

[147] McIlroy, John, *Trade Unions in Britain Today*, ..., p. 90.

[148] Ibid.

When the Government set a deadline for February 1985 for claims to be made for the funding of ballots under the 1980 Act, the AUEW and the EETPU, not withstanding TUC policy on the matter, balloted their members with both unions voting decisively in favour of accepting state funding. It then became clear that the TUC's policy of not accepting state funding was being eroded. A special TUC conference in February 1986 decided to end the boycott of Government cash to fund ballots under the 1980 Act.[149]

By the mid-1980s, it had also become clear that the trade union laws were influencing the way unions were conducting their affairs. Although in recent years, with a Labour Government having been in office since 1997, trade unions have been renewing earlier calls for the repeal of the Conservative trade union laws, which became official TUC policy in 2005 (see below), and having gained wide support for this demand from within the PLP, in the mid 1980s, it had become questionable whether such a demand, as contained in Labour's 1983 election manifesto, was a realistic option at the time. Lord McCarthy, then Opposition front bench spokesman on Employment in the House of Lords, regarded the demand for repeal as a "non-starter". He gave three reasons for this.

Firstly, despite the benefits to trade unions from the labour relations legislation of the 1974-1979 Labour Government, it was "less than perfect". One area of criticism was that judges had still been able to grant injunctions against trade unions. Another area concerned the question of trade union recognition in cases where employers, as in the Grunwick dispute in 1977, had succeeded in ignoring what the law supposedly sought. There was also controversy over picketing. In addition, a shadow was cast over the closed shop when three railwaymen, dismissed for not being union members, won their case on appeal to the European Court of Human Rights in Strasbourg in 1981 (see pages 93f).

Lord McCarthy's second argument against the call for repeal as such concerned the question of injunctions. The question arose as to how Labour should formulate criteria upon which injunctions should be granted. Were the 1974-1976 "definition of a trade dispute" to be restored, it might not prevent injunctions being granted if the plaintiff could show that there was "a serious issue to be tried" and that the "balance of convenience" favoured the preservation of the "status quo".

Thirdly, Lord McCarthy argued that the call for the traditional system of what he termed "negative immunities" to be converted into the language of "positive rights", needed rethinking. The term "immunities" had given the impression that these had put trade unions above the law. This might unintentionally strengthen the impression that the laws of the 1980s had been intended merely as a means of "redressing the balance" whereas the results, in Lord McCarthy's words, has been "the most restrictive labour code in Western Europe". So, rather than argue

[149] Ibid., pp. 90f.

for the return of "immunities" as such, he urged the labour movement to move towards a system of "positive rights" to take strike action in line with other countries in what is now the EU [150]

There is one other point which cannot be overlooked. The intense degree of industrial militancy in the early 1970s, in which the trade union movement had some notable victories and subsequently which eventually led to the downfall of the Heath Government and the repeal of the discredited Industrial Relations Act, was not repeated in the early to mid 1980s with an effect which could mirror those of ten years previously. In the early to mid 1980s, the trade union movement suffered some major defeats, even if in part self-inflicted by the failure of its most influential organs give those at the forefront of major industrial struggles at the time the degree of support necessary to win their disputes. Further, with the Labour Party having been severely weakened by the outcome of the 1983 election, with Party leaders regarding Labour's policies as too "left wing", it was felt that if there was any prospect of a Labour Government being returned to office within the foreseeable future, it would not be on the basis of the policies as advocated in the 1983 election campaign. This also included Labour's policies on trade union and labour relations law.

So very much mirroring the sentiments of Lord McCarthy, Labour, in the 1987 election campaign, committed itself to "replace" the trade union laws[151] rather than repeal them as had been pledged in the 1983 manifesto. Labour's 1987 election manifesto made commitments to restore various worker rights which had been lost or curtailed since 1979 and, in some cases, to go beyond what had previously existed e.g. to improve protection against unfair dismissal and, importantly, reinstatement should be the normal outcome of a successful claim against unfair dismissal. There, it should be noted that even in cases of successful claims against unfair dismissal before an industrial tribunal, even if the recommendation is reinstatement or just re-engagement, there was no law which could actually force employers to comply. The purpose of this commitment was intended, in part, to ensure that justice was done in cases where miners had been unfairly dismissed on account of the 1984/1985 miners' strike and to restore the right to belong to a trade union to every employee – including those at GCHQ. Pledges were also made to extend employment protection to all workers including part-timers and to restore provisions on fair pay especially the Fair Wages Resolution (which, as earlier noted, had been rescinded in 1982).[152]

This point on unfair dismissal is also important because a successful claim against this in an industrial tribunal wouldn't have been adequate enough to have

---

[150] McCarthy, (Lord) William E. J., *Freedom At Work: Towards The Reform of Tory Employment Laws*, Fabian Society (London), November 1985, Fabian Tract 508, pp. 8-11.

[151] *Britain will win: Labour manifesto June 1987*, Labour Party (London), June 1987, p. 13.

[152] Ibid.

forced an employer like British Leyland to reinstate Derek Robinson, had he chosen to fight his dismissal by legal rather than by industrial means. There, all that would have happened is that the level of compensation would have been increased – an insignificant cost for a major employer seeking to dispense with an "awkward" shop steward, in this case, someone who was then Britain's most prominent trade unionist on the shop floor.

As far as industrial action was concerned, the 1987 manifesto was rather vague. In pledging to "replace" legislation that gave employers and non-unionists the means to frustrate legitimate union activity, it pledged to bring in new laws strengthening the rights of representation, bargaining and trade unionism which are essential in a modern democracy.[153] Although the manifesto sought to ensure "that the law guarantees the essential legal freedom of workers and their unions to organise effective industrial action",[154] it did not say *how* this ought to be achieved, be this on the basis of "positive rights" or through restoring the "immunities" which had been removed or restricted in the early 1980s. Interestingly, in 1987, Labour pledged to provide "a statutory framework of measures to underpin the participative rights of union members, for example by laying down general principles for inclusion in union rule books. These will be based on a right for union members to have a secret ballot on decisions relating to strikes, and the method of election of union executives to be based on a system of secret ballots".[155]

On the surface, these commitments may appear to be plausible but one is bound to ask why there were no specific proposals on how industrial action could be pursued without workers and trade unions from coming into conflict with the law. Was the absence of any specific commitment to restore "immunities" or even to introduce "positive rights" a consequence of the hostility which Labour Party leaders, especially in government, had traditionally shown towards militant trade unionism? Be it through "positive rights" or "immunities", "the essential legal freedom ... to organise effective industrial action" would only be meaningful if neither workers nor their unions feared the prospect of repercussions in the event of an industrial dispute. Furthermore, regarding the long-established trade union practices, seen as vital in the pursuit of "effective industrial action", which the Thatcher Government had therefore curtailed, such as solidarity action and picketing, the manifesto was silent. The pledges on ballots, conforming clearly to the 1984 Act, would be consistent with this line of thinking on the part of Party leaders and of their awareness that the time taken to conduct them may well result in workers "losing the initiative" in industrial disputes.

---

[153] Ibid.

[154] Ibid.

[155] Ibid.

Admittedly, though not part of traditional trade union practice in Britain, strike ballots had become an established component of industrial action in other countries such as Germany and there, these had not in the main obstructed it. But the motive for actually legislating for such measures in Britain was in the hope of frustrating such action.

Whether Lord McCarthy's claim in 1985 that the demand for the repeal of the Conservative trade union laws at the time was really a "non-starter" or not, the outcome of the Wilson and Palmer case before the ECtHR in 2002 (see Chapter 5) has been a factor which was to influence the TUC in reviving earlier calls for repeal at its annual congress in 2005.

The traditional scepticism towards industrial militancy on the part of Labour Party leaders may also have played a part in the formulation of Labour's National Economic Assessment. This was at first a 1983 manifesto commitment[156] (having previously been formulated by the TUC-Labour Party Liaison Committee in autumn 1982), which was supposed to have formed a basis for reducing unemployment to less than a million within five years of Labour taking office (on the basis of macroeconomic measures). The intentions of the National Economic Assessment, as put before the electorate in 1983, were, on the surface reminiscent of those behind the Social Contract when it had originally been drawn up whilst Labour was in opposition in the early 1970s – an economic partnership between the trade union movement and the Labour Government, based on a redistribution of wealth and income, policies to secure and maintain "full employment" and extending trade union rights by, as a first step, repealing all restrictive trade union laws. In 1987, however, Labour once again made a pledge for a National Economic Assessment[157] but with many of the far-reaching measures of 1983 being set aside. This now needs to be considered along side the trade union policies Labour advocated in 1987.

The motive for the 1987 pledge to provide "a statutory framework of measures to underpin the participative rights of union members ..." seems unclear, even if such a pledge was really necessary. The Thatcher Government, it can be argued, had already done this through its 1984 Act. Even though the ILO Committee of Experts in 1985 rejected TUC complaints that the balloting provisions under this Act were incompatible with article 3 of ILO Convention No. 87 (see page 98), it remains remarkable that the Labour Party, which owes its very existence to the trade union movement, could make a pledge giving legitimacy to the right of the State to interfere in trade union internal affairs especially, as earlier noted, that no other country in Western Europe had such extensive regulations on such matters. It could well be that as the various balloting provisions under the 1984 Act had already taken effect, or were in the process of becoming so, Labour leaders

---

[156] *The New Hope for Britain: Labour's Manifesto 1983*, ..., p. 9.

[157] *Britain will win: Labour manifesto June 1987*, ..., p. 4.

may have intended that these provisions be applied with more flexibility. If this had been intended, the manifesto did not say so. Consequently, the motive for such a pledge remains unclear.

All the same, with Labour's proposal for a National Economic Assessment, it may have been intended that incomes policies were to be part of this. In view of this, Labour leaders would have been eager to keep down wage settlements and restrain union militancy. In fact, an overlap with some aspects of the Conservative trade union laws would suggest this. In any case, if the formulation of Labour's 1987 manifesto raised doubts regarding the aims of the Labour leadership in the field of trade union and labour relations law, these would have certainly been removed in the aftermath of Labour's policy review following its 1987 election defeat. A slimmed-down version of Labour's policy review, as approved by the 1989 Labour Party conference, was published in 1990. This document, *Looking to the Future*, was to provide the basis for Labour's 1992 election manifesto. What position did it take on the issue of trade union and labour relations law?

The 1992 manifesto pledged: "There will be no return to the trade union legislation of the 1970s".[158] But, which legislation did the manifesto refer to – the 1971 Act or the Acts of 1974 to 1978? This, the manifesto did not say specifically. However, the very next sentence read: "Ballots before strikes and for union elections will stay" and, more significantly, the following sentence added "There will be no mass or flying pickets".[159] These three sentences alone provide a clear enough indication that, rather than offering an alternative to the Conservative trade union laws, Labour would largely retain them.

In *Looking to the Future*, Labour proposed establishing an "Industrial Court" which would "deal with the whole area of industrial disputes". It would have "full powers of enforcement and damages" and have "expert" industrial members. Interestingly, "it would be headed by a senior High Court judge".[160] This may sound reminiscent of Edward Heath's short-lived National Industrial Relations Court. The claim in *Looking to the Future* that the issue was not "law or no law" but "fair or unfair law",[161] would still keep unions, in the event of industrial disputes, at the mercy of the judiciary. Therefore, they would remain to be exposed to claims for damages and hence legal costs even though, on the pretext of being "fair", legislation would "prevent the total sequestration" of a trade union's assets in a way which would paralyse its normal business.[162] On this basis, it

[158] *Labour's election manifesto April 1992: It's time to get Britain working again*, Labour Party (London), April 1992, p. 13.

[159] Ibid.

[160] *Looking to the Future*, Labour Party (London), 1990, p. 34.

[161] Ibid.

[162] Ibid. See also Kelly, John, Looking to the Future: Labour's anti-union policies, in: *Com-*

could be reasonably assumed that the code on vicarious liability, as originally introduced in the 1982 Act, would remain (see pages 91f).

The absence of a commitment to abolish this code on vicarious liability (where unions would have to distance themselves from "unlawful" and "unofficial" industrial action in order to avoid liability) should be viewed by trade unionists as a serious omission from Labour's policy review. It is this code, making the union itself the defendant, thus exposing its entire assets to the full thrust of the common law, which gave all the other legislative measures outlined in the Conservative trade union laws their biting edge.

By not making any specific proposals as to what should fall within the "definition of a trade dispute" (being one necessary condition for the remaining "immunities" provisions to apply) and not pledging the abolition of the code on vicarious liability, the conclusion can be drawn that what can be termed as the "hard core" of the Conservative trade union laws would be retained by Labour. Perhaps this, more than anything else, would confirm the traditional hostility on the part of Labour's leaders towards militant trade unionism.

Labour did, however, pledge to end the unfair procedure by which employers could secure *ex parte* injunctions without the union being able to state its case. It also committed itself to introducing a new rule by which, if an interlocutory injunction were granted, then a full hearing of the case would have to proceed immediately if this was the wish of either of the parties.[163] But how should the wide degree of discretion judges have in issuing injunctions with the result that a union could be "robbed of the initiative" in an industrial dispute be tackled – a problem which the Ethicon case in 1975 had illustrated regarding the legislation which repealed the 1971 Act (see page 121)? On this, *Looking to the Future* was silent. Furthermore, in the absence of a commitment to restore the "definition of a trade dispute" as outlined in the 1974 and 1976 Acts, Labour's pledge on injunctions would just be seen as recognising an anomaly rather than one of correcting injustices in the way they have been often issued.

In line with other countries in the EU, *Looking to the Future* pledged to restore the right of workers to take sympathy action and that in the event of workers taking part in industrial action which is lawful or, to be more precise, has the protection of the law, individual workers should have the right not to be dismissed for taking part in such action. In this, Labour was arguing that the "immunities" for trade unions in the event of industrial action should also apply to the individual workers.[164]

---

munist Review (London), No. 8, Autumn 1990, p. 9.

[163] *Looking to the Future*, ..., p. 34.

[164] See Ibid.

Labour recognised the traditional right to picket "peacefully in limited numbers"[165] – presumably the number would be "six". Where the aim of the 1980 Act had been to make "secondary" action illegal, Labour felt that "secondary" picketing should be permitted "in limited numbers" where the second employer was directly assisting the first employer in frustrating a dispute.[166] On this basis, for example, picketing at the Bury and Warrington offices (in limited numbers) during the Messenger Newspaper Group dispute might have been permitted especially as these offices were subsidiary companies of the same parent company. By contrast, mass picketing would have remained illegal.

Although the Labour Party's proposals seemed to be less restrictive than the Conservative trade union laws, it is unlikely that they would have been adequate, for example, in securing the reinstatement of the "Stockport Six" in the Messenger Newspaper Group dispute. More significantly, perhaps, Labour's proposals would have hardly made any difference to the final outcome of the miners' strike.

Labour's policy review was also significant in that support for a long-standing industrial practice in Britain – the closed shop – had been abandoned. The reason given was that this was not possible under the EC's Social Charter[167], which recognised a "freedom" not to join a trade union. Even so, this Charter, as already noted, only had the status of a political declaration rather than a legal instrument (see pages 108f) so this in itself was no reason for abandoning support for the closed shop. A more convincing reason might have been possible problems associated with the final outcome of the case of the three railwaymen, dismissed for refusing to join a trade union where a union membership agreement had been in force but won their case in 1981 on appeal to the ECtHR in Strasbourg. In this, as already noted, the Strasbourg judges interpreted the right to freedom of association under Article 11 of the ECHR to include a "freedom" of non association.

All the same, in the process of establishing the Single European Market, the support of the European trade unions was crucial, a point which the then West German Chancellor Dr. Helmut Kohl made to Margaret Thatcher at the 1988 EC Summit in Hanover.[168] Consequently, the question of social policy was important in this process. There, Labour could have used this as an opportunity to argue for support for the closed shop but chose not to do so.[169] Ironically, Labour

---

[165] Ibid.

[166] Ibid.

[167] Officially being the *Community Charter of the Fundamental Social Rights of Workers*. See page 102.

[168] See *The Social Charter: How Britain benefits*, Labour Party and British Labour Group of the European Parliament (London), 1989, p. 3.

[169] Kelly, John, Looking to the Future: Labour's anti-union policies, ..., p. 9.

abandoned support for the closed shop at the very time when the Bill, which became the 1990 Act, was going through Parliament. One of the provisions of this Act, as already noted, was to make the "pre-entry" closed shop illegal. Although *Looking to the Future* claimed to support 100% trade union membership, this cannot be compared with the advantages of a closed shop for working people. Essentially on this issue, Labour's policy on the closed shop became that of the Conservative Government.

Given the nature of Labour's "alternative" to the Conservative trade union laws, it is hardly surprising that the then Opposition spokesman on Employment in the House of Commons and later, Labour Party Leader and Prime Minister, Tony Blair, could claim that his Party's proposals were "so reasonable" that a prominent employers' body, the British Institute of Management, had endorsed them![170] All along, the constant theme going through Labour's policy review appears to have been the traditional desire of its parliamentary leaders to restrict militant trade unionism. As John Kelly pointed out in 1990, what really separates Labour and Conservative in the field of trade union and labour relations law, is not whether militant trade unionism should be curbed, but how.[171]

4.4. Conclusion

During the 1980s, the influence of the labour movement as an industrial force was weakened. But it would be wrong to assume that the back of the trade union movement had been broken, once and for all. However, it must be noted that the policies of the Thatcher Government alone cannot claim full credit for its "successes" on the industrial front. In so far as any weakening of trade union power was associated with macroeconomic policies e.g. the imposition of *cash limits* and high interest rates to force through industrial restructuring, it was more a consequence of the policies of the previous Labour Government. This was certainly the case in British Leyland and British Steel.

Where the Thatcher Government can legitimately claim success for its policies lay in the introduction of its measures to force through technological change and changes in working practices (as was shown in the Messenger Newspaper Group dispute). These can certainly be regarded as "microeconomic" measures resulting from the policies of the Thatcher Government.

The context is broader, however. One also has to consider the role of the TUC General Council and any overlap in its position with that of the Labour Party leadership. Whenever trade unionists at the forefront of any industrial struggle were confronted with the full thrust of the Conservative trade union laws, as was

---

[170] Ibid., p. 8.

[171] Ibid.

evident in the Messenger Newspaper Group dispute, the TUC General Council sought to avoid coming into conflict with the law. Even in the historic miners' strike, when the future of an entire industry was at stake and, consequently, of entire communities, TUC leaders were unwilling to implement disciplinary measures against affiliated unions which allowed their members to cross NUM picket lines; most notably against the EETPU. Yet, in the year following this strike, the TUC refrained from taking any disciplinary action against the very same union when it sided with Rupert Murdoch in the News International dispute with its members, as it were, "stealing" the jobs which had previously been done by the print workers he dismissed. Disciplinary action, as earlier noted, was eventually taken against the EETPU but only in 1988 after refusing to abide by two decisions of the TUC Disputes Committee regarding cases of a much smaller magnitude than these two strikes. But by the time the TUC had taken action against the EETPU, it had contributed to two major defeats for the trade union and labour movement.

Looking at the miners' strike from another perspective, the "battle lines" were clear: either one supported the miners and their union, the NUM, or the Thatcher Government. There was no middle road. All the same, Labour leaders missed the opportunity of taking on the Government from another perspective by putting forward an alternative energy policy based on coal and by exposing the real cause of the strike and the role of the State in this process. With hindsight, considering Britain's vast reserves of good quality coal and with North Sea oil reserves having been exhausted within a generation, Labour could have used *Plan for Coal*, as formulated by the previous Labour Government, as a basis of a viable energy policy and, in so doing, strengthening the case of the miners and their union.

Following three election defeats in a row, Labour leaders seemed convinced that the only way of getting back into office was to conduct a wide-ranging review, in effect a revision of its policies. One area where this was particularly evident was in the field of trade union and labour relations law. Yet, in the aftermath of the 1992 election, when the long-expected Labour election victory resulted in the Party's fourth defeat in a row, the question which now needs asking was whether such a policy review was needed after all and if the answer is "Yes" then did this review, and subsequently the 1992 election manifesto, go in the direction as would have been wished for by those who had "lost out" since the 1979 general election?

Chapter Five: From defeat in 1992 to the *New* Labour landslide in 1997

5.1. "Snatching defeat from the jaws of victory". Labour's policy review and the 1992 election campaign: the ERM disaster

In the Labour Party, there had long been differences between the thinking of the Party activists, as expressed in decisions of the Party's annual conferences, and what the opinions of the Party's prominent MPs were on many important issues in what can be referred to as the traditional left/right divide in the Party. This was especially noticeable from the time of the adoption of the Alternative Economic Strategy (AES) in *Labour's Programme 1973* up to the mid 1980s. In this, the Party's policies in economic and social fields were often at variance with those of Labour's parliamentary leadership. This was even more so during the period of the 1974-1979 Labour Government, especially from 1976 through incomes policies together with the impact of the IMF-imposed cuts in public expenditure. The adoption of the AES had originally come about as a result of the leftward shift in the trade union and labour movement at the end of the 1960s/-early 1970s. By 1975, these leftward advances looked to be short-lived.

In June 1975, the Labour Government secured a "Yes" vote, despite overwhelming opposition from the Party itself, in the referendum on continued EEC membership. By implication, Labour's industrial policies had to comply with the "free"-market thinking behind the Treaty of Rome, which meant that they had to be curtailed. Labour was, however, able to rescue British Leyland by bringing the company into public ownership and eventually nationalised the shipbuilding and aircraft industries. However, the fact that the Labour Government could support continued EEC membership would add weight to doubts raised earlier as to whether Labour's parliamentary leadership was committed to the economic and social policies formulated in the early 1970s in any meaningful way. In addition, by the mid to late 1970s, the advances of the left a few years earlier in the AUEW (still then Britain's second largest union) were reversed (see page 157), the left was unable to halt the return of incomes policies and subsequently the IMF-imposed public expenditure cuts as from the end of 1976.

In the aftermath of the 1979 election defeat, the left in the Party went on the offensive. It succeeded in forcing through constitutional changes in the Labour Party itself, leading to the mandatory reselection of MPs and changes in the way of electing the leader and deputy leader of the Labour Party. In addition, the left, through grass-root pressure, managed to exert sufficient pressure on the Parliamentary Labour Party (PLP) to secure the election of Michael Foot as Party Leader in autumn 1980 (under the existing method where Labour MPs alone voted) in preference to Denis Healey who then became Deputy Leader. The left also succeeded in forcing through a number of important policy positions through the

Party's annual conferences, e.g. a commitment to withdrawal from the EEC and to unilateral nuclear disarmament.

These developments led to the polarisation of the traditional left/right divide in the Labour Party already referred to. However, the degree of support for these policy positions and constitutional changes had apparently not been that deep. An indication of this can be seen in that the left suffered a number of setbacks in elections to the Party's national executive committee (NEC) at the 1981 and 1982 Party conferences.[1] Even though support for the left was far from overwhelming, this did not prevent a number of prominent people on the right of the Party from breaking away to form the Social Democratic Party (SDP) and those who remained in the Party not feeling themselves obliged in honouring conference decisions, in as far as they had ever done so. As a result, Labour found itself weakened and divided in the run-up to the 1983 election.

As Labour in this election suffered its severest defeat in the Party's postwar history, a number of prominent Party members saw this as confirmation that the Party's "left-wing" policies made it unelectable. Thus, a process began of dropping policies which were portrayed as being unpopular in the public eye. At the same time, the process began of re-establishing the power structure in the Party, which had been weakened by the advances of the left in the late 1960s/early 1970s (see page 25), so as to restore the authority the leader had traditionally had in the Party. These processes began in autumn 1983 through the election of a new Leader, Neil Kinnock. Subsequently, in autumn 1987, in the aftermath of Labour's third consecutive election defeat (where only a modest recovery was made from its severe losses in 1983), the Party leadership ordered a thorough review of the Party's policies.

In Labour's review of economic and social policies, the following areas can be identified which give an indication of how the Labour Party had moved. Firstly, abandoning the idea that "short-term" macroeconomic management was the key to "full employment". Keynesian macroeconomic management was only seen as being feasible in a closed economy. Consequently, firmer foundations for long-term investment in the productive base of the British economy was to come about by laying more stress on greater price stability and stable interest and exchange rates. This could be seen as a rerun of the policies under previous postwar governments with holding down wage settlements as being the key to any form of economic management. Secondly, existing scepticism of the European Community became one of active support. Not only was this to mean support for the "Social Charter",[2] which the Thatcher Government had refused to

1 See Shaw, Eric, *The Labour Party Since 1979*, Routledge (London and New York), 1994, p. 37.

2 Meaning the *Community Charter of the Fundamental Social Rights of Workers*, December 1989. See page 108.

sign, but, most significantly, this also meant supporting moves towards EMU of which the Party had long been critical. Thirdly, Labour abandoned the idea that nationalisation was the best way of achieving efficiency but instead argued that regulation would achieve the same results. Fourthly, rather than the state determining industrial policy as such, the state should concentrate more on providing a stronger basis for growth through more investment in training, infrastructure and research and development.[3]

In terms of actual policies, a comparison of the 1983, 1987 and 1992 election manifestos provides a good illustration of how far the Labour Party moved in its policy changes. The examples of unilateral nuclear disarmament, public ownership of industry, Labour's long-standing commitment to "full employment" and its position on what is now the European Union (EU) best illustrate this.

In its 1983 election manifesto, the Labour Party stressed the need to stop the nuclear arms race by arguing for "unilateral steps" to be "taken by Britain to secure multilateral solutions on the international level".[4] This call had an added degree of urgency in view of the decision of US President Reagan, with the full support of the Thatcher Government, to deploy Cruise and Pershing II missiles in Western Europe and the decision of the Thatcher Government to update Britain's Polaris missile system with the highly expensive American Trident system.

Despite the severity of the 1983 election defeat, the Party's annual conference, the following year, reaffirmed its call for unilateral nuclear disarmament.[5] In the 1987 election campaign, Labour made no specific call for unilateral nuclear disarmament as in 1983, even though it was still officially Party policy. Labour did, pledge to decommission Polaris, which in any case had become obsolete, and to cancel Trident. However, it argued for the money which would have been saved there to make improvements in Britain's conventional forces[6] where it could have called for some of this money to be spent on socially worthwhile causes. Whilst Labour reaffirmed support for disarmament negotiations so as to seek the removal of intermediate nuclear weapons from Europe,[7] there was a reluctance to call for any special initiatives as in 1983. At Labour's annual conference in October 1989, the Party reversed its call for unilateral nuclear disarmament

---

3 See Eatwell, John, The Development of Labour Policy, 1979-92, in: Michie, Jonathan, *The Economic Legacy 1979-1992*, Academic Press (London and San Diego), 1992, pp. 334f.

4 *The New Hope for Britain: Labour's Manifesto 1983*, The Labour Party (London), 1983, p. 35.

5 Harmer, Harry, *The Longman Companion to: The Labour Party 1900-1988*, Longman (London and New York), 1999, p. 164.

6 *Britain will win: Labour manifesto June 1987*, The Labour Party (London), 1987, p. 15.

7 Ibid., p. 16.

which also indicated a strengthening of Kinnock's position in the Party against the left.[8]

In Labour's 1983 election manifesto, there was not only a commitment to bring back into public ownership those public assets which had been privatised, but also for the State to take a stake in other industries e.g. electronics, pharmaceuticals and other important sectors.[9] By 1987, terms such as "nationalisation" or "public ownership" had been replaced by the more watered-down term "social ownership" which was to imply a "socially owned stake" where public funds would be used to support investment in the private sector.[10] So the emphasis of Labour's industrial policy had switched from the public ownership of major concerns to one of supporting industry (i.e. in the private sector).

The 1983 manifesto made a commitment to British withdrawal from the EEC on the basis that Labour's policies for reviving the British economy e.g. restoring exchange controls, regulating overseas investments, proposals for economic expansion leading to "full employment" were in contravention of the Treaty of Rome.[11] By 1987, the commitment to withdrawal from what is now the EU had not only been dropped but, especially after the election, the Party was in the process of "embracing" it. In this respect, a most notable point of Labour's change in policy on the EU was that the Party dropped its previous scepticism towards the anchoring of sterling in the European Exchange Rate Mechanism (ERM) of the European Monetary System (EMS).

This meant that countries anchoring their currencies in ERM had to tie and maintain their value against other currencies in ERM, most specifically against the deutsch mark. This then obliged governments to take any steps as required, irrespective of any adverse social or economic consequences, to maintain the value of their currencies (see pages 68-73). For this reason, the Labour Party, as well as the previous Labour Government, had been sceptical of the EMS as it would have obliged governments of countries with weaker economies to defend their currencies at what was often seen at overvalued rates, through deflationary measures and increases in interest rates. In this, the previous Labour Government only foresaw the possibility of membership of the EMS providing that it was free of its deflationary bias.[12]

---

8 Harmer, Harry, ..., p. 164.

9 *The New Hope for Britain: Labour's Manifesto 1983*, The Labour Party (London), 1983, p. 12.

10 *Britain will win: Labour manifesto June 1987*, The Labour Party (London), June 1987, p. 6.

11 See *The New Hope for Britain: Labour's Manifesto 1983*, ..., pp. 33f.

12 See *The European Monetary System*, HMSO (London), Cmnd. 7405, November 1978, p. 3, para. 10.

Labour's 1989 policy review, while emphasising the importance of exchange rate stability, recognised the potential problems of ERM and therefore set out the following conditions before sterling could join. Firstly, there had to be less reliance on interest rate adjustment and more cooperation between central banks. Secondly, there had to be an EC-wide trade policy which contributed to balance of payments stability for individual member states. Thirdly, there had to be an EC-wide growth policy and finally, sterling could only enter at a rate which ensured that British goods became and remained competitive.[13] On this question, Labour's policy review effectively restated the position of the previous Labour Government.

In a publication edited by a former Labour Cabinet Minister Douglas Jay in 1990, it was stated that "for a Labour Government to join ERM without achieving the above safeguards [from Labour's policy review] would be to court disaster".[14] Although the decision on the part of Labour leaders to support ERM may have been in part influenced by the desire to "conform" to the policies of its sister parties in Europe and at the same time of hoping to isolate Thatcher on this issue still further, one crucial matter was overlooked. When Labour supported the decision of the Thatcher Government in autumn 1990 to anchor sterling in ERM, not only were Douglas Jay's warnings ignored but, more significantly, the Labour leadership ignored the conditions for ERM membership it had set out in its *own* policy review the previous year.

On the basis of a TUC-Labour Party Liaison Committee document of autumn 1982[15] (in line with its proposed National Economic Assessment – see below), the 1983 manifesto made a commitment to reduce unemployment, then at over 3.2 million (officially) to below one million within five years of taking office.[16] This would have been consistent with the Party's long-standing commitment to "full employment". By 1987, any commitment the Labour Party had to "full employment" became one of just simply reducing unemployment. On the basis of a TUC-Labour Party Liaison Committee document of early 1987,[17] a commitment was made in the 1987 election manifesto to "reduce unemployment by one million within the first two years [of taking office] as the first instalment in beating mass unemployment".[18] However, unemployment had already been falling

---

[13] *Meet the challenge: Make the change: Final Report of Labour's Policy Review for the 1990s*, Labour Party (London), 1989, p. 14.

[14] Jay, (Lord) Douglas (Ed.), *The European Monetary System: The E.R.M. Illusion*, Labour Common Market Safeguards Committee (London), June 1990, p. 13.

[15] See *Economic Planning and Industrial Democracy: The Framework for Full Employment* (Report to the 1982 TUC Congress and Labour Party Conference), TUC-Labour Party Liaison Committee (London), 1982.

[16] *The New Hope for Britain: Labour's Manifesto 1983*, ..., p. 8.

[17] *Work to Win*, TUC-Labour Party Liaison Committee (London), March 1987, pp. 8f.

[18] *Britain will win: Labour manifesto June 1987*, ..., p. 4.

since reaching its peak, officially at over 3.4 million at the beginning of 1986 (see page 78). In December 1988, the Thatcher Government was able to claim that in the 2½ year period from July 1986, unemployment had "fallen by almost a million"[19] effectively making Labour's 1987 manifesto commitment look like one which did not require any special policy initiative.

By 1992, no target figure as such was provided for reducing unemployment though Labour laid great stress on improving training and modernising Britain's infrastructure as part of a national recovery programme, which in turn would provide the basis for tackling mass unemployment.[20] The final report of Labour's policy review for the 1990s (which formed the basis of the 1992 election manifesto) actually reaffirmed the Party's long-standing commitment to "full employment",[21] but largely only through training and modernising infrastructure. So, in the absence of any solid macroeconomic measures, the commitment to "full employment" as pledged in Labour's policy review was lacking in substance. What Labour was aiming at was for measures to encourage private sector investment by bringing Britain's level of training and infrastructure up to those of her major competitors without coming into conflict with any EU regulations. Thus any commitment the Party had to restoring "full employment", on the basis of macroeconomic measures, had to be dropped, in as far as Party leaders had any real intention of enacting such measures.

In fact, macroeconomic measures for attaining "full employment" had not only been portrayed as "unrealistic" in ruling circles, but they were also incompatible with moves towards EMU. An indication that Labour had abandoned the goal of "full employment" can be seen in that the Party leadership supported the anchoring of sterling in ERM and, like Britain's other two main parties, supported continued ERM membership despite at what was clearly an overvalued exchange rate.[22] So, Labour's support for ERM showed that the fight against inflation supplanted "full employment" as the Party's prime economic goal.[23] This implies that any support the Party had previously had for a Keynesian-based macro-economic policy had given way to one based on monetarism.

When sterling joined ERM in October 1990, at the overvalued exchange rate of £1 to 2.95DM, the official reason stated that this move was necessary to fight inflation. But this appeared to be only one reason for this move. It was also felt in a study published by the Full Employment Forum that joining ERM at such a

[19] *Employment for the 1990s*, Cm 540, HMSO (London), December 1988, p. 5, para. 1.1.

[20] See *Labour's election manifesto April 1992*, Labour Party (London), April 1992, pp. 9f.

[21] *Meet the challenge: Make the change: Final Report of Labour's Policy Review for the 1990s*, ..., pp. 26f.

[22] Kitson, Michael and Michie, Jonathan, *Coordinated Deflation – The Tale of Two Recessions*, Full Employment Forum (Watford), 1993, p. 10.

[23] Shaw, Eric, ..., p. 208.

rate would put pressure on industry to reduce costs, especially labour costs, and to force through extensive changes in working practices – very much mirroring the 1979-1981 slump which had been aggravated by high interest rates and an overvalued currency.[24]

Inevitably, the Labour's review of economic and social policies took account of "European integration" which also meant supporting the steps which lead to the Maastricht Treaty. This was also to include the "Social Chapter". Such moves were seen by the Labour leadership as the only alternative, in as far as they provided one at all, to the Conservatives' economic and "social" policies since 1979. This meant that Labour's answer to Britain's weakening position in the advanced industrial world was, similar to that of the Major Government, to endorse the "free"-market and monetarist policies of the EU – the only difference being, in as far as it was really of any significance, for Britain to adopt the "Social Chapter" (see pages 108f).

What the outcome of Labour's review of economic and social policies show is that the differences which had existed between the Party's activists and its Parliamentary leadership in the 1970s and early 1980s had largely been set aside. Not only that. The "free"-market policies of the Thatcher Government appeared to have taken a significant enough hold on public opinion for Labour to feel obliged to conform.

Parallel to the review of the Party's policies, Kinnock sought to consolidate his position and authority as Party leader. This not only meant marginalising those on the left who were critical of the direction he was leading the Party in, but interestingly, seeking to curb the influence of those forces which had originally founded the Labour Party in 1906 – the trade unions. For apart from other considerations, it was the trade unions affiliated to the Party which had been the main force in bringing about the advances of the left in the 1970s and Kinnock himself had supported these advances.

Initially, Kinnock tried to alter the procedures for the selection of prospective parliamentary candidates (PPCs) whereby the principle of "one member, one vote" (OMOV) should replace the existing procedures by which such decisions were ultimately made by CLP general management committees (GMCs), subject to endorsement by Labour's NEC. Under the existing system of selecting a PPC, all full members of the Labour Party in their CLPs had the right to take part in the selection process. In this, individual members were free to attend meetings of their local branch (normally through their ward parties) or local trade union branch or any other body which was affiliated to the local CLP. There, members were free to decide who to invite and interview from those seeking selection and then to make a nomination to their local CLP. However, the delegates these

[24] Kitson, Michael and Michie, Jonathan, ..., p. 10.

bodies sent to the GMCs were not "mandated" to support the person their ward party or local union branch had originally nominated. In preparation for the selection meeting, the CLP compiled a shortlist from those who were nominated and at this meeting, the PPC was then chosen by a secret ballot of those GMC delegates who were present.

As with any organisation, influence tends to lie with its most active members and the Labour Party has never been any exception. In the case of many CLPs, it was often alleged that influence lay with left wing activists working in close liaison with locally affiliated trade unions who would then work to secure the selection of PPCs on the left of the Party whatever the views of the ordinary Party members. So, whatever deficiencies there may have been in the previous process of selecting a PPC, the prime motive behind seeking to replace this through the "OMOV" principle becomes clearer. Thus, by implication, another motive behind the attempt to introduce the "OMOV" principle in the selection of a PPC also becomes clear – to provide some protection for Labour MPs on the right or "centre" of the Party who may have felt vulnerable owing to the introduction of the mandatory reselection of MPs just a few years earlier.

At the 1984 annual conference, Kinnock failed to secure the backing he sought for this measure.[25] However, the 1987 Party conference established the principle of an "electoral college" at CLP level which would then select PPCs. There, individual Party members were to be allocated a minimum of 60% of the votes with the remaining allocated to affiliated unions but this practice was discontinued in 1990 as it was felt to be too cumbersome.[26] Nevertheless, Kinnock was determined that the "OMOV" principle be revived and this issue reappeared at the 1993 annual conference, after his departure as Party leader. At the 1993 conference, it was decided to introduce this principle, not only in the selection of PPCs but also in the election of the constituency parties' representatives on Labour's NEC and in the process for electing the Party leader and deputy leader.[27]

In the meantime, on the pretext of "hard left" candidates being an electoral liability, especially in by-elections when individual candidates would be more prone to possible adverse media publicity than in a general election, Labour's NEC, with its weakened left influence, sought to intervene more directly in the process of selecting parliamentary candidates. One argument used centred on the Party's candidate Peter Tatchell in the by-election in the London constituency of Bermondsey in winter 1983 when a previously safe Labour seat was lost to the Liberals.[28] This process went as far as the NEC excluding specific nominees from local party short lists despite overwhelming support from within the CLP con-

25 See Shaw, Eric, ..., pp. 30f.

26 Ibid., p. 204.

27 Ibid., pp. 117f.

28 Ibid., p. 19.

cerned. One such example occurred in 1991 where the left wing Yorkshire miners' leader Ken Capstick was excluded from the short list in the safe Labour seat of Hemsworth in the Yorkshire coalfield.[29]

The process of excluding certain Party members from becoming parliamentary candidates went even further. In 1995, Labour's NEC refused to endorse a London left-wing Labour councillor Liz Davies (a future Labour NEC member) as Labour's PPC in the Leeds North East constituency despite the fact that she had been selected fully in accordance with Party rules. By implication, this was to have the effect of depriving Party members in this constituency of the parliamentary candidate of their choice.[30]

One initial target in Kinnock's plan to consolidate his position as Party leader was to take action against the Trotskyist Militant Tendency[31] which was well organised in a number of CLPs. An indication of this could be seen in the 1983 election, with two of its supporters, having become the Party's official candidates, were elected to the House of Commons. In the 1987 election, they were to be joined by another Militant supporter. Although Militant had already been subject to an investigation by the Party's NEC leading to the expulsion of five members of the editorial board of its weekly newspaper *Militant* in winter 1983,[32] it was in connection with them gaining control of the Labour group on Liverpool City Council in 1983 when attacks on them became more vigorous.[33]

---

29 Ibid., pp. 115f and 235 footnote 12.

30 See Davies, Liz, *Through the Looking Glass: A Dissenter inside New Labour*, Verso (London and New York), 2001, pp. 4ff. NB Upon a CLP selecting a PPC, he/she is subject to endorsement by the Party's NEC. This is normally a formality upon checking that the selection procedures had been fully complied with. At the same time, however, the NEC is not automatically obliged to endorse a specific candidate. So, over the years, this has led to cases of individual CLPs from being deprived of parliamentary candidates of their choice. This has also gone as far as the NEC imposing a candidate over the heads of an individual CLP. (NB Owing to spending limits for those contesting parliamentary elections, someone who is selected as a candidate by any party before an election has been called is therefore regarded as being the *prospective parliamentary candidate* (PPC). Once an election has actually been called, he/she would then be "adopted" and become the official candidate.)

31 The Militant Tendency had already been subject to an enquiry by Labour's NEC in the early 1980s. The main allegation against it, as clearly explained by a former Labour Party general secretary Jim Mortimer, was that its leaders entered the Labour Party and became active within it, not for the purpose of supporting its existing principles, programme and policies but instead to build an organisation within the Party so as to gain support and win positions of leadership for different principles, a different programme and set of policies. See Mortimer, J. E. (Jim), *A Life on the Left*, The Book Guild Ltd (Lewes, Sussex), 1998, p. 358. NB If such allegations can be made against the Militant Tendency then it can also be argued that they apply to other groups inside the Party be they on the left or on the right.

32 See Thomas-Symonds, Nick, A Reinterpretation of Michael Foot's Handling of the Militant Tendency, in: *Contemporary British History*, Routledge Taylor & Francis Group (London), Vol. 19 No. 1, Spring 2005, pp. 32f.

33 See Harmer, Harry, ..., pp. 126, 164 and 269f.

The background to the situation in Liverpool needs to be judged in the wider context of the severe social problems in the City together with the financial squeeze the Thatcher government was generally imposing on local councils as part of its programme of cutting public expenditure. In this, local councils were compelled to keep their spending levels within tight constraints. This then forced them to impose cuts in services with the effect that there was often, in the view of mostly Labour councils and councillors, inadequate provision being made in economically and socially deprived areas like Liverpool where there would be more demands on council services than in the more affluent areas. This also led to a number of local councils being "rate-capped" (having part of their funding from central government[34] withheld for failing to keep their spending within the guidelines set by central government). In addition, there was the ultimate threat of individual councillors being surcharged (being held personally liable) for the consequences of voting for budgets going beyond the constraints the Thatcher government permitted. This had the effect of putting numerous local councillors in an impossible position with them being effectively "blackmailed", as it were, to implement spending cuts against their will and the mandate they had secured from the electors. Attempts by individual local councils, principally Labour-controlled, to resist these cutbacks had little effect.

However, in 1985, in an attempt to highlight the severe social problems in Liverpool, the Labour-controlled council (under the influence of the Militant Tendency) took the extraordinary step of sending out redundancy notices to all of the council's employees although, it must be stressed, there was never the intension of actually dismissing them. Nevertheless, this angered the unions and it gave Kinnock the "green light" he had long been seeking in taking decisive action against it.[35]

Following Kinnock's forceful attack on Militant supporters in Liverpool at the 1985 Labour Party conference, the Party decided to establish an inquiry into their activities in the city (which can be broadly interpreted as yet another inquiry into the activities of the Militant Tendency generally). This was to be followed by the expulsion of seven Militant supporters in the city, the following year, together with other expulsions of Militant supporters elsewhere. Whilst there was no sympathy at all for them on the right or the "centre" of the Party, many on the left, whilst neither supportive of the policies it advocated nor of its tactics, were opposed to any form of disciplinary action against it fearing that it could have wide-ranging implications for the Party leading to a "right-wing" counter offensive against the policy and constitutional changes which had only been adopted in recent years. Indeed, as subsequent events under Kinnock's leadership were to show, such fears were not without foundation. Attacks on the Militant Tendency by Kinnock were part of his strategy for marginalising and

[34] See footnote 40.

[35] See Shaw, Eric, ..., pp. 31-36. See also Thomas-Symonds, Nick, ..., p. 34.

discrediting his critics on the left in the Party with the ultimate aim of consolidating his position and of forcing through the changes in the Party he wanted.

It was in 1990 when a Militant supporter stood against the official Labour candidate in an election in Liverpool when the Party leadership seized the opportunity to take further action against the Militant Tendency. The final break with this grouping in the Party came in winter 1992, in the run-up to the general election, with the expulsion of its MPs from the PLP and the Party itself.[36]

The general impact of Kinnock's speech to the 1985 annual conference, with his attacks on the Militant Tendency in Liverpool hitting the limelight, had the effect of him winning support from a number of people traditionally on the left of the Party whilst angering others. So with the left being divided between those supporting him and those opposing him, his position as Party leader was consolidated even if at the time he was unable to win conference votes on specific issues.[37] It was only through Labour's policy review in 1989 when Kinnock ultimately succeeded in gaining conference support for the policies which he believed would help Labour to win the following election.

It is interesting to note that up to the time of Kinnock becoming Party Leader, only two Labour leaders in Britain's post-war history had never become Prime Minister. They were Hugh Gaitskell[38] and Michael Foot. In the 1959 general election campaign, Gaitskell was up against a Prime Minister Harold Macmillan, whose party was able to capitalise on the upturn in the British economy in that year. This was despite the fact that over this decade as a whole, Britain's economic performance had been constantly held back with balance of payments deficits forcing the government to enact "stop-go" measures which largely took the form of incomes policies. In the 1983 election, as already noted, Foot was severely handicapped by the various difficulties confronting the Party under his leadership whilst not over-looking the implications of the outcome of Britain's war against Argentina the previous year.

If one could assume that in the run-up to the 1987 election, the political environment Labour found itself in wasn't yet favourable enough for it to mount a serious enough challenge to the Conservatives for power, this was certainly not the case in 1992. The question which needs asking is what actually happened in the run-up to this election?

The expectation was that after 13 years in opposition, having abandoned policies which, in the view of Party leaders and Kinnock himself, hampered the Party's

---

36 Harmer, Harry, ..., p. 172.

37 See Shaw, Eric, ..., pp. 35f.

38 Leader of the Labour Party from December 1955 up to his death in January 1963. Gaitskell succeeded the former Prime Minister Clement Attlee upon stepping down as Party Leader.

appeal to the electorate, and the Conservative Government having lost the support of many who had previously supported it, that Labour would once again become the party of government. However, this was not realised. If the causes of the 1983 election defeat were a politically divided party challenging a government which was still riding on the crest of a wave following the outcome of the war against Argentina the previous year, they surely weren't responsible for the defeat in 1987 and even less so in 1992. This would then lead to the question of whether a policy review of such a magnitude was needed at all.

By 1989/1990, public discontent with the Thatcher Government was such that it became highly questionable whether the Conservative Party under her leadership could win another term in office. The Conservatives had suffered a serious defeat in the 1989 European elections and in early 1990, Labour had been up to 20% ahead of the Conservatives in opinion polls.[39] The circumstances which influenced the outcome of the 1983 election which saved the Conservative Party from what would have almost certainly been defeat after its first term in office were unlikely to reappear.

On the economic front, by the end of the 1980s, the original strategy of the Thatcher Government of seeking to base Britain's future prosperity by strengthening the standing of the City of London as a major international financial centre had lost its credibility in the aftermath of the stock market crash in October 1987 leaving the international standing of the City of London weakened for a number of years to come (see page 73). Interest rates, after having fallen by May 1988 to their lowest levels since autumn 1977, started rising once again and by October 1989, they had risen to 15% and stayed at that level up to the day before sterling joined ERM. Thus, the slowdown in economic growth this precipitated meant that unemployment was going to rise again (see Appendix, tables 5 and 7). On top of this, there was growing public discontent due to the critical financial situation in the NHS and education (both aggravated by tight constraints in public expenditure and high interest rates) and the introduction of the "poll tax".[40] There were, as already noted, divisions within the Cabinet over Europe

[39] Junor, Penny, *The Major Enigma*, Michael Joseph Ltd (published by the Penguin Group (London)), 1993, p. 187.

[40] Up to 1989/1990, the principle sources of local government finance came from central government through the "rate support grant" and locally through the "rates" whereby those owning or renting property paid "rates" which were, in part, determined by the "rateable value" of the property they owned or rented. On this basis, local councils levied "rates" to help finance their expenditure. The "poll tax" (officially known as the Community Charge) replaced the "rates" and the principle behind this was that everyone over 18 should pay the *same* tax to the local authority in the area they lived. The introduction of the "poll tax" was a commitment in the 1987 Conservative election manifesto (see *The Next Moves Forward: The Conservative Manifesto 1987*, ..., pp. 62f). The injustice of this measure was that it neither took account of the incomes of the individual residents, nor of the fact that people living in more affluent areas found themselves paying less to fund local government services whereas people living in poorer areas, often with major social problems arising out of

especially over the anchoring of sterling in ERM, which Thatcher had been able to resist for five years until October 1990, just a few weeks before the end of her premiership.[41]

Ultimately, it was the sequence of events in that very month (October 1990) in connection with ERM which finally set in motion the process which led to the end of Thatcher's premiership.[42]

Even if Margaret Thatcher's replacement as Prime Minister and Conservative Party Leader had, on the surface, reversed the tide of public discontent long enough for the Conservatives to secure a fourth consecutive term of office, one has to assess the extent to which there had been weaknesses in the policies and campaigning strategy of the Labour Party. In the run-up to the 1992 election, the

mass unemployment, found themselves having to pay more. This problem was clearly illustrated by comparing the examples of two London boroughs, Wandsworth, where the "poll tax" in the first year of its short-lived existence was £148 (the lowest in the country) and Haringey where it was £573 (see Junor, Penny, ..., p. 188). The "poll tax" was part of the Thatcher Government's strategy to force local councils to carry out central government expenditure cuts which also included the introduction of compulsory competitive tendering for council services i.e. enabling private companies to take over the task of supplying such services e.g. refuse collection. The 1987 Conservative manifesto attempted to justify this policy on the pretext of "left-wing Labour councils" being irresponsible and resisting expenditure cuts. Owing to the unpopularity of the "poll tax" (a factor in Thatcher's downfall in autumn 1990), the problems involved in collecting it, not withstanding the large numbers of people who were unable and/or unwilling to pay it, the Major Government had little alternative other than to "replace" it. This was done through the introduction of the "council tax" whereby a "tax" was to be levied on each household, as with the "rates", but based on the number of adults living in the house as well as the value of the property. So, this tax can be seen as a combination of the previous system of the "rates" and the "poll tax" with *some* of the more open injustices of the latter being dropped.

41 Junor, Penny, ..., p. 180.

42 The tight grip Thatcher had long held over the government and party she led was, as already noted, loosened when she ultimately found herself having to give way on ERM. Nevertheless, at the EC Council summit meeting in Rome on 27 October, 1990, just three weeks after sterling entering ERM, Thatcher found herself isolated among her European counterparts when she applied the brakes on further progress towards EMU. This prompted the resignation of the Leader of the House of Commons, the former Foreign Secretary Sir Geoffrey Howe. Subsequently, the former Defence Secretary Michael Heseltine, who had resigned from the Thatcher Government in 1986, announced that he was to challenge Thatcher for the leadership of the Conservative Party and, by implication, for the premiership. Whilst she still continued to have the backing of the majority of Conservative MPs, the outcome of the ballot on 20 November was that under Party rules, she was four votes short of the majority needed to remain in office without any further voting. (See Junor, Penny, ..., pp. 189-205). The significance of this ballot result was that the grip she had long held over the Party and government was ultimately broken. Even if she had to decided to fight further and win, the outcome of this ballot was such that she could no longer continue in office with the degree of authority she had previously had. This opened the way for John Major to enter the leadership contest the following week, the outcome being that he became Thatcher's successor.

masses of ordinary people were eager that decisive measures were put forward so as to tackle the worsening problems of Britain's social infrastructure. The problems of the NHS and education highlighted the seriousness of Britain's social infrastructure.

The crisis in the NHS, on the one hand, was already apparent in terms of longer waiting lists, the cancellation of operations, ward closures and staff shortages. On the other hand, there were fears that this crisis would worsen through the Government's "reforms" of the health service. These were largely due to the NHS and Community Care Act, which came into effect in April 1991, with its emphasis was on doctors' surgeries and hospitals "managing" their own budgets and for hospitals being able to *opt out* of local area authority control with them being "managed" instead by trusts or becoming self-governing units. In this, the TUC expressed concerns that this would lead to a wide range services, having been previously administered by the NHS, being contracted out thus threatening the terms and conditions of employment of NHS employees.[43] All this gave credit to claims from the Opposition that the Government was embarking upon "creeping privatisation" of the NHS[44] and was also working towards the creation of a "two-tier" health service with the wealthier being able to get prompt treatment through taking out private insurance with everyone else having to make do with what the health service could provide on its meagre resources.

A similar picture had been emerging in education through the worsening terms and conditions of employment for teachers thus leading to a shortage of teachers and an increase in the workload of those remaining in the profession. Furthermore, there had been cutbacks in much-needed capital expenditure in schools. There then came the question of how the urgently-needed improvements in the health service and education were going to be funded and in the midst of an economic downturn. There Labour faltered.

If, on the one hand, higher social expenditure was to mean increases in taxation, Labour may well have had anxiety over possible electoral consequences. In fact, there was a forceful Conservative campaign in autumn 1991/winter 1992, capitalised upon in the mass media, depicting that Labour's expenditure plans would lead to higher taxation on the masses of ordinary people and that the Party was lacking in economic competence.[45] On the other hand, proposals for more social expenditure had to take account of the conditions for anchoring sterling in ERM, as part of the process towards establishing EMU, which then became the cornerstone of the Maastricht Treaty.

---

[43] See *Trades Union Congress 1991: General Council Report*, TUC (London), August 1991, pp. 37f, paras. 44-46 and pp. 106f, paras. 124.

[44] Shaw, Eric, ..., p. 132.

[45] Ibid., pp. 136f.

Thus, by supporting the Thatcher Government's decision to anchor sterling in ERM in October 1990 and at an overvalued rate, additionally meaning interest rates having to remain high, Labour, in effect, prevented itself from offering any serious alternative macroeconomic policies in the 1992 election.[46] Not only that. Labour also deprived itself of the opportunity of exposing the deflationary and monetarist bias of ERM, of which it had long been aware, and hence its predictable economic and social consequences.

The dilemma Labour put itself in was aggravated by the fact that when sterling entered ERM, the "Lawson boom" had already passed and there was to be yet another downturn in the British economy. This, as already noted, led to a severe economic crisis, like that of 1979 to 1981, due very much to exceptionally high interest rates defending an overvalued currency. Thus, despite the growth of real GDP declining rapidly as from 1988 with it actually being negative in 1991 and remaining negative throughout much of 1992, the pledge "to curb inflation Labour will maintain the value of the pound within the European Exchange Rate Mechanism"[47] would, as had already been predicted in an article in the *Guardian*, the previous summer, guarantee "unemployment of 2.5 million or above for the foreseeable future" thus making "Mr. Kinnock's macro-economic strategy virtually indistinguishable from Mr. Major's".[48]

The run-up to the 1992 election coincided with the conclusion of the Maastricht Treaty.[49] This was to lead to the introduction of a single European currency – the *euro* – in 12 of the 15 member states of the EU at the beginning of 2002. A precondition for an EU member state to have the *euro* introduced in its country was that its currency had to be anchored in ERM for at least two years – an issue which Margaret Thatcher had vigorously opposed for as long as she could. On this question she found herself isolated in the EC, as it was, as well as finding mounting opposition within her government. With EMU being the cornerstone of the Maastricht Treaty, it is questionable whether this Treaty could have been concluded for as long as she remained in office. This particular issue was the most significant factor which forced her out of office in autumn 1990.

With John Major replacing Margaret Thatcher as Prime Minister in November 1990, it was he who took over from her in the final stages of concluding the Maastricht Treaty. There, on this particular issue, the new Prime Minister was accredited with remarkable skill.[50] Against seemingly formidable odds, he secured *opt-outs* for Britain, most notably on phase three of EMU with its planned

---

46 Michie, Jonathan, *Maastricht: Implications for Public Services*, Nalgo (Manchester), 1993, p. 17.

47 *Labour's election manifesto April 1992*, ..., p. 12.

48 Elliott, Larry, Labour: Is this all there is?, in: *Guardian* (London), 26 August 1991, p. 10.

49 See Chapter 2, footnote 68.

50 Shore, (Lord) Peter, *Separate Ways*, Gerald Duckworth & Co. Ltd (London), 2000, p. 91.

introduction of the single European currency together with treaty constraints on the extent of future government borrowing, though he did accept phase two of EMU[51] with its so-called convergence criteria.[52] Having also secured an *opt-out* for Britain on the "Social Chapter",[53] Major could capitalise on his "success" in the Maastricht negotiations and in so doing, help unite his Party behind him in the run-up to the 1992 election. Labour, on the other hand, having tied itself to ERM, found itself cornered and unable to offer an alternative programme to the Major Government convincing enough to fully mobilise its potential voters.

Yet, the irony of Labour's position (like that of the Major Government) was finally exposed on Wednesday 16 September, 1992, barely five months after the election. On what became known as *Black Wednesday*, to the Major Government as well as to other supporters of ERM and EMU, or *White Wednesday*, to its opponents,[54] sterling was ejected from ERM. As this enabled a big drop in interest rates and thus the exchange rate of sterling to reflect more its *real* value on the world's money markets, there then came a period of modest recovery in the UK economy together with a steady fall in the number of people out of work (see page 77). Prior to ERM membership, UK economic growth had been averaging at about 2% per year and this was similar following sterling's ejection.[55]

During the period of ERM membership, the UK economy, due to high interest rates supporting an overvalued currency, was estimated to have shrunk by 3.68% in terms of GDP whilst at the same time, unemployment, using official government figures, rose by 1.2 million to 2.85 million or, on the basis of using the method calculate unemployment figures in 1979, had risen by 1.3 million to 3.99 million.[56] The cost of this fall in GDP during ERM membership has been estimated at £23.1 billion in terms of 1992 money and the costs of the extra 1.2

---

51 Ibid., pp. 91f.

52 As part of the process towards EMU and the introduction of the single European country, EU member states had to agree to the introduction of "convergence criteria" as originally defined by Article 109j of the Maastricht Treaty and explained in a protocol attached to the Treaty. This meant firstly, maintaining the country's exchange rate within ERM, secondly, achieving a high degree of price stability, thirdly, achieving long-term stable interest rates comparable with those of the best performing member states and fourthly, achieving a stable financial position. See Kenen, Peter B., *Economic and Monetary Union in Europe: Moving beyond Maastricht*, Cambridge University Press, 1995, pp. 127ff. Achieving a "stable financial position" meant in particular that the national debts of members states should not exceed 60% of GDP and, more significantly, that budget deficits should not exceed 3% of GDP. It has been this criterion above all others which has decided whether the *euro* could be introduced and whether it could be introduced in other EU member states.

53 See page 109, footnote 225.

54 Shore, (Lord) Peter, ..., p. 93.

55 Burkitt, Brian et. al., *There is an alternative: Britain and its relationship with the EU*, Campaign for an Independent Britain (London), 1996, p. 24.

56 Ibid., pp. 23f.

million unemployed claiming benefit together with the loss of tax revenue, according to Treasury estimates, were a total of £10.8 billion.[57]

Even if one wishes to question the accuracy of the above figures, one thing remains indisputable. The proposals Labour and the Liberal Democrats put forward for more expenditure on health and education in the 1992 election campaign can be seen as being modest in comparison with the economic consequences of ERM membership.

Had the Labour Party, at the very latest, by the time of the finalising of the Maastricht Treaty, questioned ERM in relation to the much-needed social expenditure plans the Party advocated, another dimension to the 1992 election campaign would have been introduced from which the Party could have benefited, given the wide degree of scepticism towards the European Community from among a large section of the electorate. All this could have put John Major on the defensive and may have prevented him from "seizing the initiative" in the run-up to this election. So there are strong grounds for arguing that support for ERM turned out to be a major cause of Labour's fourth consecutive election defeat because the monetarist constraints of ERM went unchallenged and took priority over a coherent macroeconomic policy which was needed to promote employment and much-needed improvements in public services and Britain's social infrastructure. Whilst not overlooking the damaging impact of the "Sheffield rally" on the final stages of the election campaign, in which Kinnock, as it were, had effectively celebrated victory in front of the entire media a before the campaign was actually over,[58] the "disaster" which Douglas Jay in 1990 had warned of Labour supporting ERM (see page 203) went unheeded and instead was to be suffered by the Labour Party in the 1992 election.

Comparing Thatcher's and Kinnock's positions on EMU, one can conclude the following: Thatcher's opposition to it forced her out of office whilst Kinnock's support for it kept him out of office.

One area from which Labour could have profited in the 1992 election campaign was the "peace dividend" following the recent political changes in Eastern and Central Europe and the "break-up" of the Soviet Union, the previous year. Even if only small in comparison with the economic consequences of ERM, Labour could have argued for wide-ranging disarmament measures with potential savings from military spending being diverted to areas like education and the health service but, like the other two major parties, chose not to do so. Recognising that disarmament measures could threaten the security of jobs in Britain's defence industries, as had already been the case, Labour, symbolically, advoca-

57 Ibid., p. 24.

58 See Shaw, Eric, ..., p. 143.

ted the creation of a Defence Diversification Agency[59] but the question of the "peace dividend", which could have added a new dimension to the 1992 election campaign, was kept out.

On the surface, the proposals put forward by the Liberal Democrats in the 1992 election for tackling the serious financial situation in education and the health service were more convincingly put than those of the Labour Party. Whereas Labour's election manifesto pledged that "over the next 22 months, additional resources of at least £600 million will be made available for investment in education",[60] the Liberal Democrats pledged to "increase investment in education by £2 billion in the first year, even though this [would] require an extra penny in the pound on income tax".[61] Both Labour and the Liberal Democrats pledged additional resources for the NHS and opposed the Conservative Government's health service "reforms". In this, Labour pledged that "instead of cutting income tax, we will make additional resources of at least £1 billion available for investment in the NHS over the next 22 months. Each year thereafter, we will continue to tackle underfunding".[62] But as to how the extra expenditure on education and the NHS was to be funded, Labour was rather vague which left itself exposed in the 1992 election campaign.

Even if the Liberal Democrats, taking the case of education were, on the surface, a little clearer in their proposals and more open in how they were going to be funded than Labour, ERM and the conditions attached for defending sterling's overvalued exchange rate can be seen as a reason as to why they thought an increase in income tax was necessary.

The Liberal Democrats' support for ERM was more forthright than that of the Major Government and the Labour Opposition in that it actually pledged to "put the pound into the narrow band of the Exchange Rate Mechanism".[63] Although, as already noted, the value of currencies in ERM were allowed to diverge within a range of plus or minus 2.25% against the central rate with value of sterling and the Spanish peseta being allowed to fluctuate in a wider band of plus or minus 6%, the pledge put sterling "into the narrow band" of ERM would have risked Britain having to impose even tighter financial constraints on public expenditure than those which had already been implemented. All the same, the Liberal Democrats, especially with regard to their proposals for funding improvements in education, helped to expose a weakness in Labour's manifesto which didn't go unnoticed in the election campaign.

---

59 *Labour's election manifesto April 1992*, ..., p. 27.

60 Ibid., p. 17.

61 *Changing Britain for good: The Liberal Democrat Manifesto 1992*, Liberal Democrat Publications (Dorchester, Dorset), 1992, p. 31.

62 *Labour's election manifesto April 1992*, ..., p. 15.

63 *Changing Britain for good: The Liberal Democrat Manifesto 1992*, ..., p. 18.

Following this election, Labour was confronted with a serious dilemma. Despite the extensive review of its policies in the aftermath of the 1987 election defeat, in the 1992 election campaign, the Party was unable to convince the masses of working people of the sincerity of its policies in order to bring thirteen years of Conservative rule to an end through the election of a Labour Government. Thus, what can be termed as the strategy of abandoning principles for the spoils of office, the outcome of Labour's policy review, turned out to be a failure, not only for Kinnock himself but also for the Party at large and moreover, the masses of ordinary people who felt they had lost out due to the policies of the previous thirteen years.

Looking at Labour's dilemma from another angle, Labour Party specialist Eric Shaw compared the outcome of the 1987 and the 1992 elections noting that, whereas in 1987 the Conservatives gained credit for the (apparently) booming economy, five years later, it managed to escape the blame when it faltered. The Conservative Party had succeeded in staying in power despite the two worst recessions since the 1930s with growth, investment and the balance of payments all being worse than any of its predecessors since the war.[64]

Thus, following two election defeats in a row and the failure of its policy review, Kinnock resigned as Party Leader. John Smith, with wide backing from among the Party's affiliated trade unions, the PLP and from within the Party at large, was overwhelmingly elected Party Leader in July 1992.

5.2. From Labour to *New* Labour: the impact of the change of Party leadership on the Party's development in the aftermath of the 1992 election defeat

The changes that took place in the Labour Party in the aftermath of its 1992 election defeat were a culmination in a process which can be traced back to the early 1980s through a split in the mainstream left opposition in the Party itself. This split became initially noticeable in the run-up to the 1981 Labour Party conference when a group of left Labour MPs around the future Party Leader, Neil Kinnock, refused to support the challenge of leading left Labour MP, Tony Benn, to Denis Healey for Deputy Leader of the Party. This election took place under the new method of electing the Party leader and deputy leader.[65]

[64] Shaw, Eric, ..., pp. 183f.

[65] At the 1980 Labour Party Conference, it was decided that the franchise for electing the Party leader and deputy leader be widened but could not agree upon the method at the time. So in winter the following year, a special conference was convened to resolve this problem. There, it was decided that these posts be elected through an "electoral college" which allocated 40% of the votes to affiliated trade unions, 30% to CLPs and just 30% to the PLP whereas up to then, it was the PLP alone which decided who should be in these posts. See Shaw, Eric, *The Labour Party since 1945*, Blackwell Publishers (Oxford), 1996, p. 164.

As a consequence of the left offensive in the Party following the 1979 election defeat, sufficient enough pressure, as already noted, was exerted on the PLP in autumn 1980 from the Party at large to secure the election of Michael Foot, on the left of the Party, as Leader in preference to Healey who then replaced Foot as Deputy Leader.[66] James Callaghan, who up to then had been Party Leader, stepped down before a new system of electing his successor had come into place in the hope that Healey would succeed him.[67] However, Healey, having held the key post of Chancellor of the Exchequer in the 1974-1979 Labour Government and therefore having enacted policies which had often brought it into conflict with the organised labour movement and the Party's annual conferences, eventually culminating in the "winter of discontent" in the run-up to the 1979 election, endured considerable opposition to his leadership bid from within the ranks of the Party. So, a number of Labour MPs, who may have otherwise supported him, took account of this thus giving Foot a narrow victory. Thus a major aspect of the contest to succeed Callaghan as Party Leader can be seen as apportioning blame on Healey for the 1979 election defeat. This was not the case with Foot. Even though he was up to 1980 Deputy Leader and having also served in the 1974-1979 Labour Government, continued to enjoy widespread support and sympathy across virtually the entire spectrum of the Party. However, despite this broad base of support for the new Leader, Labour's shadow cabinet, elected by the PLP alone, was largely dominated by MPs who were closely associated with the discredited policies of the previous Labour Government and therefore did not support the direction in which the Party was then moving.

All this put Foot in the unenviable position of trying to unite a Party in which there was a polarisation between the masses of ordinary members and the majority of its MPs. Whereas the Party leader could normally rely on the support of the PLP, even if the Party at large thought differently, this wasn't so noticeable under Foot's leadership. Thus during his three-year tenure in this position and hence, Leader of the Opposition, Foot found himself having to devote considerable energy in seeking to overcome the political differences between the Party's MPs and its activists. This made his main task as Opposition Leader all the more difficult.

However legitimate the call for extending the franchise for electing the Party leader and deputy leader may have been, one thing became clear which the left may not have fully considered at the time. Without the support and cooperation of the Party's MPs, no Labour leader can effectively "lead" the Party because, despite this leftward shift in the Party at large, the Party's MPs continued, as it were, to remain a powerful institution within the Party. So, whenever the Party's MPs, and even more so whenever Labour is in office, found itself in conflict

[66] See Shaw, Eric, *The Labour Party Since 1979*, Routledge (London and New York), 1994, p. 18.

[67] Ibid.

with conference decisions, as had often been the case between 1974 and 1979, at the end of the day, there was little that the Party could do to actually to "force" its MPs and any Labour government to honour conference decisions unless it could mobilise the sort of opposition in unison with the organised labour movement which ultimately defeated *In Place of Strife* in 1969/1970. So this reality added an extra degree of legitimacy to the call for the introduction of the mandatory reselection of Labour MPs.[68] However, this call should not be seen as one of intending to "blackmail" MPs but rather to increase the degree of accountability between Labour MPs and the CLPs as well as the Party at large.

Although with the introduction of mandatory reselection, a number of Labour MPs feared being vulnerable, there was no indication to show that MPs on the "right" of the Party would be deselected *en masse*. In the overwhelming majority of cases, Labour MPs could rely on the support of their CLPs even if there were differences over specific issues and Conference decisions. So for as long as the political leanings and influence of the PLP remained, there would have anyway been constraints on the extent of this leftward shift in the Party.

Nevertheless, the outcome of the 1980 Conference did not prevent a group of prominent MPs and former ministers on the right of the Party from breaking away to form the SDP which then confronted the Labour Party with its most serious split for fifty years. With the SDP subsequently forming an alliance with the Liberal Party,[69] the opposition to the Thatcher Government, both inside and outside Parliament, was weakened to the extent that this, not forgetting the outcome of Britain's war against Argentina, all but guaranteed a victory for the Conservative Party at the following general election no matter when it was going to be held.

---

[68] Up to 1980, a sitting Labour MP was automatically deemed to be the Party's PPC for his constituency unless he decided to step down or his CLP, in accordance with Party rules and subject to the approval by Labour's NEC, decided otherwise. Through the introduction of mandatory reselection, other Party members, eligible to stand for election to the House of Commons, were also free to seek nomination in a Labour-held constituency in the same way as in constituencies not held by Labour. There was nothing "revolutionary" as such about this rule change as in other countries e.g. Germany and the United States, sitting members of parliament had already had to go through various selection procedures, also being open to other party members and often to sympathisers as well so as to become their parties' official candidates at subsequent elections. So, in a sense, all the Labour Party did was to conform to what is standard practice elsewhere and this decision should be judged as an expression of the overwhelming feeling among Party members that their MPs should be more accountable to those who helped to get them elected. The controversy behind this rule change was therefore less about the change itself but more about the atmosphere in the Party at the time when it was made. In this, a number of Labour MPs felt "threatened" and there were a few cases of a sitting Labour MP, not just on the right of the Party, failing to be reselected.

[69] In the year following the 1987 election, the SDP and the Liberal Party agreed to merge and formed the Social and Liberal Democratic Party, then to become the Liberal Democrats.

So Foot's leadership was, on the one hand, overshadowed by a polarisation between the Party's MPs and by its constituency activists and, on the other hand, through this defection to the SDP. These developments set the background to the deputy leadership contest at the 1981 Labour Party conference. Put differently, the Party had to decide between seeing, publicly, to heal the political rift in the Party, in particular with its MPs, or to break clean from the sort of policies which the left viewed as being responsible for the 1979 election defeat as well as earlier general election defeats. Consequently, the significance of this contest was therefore less about *who* would win but more about the subsequent direction of the Party under Foot's leadership.

Foot, fearing that Benn's challenge for the deputy leadership would deepen the divisions within the Party still further, was bitterly opposed to his contest and a number of MPs on the left of the Party at the time, including Foot's successor as Party Leader Niel Kinnock, thought similarly. However, numerous activists in the constituency parties and a number of trade unionists thought differently. In the end, Healey was narrowly re-elected.[70] Whether or not his victory publicly led to a healing of the rift in the Party, one thing became clear. The outcome of this contest showed that the advances the left had made up to this point had reached their peak. This can be seen in that at this very Conference, no less than five left wingers lost their seats on Labour's NEC. This was to be followed by another two the following year with the result of the political composition of the NEC changing. In this, the left lost control of its most important power base in the Party[71] even if the right, then meaning those closely associated with the policies of the previous Labour Government, had not gained control of this key Party body.

So, from 1981, the influence of the left in the Party began to decline and step-by-step, this laid the basis by which a future Party leader, prepared to "take on the left", could restore the degree of authority the leader had traditionally had in the Party (based on this tight cohesion of the PLP, the Cabinet/Shadow Cabinet the NEC and the annual conference). Following Foot's resignation as Party Leader in the aftermath of the 1983 election, it was Niel Kinnock who succeeded him. By "taking on" those on the left who did not agree with the direction in which the new Leader was seeking to push the Party in, he could step-by-step, with the support of the right, restore the degree of authority the leader had long had in the Party. One aspect of this process was to integrate new people into the Party leadership who became central to the *new* Labour project as from the mid 1990s.

---

70 Shaw, Eric, *The Labour Party Since 1979*, Routledge (London and New York), 1994, pp. 18f.

71 Ibid., pp. 37f.

It is worth noting that in the contest for the Party leadership at the 1983 Conference, the majority of the left in the Party was unable to vote for the person who they would have really wanted, Tony Benn. Before the 1983 election, constituency boundaries were revised with the effect that Benn's constituency in Bristol "disappeared". By having such a strong following among the mass of Party activists, Benn would have had little difficulty in being selected in a safe Labour constituency in another part of the country. However, having represented a Bristol in constituency in the House of Commons for so many years, he felt obliged "to face the electorate" in this city, fully aware of the likely outcome given the political climate at the time. Benn contested the new constituency of Bristol East which was won by his Conservative opponent.

Thus being out of Parliament at that particular point in time, Benn was unable to contest the Party leadership. This meant that in this contest, Kinnock could rally the support of the left, despite having angered many of them two years earlier by publicly attacking Benn's bid for Deputy Leader, as well as rallying support from within the "centre" of the Party.[72] Put differently, in this contest, Kinnock turned out to be the beneficiary of Benn's defeat in the 1983 general election. Labour Party specialist Eric Shaw has indicated that had Benn been returned to Parliament in 1983 and then contested the Party leadership in the autumn of that year, Kinnock might have been eliminated from this contest after the first ballot thus improving the chances of Roy Hattersley,[73] who was supported by the right as well as from within the "centre" of the Party. Although Tony Benn won the parliamentary by-election in Chesterfield, the following year, the leadership question had already been settled.

Under Kinnock's leadership, as the 1987 election manifesto demonstrated, the Party had already begun the process of gradually distancing itself from many of the policies which the left had succeeded in forcing through only a few years previously. This process, as already noted, culminated in the Party's policy review in 1989 in the hope of making the Party "electable". But, as the outcome of the 1987 and 1992 elections show, Labour, in the words of one of the Party's former general secretaries, Jim Mortimer, "failed to convince the electorate that its policy offered an effective alternative".[74]

Whereas a major thrust of Kinnock's leadership was to marginalise the left so as to force through the various changes which he deemed as necessary for the Party to win a general election, this was neither the style of his predecessor, Michael Foot, nor that of his successor, John Smith. Smith, even though he came from

---

[72] See Shaw, Eric, *The Labour Party since 1945*, ..., p. 168.

[73] Ibid., p. 180, Note 2. At the 1983 Labour Party Conference, Roy Hattersley was elected to replace Denis Healey as Deputy Party Leader who stepped down.

[74] Mortimer, J. E. (Jim), *A Life on the Left*, The Book Guild Ltd (Lewes, Sussex), 1998, p. 396.

the right of the Party, was seen as someone who, in Mortimer's words, "sought to build bridges within the Party" and "was tolerant towards the left".[75] In this sense, Smith should not be judged as "Kinnock's successor" – the person who can be regarded as "his successor", Tony Blair, was to become Party Leader due to a tragic misfortune just two years later. For the Labour Party and the broader labour movement, John Smith's sudden death in 1994 was a severe loss.

Nevertheless, upon becoming Party Leader in July 1992, Smith announced his intention to reform the Party's relationship with the trade unions and to abolish the union "block vote"[76] at Party conferences. At the September 1992 Party conference, the strength of trade union delegates' votes was reduced from 87% to 70% but conference voted to retain union participation in leadership elections and in the selection of parliamentary candidates.[77] In September the following year, the Party conference decided to introduce the "OMOV" principle in trade union and constituency party sections of the electoral college for leadership and deputy leadership elections. At the same conference, delegates decided to change the weighting of the votes in the electoral college to one third each for affiliated trade unions, CLPs and MPs whereas previously, trade unions had 40% of the votes.[78] Even if the trade unions were to remain a major force in the Party, the outcome of the voting at the 1992 and 1993 annual conferences had by no means settled the debate about their role, precipitated by those who felt that the historic links between the trade unions and the Party should be loosed. This issue was to re-emerge a little later but with more vigour under the leadership of Smith's successor, the future Prime Minister, Tony Blair.

In the meantime, an historic change was to be made to the Labour Party's constitution which was to remove any doubt as to the Party's political direction under its new leader. Following the sudden death of John Smith in May 1994, the new Party leader Blair, set about forcing through a change to the Party's constitution through "replacing" or, more precisely, abolishing its clause IV part 4.[79] This

---

75 Ibid., ..., p. 430.

76 The "block vote" is the system by which voting has traditionally taken place in the Labour Party, especially at annual conference. This system was originally introduced by trade unions at the TUC annual conference in 1894 and was later introduced into the Labour Party itself. Organisations affiliate to the Labour Party on the basis of 1,000 members or part thereof. Whereas individual CLPs would normally affiliate to the Labour Party on the basis of just a thousand members, trade unions (at national level) would affiliate to the Party on the basis of the number of their members paying the "political levy" and therefore it was they, on account of the size of their membership, rather than the ordinary Party members, who had the decisive say in the adoption of Party policy. For brief details on the "block vote", see Harmer, Harry, ..., p. 242.

77 Harmer, Harry, ..., pp. 127f and 157.

78 Ibid., p. 128. See footnote 64.

79 Clause IV, part 4 of Labour's Constitution, originally adopted in 1918, pledged: "To secure for the workers by hand or by brain the full fruits of their industry and the most equitable

part of the constitution, in the words of former Labour Party General Secretary, Jim Mortimer, "served as a signpost, pointing the way to Labour's objective of a socialist society".[80] The significance of clause IV part 4 is that it recognised that the objective of achieving a socialist society meant a redistribution of wealth and power in favour of working people and their families. Its "replacement", despite any "fine wording", can be interpreted as an abandonment of this commitment. This decision prompted the miners' leader, Arthur Scargill, to leave the Labour Party and to found a new party – the Socialist Labour Party.

In a revealing statement in his campaign for the Party leadership, Blair claimed that "the key difference between ourselves and the Tories is not that they believe in a market economy and we do not. But rather, that while markets can and do work in the public interest, they do not guarantee it. The market economy is in the public interest".[81] Thus, the role of Government would therefore be limited to helping the "market economy" to function better. Blair went onto claim that "the difference between this approach and the perception of the Labour Party in the past, however, is that the purpose of economic intervention is not so that Government can run industry, but that it should work with it so that industry is better able to run itself. Government must concentrate on what only it can do – and do it well".[82] Blair's statement can be understood as the Conservatives and Labour, in the aftermath of its policy review, principally standing for the same thing except that Labour can run the "market economy" (or the capitalist system) better!

Thus seeking to change/abolish clause IV part 4 of the Party's constitution was the logical consequence of Blair's open support for the "market economy". However, as noted by Mortimer, Blair had made no such pledge regarding this part of the constitution in his campaign for the Party leadership. Had he done so, it would not have helped his campaign. But not to have revealed such intentions at the time was, in Mortimer's words, "an unworthy act".[83]

---

distribution thereof that may be possible upon the basis of the common ownership of the means of production, distribution and exchange, and the best obtainable system of popular administration and control of each industry and service". In its place came: "The Labour Party is a democratic socialist party. It believes that by the strength of our common endeavour, we can achieve more than we can achieve alone so as to create for each of us the means to realise our true potential and for all of us as a community in which power, wealth and opportunity are in the hands of the many not the few, where the rights we enjoy reflect the duties we owe, and where we live together, freely, in a spirit of solidarity, tolerance and respect". The new clause also pledges "a dynamic economy", "a just society", "an open democracy" and "a healthy environment". See Harmer, Harry, ..., p. 247.

[80] Mortimer, J. E. (Jim), ..., p. 455.

[81] Blair, Tony, *Leadership Election Statement 1994: Change and National Renewal*, p. 9.

[82] Ibid.

[83] Mortimer, J. E. (Jim), ..., p. 459.

Although the Labour Party, through clause IV part 4, had been constitutionally committed to "the common ownership of the means of production, distribution and exchange", the Labour Party in government, as part of "consensus"-era politics, had traditionally supported the concept of what can be regarded as a "mixed economy" which is supposed to imply a "coexistence" of industry under both public and private ownership (see page 18).

After the wave of privatisations since 1979 parallel with the Labour Party under Kinnock's leadership gradually distancing itself from any commitment to bring these privatised industries back into public ownership, open support for what Blair deemed as the "market economy", in the context of changing (or abolishing) clause IV, formally marked a clear break with a key aspect of the economic and industrial policies of previous Labour governments – their support for a "mixed economy", to mention nothing of the Party abandoning its commitment for achieving socialism. In this context, open support for the "market economy" can be seen as the cornerstone of the *New* Labour project. It can be argued that previous Labour leaders thought similarly. In fact, attempts by Hugh Gaitskell in 1959 to "revise" clause IV failed due to opposition from within the trade union movement, some CLPs and from some of the Party's MPs.[84]

Whether or not this is a coincidence, shortly before Blair became Party Leader, the Maastricht Treaty came into effect with the cornerstone of this Treaty being EMU. As member states of the EU committed themselves to co-ordinate their economic policies on the principle of "an open market economy with free competition" to mention nothing of member states being placed under pressure to privatise and open up certain publicly-owned industries to "competition" e.g. rail through an EU directive from 1991, it is questionable whether clause IV part 4 of the Labour Party's constitution as it stood, was in any way compatible with the Party's support for the Maastricht Treaty. One thing is clear. Labour's policy review did not overlook the process which eventually led to the conclusion of this Treaty which also meant the completion of the Single European Market. Thus, any commitment for a future Labour government to bring back into public ownership industries which had been privatised and to support direct state intervention in industry may well have brought it into conflict with the EU.

Blair's initial attempt at the 1994 annual conference (his first as Party Leader) to seek a "review" this clause by replacing it with "a clear, up-to-date statement of the objects and objectives of the party" was narrowly rejected when it decided to uphold the decision of the annual conference, the previous year, to retain the Party's original commitment to clause IV.[85] Not withstanding the decisions of the 1993 and 1994 annual conferences, the NEC convened a special conference

[84] See Harmer, Harry, ..., pp. 24 and 142 and Mortimer, J. E. (Jim), ..., p. 459.

[85] Harmer, Harry, ..., p. 27.

in April, the following year, in which it accepted a "rewording", in reality, the abolition of clause IV, already referred to, by a majority of almost two to one.

Leaving aside any controversy and emotions surrounding the attempt by the Party leadership to "change" this clause, there was nevertheless, an overwhelming feeling in the Party that it had to be united if it was to stand any chance of defeating the Tories at the following general election so many Party members, who would have otherwise voted to retain this clause in its original form, decided to give the new Leader "the benefit of their doubts".[86] On this particular issue, Blair succeeded where Gaitskell had failed 45 years earlier. An attempt at the 1995 annual conference to restore Clause IV in its original form was overwhelmingly defeated.[87] The 1995 annual conference also decided to reduce the trade union "block vote" at annual conference to just 50% thus giving it equal weight to the CLPs.[88] Attempts to reduce the influence of the trade unions in decision-making processes in the Party didn't stop there.

Riding on the crest of a wave following Labour's historic election victory in 1997, Blair was able to secure conference support for a fundamental reform in the Party's policy-making processes. The basis for this was through the adoption of the policy document *Partnership in Power* (PiP) at the Party's annual conference, the following September.

The principle behind PiP is that the Party's policy-making processes were to be removed from the annual conference and placed in the hands of a 175-strong National Policy Forum (NPF) which would discuss policies under a "two-year rolling programme".[89] In this, all sections of the Party were to be given more opportunities to influence policy making with the NPF being able to respond more effectively to the views of Party members in the discussion process. The NPF was to consist of representatives from all sections of the Party including its MPs (elected by the PLP) and representatives of the Cabinet (or in opposition, the Shadow Cabinet) together with members of the NEC, the Party Leader and Deputy Leader being ex-officio members.[90]

This change in the policy-making process, in the view of the left, meant that the standing of the annual conference as the Party's supreme policy-making body (which in any case had delegates from CLPs, affiliated trade unions and various socialist societies together with MPs already having speaking rights) was downgraded.[91] Although members of the NEC became ex-officio members of the

[86] Mortimer, J. E. (Jim), ..., p. 462.

[87] Harmer, Harry, p. 28.

[88] Ibid.

[89] See Ibid., pp. 277f.

[90] Ibid., see also, for example, *The Labour Party Rule Book 2004-2005*, p. 4-4.

[91] Harmer, Harry, p. 278.

NPF, the authority of the NEC as the Party's leading political organ was weakened. This, together with the influence of the left on the NEC anyway being much weaker than in the 1970s and early 1980s, was to widen the scope by which the Party leader and those closely associated with him could influence policy making in the Party, detached from the annual conference and possible pressures from the NEC, more so than previously. Although the annual conference continued to have the "final say" on Party policy and have a vote on specific issues against the wishes of the Party leadership (providing enough support can be gathered for them to get onto the conference agenda which, in turn resulted in an occasional defeat for the Blair Government e.g. Iraq, which it was then able to ignore), one can then question what role was actually envisaged for the annual conference other than to "rubber stamp" policies, which had already been formulated, and for providing a forum for public rallies in front of the mass media through "keynote" speeches by Party leaders.

Without the support of the Party's affiliated trade unions, having 50% of the votes at annual conference, these changes in the Party's policy-making progress could not have been passed. At the time, trade union leaders were in any case more supportive of the policies of the Blair Government which had only been in office for a few months than in the period running up to the end of his premiership in 2007. Although trade unionists were to sit on the NPF and play an active role in this body, their influence in formulating Party policy was to be weakened.

Whilst wanting to keep trade union influence, as it were, "in check", Blair was well aware of the fact that union support, both politically and financially, had always been crucial in securing the election and re-election of a Labour government. Consequently, in the run-up to the 2005 general election, fully aware that despite various positive points trade unions can claim from the Blair Government since taking office in 1997, there still remained a wide feeling of general discontent with the political direction of this government within the ranks of the trade union movement, a special conference at Warwick University in 2004 (see below) was convened between government ministers and trade union general secretaries.

5.3. The 1997 election victory: an historic chance for *New* Labour

In the 1997 general election, the Labour Party, presenting itself as *New Labour* won, in terms of parliamentary seats, the biggest victory ever in its history. With 418 seats compared to just 165 for the outgoing Major Government, not only did the Blair Government gain such a massive majority, the Conservative Party, in terms of seats in the House of Commons, found itself weaker than at any time since the 1906 election.[92] Not only that. As the Conservative defeat in 1997 was so severe with many of its ministers and prominent MPs failing to be re-elected in their constituencies, the Party's ability both inside and outside Parliament to function as an effective opposition was gravely impaired right up to the time when John Major's successor, Tony Blair, handed over the premiership to Gordon Brown at the end of June 2007. Even though the Labour Party had suffered setbacks in the local elections in May 2007, which speeded up the long-awaited process in bringing about a change in Party leader and hence premiership, the Conservative Party up to then, following three consecutive general election defeats, had been unable to mount a serious enough challenge for it to get back in-to power (see pages 259f).

However, in terms of how the British people actually voted, the Labour victory wasn't so spectacular. In 1997, Labour won only 43.2% of the popular vote. In comparison with other general elections in postwar Britain, it is worth noting that in 1970, Labour was voted out of office having won 43.1% of the vote, in 1951, Labour was voted out of office despite winning 48.8% of the vote (the biggest ever share of the poll in a general election in the Party's history and, incidentally, more than the "winning" Conservative Party). In the elections in 1955 and 1959, Labour lost despite receiving 46.4% and 43.8% respectively – more than the victory in 1997.[93]

Not only did Labour win the 1997 election with the biggest ever parliamentary majority in its history, it inherited what the outgoing Prime Minister John Major claimed as "the most benevolent set of economic statistics since before the First World War".[94] Labour Governments, be they in the 1920s, 1945, 1964 or 1974, had always come into office in the midst of widespread economic difficulties and whatever the actual nature of them were, they eventually fell due to discontent within the organised labour movement over the actual policies enacted to overcome them – incomes policies and cutbacks in social expenditure. In 1997, these "benevolent set of economic statistics" were largely due to the fact that following sterling's ejection from ERM, there was a steady period of economic growth. But as it was the outgoing Prime Minister himself, who during his short tenure as Chancellor of the Exchequer, shortly before taking over from Margaret Thatcher, had pushed for and succeeded in getting sterling anchored in ERM[95] and at the overvalued rate of £1=DM2,95 when the UK economy was already in

[92] Ibid., pp. 29-41.

[93] Ibid. NB It is worth noting that before 1997, there had only been two general elections in which the Labour Party had won with clear parliamentary majorities. These were in 1945 where it won 393 seats with 48.0% of the popular vote and in 1966 where it won 364 seats on 48.0% of the popular vote. For brief details of how Britain's major parties performed in general elections from 1900 to 1997, see Harmer, Harry, ..., pp. 29-42.

[94] Taylor, Robert, New Labour, new capitalism, in: Seldon, Anthony, *Blair's Britain 1997-2007*, Cambridge University Press, 2007, p. 223.

[95] Junor, Penny, ..., p. 178.

the midst of an economic downturn with the effect that a slump was to follow (see pages 74f). So, any claims of credit Major can make on the economic front by the time he left office need to be assessed in connection with the disastrous consequences of ERM on the UK economy. If the economy was really in such a favourable situation, one could then wonder why the Conservative Party was so severely defeated in 1997. On the economic front, there was still widespread unemployment and the state of Britain's social infrastructure remained seriously critical and these are crucial factors which influenced the outcome of the 1997 election.

Upon taking office, the Blair Government moved swiftly to restore trade union rights at GCHQ (abolished by the Thatcher Government in 1984) and reversed the *opt-out* Major secured for Britain on the "Social Chapter" (which then became incorporated in the EU's Treaty of Amsterdam in 1997)[96]. In an attempt to address trade union concerns regarding the abolition of various measures over the previous 18 years, which had long existed, aimed at guaranteeing minimum terms and conditions of employment, the Blair Government enacted legislation making provision for the introduction of a national minimum wage. This it did through the National Minimum Wage Act, 1998 (see below).

These measures, being welcomed by the trade union movement, as far as they went, were largely aimed at Britain conforming in some aspects to the norms of other countries in the EU in the field of workers' rights. There, the Blair Government really only sought to make some specific corrections to the policies of the Thatcher and Major Governments without having to "go against the grain" of what had been enacted over the previous 18 years.

In the field of trade union and labour relations law, Labour's 1997 election manifesto claimed that Britain needed "a sensible balance in industrial relations law – rights and duties go together", it was stated. Yet, in the very next sentence, mirroring the sentiments of Labour's policy review and the 1992 election manifesto (see page 194), it was pledged that "the key elements of the trade union legislation of the 1980s will stay – on ballots, picketing and industrial action".[97] In this, the Labour leadership was effectively saying that the Thatcher Government had principally secured "a sensible balance in industrial relations" but could have hardly said this so directly in the midst of an election campaign. So, the Labour leadership only sought to concern itself with specific anomalies which came to light over the previous 18 years.

---

[96] See page 109, footnotes 225f. NB Whilst reversing Britain's "opt-out" on the "Social Chapter", Blair pledged to take steps so as to minimise any "costly" impact of this reversal on employers. See Taylor, Robert, ..., pp. 218f.

[97] *New Labour because Britain deserves better* (1997 Labour election manifesto), Labour Party (London), 1997, p. 17.

The emphasis of the newly elected Labour Government's policies on trade union and labour relations law was, in the words of the new Prime Minister, Tony Blair, in his foreword to the Government's 1998 White Paper *Fairness at Work*, "to replace the notion of conflict between employers and employees with the promotion of partnership".[98] (In as far as "partnership" in an employer/employee context really is a reality, it should not be overlooked that in his foreword to the White Paper, Blair laid stress on "employees" rather than their representatives which, in any case, can only effectively be through trade unions, independent of employer interests, organised in the workplace and being part of the TUC. So an important motive for promoting the notion of "partnership" should be judged in the context of a continuation of long-standing governmental policy of seeking to limit trade union influence at the workplace. Only in connection with the restoration of trade union rights at GCHQ did his foreword make a specific reference towards trade unions as such.)

On the basis of this White Paper came the Employment Relations Act, 1999. Principally, this Act concentrated on three areas. Firstly, "family friendly provisions", based on union-employer talks in the EU, secondly, new protection against unfair dismissal and discrimination and thirdly, new provisions on trade union recognition and representation.[99]

In the field of "family friendly provisions", the 1999 Act extended existing provisions for "leave for family and domestic reasons". In this, improvements were made to maternity leave, provisions (on the basis of an EU directive) for parental leave were introduced and a new right to "time off for dependants" giving workers rights to take a "reasonable amount of time off" work to deal with situations whenever dependants fall ill, give birth or are injured or assaulted, attending to care arrangements for dependants and if there happen to be problems at school was also introduced.[100]

Secondly, this Act provided some protection against dismissal for those taking part in "lawful" industrial action.[101] This may appear as a correction of an anomaly but as the scope for taking "lawful" industrial action was to continue to remain restricted, largely on account of the legislation of the 1980s, the impact of this measure in the 1999 Act, however welcome it may have been, is largely symbolic. And, in any case, this measure alone could not have been of any help to the catering workers who lost their jobs due to the Gate Gourmet dispute at London Heathrow airport in summer 2005 because the spontaneousness of the

[98] Blair, Rt. Hon. Tony, Foreword to the White Paper *Fairness at Work*, Cm. 3968, Department of Trade and Industry (London), May 1998, p. 3.

[99] *The Employment Relations Act: a TUC Guide*, TUC (London), October 1999, p. 3.

[100] Ibid., pp. 31ff.

[101] Ibid., pp. 38f.

strike action which they felt they had to take could not be deemed as being "lawful" under the 1992 Act (see page 118).

The third aspect of the 1999 Act concerned the provisions for statutory union recognition. There had earlier been procedures in Britain whereby trade unions could secure recognition with the assistance of the law. This was from 1971 to 1974 and from 1978 to 1980.[102] The first period concerned the 1971 Industrial Relations Act so there, unions could have only benefited had they "registered" under it. This Act also included provisions by which employers could de-recognise trade unions (registered or not). As far as the second period was concerned, it should be recalled that on account of the House of Lords' ruling in December 1977 in the Grunwick dispute, the procedures which the 1974-1979 Labour Government enacted by which trade unions could secure recognition became inoperable (see page 56).

Under the 1999 Act, a procedure was outlined whereby a request could be made to an employer for "recognition/collective bargaining" for a "bargaining unit" by one or more independent trade unions but only where there are at least 21 workers employed. In addition, it has to show that it has at least 10% membership in the relevant "bargaining unit".[103] If the employer fails to respond to the request for recognition or rejects it there is the right of appeal to the Central Arbitration Committee (CAC).[104] For the CAC to issue a declaration for the union to be recognised, it has to be satisfied that there is a majority of workers in the "bargaining unit" who are members of that union. However, if the CAC has doubts as to the level of support for recognition among those in the "bargaining unit", it can authorise a ballot among the workers concerned. There, for a union to secure recognition, it has to get "a majority of those voting and at least 40% of those entitled to vote"[105] – a seemingly high threshold.

According to a study carried out for the TUC by Keith Ewing (professor of public law at Kings College, London) and Anne Hock in *Trade Union Recognition in Small Enterprises*, the small firms' threshold for trade union recognition has had the effect of denying more than a fifth of the British workforce of the right to trade union recognition and representation unless their employer voluntary agrees.[106] Although the Employment Relations Act, 2004, gives the Secretary of State the power to remove or amend the small firms' threshold by Order,[107]

[102] Hendy, John QC and Walton, Michael, An Individual Right to Union Representation in International Law, in: *Industrial Law Journal*, Oxford University Press (Oxford), Vol. 26 No. 3, September 1997, p. 207.

[103] *The Employment Relations Act:* ..., ..., pp. 6-9.

[104] Ibid.

[105] *The Employment Relations Act:* ..., ..., pp. 10ff.

[106] *The Employment Relations Act 2004 – a TUC Guide*, TUC (London), April 2005, p. 7.

[107] Ibid.

the high threshold of 20 employees effectively denies more than a fifth of the British workforce of the right to freedom of association in any meaningful way together with all the rights and benefits associated with this. Furthermore, the same study shows that this threshold has a had disproportionate impact on women workers.[108]

As far as the trade union movement is concerned, whatever positive points can be claimed about the 1999 Act, it was at best limited in scope for the crucial fact remained, which the Blair Government had already pledged the previous year (and before taking office!) that "the key elements of the trade union legislation of the 1980s will stay ...". This meant, in particular, the "hard core" of the 1982 Act (now incorporated in the TULRA (Consolidation) Act, 1992) through the narrowing of a "definition of a trade dispute" and the code on vicarious liability (see pages 130-133). In this, Blair could legitimately go on to claim in his foreword to this White Paper that "even after the changes we propose, Britain will have the most lightly regulated labour market of any leading economy in the world"[109] (which would be understood as workers and trade unions continuing to have fewer rights than their counterparts in Western Europe). Other aspects of the laws of the 1980s, which the White Paper pledged would stay, were the abolition of the closed shop (which, it claimed, was justified), restrictions concerning picketing, "unofficial" and "secondary" industrial action, as well as the balloting provisions and periods of notice to be given to employers before strikes could take place and have the protection of the law.[110]

A clear example of the implications of the Blair Government leaving "the key elements of the trade union legislation of the 1980s" untouched could, as already noted, be seen in summer 2005 in the Gate Gourmet dispute in which the catering workers and their union (the TGWU) were left virtually powerless to pursue their dispute in any effective way without the risk of coming into conflict with the courts. All of this would be understood as workers and their trade unions in Britain continuing to have fewer rights and more restrictions that their counterparts in the advanced industrial countries in Western Europe especially as far as taking industrial action is concerned.

Leaving aside the pledge that the "the key elements of the trade union legislation of the 1980s will stay", the Blair Government agreed to conduct a review of the 1999 Act following the 2001 general election.[111] This commitment became all the more necessary following the ruling in the Wilson and Palmer cases in the ECtHR, the following year. This review of the 1999 Act was to form the basis of the Employment Relations Act, 2004.

---

[108] Ibid.

[109] Blair, Rt. Hon. Tony, Foreword to the White Paper *Fairness at Work*, ..., p. 3.

[110] Ibid., p. 22, para. 4.8 and footnote to para. 4.8.

[111] *Trades Union Congress 2004 General Council Report*, TUC (London), 2004, p. 13.

In his foreword to the 1998 White Paper, Blair said it was "based on the rights of the individual, whether exercised on their own or with others, as a matter of their choice".[112] However important individual rights may be, one must not overlook the fact that the prime motive of portraying "the rights of the individual" (here, concerning whether or not to be a member of a trade union) has very often been associated with other motives, most notably in holding back the influence of trade unions at the workplace so as to keep down labour costs, i.e. wages – indeed, a point the Thatcher Government used when it ultimately decided to ban the closed shop altogether in 1990 (see pages 82f). For whatever *individuals* can claim to achieve on their own, this is likely to be much more limited than what could be achieved when *individuals* act in unison i.e. through being organised in a proper trade union and this is what is decisive for this, apart from anything else, concerns securing the best possible terms and conditions of employment.

But if "the rights of the individual" were to have any proper meaning at all, there was, more significantly, the crucial question of what the Blair Government was going to do to counter the problem of discrimination against trade union members at work in any meaningful way as, for example, illustrated in the Wilson and Palmer cases where trade union members refused to surrender their union membership in exchange for better terms and conditions of employment (see below).

Regarding the question of being "free to join or not to join a union", one should not overlook a slight difference in the wording between what the 1997 election manifesto said and what the Blair Government said in its White Paper in the following year. Labour's 1997 election manifesto stated (in the same paragraph as it pledged itself to retaining the "key elements of the trade union legislation of the 1980s") that "people should be free to join or not to join a union".[113] Yet, the 1998 White Paper stated that "every employee should be free to decide to join a trade union. But equally every employee should be free not to join".[114] After having already pledged that the "key elements of the trade union legislation of the 1980s" were to remain which, apart from anything else, included retaining the ban on the "closed shop", one may wonder why it was actually felt necessary to state that "every employee should be free not to join" a union.

Looking at this statement from another angle, although at the same time the Blair Government reiterated the right to join a trade union, by stressing "but equally", the 1998 White Paper effectively placed the right to freedom of association on an equal footing with an individual "right" not to associate, whether or not this was actually intended. So, the scope by which "individuals" could choose not to join a trade union and, by implication, also choose not to be repre-

[112] Blair, Rt. Hon. Tony, Foreword to the White Paper *Fairness at Work*, ..., p. 3.

[113] *New Labour because Britain deserves better* ..., 1997, p. 17.

[114] *Fairness at Work*, ..., p. 22, para. 4.8.

sented by one would continue to undermine the hard-won rights of those *individual* trade unionists who do.

Conventions at European and international level, most notably on the basis of ILO Conventions Nos. 87 and 98, have recognised the right to "freedom of association" rather than an individual "freedom" not to associate. This is also true of article 11 of the ECHR (even though, as already noted, this article makes provision whereby the public authorities in a country which has ratified this Convention can impose restrictions on this right[115] with the effect that there have been cases brought by trade unions and trade unionists before the ECtHR claiming a breach of article 11 which have failed[116]). Consequently, there is the question of whether the 1998 White Paper and the legislation which followed this (the 1999 Employment Act) had given full weight to the right to freedom of association on the basis of various conventions at European and international level which had long since been ratified by Britain. In this, one needs to determine whether a just and correct balance has been made between any proclaimed "rights of the individual" and the rights of those working in unison such that any "rights" "individuals" may claim do not undermine the collective interests of the latter. There, the question of trade union recognition and the rights of individual workers to be represented by a trade union, even if the majority of workers in a given bargaining unit are not trade union members, is of crucial importance. In this, one needs to consider the significance of article 11 and, in this context, the Human Rights Act, 1998.[117]

The significance of the Human Rights Act is that no legislation in the UK should contravene the ECHR and any of its subsequent protocols. By implication, the standing of the ECtHR in Strasbourg as a final court of appeal in cases where a breach of this Convention can be claimed, was raised, even though since 1966 individuals in Britain had already been free to take cases to this court against their own country (the UK).[118] Thus, as far as trade unions and trade unionists are concerned, the long-awaited ruling from the ECtHR in the Wilson and Palmer case on 2 July, 2002, was to be of crucial importance. Furthermore, this ruling was to give an indication as to the extent to which the 1999 Employment Relations Act had actually fulfilled the right to freedom of association as outlined in article 11 despite any limitations this article may permit.

---

115 See Chapter 2, footnotes 155 and 160. See also Ewing, K. D., Article 11 and the right to freedom of association, in: Ewing, K. D., *Human Rights at Work*, The Institute of Employment Rights (London), 2000, p. 85-89.

116 Ibid.

117 The Human Rights Act, 1998, came fully into effect in the UK on 2 October, 2002. Gearty, Conor, The Human Rights Act 1998: an overview, in: Ewing, K. D., *Human Rights at Work*, ..., p. 1.

118 Ibid., p. 3.

There, the ruling in favour of the plaintiffs in the Wilson and Palmer case in the ECtHR turned out to be of major significance in the struggle for the development of trade union rights in Britain or, more precisely, for any chance of their restoration after what had been 18 years of persistent legislative measures against them. This ruling in the ECtHR has also shown that despite any positive points that can be shown in benefiting trade unions through the 1999 Act, the right to freedom of association in Britain continued to fall way short of the limited requirements under article 11. Thus, with the Human Rights Act on the Statute Book, the ruling in the ECtHR in the Wilson and Palmer case, to mention nothing of continued trade union pressure, the Blair Government authorised a review of its 1999 Act. Out of this review came the Employment Relations Act, 2004.

In this case, the ECtHR held that: "It is of the essence of the right to join a trade union for the protection of their interests [guaranteed by Art 11 of the European Convention on Human Rights and Fundamental Freedoms] that employees should be free to instruct or permit the union to make representations to their employer or to take action in support of their interests on their behalf. If workers are prevented from so doing, their freedom to belong to a trade union, for the protection of their interests, becomes illusory".[119]

Following on from the ruling in the Wilson and Palmer case, Keith Ewing identified the following areas where the rights of workers to be represented by a trade union were strengthened. Firstly, the right of trade union members to be protected against discrimination; secondly, the right of workers (if they have to appear before their employers) to be accompanied; thirdly, the right of trade unions to organisation and representation; fourthly, the right to trade union recognition; fifthly, the right of trade unions to determine their own rules and sixthly, the right to strike.[120] All these points including the right of trade unions to determine their own rules and the right to strike are covered by ILO Convention No. 87.[121] Therefore, one needs to assess the extent to which the Blair Government adequately responded to the outcome of the ECtHR ruling in the Wilson and Palmer cases in its review of the 1999 Act in 2004.

The 1999 Employment Act had provided an opportunity to nullify the effects of the House of Lords' rulings in these cases but, in fact, this Act only dealt with

[119] Hendy, John QC and Gall, Gregor, British Trade Union Rights Today and the Trade Union Freedom Bill, in: Ewing, K. D. (Ed.), *The Right to Strike: From the Trade Disputes Act 1906 to a Trade Union Freedom Bill 2006*, The Institute of Employment Rights (Liverpool), 2006, p. 258.

[120] Ewing, K. D., The Implications of Wilson and Palmer, in: *Industrial Law Journal*, Oxford University Press (Oxford), Vol. 32 No. 1, March 2003, pp. 7-20.

[121] See Hendy, John QC, *A Law Unto Themselves. Conservative Employment Laws: A National and International Assessment* (3rd edition), The Institute of Employment Rights (London), 1st September 1993, p. 79.

"one limb" of the House of Lords' decision – being where "the detriment complained of takes the form of an act or omission"[122] meaning that "action short of dismissal" on the grounds of membership of a trade union constitutes an "omission".[123] There, the 1999 Act had the effect of reversing the ruling in the House of Lords' in the Wilson and Palmer cases in that withholding pay increases, for example, was an "omission" which was not covered by the definition of "action short of dismissal".[124]

So, of the six areas which Ewing noted as to where the rights of workers to representation were strengthened due to this ruling in the ECtHR, the 1999 Act had only dealt with the first point which he mentioned. Thus, from this angle, the 1999 Act can be judged as being limited in scope in that it did not make an adequate enough attempt to tackle the root causes of discrimination against trade unionists at the workplace. There, this Act did not go on to provide protection "where the detriment complained of relates to the services of a trade union" as illustrated in cases like Wilson and Palmer.[125] So, in this respect, the 1999 Act only limited itself to providing protection against discrimination on grounds of trade union membership. And, in any case, given the fact that the Blair Government had pledged to leave "the key elements of the trade union legislation of the 1980s" untouched, the fifth and sixth points which Ewing mentioned were going to be disregarded by the Blair Government.

However, following on from the ruling in the Wilson and Palmer cases in the ECtHR, one logical conclusion can be drawn. If the six areas which Ewing had identified as to where the rights of workers to representation had been strengthened were to be of any major significance, then this can only be realised upon the basis of a repeal of the "hard core" of the trade union legislation of the Thatcher and Major Governments. So, the ECtHR, as it were, strengthened the trade union case for repeal, whether or not this court had actually intended this.

Shortly before this ruling in the ECtHR in 2002, the Blair Government was to be confronted, with what turned out to be, the most serious industrial conflict Britain had faced since the mid 1980s – the firefighters' dispute (May 2002 to June 2003). Although the trade union laws as such were neither the point of issue nor of any relevance in its settlement, the Blair Government's handling of this dispute can be seen as being indicative of how it really judged the right of workers to freedom of association in practice.

As a result of the settlement of the nine-week firefighters' strike (1977/1978), a pay formula was agreed which linked the earnings of qualified firefighters with

[122] Ewing, K. D., ..., pp. 2f.

[123] *The Employment Relations Act* 2004 ..., ..., p. 7.

[124] Ibid.

[125] Ewing, K. D., The Implications of Wilson and Palmer, ..., p. 3.

the earnings of the upper quartile of adult male manual workers. So, in assessing the pay for firefighters, account had to be taken of the *New Earnings Survey* upper quartile figure, the average earnings index and the earnings of qualified firefighters. So, on the basis of this formula, the Fire Brigades Union (FBU) and the firefighters' employers (local authorities) carried out a joint survey each year so as to determine the pay for qualified firefighters and to ensure that their earnings did not fall relative to those of other skilled workers.[126]

Following the nine-week strike right up to the mid 1990s, the pay formula was seen as having served the FBU and its members "relatively well".[127] At the same time, it is also worth noting that in this period, whilst many trade unions endured a considerable loss of membership and influence, the FBU was fairly successful in protecting its members' terms and conditions of employment, fighting off attempts to impose cuts in the firefighting service and was one of the few unions to record an increase in its membership.[128]

However, by the mid 1990s, "cracks" in the pay formula were beginning to show. This was due to manufacturing declining together with an acceleration of occupational changes in the profession involving more use of computers and other forms of modern technology coupled with a greater emphasis on fire prevention and special services.[129] So the effect of all this was that "the relative level of craft workers' earnings" (the upper quartile of male manual earnings on which the pay formula was based) began to fall due to average earnings rising faster than the pay for fully trained firefighters. Inevitably, pay negotiations became increasingly complicated to mention nothing of continued government attempts to impose cuts in the firefighting service.

On the basis of this formula, a pay increase of 3.9% in 2001 was agreed[130] but, when the FBU made its pay claim in May the following year, the earnings of a qualified firefighter (without overtime and despite four years training and experience), according to the then president of the Chief and Assistant Chief Fire Officers' Association Richard Bull, did not bear comparison with those of other skilled workers or a police constable.[131] Furthermore, the question of low pay for many employed in the fire service affecting administrative staff and parttime workers, in particular women, also had to be addressed. So, in its endeavours to secure pay parity with other skilled and professional workers, the FBU's pay claim in 2002 not only meant substantial pay increases (from around £20,000 to

[126] See Seifert, Roger and Sibley, Tom, *United They Stood: The Story of the Firefighters' Dispute 2002-2004*, Lawrence & Wishart (London), 2005, pp. 29f.

[127] Ibid., p. 72.

[128] Ibid., p. 33.

[129] Ibid., p. 72.

[130] Ibid., pp. 29f.

[131] Ibid., pp. 72f.

£22,000 per annum to £30,000)[132] but, by implication, the pay formula itself had to be updated so as to prevent any future erosion of firefighters' pay in comparison with that of other professional workers. Whilst there was sympathy for the FBU from the local authority employers, the Blair Government made it clear that it would oppose what it saw as any large pay claim.[133]

With no sign of a pay agreement in sight, the FBU announced on 12 September that it was going to conduct a ballot (in accordance with the provisions of the 1992 Act) for industrial action and secured overwhelming support. Owing to frustration over the lack of progress in the pay negotiations some "unofficial" industrial action at a number of fire stations took place in early November[134] but to no avail. Subsequently, the FBU embarked upon a 48-hour strike as from 12 November – this being the first national firefighters' strike since the 1977/1978 strike.[135] This was to be followed by an eight-day strike which had been planned to begin in the morning of 22 November. However, in the night of 21/22 November, FBU leaders had almost succeeded in securing a basis with the employers by which negotiations could have begun for bringing about a final settlement to the dispute. This would have paved the way for a pay increase of 16% by the following November and would have enabled the FBU to suspend its planned eight-day strike. As this was blocked by the Government, the eight-day strike, as originally planned, went ahead.[136] So troops had to be deployed in the providing emergency fire cover.

In what can be portrayed as an "attempt" to break the deadlock over the pay negotiations, the Government set up an "Independent Review of the Fire Service" under Sir George Bain. In fact, its terms of reference were to go beyond the dispute itself so as to make recommendations on the future organisation and management of the fire service in general with a view to future legislation. In this, two major purposes of this inquiry become clear. Firstly, pay increases should principally be linked to job cuts in the fire service. Secondly, working practices in the fire service should be "modernised" and thereby recommending ways in how all this could be achieved. Thus, the interim report of the Bain inquiry, released on 12 November, recommending pay rises of just 11.3% over two years, conditional on wide-ranging "reforms" in working practices together with the fire authorities having to fund any pay increases from within their current budgets, was therefore judged as provocative.[137]

---

[132] See Ibid., pp. 28ff and 75ff.

[133] Ibid., p. 73.

[134] Ibid., p. 204.

[135] Ibid., p. 126.

[136] Ibid., pp. 124f and 137f.

[137] Ibid., p. 125.

The final report of the Bain inquiry, presented to Deputy Prime Minister John Prescott on 16 December, was to form the basis of the 2004 Fire Services Act. This made provision whereby the fire service could be placed under central government control. In this, the Act also made it possible for the Government to be able to impose terms and conditions of employment on those employed in the fire service,[138] reminiscing what the Thatcher Government actually did when it withdrew teachers' negotiating rights in 1987 (see page 104), disregarding ILO convention 151. (This convention stipulates that disputes about conditions of employment of public employees should be resolved through negotiation or through independent and impartial machinery.)[139]

It should not be overlooked that when on the following 28 January Prescott announced that legislation was going to be introduced so as to give the Government powers to be able to impose terms and conditions of employment on those working for the fire service, preparations were already being made for what was to become a military intervention in Iraq. With 19,000 members of the armed forces, according to Prescott, having to be deployed in providing fire emergency cover at home, the Government was aware that any escalation of this dispute would have imposed additional strains on the armed forces in their preparations for intervening in Iraq. For whenever participation in a war is contemplated, no government can ignore the logistical and political implications of having so many troops "grounded", as it were, for "domestic" purposes. This, together with the level of support the firefighters enjoyed within the trade union movement as a whole and from the general public to mention nothing of the determination of the firefighters themselves to secure what they saw as a "just" settlement as well as the rising costs of the dispute increased pressure on the Government to reach a settlement.[140]

Yet, on 19 March, with the spectre of war and concerned that the Government was contemplating the imposition of a settlement, coupled with a possibility of intervention by the Attorney General of deeming the strike action as a threat to public safety with the consequences of the full thrust of the State apparatus being deployed so as to "crush" the union, an agreement was reached with local authority employers on a pay settlement of 16% over three years. This was conditional of there being a return of overtime and rest-day working and was therefore rejected by the union's national delegate conference.[141] In seeking to reach a settlement, union leaders set new dates for strike action whilst exploring ways for negotiations to be reopened but at the same time, decided, as it were, not to "widen" the dispute through authorising further strikes whilst UK troops were in Iraq.

---

[138] Ibid., p. 212.

[139] Ibid., p. 194f.

[140] See Ibid., pp. 173-182.

[141] Ibid., p. 182.

Eventually, the firefighters' dispute was settled in June 2003 when the FBU, despite opposition from a number of firefighters, accepted a pay increase of 16% for fulltime firefighters which was to be phased in over two-and-a-half years. With this, a new pay formula was agreed aimed at linking future improvements in the earnings of firefighters to those achieved by other associate professional and technical workers in the country. An additional point worth noting about this settlement is that considerable progress was made towards securing pay equality with increases of 17% to 20% going to the largely female control room workers and part-time retained firefighters. This settlement, even though it fell short of what the union had originally demanded, represented the best pay increase for a significant group of public sector workers at the time.[142]

So, although the trade union laws as such may not have been of any special importance in influencing the outcome of this dispute, the passing of legislation which could be used against the firefighters in the event of future disputes is a further indication showing that the Blair Government's policy on trade union and workers' rights remained to be broadly similar to that of the Thatcher and Major Governments. So, through the Fire Services Act, the State secured additional powers to intervene in industrial disputes.

Following on from its policy review at the end of the 1980s, the Labour Party, as noted earlier, had dropped its earlier calls for the repeal of the Thatcher Government's trade union laws and trade union leaders, as it were, "complied". The reasoning behind this "compliance" can be understood in the context of the need for the labour movement to be united behind the Labour Party if it was to stand any chance of getting back into office at the following election. As it turned out, it was not until 1997 when Labour eventually got back into office. By then, the Conservative Party, after 18 years in government, had become so discredited that a Labour victory at the polls would have been all but certain with or without its policy review. All the same, there remained the feeling that injustices the trade union movement felt it suffered through the trade union laws since 1979 should be put right and despite the longest period ever of the Labour Party in Britain being in government, these injustices have not in any way been corrected so as to put trade union and workers' rights on a par with what they were in 1979 or with the norms that exist in other advanced industrial countries in Europe.

However, in the aftermath of various industrial disputes, especially the Gate Gourmet dispute, together with the ECtHR ruling in the Wilson and Palmer cases and, not overlooking the fact that in a number of prominent trade union elections since the end of the 1990s, a new generation of trade union leaders, who have been more critical of the Blair Government than their predecessors,

142 See Sibley, Tom, What other option did the FBU have? in: *Morning Star* (London), 14 January 2005, p. 8.

have been elected,[143] calls for the repeal of the Conservative trade union laws grew. Out of this, the TUC was to drop its previous scepticism towards calls for the repeal of these laws when it unanimously supported the call for a *Trade Union Freedom Bill* at the TUC annual congress in 2005 (resolution 'Composite 1').[144] By the end of 2005, no fewer than 187 MPs (almost all of them Labour) signed an "Early Day Motion" in the House of Commons to this effect which, incidentally, was also to mark the centenary of the 1906 Trade Disputes Act.[145]

In its call for a trade union freedom Bill, the TUC called for the abolition of restrictive balloting and industrial notice procedures, the right to strike and the right to automatic reinstatement for taking lawful industrial action, the freedom to take solidarity action for workers who are in dispute and sectoral forums to establish minimum terms and conditions [of employment]. Following on from the Gate Gourmet dispute, the resolution also called for amendments in the law so as to permit supportive action at least where there is a close connection between those involved [on the basis of ILO Conventions], simplifying balloting procedures, protecting strikers from dismissal and barring the replacement of workers in dispute. Following on from these initiatives, a Private Member's Bill (the Trade Union Freedom Bill) was presented to Parliament in 2007 by the Labour MP John McDonnell, which sought some modest changes to the trade union laws. However, this Bill failed to secure adequate time for debate in the House of Commons after it met strong governmental disapproval despite it having widespread trade union support.[146]

Through the Human Rights Act, UK law, as already noted, should not contravene the ECHR. In this, one area of particular importance is Article 11 where the principle of freedom of association, leaving aside any security considerations which the public authorities in a particular country may claim, is anchored. Over the years, rulings in the ECtHR under Article 11 had tended to strengthen the "rights" of non-union members rather than those rights of union members as the principle of freedom of association had originally intended and out of this, the right to freedom of association has been construed to include a "freedom" of non-association (see pages 94f). However, in the Wilson and Palmer cases, the ruling in the ECtHR was a landmark in another aspect in that it very much went against the trend of earlier rulings in this court with the effect that the right to freedom of association had, as it were, secured a new degree of impetus. Consequently, in its review of its 1999 Act, the question which needs to be considered

---

143 See Murray, Andrew, *A New Labour Nightmare: The return of the awkward squad*, Verso (London and New York), 2003.

144 Hendy, John and Gall, Gregor, *The Right to Strike: From the Trade Disputes Act 1906 to a Trade Union Freedom Bill 2006*, ..., p. 247.

145 This was Early Day Motion 1170. See Appendix 4, Early Day Motion and signatories, in: Ewing, K. D. (Ed.), *The Right to Strike: ...*, pp. 301-304.

146 See Taylor, Robert, ..., p. 230.

is to what extent did the Blair Government take advantage of the opportunities the ECtHR ruling opened in the Wilson and Palmer cases such that the right to freedom of association could be widened to ensure that Britain conformed more to the norms already attained under various European and international conventions and what had already been attained in other advanced industrial nations or, more precisely, to what extent did it feel compelled to respond to this ruling in any positive way.

The 2004 Act gives workers a right not to have offers made to them by their employers where the sole or main purpose is not to be or seek to be a member of an independent trade union and therefore not to take advantage of the benefits of membership. By implication, this strengthens the rights of workers to take part in the activities of an independent trade union, to take advantage of the services it offers at an appropriate time. In this, a worker was then given the right to complain to an industrial tribunal in the event of he or she believing that his or her employer made an offer in the nature of an unlawful inducement. In work places where unions are recognised or are in the process of seeking recognition, more protection was made available to protect unions from the effects of seeking to personalise employment contracts with additional rights to complain to an industrial tribunal. Following on from this, the 2004 Act provides additional protection from detriment and dismissal relating to the use of union services or refusal of an inducement.[147]

However welcome these measures may be, all the 2004 Act really did was to strengthen the rights of workers to representation. The key question of the repeal of the Conservative employment laws, as far as the trade union movement is concerned, has yet to be resolved for this remains *the* criterion for ensuring that the right to freedom of association and all the benefits associated with this can be fulfilled. For as long as the "hard core" of the various trade unions laws enacted since 1980 remain on the Statute Book, the right in Britain to freedom of association will continue to fall way short of what has been attained in other countries in the advanced industrial world.

Although there are conventions at international and European level whereby everyone, through the right to freedom of association, has the right to join and form trade unions for the protection of his interests e.g. Article 23(4) of the UN *Universal Declaration of Human Rights* of 1948, Article 8(1) of the *International Covenant on Economic, Social and Cultural Rights* of 1966, Article 11 of the ECHR of 1950 and Article 5 of the *European Social Charter* of 1961,[148] as well as Conventions 87 and 98 of the ILO,[149] the 1999 Act missed an opportunity for the key provisions of these various charters and conventions to be enacted

[147] See *The Employment Relations Act 2004 – a TUC Guide*, ..., pp. 51-56.

[148] See Hendy, John QC and Walton, Michael, ..., pp. 214-220.

[149] Ibid., pp. 220ff.

into British law with the effect that had originally been intended. This was mainly due to the high thresholds this Act set for requiring employers to recognise trade unions (see pages 230f). While the 1999 Act sought to limit the scope by which employers can arbitrarily seek to withdraw recognition from a trade union, a "right" to non-representation by a trade union continued to go as far as workers actually being denied rights to representation which these various charters and conventions had never intended.

However, as already noted, there is provision whereby an employer can seek to de-recognise a trade union. In this, there is provision for "swift de-recognition" if the number of workers in the bargaining unit falls below 21. There is also a procedure involving an application to the CAC whereby an employer can seek to de-recognise a trade union if this is the wish of at least *one* worker in the "bargaining unit".[150] By implication, this gives any dissident worker the opportunity of trying to deny the right to freedom of association to his workmates.

From another angle, the right to freedom of association was underlined by a more recent ruling in the ECtHR. This was in 2007 in the case of *ASLEF v. United Kingdom.* This case came about because the train drivers' union, Associated Society of Locomotive Engineers and Firemen (ASLEF), expelled from membership a member of the extreme right British National Party (BNP). Through the 1993 Act, an amendment was inserted into the 1992 Act whereby persons who are excluded from or expelled from membership of a trade union on grounds of membership of a political party could bring litigation against the union concerned and there, this provision in the 1992 Act was deemed as being in breach of Article 11 of the ECHR.[151] This expulsion took place on the grounds that membership of this particular party or similar fascist organisations was in fundamental conflict with the aims and objects of the union and there, the ECtHR ruled that ASLEF was entitled to do this.

The right to freedom of association, on the basis of ILO Convention No. 87, gives trade unions the right to draw up their constitutions and rules without interference by the public authorities. In the ASLEF case, the ECtHR ruled that "Article 11 cannot be interpreted as imposing an obligation on associations or organisations to admit whosoever wishes to join. Where associations are formed by people, who, espousing particular values or ideals, intend to pursue common goals, it would run counter to the very effectiveness of the freedom at stake if they had no control over their membership".[152] Through this ruling, the ECtHR has recommended that Section 174 of the 1992 Act be amended so that UK law conforms to article 11 of the ECHR. This does not mean that unions should be

[150] Ibid., pp. 18-23.

[151] See Ford, Michael and Hendy, John QC, *Briefing note: ASLEF v UK*, The Institute of Employment Rights (Liverpool), 26 June 2007.

[152] Ibid., p. 4.

automatically free to expel or exclude from membership anyone for simply being a member of a certain political party but that they should have this right in the event of this party having objectives and beliefs which are in fundamental conflict with the values of the union.[153]

So, following on from the implications of the ruling in the Wilson and Palmer case in the ECtHR in 2002, this ruling in the same court in the ASLEF case five years later has reaffirmed the rights of trade unions to determine their own rules (see page 234). And once again, this court has made a ruling which confirms that the trade union laws in the UK, which had originally been enacted by the Thatcher and Major Governments, do not fulfill the limited rights to freedom of association as defined by article 11 of the ECHR.

However one assesses the record of the Blair Government, after almost two legislative periods and with it wanting to be re-elected at the following election (which took place in 2005), it could not be overlooked that within the ranks of the trade union and labour movement there emerged (and continued to remain) a wide degree of discontent over many aspects of the policies of this Government.

In its endeavours to secure re-election and of the need to reassure active trade unionists that their interests are best served by a Labour government, despite any misgivings there may have been, a meeting at Warwick University in 2004 between government ministers and trade union general secretaries took place and out of this came a whole package of measures which government ministers agreed to enact. This package became known as the *Warwick Agreement*. On the basis of this agreement, the Blair Government had agreed to implement a package of no fewer than 110 measures ranging from employment rights and pensions to manufacturing and public services by the following election.[154] One of the biggest successes was the agreement to end the practice by which some employers counted statutory holidays against the statutory entitlement to four weeks' annual leave. Out of this, up to two million workers would benefit, once legislation is passed. However, unions became less satisfied with the actual plans the Government had for implementing this agreement.[155] This example, as well as the position the Government took on the Trade Union Freedom Bill in 2007 (see above), would imply that unions were to have a constant battle in ensuring that the Government fulfills its obligations under the *Warwick Agreement* in a meaningful way.

---

[153] Ibid.

[154] See The unions take stock of Warwick, in: *Labour Research*, Labour Research Department (London),Vol. 95 No. 10, October 2006, pp. 9-13. See also Has Warwick saved the link?, in: *Labour Research*, ..., Vol. 94 No. 1, January 2005, pp. 9-12.

[155] The unions take stock of Warwick, ..., p. 9.

One important area of policy from the Blair Government which the trade union movement welcomed was the introduction of a national minimum wage together with minimum rates of pay being reviewed every year. With this, the Blair Government decided that Britain should conform to what had already been introduced in many other countries in Europe. Although this measure has not resolved the problem many workers endure of having to "live" off low pay, in the run-up to the 2005 general election, the Blair Government was able to show that 1.6 million workers from the age of 16 have benefited from this measure.[156] As to long-standing claims that such regulations endanger jobs (see page 80), an argument which is still being used in prominent political and industrial circles in Germany in an attempt to prevent the extension of such regulations there, in the run-up to the 2005 general election, the Blair Government was also able to show that in the period from 1997 to 2005, the number of full-time permanent jobs in the UK had increased by 1.9 million to a record of 28.4 million people in work with unemployment at the lowest level for 30 years.[157] This example alone of the UK would more than adequately refute claims that minimum wage regulations lead to job losses.

However, one crucial area of assessing the record of the Blair Government is its position of the question of the EU. On this issue, opinions within the ranks of the trade union and labour movement are divided.

In line with the process of establishing European EMU where, apart from other matters, stress is laid on central bank "independence", as had already been stipulated in the Maastricht Treaty,[158] the new Chancellor of the Exchequer, Gordon Brown, moved swiftly and made the Bank of England "operationally independent".[159] Most significantly, this was to mean that the criteria by which the Bank would intervene in the money markets, especially in determining lending rates, was to lie with the Bank itself whereas up to then, final decisions on such matters lay with the Chancellor of the Exchequer.

However, whereas other member states of the EU were then striving to proceed to phase three of EMU with the introduction of the single European currency, which in any case had already been delayed due to the inability of almost all EU

---

[156] See Labour's achievements for working people, in: *Amicus: the magazine*, Issue 6, Amicus (London), Summer 2005, p. 18.

[157] Ibid. See also Appendix, tables 4, 7 and 14.

[158] Article 107 of the Maastricht Treaty stipulates that the European System of Central Banks, the European Central Bank as well as national central banks are to be "independent" and actually prohibits governments from seeking to influence decisions taken by these banks. For further information on the implications of central bank "independence" under the Maastricht Treaty, see Kenen, Peter B, *Economic and Monetary Union in Europe: Moving beyond Maastricht*, Cambridge University Press (Cambridge), 1995, pp. 39-43.

[159] See Brittan, Samuel, Beyond independence, in *Financial Times* (London), 8 May 1997, p. 24.

member states to fulfill Maastricht's so-called convergence criteria, the newly-elected Blair Government, whilst pledging Britain's continued support for EMU, decided "to keep its options open". In this, Blair was aware that under the Maastricht Treaty, Britain was not obliged to proceed to stage three of EMU owing to the *opt-out* his predecessor Major had secured in the final stages of the Maastricht negotiations in autumn 1991 (see pages 213f) and is still not obliged to do so. More significantly, however, Blair, like his predecessor, was well aware of the wide degree of scepticism among the British people on this crucial issue with the likelihood of it not securing their support in any referendum in the event of one ever being held on this issue.

In this, in deciding whether to recommend the introduction of the *euro* in Britain in a referendum, which had in any case been promised on this issue by both the outgoing Major Government as well as the Labour Party in the 1997 election campaign,[160] the Blair Government decided to introduce "five economic tests" as criteria before making any such recommendation. The criteria the Government set for these tests are: firstly, there would have to "be sustainable convergence between Britain and the economies of the single currency"; secondly, whether "there is sufficient flexibility to cope with all the economic change" and for Britain's ability "to change and adjust to unexpected economic events in any part of that monetary union"; thirdly, "it must be good for investment"; fourthly, its effect on the financial services industry; and, finally, "whether it is good for employment".[161] The fourth point principally refers to the City of London. In this, one can question as to whether there is a contradiction between the fourth and fifth points of these "five economic tests" in that the initial aim of the City of London in seeking to maximise profits would be at variance with the need to create and maintain jobs.[162] In any case, as the principle aim of EMU is "price stability", the question of job stability would only be of secondary importance. Following the voters' rejection of their governments' recommendation for the introduction of the *euro* in referenda held in Denmark in 2000 and Sweden in 2003, discussion over the possible introduction of this currency in the UK has receded for the time being.

In the meantime, the question of the EU seeking the adoption of a constitution has taken centre stage. In the general election campaign in May 2005, all three major parties promised a referendum on the proposed *Treaty establishing a*

---

160 See *You can only be sure with the Conservatives: The Conservative Manifesto 1997*, Conservative Central Office (Westminster, London), 1997, p. 47, and *New Labour because Britain deserves better ...*, ..., pp. 37f.

161 See speech by Brown, Rt. Hon. Gordon (Chancellor of the Exchequer), in: *Unions and the Euro: TUC Euro Briefing* (Special Issue – No. 8), TUC (London), July 1999, pp. 5f.

162 See *EU Economic and Monetary Union: Euro Fallout*, Campaign against Euro-federalism (Merseyside), 1999, p. 12.

Constitution for Europe[163] which was signed at the European Council meeting in Rome on 29 October, 2004. Shortly after this election this proposed treaty was rejected in referenda held in France and the Netherlands with the effect that there was little chance of it being put into effect as it stood so it was "withdrawn".

Not withstanding the decision of the people in these two countries (to mention nothing of those in other EU member states who have never been and are never likely to be consulted on this issue), the question of the EU adopting a constitution has been reactivated, with Germany, in particular, "taking the initiative" during her presidency of the EU in the first half of 2007. Out of this came the proposed EU Reform Treaty which was signed at the European Council meeting in Lisbon in December 2007 and the process of this treaty (otherwise known as the Treaty of Lisbon) being ratified in the individual member states of the EU has already begun. Although the term "constitution" is avoided, the purpose of this "new" draft treaty remains the same as the one which was rejected in France and the Netherlands. Consequently, the original commitments made in the 2005 election campaign to hold a referendum would surely remained valid. However, this "new" draft treaty has been formulated in such a way (principally through numerous amendments to existing treaties) with the aim of it being ratified without referenda (except in Ireland where a referendum is necessary whenever there are matters requiring changes to the country's constitution).

An attempt to make ratification of the Treaty of Lisbon in Britain conditional upon the support of the British people through a referendum failed when on 6 March, the House of Commons rejected a Conservative motion to this effect. So this can be interpreted as the Labour Government (under Blair's successor Gordon Brown) as well as the Liberal Democrats, voting to disregard their election pledges (apart from the individual MPs of these two parties who voted to honour them). Brown argued that a referendum was not necessary by claiming that there are no constitutional implications for the UK but the House of Commons EU Scrutiny Committee thought differently.[164]

---

[163] Blair pledged to put the constitutional treaty "to the British people in a referendum and campaign whole-heartedly for a 'Yes' vote", see *Britain forward not back: The Labour Party manifesto 2005*, Labour Party (London), 2005, p. 84. Arguing similarly, the Liberal Democrats also pledged that "ratification must be subject to a referendum of the British people", see *The Real Alternative: Manifesto Text*, Liberal Democrats (London), undated (2005), p. 27. The Conservative Party declared its opposition to the treaty and pledged to "give the British people the chance to reject its provisions in a referendum within six months of the General Election". See *Are you thinking what we're thinking? It's Time for Action: Conservative Election Manifesto 2005*, p. 26.

[164] See House of Commons EU Scrutiny Committee says: Britain will be subject to "new and unquantifiable risks" from EU Constitution and 'red-lines' will not work, in: *The Democrat*, Campaign against Euro-federalism (London), No. 105, November-December 2007, p. 2.

A contentious issue in the process of the EU seeking to adopt a constitution has been *The Charter of Fundamental Rights of the Union* from 2000,[165] especially regarding its provisions on workers' rights. Basically, the question has been whether the incorporation of workers' rights are necessary to secure the support of the European trade unions for the EU to adopt a constitution as, for example, has been the view of Germany, France and the Benelux countries or whether these would impose additional costs on employers – a line of argument Britain has regularly taken on such matters in the EU.

However, little attention has been given to the question of whether workers' rights, in as far as they are really incorporated in the Fundamental Rights Charter, fulfill the norms which had already been achieved at European and international level as well as in the constitutions of various countries in Western Europe. A most notable omission in this Charter is "the right to work"[166] – a point which was also evident in the *Community Charter of the Fundamental Social Rights of Workers* from 1989 (see page 108). Instead of "the right to work", the Fundamental Rights Charter merely proclaims "the right to engage in work".[167] Although the Charter from 1989 reaffirmed the right of workers "to just and favourable remuneration",[168] the Charter from 2000 is notable for the fact that there is neither "the right to work" nor the right "to just and favourable remuneration".[169] On these crucial points alone, one can assume that the entire process of the EU seeking to adopt a constitution has been accompanied by a steady erosion of workers' rights.

"The right to work" is of special importance for it is only on this basis where the best possible employment policies can be implemented even if this does not lead to a job of one's personal choice.[170] In this, governments are obliged to formulate

[165] *The Charter of Fundamental Rights of the Union* was originally drafted by a convention under the chairmanship of the former German President and former President of Germany's Constitutional Court Professor Roman Herzog. This Charter was adopted at the European Council meeting in Nice on 7 December, 2000. It later became Part II, incorporating Articles II-61 to II-114, of the EU Constitutional Treaty, which has been "withdrawn". It has now become a Protocol which is annexed to the Treaty of Lisbon with its provisions not legally binding on the UK and Poland.

[166] "The right to work" is incorporated, for example, in the *Universal Declaration of Human Rights* from 1948 (Article 23 (1)), the *European Social Charter* from 1961 and also in its revised form 1996 (Part II, Article 1), the *International Covenant on Economic, Social and Cultural Rights* from 1966 (Part III, Article 6) as well as in the constitutions of a number of European countries.

[167] NB Article 15 of *The Charter of Fundamental Rights of the Union* (but Article II-75 of the "withdrawn" Constitutional Treaty).

[168] Also incorporated in the various conventions and charters at European and international level as noted in footnote 164.

[169] Barlow, Keith, The EU Constitution's Implications on the Right to Work, in: *Communist Review*, Communist Party of Britain (London), No. 44, Summer 2005, pp. 20f.

[170] Schachtschneider, Karl Albrecht, Eine Charta der Grundrechte für die Europäische Union,

their economic and social policies such that proper work with proper terms and conditions of employment are provided for those wanting to work.[171] In this, policies based on "the right to work" would clash with a key objective of EMU, price stability (see above), so the reason behind the exclusion of this right from the Fundamental Rights Charter becomes evident.

So, whereas Article 15 of the Fundamental Rights Charter merely proclaims "the right to engage in work", one cannot overlook the fact that the very next article proclaims a "Freedom to conduct a business".[172] Commenting on this Charter, almost immediately after it was signed in December 2000, in obvious anticipation of what was likely to follow, German public law professor Karl Albrecht Schachtschneider wrote that a Fundamental Rights Charter which recognises "the right to conduct a business" but not "the right to work" fundamentally changes the economic constitution. It changes from a "social market economy" to a "competitive market economy" which will not lay a stone in the path of the "global revolution of capital".[173]

A further matter concerning workers' rights, which now has an added degree of importance, due to the rulings in the European Court of Justice in Luxembourg (ECJ) in December 2007 in the Viking and Laval cases, concerns "the right to strike". The social rights of workers, as set out in the *European Social Charter* from 1961 and in *Community Charter of the Fundamental Social Rights of Workers* from 1989 have been incorporated in Article 151 of the consolidated Treaty on the Functioning of the European Union, as amended in December 2007.[174] This would also include "the right to strike".

In the first case, Viking owned a ship called the *Rosella* which operated under a Finnish flag between Tallin and Helsinki. The ship was making a loss so the owner sought to "re-flag" it so as to operate under a "flag of convenience" in Estonia or Norway so as to enable the employer to avoid collective agreements with the Finnish trade unions, thereby cutting jobs and undermining terms and conditions of employment. Following a request from the Finnish seamen's union, the International Transport Workers' Federation instructed all affiliates to boycott Viking and the Finnish seamen's union issued a call for strike action by its members. Viking brought proceedings in the High Court in London arguing

in: *Beilage zur Wochenzeitung Das Parlament*, Bundeszentrale für politische Bildung (Bonn), 22 December 2000, p. 19.

[171] Barlow, Keith, ..., p. 22.

[172] Under the "Freedom to conduct a business", Article 16 of *The Charter of Fundamental Rights* ... states that the "freedom to conduct a business in accordance with Union law and national laws and practices is recognised."

[173] See Schachtschneider, Karl Albrecht, ..., p. 19.

[174] Arthur, Richard (Thompsons Solicitors), *Viking and Laval: A Collision Waiting to Happen*, paper delivered to the Scottish Trades Union Congress, 29 February 2008.

that its "right to freedom of establishment" was being infringed upon by strike action and the case was eventually referred to the (ECJ).[175]

In the second case, the Latvian company Laval was contracted to build a school at Vaxholm in Sweden and for this purpose, workers from Latvia were recruited. The Swedish construction unions attempted to get Laval to sign up to collective agreements in the construction sector in Sweden covering terms and conditions of employment comparable to those in Sweden. Laval refused so the Swedish construction unions blockaded Laval's sites in Sweden and also secured the solidarity of the Swedish electrician's union. Eventually, the Swedish subsidiary of Laval was declared bankrupt and the parent company brought proceedings in the Swedish courts arguing that its "freedom to provide services" had been infringed upon and that it had been discriminated against because of the failure of Swedish national provisions to take account of collective agreements entered into between it and the unions in Latvia. Eventually, the case was handled by the ECJ.[176]

So, whereas the Viking case concerned an employer's "right to freedom of establishment", as laid down by Article 43 of the EC Treaty, prior to its amendment, the Laval case concerned an employer's "freedom to provide services", as laid down by Article 49 of the same treaty, prior to its amendment. In the first case, the ECJ ruled on 11 December 2007, that the Treaty's provisions protecting the "right to freedom of establishment" applies to industrial action and that such action represents a restriction of this right if it makes the exercising thereof "less attractive". Although the ECJ ruled that a restriction of this right is acceptable where industrial action pursues a legitimate aim and is justified by overriding reasons of public interest, this, in the view of this court, was not so in the Viking case. On 18 December, 2007, the ECJ ruled similarly in the Laval case.[177] There, the ECJ also ruled that the protection of workers from social dumping can amount to an overriding reason of public interest but, in the context of posted workers, industrial action in support of a demand that an employer exceeds the level of protection guaranteed by the Posted Workers Directive cannot be justified and that an employer is discriminated against if national rules do not take account of collective agreements in the employer's state of origin.[178] So, in these two cases, employers' "economic freedoms" secured more weight before the

---

[175] Ibid. (NB The European Court of Justice (ECJ) in Luxembourg should not be confused with the European Court of Human Rights (ECtHR) in Strasbourg. Whereas the ECJ acts as a final court of appeal on matters within the EU, as regulated under the various treaties and directives in the EU, the ECtHR was established under the ECHR and acts as a final court of appeal on cases alleging breaches of it from and within those countries which have signed this convention.)

[176] Arthur, Richard, ...

[177] Ibid.

[178] Ibid.

ECJ than the social rights of workers which had already been laid down and ratified in various charters and convention at European and international level.

Following on from the rulings in the Laval and Viking cases, clarification is necessary on the extent to which "the right to strike" exists in the EU and, in as far as this right exists, whether it fulfills the norms which had already been laid down in the Charters from 1961 and 1989 (see above). In this, one also needs to assess the validity of "the right to strike" as laid down in Article 28 of the Fundamental Rights Charter,[179] to mention nothing of the existence of this right, to varying degrees, in the constitutions or labour codes or in other forms in the individual member states of the EU.

As things stand, strike action in the UK has the protection of the 1992 Act providing that it's undertaken "in contemplation or furtherance of a trade dispute", the definition of which having originally been narrowed in the early 1980s, most notably through the 1982 Act in that it has to be "wholly or mainly" about the terms and conditions of employment (see pages 91f). Following on from the rulings in the ECJ in the Viking and Laval cases, even though they can be seen as being "wholly or mainly" about the terms and conditions of employment, it is therefore possible that in the UK, the "definition of a trade dispute" could be narrowed further in that industrial action which is deemed as being in breach of the rules governing the EU's internal market would have no legal protection. This could then expose the organisers of such action and the trade unions themselves to claims for damages in tort for strike action which (still) falls under the protection of the 1992 Act which, by implication, could impose further constraints on the right of workers to freedom of association.

Under Article 28 of the Fundamental Rights Charter, the right to take strike action "in accordance with Union law and national laws and practices" would mean that in the case of the UK, this "right" would only be possible within the constraints of the Conservative trade union laws which, in effect, have secured a degree of legitimacy under this Charter (whether or not its provisions are legally binding on the UK). This point is qualified further through an Explanation in Declaration 12 in the Treaty by stating that the limits for the exercise of collective action, come under national laws and practices.[180] The rulings in the Viking and Laval cases may impose further constraints upon the right to take strike action in accordance with the Fundamental Rights Charter. In this, another question which needs to be considered is how does one assess employers' rights "to take

[179] Under the "Right of collective bargaining and action", Article 28 of *The Charter of Fundamental Rights* ... states that "Workers and employers, or their respective organisations, have, in accordance with Union law and national laws and practices, the right to negotiate and conclude collective agreements at the appropriate levels and, in cases of conflicts of interest, to take collective action to defend their interests, including strike action."

[180] Denny, Brian, Rights? What Rights?, in: *Morning Star* (London), 18 December 2007, p. 8.

collective action ... including strike action" as laid down in this Charter? Article III-210 paragraph 6 (although not actually part of the Fundamental Rights Charter) of the withdrawn Constitutional Treaty, for example, had already acknowledged the existence of "the right to impose lockouts"!

It is therefore apparent that within the EU, there are uncertainties, together with wide differences among the member states themselves, as to the extent to which strike action is possible. Following on from the rulings in the ECJ in the Viking and Laval cases, it is possible that the ratification of the Treaty of Lisbon could lead to restrictions on the extent to which strike action is possible within the EU as a whole. In view of this, there is a strong case for trade unions and trade unionists in the member states of the EU to press for a delay in the ratification of the Treaty of Lisbon until there is clarity over the extent to which strike action is possible and protected, especially in Britain where the right to take strike action is not as wide as in other countries in the EU.

5.4. Conclusion

In its endeavours to get back into office following the general election defeats in 1979 and 1983, the Labour Party, initially under the leadership of Neil Kinnock and later under the leadership of the future Prime Minister Tony Blair, underwent profound changes. Principally, these changes took place on two fronts. Firstly, following the election defeat in 1987, the Party leadership undertook a fundamental review of the Party's policies which had the aim of either dropping or altering those which, in their view, hampered the Party's electoral appeal. Apart from anything else, this included abandoning earlier commitments to bring back into public ownership industries which had been privatised since 1979 and to repeal the Conservative trade union laws. Secondly, the Party "modified" its relationship with the trade unions affiliated to the Party so as to reduce their influence. This ranged from reducing their share of votes at annual conference to reducing their influence in the selection of PPCs.

Feeling the need for the Party to be united in preparation for a general election campaign, trade union leaders, leaving aside any personal reservations and those of union members on specific issues, went along with the wishes of Party leaders and gave them the necessary support in the key votes at annual conference. The outcome of the 1992 election when the Major Government, as it were, escaped the defeat which had long been predicted, shows that Labour's policy review failed. This review, which then formed the basis of Labour's 1992 election manifesto, was unconvincing in that it failed to mobilise the mass potential of Labour voters to vote for the Party despite them wanting to see an end to 13 years of the Conservative Party in government.

During the course of the policy review, preparations for EMU, which was to become the cornerstone of the future Maastricht Treaty, were advancing. In this, there was then the question of how Labour leaders, having already dropped the Party's long-held scepticism towards the EU, was going to position itself on the question of anchoring sterling in ERM which Thatcher and her closest allies in the Government she led, for reasons totally different from those of the broad labour movement, opposed. On this issue, Labour leaders made a fatal mistake – the consequences of which were to overshadow its election campaign in 1992.

Above all else, Labour's support for the anchoring of sterling in ERM and at the overvalued rate of £1 to DM 2,95 in October 1990, in the midst of an economic downturn, meant that unemployment rose to levels higher than they would have and the loss of output was likewise higher than it have otherwise been. So, this support for ERM and the pledge to maintain the value of sterling there at this overvalued rate in the election campaign itself meant that the Party's costing for much needed improvements in Britain's social infrastructure, most notably in health and education, were needlessly placed in a financial straight jacket. This in turn left Labour exposed to questions of how its spending plans were going to be financed without raising taxes. Even if Labour was not prepared to oppose ERM in principle, it could have made support for it being conditional of it being free of its deflationary bias, in line with its own policy review. Thus, on this crucial question, the policy of the Labour opposition appeared identical to that of the Major Government and the Liberal Democrats. In other words, the "fight against inflation" took priority over the need for a coherent macro-economic strategy for growth and employment.

Despite the failure of Labour's policy review, the strategy of "reforming" the Party, both in terms of policy and in connection with its relations to the affiliated trade unions, continued after Kinnock stepped down as Party leader. Not withstanding the failure of Labour's policy review, trade union leaders at the time continued to go along with the "reforms" initiated by the Party leadership so that the Party, even if only on the surface, continued to remain united. As well as agreeing to further reductions in their share of votes at annual conference and in the "electoral college" for the election of Party leader and deputy leader, trade union leaders also agreed to a "revision" which, to all intents and purposes, amounted to the abolition of Clause IV, part 4 of the Party's constitution. This change to the constitution came about despite widespread apprehension within the ranks of the unions themselves and among the mass of Party activists.

Yet, by the time Labour got back into office, public discontent with the Major Government had become so widespread that a Labour victory was all but certain no matter when the election was going to be called. This then leads to the question of whether the wide-ranging "reforms" and policy changes which Party leaders initiated were necessary at all?

On the question of trade union and labour relations law and workers' rights, the Blair Government enacted some preliminary measures which were welcomed by the trade union movement. These included the reversal of Britain's *opt-out* from the "Social Chapter" (however significant this really was), the restoration of trade union rights at GCHQ, the 1988 Human Rights Act and legislation enabling the introduction of national minimum wages. However, the "hard core" of the trade union laws dating back to the early 1980s were going to remain untouched.

Following the ruling in the Wilson and Palmer case in the ECHR in 2002, the Blair Government, on the "moral authority" of this court, had an opportunity and, in fact, an obligation, to enact legislation so as to tackle deficiencies in the right to freedom of association this court highlighted in a meaningful way so as to bring this right up to levels comparable with those of other countries in Europe. Its handling of the firefighters' dispute is in itself indicative that no such legislation was going to be contemplated. Yet, had such an opportunity been fully exploited, it would have won wide acclaim from within the organised labour movement. Furthermore, as it was Conservative legislation which this court rebuked, it would not have been easy for the Conservative opposition, still weakened by two severe election defeats in a row, to oppose legislation in this direction in any convincing way. Another reason for believing this is quite simple. This ruling in the Wilson and Palmer case in the ECtHR as well as the ruling in the ASLEF case in the same court in 2007 showed that the right to freedom of association in the UK failed (and still fails) to fulfill the minimal requirements under the European Convention on Human Rights. The rulings in the ECtHR in 2002 and 2007 would in any case be overshadowed by the rulings in the ECJ in the Viking and Laval cases in December 2007.

However, legislating so as to bring the right to freedom of association up to the levels attained in other countries in Western European would have effectively meant "going against the grain" of the key elements of the Conservative trade union laws. This is something which the Blair Government was unwilling to do and, to date, this also appears to be the case under Brown.

So, after the longest period ever of the Labour Party in Britain in government and after three general election victories in a row, Blair's position, like that of his successor Brown, be it just on the questions of privatisation and trade union and labour relations law, are indicative of the legacy of *New* Labour in that the political agenda which the Thatcher Government had begun to put into effect upon taking office in 1979 was, to all intents and purposes, either to remain untouched or pursued further.

Chapter Six: Conclusion

The Conservative Party and the Government it led from 1979 to 1997 put the root causes of Britain's economic difficulties down to two areas. Firstly, "high" levels of state involvement in the economy had led to a lack of monetary discipline on the part of the public authorities which in turn led to inflationary pressures. Secondly, the influence of the organised labour movement under conditions of "full employment" meant that for many groups of workers, working practices, terms and conditions of employment had been secured beyond what would have been permitted had there been a "free" market for labour.

These two factors are interrelated. The influence of the organised labour movement at a time in which there was a shortage of skilled workers, as during the Second World War, was a factor which resulted in a governmental commitment to enact macroeconomic measures so as to maintain "full employment" once the War was over. Parallel to this, so as to prevent any return of widespread poverty and deprivation, wide ranging reforms in social welfare were enacted. These measures provided the basis of what has often been referred to as the post-war "consensus". But, in the view of the Conservative Party, these reforms caused two problems.

Firstly, the State, it was claimed, committed itself to spending levels it could not afford. Secondly, the existence of "full employment" meant that there was no large pool of unemployed labour which could be exploited to keep down labour costs. Consequently, the balance of forces in society were tilted more favourably towards the organised labour movement. Not only that. This greater influence of the labour movement led to constraints upon the State whenever it sought to impose limits on its commitment to maintain "full employment" and social welfare.

Thus, the end of an era of "full employment", which had actually occurred under the previous Labour Government (1974-1979), whose economic policies had become discredited in the eyes of many Labour voters, enabled the economic "initiative" to pass into the hands of the Conservative Opposition which, in early 1975, had elected a "New" Right leader. So, the re-emergence of large scale unemployment in the latter half of the 1970s opened the way for the Conservative Opposition to set an agenda which was to pave the way for a comprehensive challenge to the whole basis of "consensus" politics upon it getting into office, in as far as "consensus" had really existed at all.

For the Conservative Party, policies seeking or maintaining "full employment" had then become officially regarded as the main reason for Britain's declining position in the advanced industrialised world. Abandoning any commitment to "full employment" by pursuing "free" market economic policies within a tight monetary framework became part of the "new" Conservative strategy to force working people and trade unions to conform to "new" realities. Had this been the only factor, such policies, given the experience of the 1930s, might appear to have been misconceived in view of its likely impact on manufacturing industry. However, the Thatcher Government saw Britain's longer term economic prosperity through strengthening the standing of the City of London as a major international financial centre and based its economic policies accordingly. There was already a basis for this as Britain already had vast holdings of assets overseas in comparison with other countries. Indeed, her balance of payments by the end of the 1970s was being bolstered by becoming an oil-producing nation at a time when oil prices were high on the world market. There was also the hope that new employment opportunities in London and the South-East of England, in an expanded financial services sector, would partially offset some of the job losses in manufacturing.

However, for the City of London to gain the maximum benefit of the North Sea oil revenues, interest rates had to be "competitive", sterling had to be "strong and stable" which meant inflation and monetary expansion having to be tightly controlled. Thus within the tight constraints the Thatcher Government set itself, industry could only survive by becoming "leaner and fitter". Management had to have the "right to manage". Industrial restructuring had to be forced through no matter what side-effects this may have. So reasons for allowing interest rates to rise the way they did from June 1979 become evident.

By officially having no incomes policy, the Thatcher Government could "keep its distance" in pay negotiations, especially in the private sector. At the same time, the large increases in interest rates from the middle of 1979 had the effect of increasing the cost of credit as well as industrial fixed costs. This not only hit investment in manufacturing industry, it also hit those buying their own homes. All these factors depressed domestic demand and additionally, British goods, initially through a high if not over-valued exchange rate, became uncompetitive on both domestic and world markets. All this also led to a considerable loss of productive industrial capacity which inevitably forced industry, both in the public and private sectors, to shed labour.

The question which needs asking is whether higher interest rates were necessary for the City of London to gain the maximum possible benefit from the North Sea oil revenues even if this was to mean allowing a rundown of much of the UK's manufacturing base with its inevitable consequences on the labour market. If higher interest rates were necessary to maximise the benefit of these revenues, this would then lead to the question of whether higher unemployment was the price which had to be paid for this. In this, there is one additional point which would not have been overlooked. If "full employment" had brought about "a sellers' market for labour", thereby a strengthening of the influence of organised labour, and if abandoning any commitment to this was a necessary condition for the implementation of a "free" market economic strategy within a tight monetary framework, this would raise the question. Was a high unemployment strategy deliberately pursued from May 1979?

Whatever view one takes on this, one thing is certain. The policies of the Thatcher Government appeared to disregard the lessons of the inter-war depression almost fifty years earlier. Upon taking office in 1979, it pursued deflationary measures coupled with two drastic rises in interest rates in that year – both at a time when a downturn in the world economy had already become evident. The fact is that after the Thatcher Government took office, there was a rapid increase in unemployment and little was done to prevent this. Moreover, when the economy started to recover from the 1979-1981 slump, unemployment continued to rise up to the beginning of 1986. So, whether or not a high unemployment strategy was actually intended, a large pool of unemployed labour was the outcome of this slump and this subsequently became and remained a permanent feature of economic and social life in Britain.

Following the outcome of the war against Argentina in 1982, any serious opposition to Margaret Thatcher's authority as Prime Minister and Leader of the Conservative Party, within or outside her Party and Government, crumbled. With the possible exception of the year-long miners' strike, it seemed as if her tenure in office had become unchallengeable. Yet, as from around the time of the end of this strike, divisions were opening up within the Thatcher Government on the controversial question of how Britain should position herself on moves towards establishing EMU which became the cornerstone of the Maastricht Treaty. This issue was to overshadow the remaining years of her premiership and eventually became a key factor in her downfall in autumn 1990.

In any case, from the time following the 1987 election, there was rising public discontent over the critical social situation as shown by the worsening state of Britain's social infrastructure. In addition, there was widespread opposition to the introduction of the "poll tax". Furthermore, 1990 saw the end of the fall in joblessness which the "Lawson boom" had temporarily sustained. As a result, it became increasingly questionable whether the Conservative Party under Thatcher's leadership could win another term in office. As it turned out, it was her opposition at the European Community summit meeting in Rome in October 1990 to further moves towards establishing EMU which ultimately set in motion the process which led to the end of her premiership.

Whilst Conservative Party leaders were seeking to resolve their differences over EMU, the Labour Party was in the process of "reviewing" its policies which appeared to have an added degree of urgency following its 1987 election defeat. The thinking behind this policy review was that if Labour had any chance of getting back into office, it had to drop or modify those policies which Party leaders regarded as making it unelectable.

One aspect of Labour's policy review was that the Party's long-standing scepticism towards EMU and the anchoring of sterling in ERM became one of actual support, providing it was free of its deflationary bias. Yet, when in October 1990 Thatcher was forced to concede to sterling joining ERM, Labour leaders, as well as the Liberal Democrats, supported this decision. Yet, Labour's decision to support ERM took no account of the terms it set out for membership in its policy review which had only been adopted the previous year. As the "Lawson boom" had already passed with there being yet another downturn in the UK economy, the decision to join ERM with sterling being fixed at the overvalued rate of £1=DM2,95 led to the UK economy being plunged into another slump – this being on a magnitude almost comparable to that of 1979 to 1981.

As Labour had not considered the economic implications of ERM seriously when sterling joined, this issue did not feature prominently in the run-up to the 1992 election. Thus, its plans for financing much-needed improvements in Britain's social infrastructure notably for health and education had not taken account of the cost of ERM. So, Labour was exposed to allegations of having to raise taxes without it having the courage to say so. Yet the costs of Labour's plans for funding improvements in health and education would have been small in comparison to the actual costs of ERM on the UK economy given the steep rise in unemployment and the big loss of output this precipitated.

Had Labour questioned ERM, it could have added another dimension to the 1992 election campaign from which it could have profited given the wide degree of scepticism towards the EU under a large number of voters. Labour didn't do this so support for ERM turned out to be a major factor which overshadowed its election campaign even if this went unnoticed. This, not overlooking the damaging impact of the "Sheffield rally" shortly before the election, leads to one important conclusion: one cannot say that John Major "won" the 1992 election, rather Neil Kinnock lost it. In this, Major "escaped" what had long been predicted as a certain defeat. Thus, the policy review Kinnock authorised after the 1987 election defeat was neither honoured nor endorsed by the electorate.

Parallel to Labour reviewing its policies were moves towards "reforming" the Party itself. This had two main features. Firstly, "reform" was to mean reducing the influence of the trade unions in the Party's main decision-making processes. Secondly, as a "logical follow-on" from its policy review, coupled with pressure form the new Party Leader Tony Blair, "reform" also meant the Party having to formally abandon its long-standing commitment to bringing about a socialist society through, to what to all intents and purposes was, the abolition of Clause IV, part 4 of the Party's constitution. But as to whether any of these measures were necessary at all, one thing became certain. After having "escaped" defeat in 1992, the Major Government became so discredited that a Labour victory at the following general election was all but certain no matter when it was going to be held.

With Labour winning the biggest ever parliamentary majority in its history in the 1997 election and winning a similar majority at the following election four years later, Tony Blair had a "free hand" to reverse many of the Conservative policies of the previous 18 years which had become unpopular within the ranks of the organised labour movement, had he had the intention of doing so. Had he done so, he would have won wide acclaim. Furthermore, as the Conservative Party was so severely defeated in 1997 with a number of its prominent leaders failing to be re-elected in their constituencies, it would have had difficulty in mounting any serious opposition to such measures. But, despite any positive points trade union leaders were able to make about the Blair Government as part of their attempt to mobilise the votes of trade unionists in the general election campaigns in 2001 and 2005, Blair had principally left the key policies enacted under Thatcher and Major untouched. This was especially so in the fields of privatisation and trade union and labour relations law. To date, Blair's successor Gordon Brown has not indicated any change in course.

Whereas under Blair's premiership, the Conservatives had not been able to mount any serious challenge to the Labour Party, opinion polls as from autumn 2007 have shown that they have been able to do this on the biggest scale since their severe defeat in 1997. This recovery in lost Conservative support became all too clear when the Labour Party suffered major losses in the local elections in England and Wales on 1 May, 2008. This confirms that since autumn 2007, the Conservative Party has been able to capitalise on the discontent among the masses of ordinary people over many of the policies associated with *New* Labour thus winning back support it had lost following the 1992 election. At the time of writing, Labour's prospects for the next general election, which has to be held by mid 2010 at the very latest, look critical. The key to Labour winning a fourth consecutive term in office depends on its willingness to seriously attend to the grievances under the mass of its traditional supporters. Put differently, if Labour is to win the next election, there have to be "positive" reasons for voting Labour and one aspect in this is for trade union leaders to ensure that there is no departure from the spirit behind the *Warwick Agreement* of summer 2004.

The critical situation which Labour currently finds itself in may have been eased had it agreed to hold a referendum on the EU's "Reform Treaty", given the wide degree of scepticism towards the EU among the British people. As Labour, as well as the Conservatives and Liberal Democrats, had made such a pledge on the EU's Constitutional Treaty in the 2005 election campaign, any failure to hold a referendum on the "Reform Treaty" can be judged as a breach of its manifesto commitment as the aims and contents of this Treaty are almost identical to those of the Constitutional Treaty, which was withdrawn owing to its rejection in France and the Netherlands in referenda shortly after the 2005 election. A key factor in influencing the outcome of the referenda in these countries was that people there rejected the neo-liberal contents of this treaty as well as moves to further the militarisation of the foreign policy of the EU. In fact, Labour's support for such policies is the reason for the big drop in its support.

There remains the question of whether a large pool of unemployed labour is a condition for implementing a "free" market economic strategy. If such a strategy requires a "free" market for labour, the Thatcher Government may well have seen mass unemployment as an opportunity for undermining the influence of organised labour as a whole. But on the other hand, there were still industrial sectors where trade union organisation was strong and well developed as, for example, among skilled workers in the British printing industry. There, mass unemployment alone would not have been enough to break the influence of the unions. What was additionally needed were "special measures" – hence the central importance of the trade union laws, particularly those enacted in the early the 1980s.

These laws, particularly the 1980 and 1982 Acts, were designed to assist the employer at the level of an individual firm or company in forcing through changes in working practices and in the introduction of new technology over the heads of the unions. This was to be done, as Lord Wedderburn puts it, by readmitting "the tides of the common law" into industrial cases.

Established trade union practices which were regarded as disrupting the "free" market order were either made illegal or they lost their "immunity". If the initial remedy against an "obstruction" to the "free" market order by a trade union is the injunction, the common law could force compliance with it in a way which had not been possible since 1906 (with the exception of the period of the short-lived 1971 Industrial Relations Act) with the assets of the union being liable to sequestration in the event of it being in "contempt of court". In this, there was nothing especially "new" about the policies of the Thatcher Government as the term "Thatcherism" is supposed to imply. Rather, it was a reactivation of older principles by readmitting "the tides of the common law" into industrial cases as part of the overall strategy of "taking back" from working people various reforms and rights which had been conceded so that the "free" market order, as envisaged by the Thatcher Government, could be realised. The "leeway" it had for doing this, being under conditions of mass unemployment, was denied to earlier post-war Conservative governments.

All this was to have the effect of exposing trade unions and their assets to the mercy of judges whenever unions took measures to protect the livelihoods of their members by using industrial means which became illegal by these Acts. In this, the trade union legislation of the 1980s was the microeconomic strategy of the Thatcher Government and thus a continuation of its macro-economic strategy which had initially had the effect of creating a large pool of unemployed labour. There, it is worth remembering that although attempts were made to use these laws against the miners in the year-long miners' strike, they were of no influence in determining its final outcome. It was most notably in the printing industry, in the Messenger Newspaper Group and News International disputes where these laws were effectively used.

Thus, the first stage in the Thatcher Government's economic strategy can be seen to be its macroeconomic strategy out of which a large pool of unemployed labour emerged. This, judged from a quantitative standpoint, would in itself weaken the organised labour movement. The second stage involved more of a qualitative aspect in that it had to deal with "specific problems" at the level of individual firms or companies. On this basis, the second stage can be described as the Thatcher Government's microeconomic strategy.

If the creation of what then turned out to be a permanent pool of unemployed labour was a precondition of economic and industrial restructuring in the 1980s, how was the trade union movement going to defend the jobs and livelihoods of its members? How was it going to defend the rights it had gained over decades of struggle? Initially, the TUC pledged itself to "resist" the Conservative trade union laws. However, what on the surface appeared to be the high point of the TUC's stand, the Wembley Conference decisions of April 1982, turned out to be largely symbolic because all this conference really did was to confirm the powers the TUC had already had.

Initially, the trade union laws of the 1980s did not place obligations on unions to actually do anything and the Thatcher Government itself refrained from using these laws. At first, the latter merely sought to establish a "new" legal framework or, more precisely, re-establish an old one at a time when the labour market situation for working people was deteriorating. So, in the initial period in which these laws were being put in place, nothing more than relatively minor skirmishes took place under them.

As far as any commitment to resist these laws existed, the impact of mass unemployment, following on from union defeats in British Leyland and the British Steel Corporation and from Labour's electoral humiliation in 1983, brought divisions of opinion among key trade unions into the open. This was in complete contrast to the experience of the 1971 Industrial Relations Act under the Heath Government. Indeed, the Thatcher Government in the 1980s, as far as its trade union laws were concerned, enjoyed "advantages" which would have been the envy of the Heath Government, namely, a labour movement weakened by mass unemployment, and divisions among leading trade unions which prevented the TUC from taking any effective measures to force all affiliated unions to "toe the line" against these laws. The Thatcher Government also profited from the lessons of the 1971 Act, in particular by avoiding the "all at once" approach of the Heath Government in favour of introducing these laws on a "step-by-step" basis.

One major difference between the 1971 Act and the legislation of the 1980s was that the former bore no direct relation to Government economic and political strategy and was purely directed against trade unions, at least as far as specific features of Britain's industrial relations problems were concerned. In contrast, the laws of the 1980s were an integral part of a broad economic and political strategy which was based on the assumption that a "free" market for labour was a necessary precondition for economic and industrial restructuring. This presupposed that employers should be able to force through changes in working practices and introduce new technology on their own terms irrespective of the consequences for the jobs and livelihoods of working people, their families and the communities in which they live.

When the full thrust of the trade union laws was felt for the first time, namely in the Messenger Newspaper Group dispute in autumn 1983, the TUC refrained from giving the NGA the vital support it needed. So, the TUC's decision in this dispute represented the first major victory for the Thatcher Government under these laws. This dispute also showed the extent to which the TUC would provide the necessary support in the event of an affiliated union finding itself exposed to the full thrust of these laws, even if its very existence was brought into question, as was the case there with the NGA in autumn 1983.

The TUC *did* support the NGA, but only in as far as the law permitted. An NGA victory there would have required the TUC to break the law and to ensure that other affiliated unions did likewise. It was this refusal of the TUC to sanction the law being broken which brought about the defeat of the NGA in this dispute. This dispute also showed that the TUC's "opposition" to these laws on the basis of the Wembley Conference decisions had effectively been abandoned. The TUC's decision in this dispute was to mark the first stage in a process whereby the initial policy of opposing these laws was going to become one of compliance by the end of the 1980s. Three other factors were also to influence this process.

Firstly, the outcome of the 1984/1985 miners' strike and the News International dispute of 1986/1987 clearly showed the TUC failing to respond adequately to what was also a political confrontation on the part of the employers and the Government with the most influential sections of the trade union movement. Apart from other considerations, there was the failure of the TUC to take disciplinary action against the electrician's union (EETPU) for allowing its members to cross NUM picket lines, fully disregarding long-standing trade union practices of not crossing the picket lines of other unions in industrial disputes. In a similar manner, there was the failure of the TUC to take such action against the same union for recruiting its own members to work for News International by doing the very jobs which had previously been done by the print workers whom the company had dismissed thus provoking this dispute.

Secondly, despite the political fund ballots totally backfiring on the Thatcher Government, the fact that these and other balloting provisions under the trade union laws were being acted on at all meant that these Acts were being complied with by individual trade unions. Although a case for their repeal has always been argued and has continued to remain the policy of a number of individual trade unions, the call for repeal in the absence of mass defiance by the trade union movement as a whole was deemed as being harder to achieve when there was little prospect of the Thatcher Government being voted out of office within the foreseeable future and when trade unions, compelled or otherwise, found themselves "complying" with their key provisions. Only at the TUC annual congress in 2005, under the influence of a new generation of trade union leaders, did the TUC eventually drop its previous scepticism to calls for repeal when it unanimously supported a resolution calling for this. So the demand for the repeal of the Conservative trade union laws is now back on the political agenda.

Thirdly, the outcome of the 1987 election, in which Labour suffered its third consecutive election defeat, precipitated a fundamental review of its policies. In the background of this development and in the endeavour to secure the return of a Labour Government, a "new realist" Labour Party leadership under Neil Kinnock managed to persuade a number of key trade unions and the Party itself to drop policies which were seen to be "controversial". This compliance with "reality" included the acceptance of the key provisions of the Conservative trade union laws despite them curtailing the ability of trade unions to take industrial action. Given the outcome of the 1992 election, one can then question whether such a review was necessary at all as Labour had dropped any remaining policies which allegedly hampered its electoral appeal and still lost the election.

It can be said that the outcome of Labour's policy review was that the Party appeared to move closer to the position of the Conservative Party and Government on a number of key issues. On this basis, one can conclude that many of the key economic, industrial and a whole range of other policies enacted since 1979, including the trade union laws, would largely remain unaltered by a future Labour Government and this has been the case after eleven years in office with little prospect of a change in course under Gordon Brown.

One major difference between the Labour Party and the Thatcher Government concerned developments leading up to the conclusion of the Maastricht Treaty. Although Labour supported these developments, it argued, contrary to the Thatcher and Major Governments, for Britain to conform to moves in the EU to "harmonise" various social rights for working people as originally laid down by the *Community Charter of the Fundamental Social Rights of Workers* from 1989 (incorporated into the Treaty of Amsterdam following Labour's election victory in 1997) whilst at the same time complying with the key elements of the Conservative trade union laws. In this, Labour saw in this Charter an alternative, in as far as it really provided one, to earlier calls for the repeal of these trade union laws.

Yet, on the question of workers' rights, the new Prime Minister gave a clear indication where he really stood when it came to the conclusion of the EU "Reform Treaty" at the European Council meeting in Lisbon in December 2007. There, Brown secured an *opt-out* for Britain on the EU's Charter of Fundamental Rights, in as far as this Charter is really of any significance on the questions of workers' rights.

Whilst Labour Party leaders may have defended the policy changes they forced through on the basis of "reality", the reason for wanting to retain the key provisions of the Conservative trade union laws must also be judged in the context of the long-standing scepticism on the part of Party leaders, like that of the Conservative Party itself, towards militant trade unionism. However, "reality" itself is not static and in view of the ruling in the ECtHR in Strasbourg in 2002 in the Wilson and Palmer case, "reality" attained another dimension by showing that key aspects of the Conservative trade union laws do not fulfill the limited rights to freedom of association under article 11 of the ECHR. But, overshadowing this ruling in Strasbourg are the rulings in the ECJ in Luxembourg in December 2007 in the Viking and Laval cases.

The ruling in the Wilson and Palmer case is therefore a reminder in that freedom of association is a human right. This means that trade union and workers' rights, including the right to strike, must also be seen and judged in this context. So this ruling provides a powerful argument for the trade union movement to press its case for the repeal of these laws. Any serious move in this direction would, no doubt, face fierce opposition from the Conservative Party, employers' associations and from within the mass media. On the other hand, such an initiative is what is needed if the Brown Government is to secure the active support of the entire trade union and labour movement in the run-up to the next election and if it makes such an initiative, a fourth consecutive victory for Labour would be more likely.

Appendix One: Tables

Table 1: Rates of Growth of GDP and GDP per Capita among member states of the OECD in the period 1950-1973 (annual average compound growth rates)

	Growth of GDP % 1950-1973	Growth of GDP per Capita % 1950-1973
Japan	9.29	8.05
Germany (West)	5.68	5.02
Italy	5.64	4.95
Austria	5.35	4.94
Finland	4.94	4.25
France	5.05	4.05
Belgium	4.08	3.55
Netherlands	4.74	3.45
Norway	4.06	3.19
Denmark	3.81	3.08
Switzerland	4.51	3.08
Sweden	3.73	3.07
USA	3.93	2.45
UK	2.93	2.44

Source: Maddison, Angus, *The World Economy: A Millennial Perspective*, Development Centre of the Organisation for Economic Co-operation and Development (Paris), 2001; for the Rates of Growth of GDP, p. 262 Table B-19; for the Rates of Growth of GDP per Capita, p. 265 Table B-22.

Table 2: Main strike statistics, UK 1946-1980 (annual averages and totals).

Year	Strike frequency	Workers directly involved (000)	Striker days (000)	% strikes over wages
1946-52	1,698	444	1,887	44.2
1953-59	2,093	551	3,950	46.5
1960-64	2,512	1,499	3,180	47.5
1965	2,354	874	2,925	50.1
1966	1,937	544	2,398	45.6
1967	2,116	734	2,787	46.5
1968	2,378	2,258	4,690	51.7
1969	3,116	1,665	6,846	57.2
1970	3,906	1,801	10,980	63.1
1971	2,228	1,187	13,551	51.8
1972	2,497	1,734	23,909	59.2
1973	2,873	1,528	7,197	50.9
1974	2,922	1,626	14,750	65.8
1975	2,282	809	6,012	57.8
1976	2,016	668	3,284	43.4
1977	2,703	1,166	10,142	57.6
1978	2,471	1,042	9,405	61.1
1979	2,080	4,608	29,474	59.1
1980	1,330	834	11,964	47.4

NB Strike frequency means number of strikes beginning. The figures for 1946-1952, 1953-1959 and 1960-1964 are the averages taken over these time periods.

Source: Kelly, John, *Trade Unions and Socialist Politics*, Verso (London & New York), 1988, p. 105 (1946-1974) & p.115 (1975-1980).

Table 3: Comparison of the Number of Official Strikes with the Number of Strikes beginning in the Period 1960-1967

Year	No. of Official Strikes	Strike Frequency
1960	68	2,382
1961	60	2,686
1962	78	2,449
1963	49	2,068
1964	70	2,524
1965	97	2,354
1966	60	1,937
1967	108	2,116

NB The figures in the number of official strikes include "partly official" strikes, i.e. strikes involving more than one union and recognised as official by at least one but not all the unions involved. These figures, in themselves, were not very significant but were used by the 1964-1970 Labour Government in an attempt to justify the policies it had hoped to enact so as to curb the problem of "unofficial" strikes. The figures for the strike frequency match those which are quoted in Table 2.

Source: For the number of official strikes, *In Place of Strife*, HMSO (London), Cmnd. 3888, January 1969, p. 40; for the strike frequency, *Annual Abstract of Statistics*, Central Statistical Office (London), 1971, p. 144, Table 155.

Table 4: Unemployment in the UK 1959 – 1979 (at mid-June each year)

Year	Total working populati-on (000)	Total unem-ployed (000)	% of working populati-on un-employ-ed	Year	Total working populati-on (000)	Total unem-ployed (000)	% of working populati-on un-employ-ed
1959	24,765	420	1.7	1970	25,308	555	2.2
1960	25,100	326	1.3	1971	25,123	724	2.9
1961	25,345	287	1.1	1972	25,195	804	3.2
1962	25,633	406	1.6	1973	25,547	575	2.3
1963	25,744	497	1.9	1974	25,601	542	2.1
1964	25,887	349	1.3	1975	25,798	866	3.4
1965	26,049	299	1.1	1976	26,097	1,332	5.1
1966	25,632	281	1.1	1977	26,282	1,450	5.5
1967	25,490	503	2.0	1978	26,407	1,446	5.5
1968	25,378	542	2.1	1979	26,464	1,344	5.1
1969	25,370	518	2.0				

Source: *Annual Abstract of Statistics*, Central Statistical Office (London); for the years 1959-1964, edition 1971, p. 125, Table 140; for 1965-1969, edition 1976, p. 149, Table 149; for 1970-1977, edition 1981, p. 150, Table 6.1; for 1978/-1979, edition 1982, p. 150 Table 6.1.

NB In later editions of the *Annual Abstract of Statistics*, the figures for the total working population and the total number of people unemployed were subject to minor adjustments so in the above table, the figures used were the latest listed on the basis of assessing the unemployment statistics at the time. For the above period, there were no changes in the criteria for calculating the unemployment statistics which would in any way alter the trend shown. Following 1979/1980, there were a number of changes in the method of calculating the unemployment figures which warrants separate tables (see tables 7 and 13).

Table 5: Rates of Change of United Kingdom GDP at constant (1995) market prices as % over the previous year (1960-2001)

Year	% change on previous year	Year	% change on previous year
1960	5.4	1981	- 1.5
1961	2.5	1982	2.0
1962	1.3	1983	3.6
1963	5.0	1984	2.5
1964	5.4	1985	3.6
1965	2.4	1986	3.9
1966	1.9	1987	4.5
1967	2.5	1988	5.2
1968	4.1	1989	2.2
1969	2.0	1990	0.8
1970	2.3	1991	- 1.4
1971	2.1	1992	0.2
1972	3.6	1993	2.5
1973	7.2	1994	4.7
1974	- 1.6	1995	2.9
1975	- 0.6	1996	2.6
1976	2.8	1997	3.4
1977	2.3	1998	2.9
1978	3.3	1999	2.4
1979	2.6	2000	3.1
1980	- 2.2	2001	1.9

Source: *United Kingdom National Accounts: The Blue Book 2002*, HMSO (London), 2002, p. 267, Table 8.7.

Table 6: Industry's shrinking base: £million at 1980 prices

Year	New investment	Rundown of capital stock	Net investment
1979	7468	6190	1275
1980	6445	6270	175
1981	4865	6275	-1410
1982	4475	6286	-1830

Source: *TUC Economic Review 1984*, Trades Union Congress (London), 1984, p. 6, fig.2.2.

Table 7: Unemployment in the UK 1977-1996 (at mid-June each year)

Year	Total working populati-on (000)	Total unem-ployed (000)	% of working populati-on un-employ-ed	Year	Total working populati-on (000)	Total unem-ployed (000)	% of working populati-on un-employ-ed
1977	26,224	1,359	5.2	1987	28,803	2,836	9.8
1978	26,357	1,343	5.1	1988	28,430	2,294	8.1
1979	26,627	1,234	4.6	1989	28,731	1,786	6.2
1980	26,839	1,513	5.6	1990	28,813	1,615	5.6
1981	26,740	2,395	9.0	1991	28,614	2,301	8.0
1982	26,677	2,770	10.4	1992	28,476	2,734	9.6
1983	26,594	2,984	11.2	1993	28,270	2,919	10.3
1984	27,297	2,897	10.6	1994	28,131	2,644	9.4
1985	27,702	3,019	10.9	1995	28,064	2,313	8.2
1986	27,838	3,120	11.2	1996	27,969	2,150	7.7

Source: *Annual Abstract of Statistics*, Central Statistical Office (London); for the years 1977-1983, edition 1988, p. 108, Table 6.1; for 1984-1985, edition 1995, p. 102, Table 6.1; for 1986-1996, edition 1997, p. 124, Table 6.1 (the figures for 1984 onwards have been *seasonally adjusted*).

NB The above table gives a picture of the unemployment statistics in the UK, on the basis of the criteria the Conservative Government (1979-1997) used, spanning the period from 1977 (two years before coming into office) up to 1996 (the year before it left office). Comparing the figures for 1977-1979 in table 4 with those in the above table, the rise in unemployment, due to the slump of 1979-1981, is statistically sharper. The above table also shows that much of the above period is characterised by *mass unemployment* even though there had been many changes in the way these figures were calculated with the effect that many categories of people out of work were no longer included in the figures. One such example is that as from April 1983, many unemployed men over the age of 60 were no longer required to "sign on" at an unemployment office with the effect that by summer of that year, there was an estimated reduction in the unemployment count of almost 162,000 See *Annual Abstract of Statistics*, ..., 1988, p. 108.

Table 8: Projections and Outruns for £M3 according to the MTFS

Financial year	1980/1981	1981/1982	1982/1983	1983/1984
Projected (MTFS 1980)	7 - 11%	6 - 10%	5 - 9%	4 - 8%
Actual (MTFS)	18.5%	14.5%	-	-

Financial year	1982/1983	1983/1984	1984/1985	1985/1986
Revised (MTFS)	8 - 11%	7 - 11%	6 - 10%	5 - 9%
Actual (MTFS)	11.2%	9.4%	11.9%	16.9%

Financial year	1986/1987
Revised (MTFS)	11 - 15%
Actual (MTFS)	19.0%

Source: Busch, Andreas, *Neokonservative Wirtschaftspolitik in Großbritannien*, Peter Lang (Frankfurt am Main), 1989, p. 66.

Table 9: Main strike statistics, UK 1979-2005 (annual averages and totals).

Year	Strike frequency	Workers directly and indirectly involved (000)	Striker days (000)
1979	2,080	4,583	29,474
1980	1,330	842	11,964
1981	1,344	1,513	4,266
1982	1,538	2,103	5,313
1983	1,364	574	3,754
1984	1,221	1,391	27,135
1985	903	791	6,402
1986	1,074	720	1,920
1987	1,016	887	3,546
1988	781	790	3,702
1989	701	727	4,128
1990	630	298	1,903
1991	369	176	761
1992	253	148	528
1993	211	385	649
1994	205	107	278
1995	235	174	415
1996	244	364	1,303
1997	216	130	235
1998	166	93	282
1999	205	141	242
2000	212	183	499
2001	194	180	525
2002	146	943	1,323
2003	133	151	499
2004	130	293	905
2005	116	93	157

NB In Table 2, figures quoted from the book *Trade Union and Socialist Politics* refer to the number of workers *directly involved* in industrial stoppages whereas the figures in the above table from the *Annual Abstract of Statistics* refer to the number of workers *directly and indirectly involved* in industrial stoppages.

Source: *Annual Abstract of Statistics*, Central Statistical Office (London); for the years 1979-1980, edition 1984, p. 122, Table 6.14; for 1981-1982, edition 1987, p. 120, Table 6.14; for 1983-1985, edition 1990, p. 120, Table 6.14. For the years 1986-1997, *Annual Abstract of Statistics*, Office for National Statistics, HMSO (London), edition 2001, pp. 101f, Table 7.18. For the years 1998-2004, *Annual Abstract of Statistics*, Office of National Statistics, Palgrave Macmillan (Basingstoke and New York), edition 2006, p. 106, Table 7.18. For the year 2005, *Annual Abstract of Statistics*, Office of ..., ..., p. 106, Table 7.19.

Table 10: Total number of people belonging to TUC-affiliated unions 1970-2006

Year	No. of Members (million)	Year	No. of Members (million)	Year	No. of Members (million)
1970	9.4	1983	10.5	1996	6.8
1971	10.0	1984	10.1	1997	6.8
1972	9.9	1985	9.9	1998	6.6
1973	10.0	1986	9.6	1999	6.7
1974	10.0	1987	9.2	2000	6.7
1975	10.4	1988	9.1	2001	6.7
1976	11.0	1989	8.7	2002	6.7
1977	11.5	1990	8.4	2003	6.7
1978	11.9	1991	8.2	2004	6.4
1979	12.1	1992	7.8	2005	6.5
1980	12.2	1993	7.3	2006	6.5
1981	11.6	1994	7.3	2007	6.5
1982	11.0	1995	6.9		

Source: *Report of Congress 2007*, TUC (London), March 2008, pp. 197f.

Table 11: Grounds for Seeking Injunctions 1980 – 2005 in Industrial Disputes

Year	Picketing	Secondary action	Balloting	Other	Total
1980	1	-	-	-	1
1981	5	-	-	5	10
1982	5	1	-	4	10
1983	5	6	-	1	12
1984	2	9	5	4	20
1985	2	7	12	4	25
1986	4	9	4	5	22
1987	2	3	3	3	11
1988	3	2	1	2	8
1989	2	1	9	5	17
1990	-	-	4	7	11
1991	4	1	4	1	10
1992	1	-	3	1	5
1993	3	-	1	4	8
1994	-	-	14	1	15
1995	-	-	8	5	13
1996	1	-	7	6	13
1997	1	-	1	2	4
1998	1	-	6	6	12
1999	-	-	2	5	6
2000	-	-	2	4	4
2001	2	-	4	10	13
2002	1	-	-	4	4
2003	-	-	2	3	4
2004	-	-	2	3	5
2005	1	-	2	1	4

NB The figures quoted for 2005 are those just to the end of August. Between 1996 and 2004, a number of applications were made for injunctions on the basis of more than one ground so the *total* number of injunctions sought is less than the number of items a ground was used for seeking an injunction.

Source: Gall, Gregor, Research Note: Injunctions as a Legal Weapon in Industrial Disputes in Britain, 1995-2005, in: *British Journal of Industrial Relations*, Blackwell (Oxford), Vol. 44 No. 2, June 2006, p. 330.

Table 12: Sectoral Distribution of Injunctions: May 1984 - April 1987

Printing	29
Shipping/Transport	18
Public Services	14
Engineering/Shipbuilding	5
Professional	3
Chemicals (inc. 2 in the same dispute)	3
Communications	3
Retail/Distribution	2
Construction	2
Coal	1
TOTAL	80

Source: Evans, Stephen, The Use of Injunctions in Industrial Disputes May 1984 - April 1987, *British Journal of Industrial Relations*, Blackwell (Oxford), Vol. XXV No. 3, November 1987, p. 425.

Table 13: EEC Steel Production and Producing Capacity Tonnes (Million)

	Production		Capacity	
	1972	1984	1973	1983
UK	25	15	30	25
Germany (West)	44	40	59	68
Italy	20	24	28	40
France	24	19	28	40
Belgium	15	11	17	19

Source: Gould, Bryan (Ed.), *Jobs or the Treaty of Rome: The Choice for Labour*, Labour Common Market Safeguards Committee (London), September 1985, p.9.

Table 14: Labour force summary

Year	Total economically active (000)	Total in employment (000)	Total unemployed (000)	Rate of unemployment as a % of the total economically active
1995	28,202	25,731	2,470	8.8
1996	28,345	26,000	2,344	8.3
1997	28,492	26,448	2,045	7.2
1998	28,497	26,713	1,783	6.3
1999	28,811	27,052	1,759	6.1
2000	29,071	27,434	1,638	5.6
2001	29,122	27,691	1,431	4.9
2002	29,399	27,866	1,533	5.2
2003	29,643	28,167	1,476	5.0
2004	29,835	28,409	1,426	4.8
2005	30,101	28,676	1,425	4.7

NB The above statistics are for spring, each year, and have been *seasonally adjusted*. The unemployment statistics for 1995 and 1996 differ from those given in Table 7. Whereas the statistics in Table 7 are for mid-June, each year, in the above table, they are for spring.

Source: *Annual Abstract of Statistics*, edition 2006, No. 142, Office of National Statistics, published by Palgrave Macmillan (Basingstoke, Hampshire and New York), 2006, p. 87, Table 7.1.

Appendix Two: Bibliography

Primary Sources

1.i. Government and Parliamentary Papers and Reports (London):

Employment Policy, Cmd. 6527, 1944

Royal Commission on Trade Unions and Employers' Associations 1965-1968, Cmnd. 3623, June 1968

Hansard: Parliamentary Debates (Hansard), Fifth Series - Volume 768, Session 1967-68 Comprising Period from 8th - 19th July 1968

In Place of Strife, Cmnd. 3888, January 1969

Annual Abstract of Statistics (editions 1971, 1976, 1981, 1982, 1984, 1987, 1988, 1990, 1995), Central Statistical Office (London); (editions 1997 and 2001), Office for National Statistics (London); (editions 2006 and 2007), Office of National Statistics, published by Palgrave Macmillan (Basingstoke, Hants. and New York)

Advisory Conciliation and Arbitration Service (*Annual Report*(s)) 1976-1990

The Challenge of North Sea Oil, Cmnd. 7143, March 1978

The European Monetary System, Cmnd. 7405, November 1978

Working Papers for Consultation on Proposed Industrial Relations Legislation, Secretary of State for Employment, July 1979 (unpublished)

Report of Inquiry into certain Trade Union Recruitment Activities, Cmnd. 7706, October 1979

House of Commons, The Employment Committee Session 1979-1980, The Legal Immunities of Trade Unions and other related matters, Minutes of Evidence 20 February 1980 (The Rt. Hon. James Prior MP), HMSO, 462-i

Trade Union Immunities, Cmnd. 8128, January 1981

Democracy in Trade Unions, Cmnd. 8778, January 1983

Report of the Security Commission, Cmnd. 8876, May 1983

Employment Gazette June 1984, Employment Department, June 1984

Employment: The Challenge for the Nation, Cmnd 9474, March 1985

Consultative Paper on Wage Councils, Department of Employment, 1985

Trade Unions and Their Members, Cm 95, February 1987

Employment for the 1990s, Cm 540, December 1988

Removing Barriers to Employment, Cm 655, March 1989

Unofficial Action and The Law: Proposals to reform the law affecting unofficial industrial action, Cm 821, October 1989

Fairness at Work, Cm 3698, Department of Trade and Industry, May 1998

United Kingdom National Accounts: The Blue Book 2002, HMSO, 2002

1.ii. Conservative Party Documents (Westminster, London SW1):

A Giant's Strength, The Inns of Court Conservative and Unionist Society, undated (published in 1958)

Trade unions for tomorrow, CPC Number 346, September 1966

Fair Deal at Work, CPC Number 400, April 1968

'Fair Deal' Takes Shape, December 1970

The Right Approach, October 1976

Maude, Angus (Ed.), *The Right Approach to the Economy*, October 1977

The Conservative Manifesto 1979

The Conservative Manifesto 1983

Our First Eight Years, May 1987

The Next Moves Forward: The Conservative Manifesto 1987, May 1987

The Trade Union Problem, *Politics Today*, No 17, November 1987

You can only be sure with the Conservatives: The Conservative Manifesto 1997

Are you thinking what we're thinking? It's Time for Action: Conservative Election Manifesto 2005

1.iii. Labour Party Documents (London):

Labour's Programme 1973

Let us work together - Labour's way out of the Crisis: Labour Party Manifesto 1974, (February) 1974

Britain Will Win with Labour - Labour Manifesto October 1974

Labour Party Conference Report, 1976

The Labour Party Manifesto 1979: The Labour Way is the Better Way

The New Hope for Britain: Labour's Manifesto 1983

Britain will win: Labour Manifesto 1987

The Social Charter: How Britain benefits, (published jointly by the Labour Party and the British Labour Group of the European Parliament), 1989

Meet the Challenge: Make the Change: Final Report of Labour's Policy Review for the 1990s, 1989

Looking to the Future, 1990

Labour's election manifesto April 1992: It's time to get Britain working again

New Labour because Britain deserves better (1997 Labour election manifesto), 1997

The Labour Party Rule Book 2004-2005

Britain forward not back: The Labour Party manifesto 2005

1.iv. Trades Union Congress Documents (London):

Report of 103rd Annual Trades Union Congress, 1971

The Economy, the Government and Trade Union Responsibilities, 1979

TUC's letter and responses to the Government's working papers on proposed industrial relations legislation, 30 July 1979 (unpublished)

The TUC case against the Employment Bill, London, 1980

TUC Economic Review, 1984

Industrial Relations Legislation: The Employment Act 1980 and Employment Bill 1982, 1982

TUC Handbook on the Employment Act 1982, 1982

1984 Trade Union Act: The Trade Union Response to the new Legislation, August 1984

Industrial Relations Legislation A TUC Consultative Document, London, 1986

TUC Guide to the Wages Act 1986, December 1986

Green Paper: "Trade Unions and Their Members" TUC Responses, 1987

The TUC Guide to the Employment Bill, 1987

Trades Union Congress General Council Report(s) 1987-1991, 2004

The EETPU Suspension: A TUC Information Note, 1989

Employment Law: A TUC Briefing, Spring 1992

Guide to the Trade Union Reform & Employment Rights Act 1993, 1993

Unions and the Euro: TUC Euro Briefing (Special Issue – No. 8), July 1999

The Employment Relations Act: a TUC Guide, October 1999

The Employment Relations Act 2004: A TUC guide, April 2005

Report of Congress 2007, March 2008

1.v. TUC-Labour Party Liaison Committee Documents (London):

Economic Policy and the Cost of Living, February 1973

Economic Planning and Industrial Democracy: The Framework for Full Employment, 1982

Work to Win, March 1987

1.vi. Labour Research Department (LRD) Documents, (London):

New Tory attack on union rights, April 1982

Tory Attack on Union Rights, 1982

Unions Attacked: LRD's Guide to the Trade Union Bill, December 1983

Unions' Freedom under Threat, 1983

Economic Notes, in: *Labour Research*, Vol. 73 No. 1 – Vol. 77 No. 12, January 1984 – December 1988

The miners' case, October 1984

Rise in Legal Actions against Unions, in: *Labour Research*, Vol. 74 No. 10, October 1985, pp. 259ff

Employment Law under the Tories, August 1986

A State of Collapse - The UK Economy under the Tories, 1987

The Tories' inflated record, in: *Labour Research*, Vol. 78 No. 5, May 1989

Making the Unions Pay: A Guide to the 1990 Employment Act, June 1991

Unions in a Legal Minefield, in: *Labour Research*, Vol. 80 No. 10, October 1991, pp. 19ff

Employers Step Up Legal Challenges, in: *Labour Research*, Vol. 83 No. 9, September 1994, pp. 7ff

Eighteen Years of Worker-Bashing, in: *Labour Research*, May 1997

Ballot Laws cause Legal Attacks, in: *Labour Research*, Vol. 87 No. 10, October 1998, pp. 15f

Has Warwick saved the link?, in: *Labour Research*, Vol. 94 No. 1, January 2005, pp. 9-12

The unions take stock of Warwick, in: *Labour Research*, Vol. 95 No. 10, October 2006, pp. 9-13

Law at work, May 2007

2.i. Miscellaneous Sources (in alphabetical order by author):

Blair, Tony, *Leadership Election Statement 1994: Change and National Renewal*

Brown, Gordon (Chancellor of the Exchequer), in: *Unions and the Euro: TUC Euro Briefing* (Special Issue – No. 8), TUC (London), July 1999, pp. 5f

Craig, F. W. S., *British General Election Manifestos 1900-1974*, Macmillan (London and Basingstoke), 1975

Address by Michael Edwardes to BL management and employee representatives in Birmingham on 1 February 1978 (unpublished)

Edwardes, Michael, Statement to all BL employees from the Chairman, 10 September 1979 (unpublished)

Gill, Ken, Secret NIRC documents show how union solidarity beat the Tory Act, in: *Tribune* (London), 8 June 1973, p. 8

Ramelson, Bert, *Donovan Exposed: A critical analysis of the Report of the Royal Commission on Trade Unions*, CPGB (London), 1968

Robinson, D., et al., *The Edwardes Plan and your job*, Leyland Combine Trade Union Committee (Cookley, Nr. Kidderminster), undated (published in autumn 1979)

Maddison, Angus, *The World Economy: A Millennial Perspective*, Development Centre of the OECD (Paris), 2001

2.ii. Miscellaneous Sources (without author – listed in date order):

The Industrial Relations Act: What the Engineering Employers think, in: *Tribune* (London), 18 May 1973, p. 2

Plan for Coal, National Coal Board, June 1974

Economic Policy Review, No. 4, University of Cambridge Department of Applied Economics, March 1978

Appomattox or Civil War, *The Economist* (London), 27 May 1978, pp. 21f

Budget Summary, *Financial Times* (London and Frankfurt), 13 June 1979

The Backlash Looms, in: *SLADE Journal*, SLADE (London), No. 81, November 1979, p. 1

Man and Metal, The Journal of the Iron and Steel Trades Confederation, Vol. 56 No. 10, December 1979, p. 293

Cambridge Economic Policy Review, Vol. 6 No. 1 University of Cambridge Department of Applied Economics, April 1980

Action Defeats the Bill, Liaison Committee for the Defence of Trade Unions (Barking, Essex), undated (published in 1982)

The two faces of recession, in: *Financial Times* (London and Frankfurt), 19 July 1980

Why the left must fight on, in: *Morning Star* (London), 24 May 1982, p. 2

British Print: Victims of Marauders, CPGB (London), 1982

Composition of monetary and liquid aggregates, and associated statistics, in: *Bank of England Quarterly Bulletin*, Vol 22 No 4, Bank of England (London), December 1982, pp. 530-537

Coal, Rail and Steel, NUM et. al. (London), 1983

The Way Forward – New Technology in the Provincial Newspaper Industry, NGA (1982) (Bedford), 1984 (unpublished)

Consultative Paper on Wages Councils, Department of Employment (London), 1985 (unpublished)

The Wolverhampton Express and Star Dispute (a briefing paper), NGA (1982) (Bedford), 1985 (unpublished)

An NGA (1982) Briefing Paper: News International Dispute, February 1986 (unpublished)

Murdoch deceit unmasked, in: *Morning Star* (London), 4 February 1986, p. 4

SOGAT Journal – Special Issue: Union in Crisis, SOGAT (Hadleigh, Essex), November 1986

Financial Times (London and Frankfurt), 18 March 1987

Financial Times (London and Frankfurt), 16 March 1988

OECD Economic Surveys 1988/1989: United Kingdom, OECD (Paris), August 1989

The Budget: Red Book Details, *Financial Times* (London and Frankfurt), 20 March 1991, pp. 22-26

OECD Economic Surveys 1990/1991: United Kingdom, OECD (Paris), August 1991

Changing Britain for good: The Liberal Democrat Manifesto 1992, Liberal Democrat Publications (Dorchester, Dorset), 1992

Not Major or Thatcher, in: *Morning Star* (London), 6 July 1992

EU Economic and Monetary Union: Euro Fallout, Campaign against Eurofderalism (Merseyside), 1999

Bank of England Money Market Intervention Rates: Changes in Bank Rate, Minimum Lending Rate, Minimum Band 1 Dealing Rate and Repo Rate, in: *Bank of England Statistical Abstract Part 1*, Bank of England (London), December 2002

The Real Alternative: Manifesto Text, Liberal Democrats (London), undated (2005)

Labour's achievements for working people, in: *Amicus: the magazine*, Issue 6, Amicus (London), Summer 2005

European Economy, European Commission (Brussels), Number 6, 2006

House of Commons EU Scrutiny Committee says: Britain will be subject to "new and unquantifiable risks" from EU Constitution and 'red-lines' will not work, in: *The Democrat*, Campaign against Euro-federalism (London), No. 105, November-December 2007

Secondary sources

1. Books/Pamphlets/Papers in alphabetical order by Author

Aaronovitch, Sam, *The Road from Thatcherism*, Lawrence & Wishart (London), 1981

Arnison, Jim, *The Shrewsbury Three*, Lawrence & Wishart (London), 1974

Arthur, Richard (Thompsons Solicitors), *Viking and Laval: A Collision Waiting to Happen*, paper delivered to the Scottish Trades Union Congress, 29 February 2008

Baimbridge, Mark et. al, *Britain and the European Union: alternative futures*, Campaign for an Independent Britain (London), April 2005

Barlow, Keith, *The Labour Movement in Thatcher's Britain*, Peter Lang (Frankfurt am Main), 1997

Barnes, Denis and Reid, Eileen, *Government and Trade Unions*, Heinemann (London), 1980

Beveridge, William H., *Full Employment in a Free Society*, Allen & Unwin (London), 1944

Bullock, Alan, *The Life and Times of Ernest Bevin - Vol 2 Minister of Labour 1940-1945*, Heinemann (London), 1967

Burkitt, Brian et. al., *From Rome to Maastricht: A reappraisal of Britain's membership of the European Community*, Campaign for an Independent Britain (London), June 1992

Busch, Andreas, *Neokonservative Wirtschaftspolitik in Großbritannien*, Peter Lang (Frankfurt am Main), 1989

Coates, David, *The Crisis of Labour*, Philip Allan (Oxford & New Jersey), 1989

Davies, Liz, *Through the Looking Glass: A Dissenter inside New Labour*, Verso (London and New York), 2001

Deakin, Simon et. al., *Inflation, Employment, Wage-bargaining and the Law*, The Institute of Employment Rights (London), March 1992

Degen, Günther R., *Shop Stewards: ihre zentrale Bedeutung für die Gewerkschaftsbewegung in Großbritannien*, Europäische Verlagsanstalt (Frankfurt – Köln), 1976

Dickinson, Mark, *To Break a Union*, Booklist Ltd. (Manchester), 1984

Donaldson, Peter, *Guide to the British Economy* (Fourth Edition), Penguin (Harmondsworth), 1976

Dunn, Stephen and Gennard, John, *The Closed Shop in British Industry*, Macmillan (London & Basingstoke), 1984

Ewing, K. D. (Ed.), *Human Rights at Work*, The Institute of Employment Rights (London), 2000

Ewing, K. D., *Britain and the ILO* (Second Edition), The Institute of Employment Rights (London), July, 1994

Fine, Bob and Millar, Robert, *Policing the Miner's Strike*, Lawrence & Wishart (London), 1985

Flanders, Allan, *Management and Unions*, Faber and Faber (London), 1975

Florio, Massimo, The Great Divestiture: Evaluating the Welfare Impact of the British Privatizations 1979-1997, MIT Press (Cambridge, Massachusetts and London), 2004

Foley, Tony, *A Most Formidable Union: The History of DATA and TASS*, Manufacturing Science Finance (London), 1992

Ford, Michael and Hendy, John QC, *Briefing note: ASLEF v UK*, The Institute of Employment Rights (Liverpool), 26 June 2007

Forrest, David, *Low Pay or No Pay?*, Institute of Economic Affairs (Westminster, London), Hobart Paper 101, July 1984

Frow, Edmund et. al., *Democracy in the Engineering Union*, Institute of Workers' Control (Nottingham), 1982

Gamble, Andrew, *The Free Economy and the Strong State* (Second Edition), Macmillan (Basingstoke & London), 1994

Geary, Roger, *Policing Industrial Disputes 1893-1985*, Cambridge University Press, 1989

Glyn, Andrew, *The Economic Case Against Pit Closures*, National Union of Mineworkers (Sheffield), undated (published in 1984)

Gould, Bryan (Ed.), *Jobs or the Treaty of Rome: The Choice for Labour*, Labour Common Market Safeguards Committee (London), September 1985

Griffith, J. A. G., *The Politics of the Judiciary* (Fifth Edition), Fontana Press (Hammersmith, London), 1997

Griffiths, Robert, *Driven by ideals – a history of ASLEF*, Associated Society of Locomotive Engineers and Firemen (London), 2005

Hain, Peter, *Political Strikes*, Penguin (Harmondsworth, Middlesex), 1986

Hall, Stuart and Jacques, Martin (Ed.), *New Times*, Lawrence & Wishart (London), 1989

Hamilton, Malcolm B., *Democratic Socialism in Britain and Sweden*, Macmillan Press (Basingstoke), 1989

Hanson, Charles G and Mather, Graham, *Striking Out Strikes*, Institute of Economic Affairs (London), Hobart Paper 110, 1988

Harmer, Harry, *The Longman Companion to: The Labour Party 1900-1988*, Longman (London and New York), 1999

Hayek, F. A., *The Constitution of Liberty*, Routledge and Kegan Paul Ltd. (London and Henley), 1960

Hayek, F. A., *Law, Legislation and Liberty (Vols 1-3)*, Routledge & Kegan Paul (London), 1982

Healey, Denis, *The Time of My Life*, Michael Joseph (London), 1989

Hendy, John QC, *A Law Unto Themselves. Conservative Employment Laws: A National and International Assessment* (3rd edition), The Institute of Employment Rights (London), 1993

Hepple, Bob, *European Social Dialogue – Alibi or Opportunity*, The Institute of Employment Rights (London), August 1993

Hickson, Kevin, *The IMF Crisis of 1976*, Tauris Academic Studies (London and New York), 2005

Hobsbawm, Eric, *Politics for a Rational Left*, Verso (London & New York), 1989

Hutt, Allen, *A Short History of British Trade Unionism*, Lawrence & Wishart (London), 1975

Jacobi, Otto and Kastendiek, Hans (Hg.), *Staat und industrielle Beziehungen in Großbritannien*, Campus Verlag (Frankfurt/New York), 1985

Jay, (Lord) Douglas (Ed.,), *The European Monetary System: The E.R.M. Illusion*, Labour Common Market Safeguards Committee (London), June 1990

Jessop, Bob et. al., *Thatcherism: A Tale of Two Nations*, Polity Press (Cambridge), 1988

Joseph, (Rt. Hon. Sir) Keith, *Solving the Union Problem is the Key to Britain's Recovery*, Centre for Policy Studies (London), 1979

Junor, Penny, *The Major Enigma*, Michael Joseph Ltd. (London), 1993

Keegan, William, *Britain Without Oil*, Penguin Books Ltd. (Harmondsworth), 1985

Kelly, John, *Labour and the Unions*, Verso (London & New York), 1987

Kelly, John, *Trade Unions and Socialist Politics*, Verso (London & New York), 1988

Kenen, Peter B., *Economic and Monetary Union in Europe: Moving beyond Maastricht*, Cambridge University Press, 1995

Kitson, Michael and Michie, Jonathan, *Coordinated Deflation - The Tale of Two Recessions*, Full Employment Forum (Watford), 1993

Laybourn, Keith, *British Trade Unionism c.1770-1990*, Alan Sutton Publishing Limited (Stroud, Gloucestershire), 1991

Marsh, Arthur and Ryan, Victoria, *Historical Directory of Trade Unions* (Volume 2), Gower Publishing Company Ltd. (Aldershot, Hants.), 1984

McCarthy, (Lord) William E. J., *Freedom At Work: Towards the Reform of Tory Employment Laws*, Fabian Society (London), November 1985, Fabian Tract 508

McCarthy, (Lord) William E. J. (Ed.), *Legal Intervention in Industrial Relations: Gains and Losses*, Blackwell Publishers (Oxford, UK and Cambridge, USA), 1992

McIlroy, John, *Trade Unions in Britain Today*, Manchester University Press (Manchester and New York), 1988

McIlroy, John, *The permanent revolution?: Conservative law and the trade unions*, Spokesman (Nottingham), 1991

Michie, Jonathan (Ed.), *The Economic Legacy 1979-1992*, Academic Press (London & San Diego), 1992

Michie, Jonathan, *Maastricht: Implications for Public Services*, Nalgo (Manchester), 1993

Miller, Robert and Wood, John B., *What Price Unemployment? An Alternative Approach*, Institute of Economic Affairs (Westminster, London), Hobart Paper 92, January 1982

Mills, John, *Europe's Economic Dilemma*, Macmillan Press Ltd. (Basingstoke), 1998

Mortimer, J. E. (Jim), *A Life on the Left*, The Book Guild Ltd. (Lewes, Sussex), 1998

Murray, Andrew, *A New Labour Nightmare: The return of the awkward squad*, Verso (London and New York), 2003

Musson, A. E., *The Congress of 1868: The origins and establishment of The Trades Union Congress*, Trades Union Congress (London), July 1982

Peak, Steve, *Troops in Strikes: Military Intervention in Industrial Disputes*, The Cobden Trust (London), 1984

Pelling, Henry, *A Short History of the Labour Party* (Fourth Edition), The Macmillan Press Ltd. (London and Basingstoke), 1972

Ramelson, Bert, *Consensus or Socialism?: The 1986 Ralph Fox Memorial Lecture*, Ralph Fox Memorial Committee (Halifax), 1986

Richards, Andrew J., *Miners on Strike: Class Solidarity and Division in Britain*, Berg (Oxford and New York), 1996

Rogers, W. V. H., *Winfield and Jolowicz on Tort*, Sweet & Maxwell (London), (13th Edition), 1989; (16th Edition), 2002; (17th Edition) 2006

Rohe, Karl and Schmidt, Gustav (Hrsg), *Krise in Großbritannien? Studien zu Strukturproblemen der britischen Gesellschaft und Politik im 20. Jahrhundert*, Studienverlag Dr. N. Brockmeyer (Bochum), 1987

Seifert, Roger and Sibley, Tom, *United They Stood: The Story of the Firefighters' Dispute 2002-2004*, Lawrence & Wishart (London), 2005

Shaw, Eric, *The Labour Party Since 1979*, Routledge (London & New York), 1994

Shaw, Eric, *The Labour Party since 1945*, Blackwell Publishers (Oxford), 1996

Shore, (Lord) Peter, *Separate Ways*, Gerald Duckworth and Co. Ltd. (London), 2000

Steinmetz, Willibald, *Begegnungen vor Gericht: Eine Sozial- und Kulturgeschichte des englischen Arbeitsrechts (1850-1925)*, R. Oldenbourg Verlag (München), 2002

Sturm, Roland, *Großbritannien: Wirtschaft – Gesellschaft – Politik*, Leske und Budrich (Opladen) 1991

Sugden, Philip, Dissertation: A Post-war British Conservative Party economic, political and ideological strategy, with particular reference to the period 1974 to 1979, Humboldt University (Berlin), 1985 (unpublished)

Taylor, Robert, *The Future of Trade Unions*, André Deutsch Limited (London), 1994

Thatcher, (Baroness) Margaret, *Margaret Thatcher: The Downing Street Years*, HarperCollins (London), 1993

Trask, Roger, *Anti-trade union legislation in Britain*, International Centre for Trade Union Rights (London), 1989

Warren, Des, *Shrewsbury: Whose conspiracy? The Need for an Inquiry* (Second Edition), New Park Publications Ltd. (London), 1980

Webb, Sidney and Beatrice, *The History of Trade Unionism*, Longmans Green and Co (London), 1920

Wedderburn, (Lord) K. W., *The Worker and the Law* (Third Edition), Penguin (Harmondsworth), 1986

Weeks, B. C. M. et. al., *Industrial Relations and the Limits of the Law*, Blackwell (Oxford), 1975

Weiss, Manfred, *European Employment and Industrial Relations Glossary: Germany*, Sweet & Maxwell (London), 1992

Winterton, Jonathan and Ruth, *Coal, crisis and conflict: The 1984-85 miners' strike in Yorkshire*, Manchester University Press (Manchester and New York), 1989

2. Articles, in alphabetical order by author:

Adams, Jack, Where are we now? A Roundtable Discussion, in: *Marxism Today* (London), Vol. 24 No. 9, September 1980, pp. 17-23

Adams, J. J., The exchange rate mechanism of the European monetary system, in: *Bank of England Quarterly Bulletin*, Bank of England (London), November 1990, pp. 479ff

Barlow, Keith, The EU Constitution's Implications on the Right to Work, in: *Communist Review* (London), Summer 2005, pp. 20-24

Begg, Iain and Rhodes, John, Will British industry recover?, in: *Cambridge Economic Policy Review*, Vol. 8 No. 1, University of Cambridge Department of Applied Economics, April 1982, pp. 18-26

Bleaney, Michael, The Tories' Economic Strategy, in: *Marxism Today* (London), Vol. 23 No. 11, November 1979, pp. 12-16

Brittan, Samuel, Beyond independence, in *Financial Times* (London), 8 May 1997, p. 24

Carty, Hazel, The Employment Act 1990: Still Fighting The Industrial Cold War, in: *Industrial Law Journal*, Oxford University Press, Vol. 20 No. 1, March 1991, pp. 1-20

Christian, Louise, Restriction without Conviction: The Role of the Courts in Legitimising Police Control in Nottinghamshire, in: Fine, Bob and Millar, Robert, *Policing the Miners' Strike*, Lawrence & Wishart (London), 1985, pp. 120-136

Coakley, Jerry and Harris, Laurence, Financial Globalisation and Deregulation, in: Michie, Jonathan (Ed.), *The Economic Legacy 1979-1992*, Academic Press (London & San Diego), 1992, pp. 37-57

Coutts, Ken and Godley, Wynne, Does Britain's Balance of Payments Matter Any More, in: Michie, Jonathan (Ed.), *The Economic Legacy 1979-1992*, Academic Press (London & San Diego), 1992, pp. 60-67

Denny, Brian, Rights? What Rights?, in: *Morning Star* (London), 18 December 2007, p. 8

Eatwell, John; The Development of Labour Policy, 1979-92; in: Michie, Jonathan (Ed.), *The Economic Legacy 1979-1992*, Academic Press (London & San Diego), 1992, pp. 333-339

Elliot, Larry, Labour: Is this all there is?, in: *Guardian* (London), 26 August 1991, p. 10

Evans, Stephen, The Use of Injunctions in Industrial Disputes May 1984-April 1987, in: *British Journal of Industrial Relations*, Blackwell (Oxford), Vol. XXV No. 3, November 1987 pp. 419-435

Ewing, K. D., Article 11 and the right to freedom of association, in: Ewing, K. D. (Ed.), *Human Rights at Work*, The Institute of Employment Rights (London), 2000, pp. 85-111

Ewing, K. D., The Implications of Wilson and Palmer, in: *Industrial Law Journal*, Oxford University Press, Vol. 32 No. 1, March 2003, pp. 1-22

Ewing, Keith (K. D.) and Hendy, John, Why Mr Brown should back the Bill, in: *Morning Star* (London), 18 October 2007, p. 7

Fine, Ben and Poletti, Clara, Industrial Prospects in the Light of Privatisation, in: Michie, Jonathan (Ed.), *The Economic Legacy 1979-1992*, Academic Press (London & San Diego), 1992, pp. 315-330

Fine, Bob and Millar, Robert, Introduction: The Law of the Market and the Rule of Law, in: Fine, Bob and Millar, Robert, *Policing the Miners' Strike*, Lawrence & Wishart (London) 1985, pp. 1-22

Gall, Gregor, Research Note: Injunctions as a Legal Weapon in Industrial Disputes in Britain, 1995-2005, in: *British Journal of Industrial Relations*, Blackwell (Oxford), Vol. 44 No. 2, June 2006, pp. 327-349

Gamble, Andrew, Mrs Thatcher's Bunker: the reshuffle and its consequences, in: *Marxism Today* (London), Vol. 25 No. 11, November 1981, pp. 6-11

Gamble, Andrew, Thatcher: The Second Coming, in: *Marxism Today* (London), Vol. 27 No. 7, July 1983, pp. 7-14

Gearty, Conor A., The Human Rights Act 1998: an overview, in: Ewing, K. D. (Ed.), *Human Rights at Work*, Institute of Employment Rights (London), 2000, pp. 1-23

Gennard, John and Dunn, Steve, The Impact of New Technology on the Structure and Organisation of Craft Unions in the British Printing Industry, in: *British Journal of Industrial Relations*, Blackwell (Oxford), Vol. XXI No.1, March 1983, pp. 17-32

Gennard, John, The implications of the Messenger Newspaper Group Dispute, in: *Industrial Relations Journal*, Vol. 15 No. 3, Blackwell (Oxford), Autumn 1984, pp. 7-20

Gennard, John, The NGA and the impact of new technology, in: *New Technology, Work and Employment*, Vol. 2 No 2, Blackwell (Oxford), Autumn 1987, pp. 126-141

Grahl, John, The Liberal Revolutionary, in: *Marxism Today* (London), Vol. 27 No. 6, June 1983, pp. 18-24.

Hall, Stuart, The Great Moving Right Show, in: *Marxism Today* (London), Vol. 23 No. 1, January 1979 pp. 14-20

Hanson, Charles G., Economic Significance of British Labor Law Reform, in: *Cato Journal*, Vol. 6(3), Cato Institute (Washington D.C., USA), Winter 1987, pp. 851-868

Hart, Moira, Why the bosses love the closed shop, in: *New Society* (London), Vol. 47 No. 854, 15 February 1979, pp. 352ff

Hendy, John and Gall, Gregor, British Trade Unions Today and the Trade Union Freedom Bill, in: Ewing, K. D. (Ed.), *The Right to Strike: From the Trade Disputes Act 1906 to a Trade Union Freedom Bill 2006*, The Institute of Employment Rights (Liverpool), 2006, p. 247-277

Hendy, John QC and Walton, Michael, An Individual Right to Union Representation in International Law, in: *Industrial Law Journal*, Oxford University Press (Oxford), Vol. 26 No. 3, September 1997, pp. 205-223

Hodgson, Godfrey, Private Power and the Public Interest: The Case of Times Newspapers, in: *The Political Quarterly*, Blackwell (Oxford), Vol. 52 No. 4, October-December 1981, pp. 403-415

Jacques, Martin, Thatcherism: The impasse Broken?, in: *Marxism Today* (London), Vol. 3 No. 10 October 1979, pp. 6-14

Kastendiek, Hans, "Gewerkschaftsmacht" und Arbeitskonflikte als Hauptthema der britischen Politik, in: Jacobi, Otto and Kastendiek, Hans (Hg.), *Staat und industrielle Beziehungen in Großbritannien*, Campus Verlag (Frankfurt/New York), 1985, pp. 11-30

Kavanagh, Dennis, Political Crisis in Britain; in Rohe, Karl and Schmidt, Gustav (Hrsg), *Krise in Großbritannien? Studien zu Strukturproblemen der britischen Gesellschaft und Politik im 20. Jahrhundert*, Studienverlag Dr. N. Brockmeyer (Bochum), 1987, pp. 219-229

Kelly, John, Steel – an irreversible decline?, in: *Marxism Today* (London), Vol. 25 No. 6, June 1981, pp. 10-16

Kelly, John, TUC Reforms, in: *Marxism Today* (London), Vol. 25 No. 11, November 1981, pp. 4f

Kelly, John, Tebbit changes tack, in: *Marxism Today* (London), Vol. 27 No. 3, March 1983 pp 22-25

Kelly, John, Communists and the Unions, in: *Communist Campaign Review*, (London), Vol. 2 Issue 3, Spring 1988, pp. 10-14

Kelly, John, Looking to the Future: Labour's anti-union policies, in: *Communist Review* (London), No. 8, Autumn 1990, pp. 8-11

Kettle, Martin, The National Reporting Centre and the 1984 Miners' Strike, in: Fine, Bob and Millar, Robert, *Policing the Miners' Strike*, Lawrence & Wishart (London), 1985, pp. 22-33

Kimmig, Karl H., Politische und ökonomische Aspekte der "britischen Krise", in: Rohe, Karl and Schmidt, Gustav (Hrsg), *Krise in Großbritannien? Studien zu Strukturproblemen der britischen Gesellschaft und Politik im 20. Jahrhundert*, Studienverlag Dr. N. Brockmeyer (Bochum), 1987, pp. 157-170

Leopold, John W., Trade unions and the third round of political fund review balloting, in: *Industrial Relations Journal*, Vol. 37 Issue 3, Blackwell Publishing Ltd. (Oxford), May 2006, pp. 190-208

Marx, Karl, Bloody Legislation against the Exploited, from the end of the 15th Century. Forcing Down of Wages by Acts of Parliament, in: Marx, Karl, *Capital* (Volume 1), Progress Publishers (Moscow), first published in 1954 (reprinted edition from 1986), Part VIII, Chapter XXVIII, pp. 686-693

McColgan, Aileen, Recent Legislation: Trade Union and Labour Relations (Consolidation) Act 1992, in: *Industrial Law Journal*, Oxford University Press (Oxford), Vol. 22 No. 1, March 1993, pp. 32f

McIlroy, John, The Unions: is There Life after Warrington?, in: *Marxism Today* (London), Vol. 28 No. 2, February 1984 pp. 30ff

McIlroy, John, The Belfast Butchers: *Quinn v Leathem* after a Hundred Years, in: Ewing, K. D. (Ed.), *The Right to Strike: From the Trade Disputes Act 1906 to a Trade Union Freedom Bill 2006*, The Institute of Employment Rights (Liverpool), 2006, pp. 31-67

Meggison, Doug, The rise and fall of wages councils, in: *Communist Review* (London), No. 18, 1993, pp. 28-32

Morton, Gary, Labour's anti-union laws, *Communist Review*, No. 30, Autumn 1999, p. 23-26

Pike, Alan, Massive backing for BL recovery plan, in: *Financial Times* (London and Frankfurt), 2 November 1979, p. 1

Pike, Alan, Man of the Week: Back from the brink, in: *Financial Times* (London and Frankfurt), 1 December 1979, p. 36

Pliatzky, (Sir) Leo, Cash Limits and Pay Policy, in: *The Political Quarterly*, Blackwell (Oxford), Vol. 53 No. 1, January-March 1982, pp. 16-23

Power, Mike, A Tale of Wapping Woe, in: *Marxism Today* (London), March 1987, pp. 40f

Robinson, Derek (interview with), in: *Marxism Today* (London), Vol. 24 No. 3, March 1980, pp. 5-10

Rowthorn, Bob, Corby and the Steel Crisis, in: *Marxism Today* (London), Vol. 23 No. 12, December 1979, pp. 2f

Schachtschneider, Karl Albrecht, Eine Charta der Grundrechte für die Europäische Union, in: *Beilage zur Wochenzeitung Das Parlament*, Bundeszentrale für politische Bildung (Bonn), 22 December 2000, pp. 13-21

Sibley, Tom, What other option did the FBU have? in: *Morning Star* (London), 14 January 2005, p. 8

Simpson, Bob, A Milestone in the Legal Regulation of Pay: The National Minimum Wage Act 1998, in: *Industrial Law Journal*, Oxford University Press, Vol. 28 No. 1, March 1999, pp. 1-32

Smith, Arthur, The Sacking of Derek Robinson: Why BL risks crossing a bridge too far, in: *Financial Times* (London and Frankfurt), 24 November 1979, p. 20

Taylor, Robert, New Labour, new capitalism, in: Seldon, Anthony, *Blair's Britain 1997-2007*, Cambridge University Press (Cambridge and New York), 2007, pp. 214-240

Therborn, Göran, The two-Thirds, One-Third Society, in: Hall, Stuart and Jacques, Martin (Ed), *New Times*, Lawrence & Wishart (London), 1989, pp. 103-115

Thomas-Symonds, Nick, A Reinterpretation of Michael Foot's Handling of the Militant Tendency, in: *Contemporary British History*, Routledge Taylor & Francis Group (London), Vol. 19 No. 1, Spring 2005, pp. 27-51

Tyler, Christian, Tebbit's Law: A Tory Dream Come True?, in: *Marxism Today* (London), Vol. 26 No. 4 April 1982, pp. 23-28

Wareing, Robert, How the EC pushed Yugoslavia towards civil war, in: *Socialist Campaign Group News*, No. 78, Campaign Group News Ltd. (London), May 1993, p. 7

Wedderburn (Lord) K. W., Freedom of Association and Philosophies of Labour Law, in: *Industrial Law Journal*, Oxford University Press, Vol 18 No. 1, March 1989, pp. 1-38

Wedderburn, (Lord) K. W., Laws about Strikes, in: McCarthy, (Lord) William E. J. (Ed.)., *Legal Intervention in Industrial Relations: Gains and Losses*, Blackwell Publishers (Oxford, UK & Cambridge, USA), 1992, pp. 147-208

Weinmann, Georg, Wandel oder Kontinuität? Britische Gewerkschaften in der Ära Thatcher, in: *1999 Zeitschrift für Sozialgeschichte des 20. und 21. Jahrhunderts*, Hamburger Stiftung für Sozialgeschichte des 20. Jahrhunderts (Hamburg), 6. Jahrgang Heft 3, Juli 1991, pp. 54-77

Welch, Roger, Judicial Mystification of the Law: Rookes v Barnard and the Return to Judicial Intervention, in: Ewing, K. D. (Ed.), *The Right to Strike: From the Trade Disputes Act 1906 to a Trade Union Freedom Bill 2006*, The Institute of Employment Rights (Liverpool), 2006, pp. 195-218

Wells, John, Ministers burying heads in sand over unprecedented trade deficit, in: *The Guardian International* (London), 15 June 1992, p. 11

Westacott, Fred, Struggle for miners' unity, in: *Morning Star* (London), 19 February 1987, pp. 6f

Whitfield, David, Murdoch multi-media dictator, in: *Communist Campaign Review* (London), Winter 1986-87, pp. 25f

Winchester, David, Trade Unions and the Recession, in: *Marxism Today*, (London), Vol. 25 No. 9, September 1981, pp. 20-25

Appendix Three: Glossary of Abbreviations

ACAS	Advisory Conciliation and Arbitration Service (established 1974)
AES	Alternative Economic Strategy
AEEU	Amalgamated Engineering and Electrical Union upon the amalgamation of the AUEW and the EETPU (becoming part of AMICUS upon the amalgamation with the MSF)
AEU	Amalgamated Engineering Union (formed in 1921 upon amalgamations with the Amalgamated Society of Engineers and several smaller unions, (became the AUEW – see Chapter 1, footnote 30)
AMICUS	Name given to the union which came into being in 2002 owing to the amalgamation of the AEEU and MSF. (AMICUS, Latin for friend, supporter, partner, counsellor, ally was chosen by the executives of the two unions as the name for this new union. Since May 2007, part of the new trade union "Unite" upon amalgamation with the TGWU)
APEX	Association of Professional, Executive, Clerical and Computer Staff (since 1989 part of the general union GMB due to an amalgamation. The GMB had previously been known as the General, Municipal, Boilermakers and Allied Trades Union (GMBATU))
ASLEF	Associated Society of Locomotive Engineers and Firemen
AUEW	Amalgamated Union of Engineering Workers (becoming the AEEU upon the amalgamation with the EETPU)
BA	British Airways
BL	British Leyland
BoE	Bank of England
BSC	British Steel Corporation
CAC	Central Arbitration Committee
CIR	Commission on Industrial Relations (established 1969, abolished 1974)
CLP	Constituency Labour Party
CPAUIA	Commissioner for Protection Against Unlawful Industrial Action
CPGB	Communist Party of Great Britain
CPSA	Civil and Public and Services Association
CROTUM	Commissioner for the Rights of Trade Union Members
CSEU	Confederation of Shipbuilding and Engineering Unions

CWU	Communications Workers' Union
EC	European Community (originally the EEC, became known as the European Union upon the conclusion of the Maastricht Treaty)
ECHR	European Convention on Human Rights (adopted by the Council of Europe in Rome in 1950 – officially being the *Convention for the Protection of Human Rights and Fundamental Freedoms*)
ECtHR	European Court of Human Rights
ECJ	European Court of Justice
ECU	European Currency Unit
EEC	European Economic Community
EETPU	Electrical, Electronic, Telecommunications and Plumbing Union (see AEEU)
EFTA	European Free Trade Association
EMS	European Monetary System
EMU	Economic and Monetary Union
Epoc	TUC Employment Policy and Organisation Committee
ERM	European Exchange Rate Mechanism (of the EMS)
EU	European Union
FBU	Fire Brigades Union
FT	Financial Times
GCHQ	Government Communications Headquarters
GDP	Gross Domestic Product
GMBATU	General, Municipal, Boilermakers and Allied Trades Union (now known as GMB)
GMC	General Management Committee (policy-making body of CLPs)
GNP	Gross National Product (GNP and GDP are two methods of assessing the total value of goods and services produced by an economy over a specific period of time – normally a year. GNP is equal to GDP plus net income of domestic residents from abroad)
GPMU	Graphical Paper and Media Union (upon the amalgamation of the NGA (1982) and SOGAT '82 in 1991) – became part of AMICUS in 2004
HMSO	Her Majesty's Stationery Office
ILO	International Labour Organisation (originally established 1919)
IMF	International Monetary Fund (established 1944)

IPCS	Institute of Professional Civil Servants
IR Act	Industrial Relations Act, 1971 (repealed 1974)
ISTC	Iron and Steel Trades Confederation
LRC	Labour Representation Committee
LRD	Labour Research Department
MFGB	Miners' Federation of Great Britain (forerunner to the NUM)
MLR	Minimum Lending Rate
MSF	Manufacturing Science Finance (formed, 1988 upon amalgamation of the Association of Scientific, Technical and Managerial Staffs (ASTMS) and the Technical, Administrative and Supervisory Union (TASS) – (previously AUEW (Technical, Administrative and Supervisory Section)), becoming part of AMICUS upon amalgamation with the AEEU)
MTFS	Medium Term Financial Strategy
NALGO	National and Local Government Officers' Association
NATSOPA	National Society of Operative Printers, Graphical and Media Personnel (amalgamated with SOGAT in 1982)
NCB	National Coal Board
NEC	National Executive Committee
NGA	National Graphical Association (becoming National Graphical Association (1982) upon the amalgamation with SLADE in 1982, then to become part of the GPMU in 1991 upon the amalgamation with SOGAT '82)
NHS	National Health Service
NIRC	National Industrial Relations Court (established 1971, abolished 1974)
NMA	Nottinghamshire Miners' Association (part of the then MFGB)
NMW	National Minimum Wage
NMWA	National Minimum Wage Act
NPF	National Policy Forum
NUJ	National Union of Journalists
NUM	National Union of Mineworkers
NUR	National Union of Railwaymen (now RMT through amalgamation with the National Union of Seamen (NUS) in 1991)
OECD	Organisation for Economic Co-operation and Development

OMOV	One Member, One Vote
PiP	Partnership in Power
PLP	Parliamentary Labour Party
POEU	Post Office Engineering Union (became the National Communications Union (NCU) which in January 1995 amalgamated with the Union of Communication Workers to become the CWU)
PSBR	Public Sector Borrowing Requirement
PSU	Police Support Units
RMT	National Union of Rail, Maritime and Transport Workers
RPI	Retail Price Index
SAU	Slade Art Union
SEA	Single European Act
SLADE	Society of Lithographic Artists, Designers, Engravers and Process Workers
SOGAT	Society of Graphical and Allied Trades (becoming SOGAT '82 upon amalgamation with NATSOPA in 1982, then to become part of the GPMU upon the amalgamation with NGA (1982) in 1991)
SPG	Special Patrol Groups
Sterling M3	"Broad" money supply
TSSA	Transport Salaried Staffs' Association
TGWU	Transport and General Workers' Union (formed 1921, since May 2007, part of the new trade union "Unite" upon amalgamation with AMICUS)
TUC	Trades Union Congress
TULRA	Trade Union and Labour Relations Act
UCATT	Union of Construction, Allied Trades and Technicians
UDM	Union of Democratic Mineworkers
UN	United Nations

Index

Name index

Subject index